Early Baseball
in New Orleans

Also by S. Derby Gisclair

*The Olympic Club of New Orleans:
Epicenter of Professional Boxing,
1883–1897* (McFarland, 2018)

Early Baseball in New Orleans

A History of 19th Century Play

S. Derby Gisclair

McFarland & Company, Inc., Publishers
Jefferson, North Carolina

LIBRARY OF CONGRESS CATALOGUING-IN-PUBLICATION DATA

Names: Gisclair, S. Derby, author.
Title: Early baseball in New Orleans : a history of 19th century play / S. Derby Gisclair.
Description: Jefferson, North Carolina : McFarland & Company, Inc., Publishers, 2019 | Includes bibliographical references and index.
Identifiers: LCCN 2019003391 | ISBN 9781476677811 (paperback : acid free paper) ∞
Subjects: LCSH: Baseball—Louisiana—New Orleans—History—19th century. | Baseball—Social aspects—United States—History—19th century. | Baseball teams—Louisiana—New Orleans—History—19th century.
Classification: LCC GV863.L82 G57 2019 | DDC 796.35709763/35—dc23
LC record available at https://lccn.loc.gov/2019003391

BRITISH LIBRARY CATALOGUING DATA ARE AVAILABLE

ISBN (print) 978-1-4766-7781-1
ISBN (ebook) 978-1-4766-3598-9

© 2019 S. Derby Gisclair. All rights reserved

No part of this book may be reproduced or transmitted in any form or by any means, electronic or mechanical, including photocopying or recording, or by any information storage and retrieval system, without permission in writing from the publisher.

Front cover image: "Safe at third," cabinet style baseball card portrait Turkey Red (T3; American Tobacco Company), 1911 (Library of Congress)

Printed in the United States of America

McFarland & Company, Inc., Publishers
  Box 611, Jefferson, North Carolina 28640
    www.mcfarlandpub.com

For Claire

Table of Contents

Preface	1
Introduction	7
One—The Game They Played	23
Two—Equipment	44
Three—Where They Played	57
Four—Teams and Leagues	105
Five—The Business of Baseball	149
Appendix: What's in a Name?	207
Chapter Notes	236
Bibliography	240
Index	243

Preface

"The birth of baseball is a term that contradicts itself."
—Mark Rucker and John Fryer

This book is an extension of my search for the origin and history of New Orleans' first professional baseball team—the New Orleans Pelicans. This search inevitably led me to the roots of baseball itself and the story of early baseball in New Orleans. Unfortunately, that story begins with an unclear and uncertain past and, as such, an exact starting point is difficult to mark. The first mention of baseball in New Orleans occurs in July of 1859, so everything prior to that time is largely apocryphal. Did people play baseball in New Orleans before July of 1859? Of course they did, but there simply was no mention of it in the press or other contemporary accounts.

By comparison, the New York press was at least aware of and frequently mentioned the activities of the New York Base Ball Club almost from the day it was founded in 1845, covering their games on the playing fields of Hoboken, New Jersey. "We stated yesterday that the proposed Base Ball match between eight players of New York against eight players of Brooklyn, would turn out to be a failure; and so it was, for the New Yorkers did not make their appearance on the ground, and the supper provided by their order was necessarily untouched."[1] Whatever caused the delay, the game eventually came off on Tuesday, October 21, 1845, at the Elysian Fields in Hoboken, won by the New York club 24 to 4 in four innings—twenty-one aces (runs) being necessary to win the match. As many of the clubs in New York played multiple types of ball games, one wonders if game being described with the eight-man teams and twenty-one-run limit might not actually be a game of townball instead of baseball.

Similarly, details of the events of the last half of the 19th century in New Orleans are no less murky and are often in dispute when it comes to the subject of baseball. For instance, the vast majority of 19th century players are virtually unknown outside of a handful of historians and writers. There is certainly no one alive today who remembers Asa Brainard, Ross Barnes, or Cal McVey, much less Abner Powell, Count Campau, Mark Polhemus, Lucien Smith, or Perry Werden. That is why presenting the stories of these players and their teams is so important, and in so doing glean and verify from their activities and then set the record straight whenever possible to correct the absence of information.

In most cases, this absence of information can to a large extent be traced to a general lack of awareness about the game of baseball but also indirectly to the disapproval of the community's thought leaders trying to establish and enforce a staunch moral standard rather than any specific deficiency in the game of baseball itself. It was a value judgment as to what was and what was not newsworthy, particularly since *The Daily Picayune* had to shoe-horn the international, national, and local news into a scant four-page edition in 1859. I suppose this lack of coverage of local baseball is understandable given not only the paucity of column space, but also with the social posturing that was prevalent in New Orleans then. At the same time, there were significant social, ethnic, economic, and political changes during the latter half of the 19th century in New Orleans taking place, from the tragedy of the Civil War through the upheaval of Reconstruction to the ongoing economic struggles of the last three decades of the century. During this period in our history nearly every aspect of society was undergoing change, both positive and negative. Baseball was just in its infancy, but it was impacted by the world around it like everything else. In many respects, baseball was a mirror of American society in the last half of the 19th century.

As baseball was first catching on in New Orleans, the city had long since found a foothold along the Mississippi River and had successfully absorbed several large waves of immigration, each of which more than doubled the population of New Orleans. This influx of immigrants brought with them the related tangle of different cultures, different languages, and different customs. In the process they had to work through the details of learning how to live together. And while we know a great deal about how New Orleans developed, the true origin of baseball in New Orleans has been lost in the mists of time. Even the early years of baseball in New York City underwent a prolonged and rigorous discussion for nearly a century before the Doubleday–Cartwright debate on the origin of baseball was settled, at least in some people's minds. But rather than lamenting what we do not know about early baseball in New Orleans, I have elected to celebrate what we do know about the formative years of baseball in New Orleans.

There is a certain grain of truth that baseball in New Orleans was influenced by cricket, but on a parallel development path rather than as a direct result of cricket players proactively electing to systematically and purposefully change the rules, the field proportions, and the equipment from cricket to baseball. So it begs the question—why did young men in New Orleans overwhelmingly turn to baseball instead of cricket? In the late 1850s neither sport could lay claim to being "an American game." In fact, cricket was a complicated game whose rules could quickly cross the eyes of anyone who had not grown up with the game. It also required a high degree of skill to master, but so did baseball. But baseball's structure and rules were much easier to absorb than cricket. Finally, a single cricket match could take several days to complete, while a baseball game could be finished in a matter of hours and that, in the end, swung the scales in favor of baseball. It was accessible. It was efficient, and, above all, it was fun.

A review of early rosters shows no overlap of players between cricket and baseball teams. In New Orleans, at least, both sports enjoyed their own individual evolution. The pastoral images portrayed of the early game of cricket and baseball that dominated the press coverage of the day were more probable than one might imagine. It would be several years before anyone thought to enclose the playing fields behind a wooden fence so they could charge admission. Further, both sports were popular and did not rely on one another for inspiration. Simply put, cricket and baseball are distant cousins, very different branches of the same family tree. The roots of embracing the social nature and origins of both cricket and baseball as an expansion of the search for outdoor physical exercise and social engagement flows from the growth of New Orleans' residential and commercial footprint. New Orleans quickly became the central hub of baseball in the South, which was in keeping with its position as the largest city in the South and among the largest cities in the United States in the latter part of the 19th century. While Americans readily accepted baseball as their game, cricket was always considered a British game that was popular in only the largest, most cosmopolitan cities. Cricket was fashionable in New Orleans before the Civil War but tapered off after the war.

Baseball in the 19th century was a far cry from the game we know today, but no more so than any other aspect of society. While the game of baseball itself has only changed incrementally, the outside world changed rapidly. A crowd of 3,000 to 5,000 at the ballpark every day would have electrified the owners and players in 1870 or 1880. It might also have kept some of the clubs out of the soup. Compare that with the 35,000 to 40,000 fans that fill the seats of today's colossal ballparks. Changes in lifestyle, diet, and training are only some of the transformations that have made players bigger, stronger, and faster. The inclusion of Latino-Americans and African Americans baseball players would have been fundamentally impossible in the 19th century. Transportation, clothing, agriculture and nutrition, housing, industry, and even war-fighting have been refined and improved with the passage of time. The ability to harness electricity led to the proliferation of the telegraph, allowing news to be transmitted across the country today and printed in a local newspaper tomorrow. A delay of two or three days in receiving the newspapers from out of town would have been of little concern for 19th century New Orleanians who would have been happy just to receive this information. But in today's world of instant information and the expectation of immediate access to news, such a delay would be unthinkable.

As society evolved, the progress and advances in the world around baseball eventually became engrained in the game. One can only wonder what legendary 19th century manager Abner Powell of the New Orleans Pelicans would think of pitch counts, spray charts, instant replay, launch angles, or any of the elements of today's game that we take for granted. Baseball was no different from our broader society in that it too was a constant work in progress. The initial push to popularize a sport was typically led by the upper crust who had both the time and resources to devote to leisure activity. But unlike most of the urban centers in the United States, New Orleans moved to its own vibrant rhythm. While the upper-class tended to set the moral and social standard for New Orleans society, they also had a unique relationship with vices such as gambling and prostitution.

New Orleans has always served as a study in stark contrasts, from staunch Catholic moralism to the ready acceptance of prostitution and gambling. In March of 1857, New Orleans became the first and only American city to license prostitution with the adoption of City Ordinance 3267, which raised more than a few eyebrows while at the same time also raising between $75,000 and $100,000 annually for the city's coffers. This social experiment would only last two years, being repealed following a barrage of lawsuits filed by the city's furious madams who detested the municipal oversight, not to mention the outstretched palms of city officials and police. Prostitution was actually encouraged throughout the Union occupation of New Orleans during the Civil War. It was even expanded during Reconstruction by ambitious carpetbaggers who explored every possible form of graft and corruption during their temporary assignation in what they believed to be a true cesspool of sin. Brothels were no longer limited to being located "back of town," but could increasingly be found near residential and business areas. Indeed, the motivation behind Abner Powell's introduction of a regularly scheduled, recurring Ladies' Day in 1887 at New Orleans Pelicans baseball games was not only to gain a whole new cadre of fans, but also, and more importantly, it was to tone down the swearing, drinking, and gambling in the grandstands at Sportsman's Park. As luck would have it, newspaper accounts indicated that Powell's event was a success, but that many of the ladies in attendance were *working girls* who enjoyed the atmosphere of the grandstand just the way it was. There were, however, enough husbands who brought their wives, respectable ladies who, despite their ignorance of the game, ignored the presence of these fallen women and became fully engaged in the game midway through the contest. This was just another shade of the many complexities of the social structure in New Orleans.

For instance, the scions of silk stocking society, many of whom disapproved of baseball, openly kept their quadroon mistresses housed, fed, and clothed comfortably in cottages along Rampart Street. Their friends viewed this with a wink and a nod, while their wives often turned an indifferent eye to their husband's indiscretions as long as they and their children were well provided for first. There were complex boundaries drawn between the public and private lives of the city's social elite who would condemn baseball in public but who enjoyed a certain anonymity when they attended a game at the ballpark with their social peers. Such a social paradox was not unusual in New Orleans where gentlemen often split their time between their storybook families at home and their quadroon mistresses in the modest one-story cottages back of town provided for them by their "protectors." Bachelors and married men alike attended one or more of the notorious Quadroon Balls, lavish affairs held periodically at the Orleans Theatre, just a few paces from the St. Louis Cathedral. The families of these mixed race young ladies dressed them to the nines, showcased them in ornate tableaus, and negotiated a suitable arrangement with an interested gentleman who would become her protector. Such unmentionable arrangements were, in fact, quite well known and were responsible, in great part, for the city's escalating problem with dueling, when two gentlemen disagreed over who should "protect" a certain young lady.

There is so much about New Orleans that is multi-faceted, confounding, and even byzantine socially, ethnically, economically, and politically. The introduction of baseball into New Orleans was no different. Most participant sports relied on the ready acceptance and support of the city's well-heeled citizens. It was important to gain the confidence and, later, the patronage of every right-minded and influential New Orleanian. So, unlike most sports in New Orleans, it was not always the city's upper-class who championed the development of baseball. Rather, more often than not it was the middle-class who led the charge. Now they had an unexpected new problem: how to position the game as the very citadel of Victorian propriety with a sternly implied caution to cater the "proper element."

The Southern League, the first professional baseball league to operate below the Mason-Dixon Line, did not come into being until 1885, and New Orleans did not join the league until 1887. Its tenuous existence was an on-again, off-again affair, alternating between periods of strong fan support with only fleeting financial security and painful periods with row after row of half-empty bleachers due to non-stop economic recession and depression that characterized the national economy of the last half of the 19th century.

Despite a conscientious effort to chronicle the high points and significant events of 19th century baseball in New Orleans, there may be intervals in the story where the unfortunate absence of information limits our full understanding and greater appreciation of the actual events. This is a regrettable by-product of the available research resources upon which we must rely. I always strive to use primary sources whenever possible, and then pray that the information is accurate. So many sources have been found to be less than accurate—names are often misspelled, players misidentified, locations assumed, and statistics presented such as they are. These are the details that haunt the historian in me. Sources can often conflict and will sometimes contradict each other as to dates and names, especially when it concerns black players, so being able to verify what happened and why becomes vitally important.

I would like to gratefully acknowledge my indebtedness to my mentor, the late Arthur O. Schott, and the dedicated and diverse members of the Schott-Pelican Chapter of the Society for American Baseball Research (SABR) for their ongoing support. Also, a world of thanks to my many friends at the Library of Congress, the Historic New Orleans Collection, and the New Orleans Public Library for their ongoing assistance in my research and in acquiring many of the images that appear in the book and, where applicable, for providing their permission to use these images. I also wish to thank Brian Boyles of the Louisiana Endowment for the Humanities for allowing me to rework portions of articles and essays that I contributed to *Louisiana Cultural Vistas* and their online encyclopedia KnowLouisiana (www.KnowLouisiana.org).

Introduction

"The whole history of baseball has the quality of mythology."
—Bernard Malamud

Several years ago I came across a copy of an interesting newspaper article from a Cameron Parish newspaper from the late 1840s which described a "game of ball" that had been played between two Indian tribes in southern Louisiana. The players and the families of the losing tribe went home naked, having wagered and lost everything they owned on the outcome of the contest. Just exactly what type of game the Indians played is not mentioned, it was simply described as "a game of ball." It might have been some early variation of lacrosse, or an imitation of a game that they had seen white men playing such as stoolball or townball, or even a game of their own design. Whatever the form of the game, the foundational fact is that men, women, and children have been playing a variety of stick and ball games for thousands of years. They are also known as safe-haven games, where a player reaches a stake, a post, or a base and is declared safe from being called out, thus losing a chance to continue playing or to score. But stick and ball and safe-haven games are not unique to America, or even to the 19th century.

There are engravings that depict a ball ceremony on the north wall of the main chamber of tomb fifteen at Beni Hasan in Egypt that date to before 2,000 BCE in the time of Pharaoh Thothmes III. There are similar images on the eastern wall of the entrance hall in the shrine of Hathor in the temple of Deir-er-Bahari that date to 1,500 BCE.[1] These images all depict two opposing sides engaged in ritual combat and were staged as agricultural and fertility rites. Indeed, most of the earliest stick and ball games have their origin not in recreation, but in religious symbolism and sacred rites. Many of these rituals revolved around mock combat where teams represented the opposing sides in the conflict, not simply for recreation or for the pleasure of the Pharaoh and his court.

Over the years, man has tinkered with the warp and woof of stick and ball games, designing and developing games as diverse as polo, golf, lacrosse, tennis, billiards, and of course, baseball. There were many variations on each of these games, particularly on the game we now know as baseball. Despite the best efforts of Al Spalding, who took up the gauntlet thrown at an 1889 banquet at Delmonico's Restaurant in New York which included luminaries of the day such as Mark Twain and Theodore Roosevelt, during which American Nationalism entered the discussion concerning the origins of the game of baseball. The origin of the controversy was an ongoing dispute between Spalding and Henry Chadwick, the British-born sportswriter for the *New York Clipper*. Even as the popularity of baseball was still exploding in 1889 and had not even begun to reach its peak, the subject of its pedigree was seriously being questioned.

Sixteen years later, to settle the question once and for all, Spalding bankrolled the Mills Commission, a group of seven former players and league officials, headed by Abraham G. Mills, a New York attorney who played baseball during and after the Civil War, and who was also present at the 1889 Delmonico's banquet. He had been the fourth President of the National League (1883–1884). However, to most observers, the determinations of the Commission appeared to be nothing more than a solution in search of a question. After two years of thoughtful deliberations, the Commission determined on December 30, 1907, that the origin of baseball had spontaneously taken place in 1839 when a young local resident, Abner Doubleday, suddenly and instinctively invented the game along the scenic shores of Otsego Lake in Cooperstown, New York, teaching it to the students of the Otsego Academy and Green's Select School who unknowingly were present at the birth of baseball. At least this was the fanciful version of events according to a seventy-one-year-old mining engineer named Abner Graves who wrote to the Commission to inform them that he personally witnessed the actual game during which Doubleday invented baseball. What Graves described in his letter was nothing more than an improved version of townball and was more like a popular variation on old cat commonly called "scrub." The Commission, with only a cursory and perfunctory investigation of Graves' testimony, accepted his claim with a minimum amount of investigation, despite a mountain of evidence to the contrary. For instance, there was the inconvenient fact that the twenty-year-old Doubleday was thoroughly ensconced in his duties during the spring semester of his freshman year at West Point during the very time he was supposedly inventing baseball. Doubleday died in 1893 so he was never aware of the controversy surrounding his alleged participation, at least not to the extent that he would have felt compelled to mention baseball in any of his extensive personal diaries. Webster defines a myth as "a traditional story of unknown authorship, ostensibly with a historical basis, but serving usually to explain some phenomenon of nature." That fairly well describes the origins of baseball. Long after Spalding realized the truth about Alexander Cartwright and Abner Doubleday, he never expressed any inclination or obligation to set the record straight.

While America is deservedly known for bearing the inventive engine of the world, the history of that invention myth alone could encompass volumes and it is not my intent to reengage the reader in that argument. Rather, our purpose is to explore the early history of baseball in New Orleans. The city enjoyed a long and rich history of sports of all kinds, particularly baseball, long before the title of "Sportsmen's Paradise" was first added to Louisiana's automobile license plates in 1954, a declaration of the state's reputation as a premiere destination for outdoorsmen. Along with the natural bounty available to hunters and fishermen, Louisiana has long been the home to storied traditions in team and individual sports, games, and other forms of recreation.

The indigenous tribes of pre-colonial Louisiana almost certainly knew who among them was the most accurate archer, who could throw a knife or a tomahawk with deadly precision, and who was the most skilled horseman. But these were merely utilitarian pursuits. The preferred recreational game among the Indians was a stick and ball game we know today as lacrosse. Documented in 1637 by Jean de Brebéuf, one of the very first Jesuit explorers, it was dubbed *"le jeu de la crosse,"* the game is widely believed to have been developed much earlier, perhaps as early as from 1100. It is a variant on one of many stick and ball games that have been popular since the involvement and innovation of the ancient Egyptians, Romans, Greeks, and other cultures. The Indian's games were attended by large crowds and brought together members of different tribes for competition, cultural exchange, and tribal practices that included songs and dancing.

Given the physical nature of everyday work during the French and Spanish colonial periods in Louisiana, it is highly probable that most adults felt little need to engage in further physical activity solely for recreation. Hunting, shooting, and fishing were every day, practical undertakings rather than discretionary recreational endeavors. The basic reality is that life in colonial Louisiana was extremely hard for the average citizen of New Orleans. During the Colonial Period and well into the Antebellum Period, New Orleans was a dark, smelly place that was under constant siege by frequent hurricanes, horrific floods, devastating fires, and diseases such as yellow fever, cholera, and malaria brought into their midst by swarms of determined mosquitos. Nearly everything these colonists encountered would either stick, bite, or sting them non-stop day and night. And surprisingly, regardless of the odds and the unlikely location of New Orleans, its perils and problems, the city actually began to thrive along the banks of the Mississippi River.

For the resolute citizens of New Orleans, their few recreational diversions were generally limited to those brief social occasions where music and dancing could afford them with a brief reprieve from the burden and grind of daily life. What leisure time remained for adults might be spent at home reading, playing card games such as whist or cribbage, or enjoying board games such as backgammon, dominoes, or chess. Theatre, vaudeville, and puppet shows were presented at any number of public venues from taverns to town squares. Popular songs and ballads touched on common themes such as politics, love, and sports like boxing, cricket, fencing, and horse racing. Children in colonial Louisiana played games such as fox and geese, hare and hounds, hopscotch, hide and seek, leapfrog, marbles, and jacks. One of the stick and ball games the French introduced was called "*croquet*" while the Spanish popularized a counting game called "*cuantas naranjas*," that translates to "how many oranges."

It is safe to assume that none of the eighty ragtag salt bootleggers who were salvaged from French prisons in 1718 for the singular privilege of traveling across the ocean to New Orleans as colonists for a promised life of relative comfort and ease would have known anything whatsoever about "*la soule*," another stick and ball game played by the French nobility that was similar in many respects to lacrosse. It is quite possible, however, that Jean-Baptiste Le Moyne de Bienville and Pierre Le Moyne d'Iberville, the two brothers who oversaw France's ambitious colonization project for the crown in the New World, may have played *la soule* themselves. Of the stick and ball games played in the towns and villages across colonial Louisiana, the French did, however, introduce "*la balle empoisonée*" or "poison ball" to the broader citizenry. For their part, the British introduced rounders, peckers, and townball, and the Spanish brought "*pelota*." Each of these games were played with an endless number of variations and rule revisions such that a game of rounders played in New Orleans could be markedly different from a game of rounders played ninety miles upriver in Baton Rouge. The shape of the playing field, the number of players, the number of posts or safe-haven bases, and the distance between the posts are some of the common variations that might distinguish a game of rounders or townball in different cities. Changes that occurred in sports between 1820 and 1870 were a result of the considerable influence of the waves of immigration that began in 1791, then again in 1809, and yet again in the 1830s that brought with them broader attitudes toward leisure and recreation.

New Orleans, like most cities during the 19th century, had its own unique social structure wherein everything was divided socially, ethnically, economically, and politically. Sports were generally separated into two types—sports for the upper-class and sports for the hoi polloi. The upper-class constituted an influential minority that sought to establish a social and spiritual standard for the society in which they lived. Anyone and anything that puckered their blue-blooded brows and that, in their opinion, threatened to adversely impact or to unfavorably modify that social order was immediately considered suspect and was therefore to be avoided. The stability of their social standing in New Orleans often revolved around their devotion to the pursuit and possession of wealth, and their commitment to the quest for amusement was handled with the same degree of intensity. One way to establish and perpetuate their social standing was by promoting and controlling expensive sporting pastimes such as yachting, golf, and horse racing. The suspicion of other sports as a possible negative influence on their society had its origin in the Puritan legacy adhered to chiefly by the city's Anglo-American citizens but had already begun to dissolve in New Orleans and indeed across the country following the Civil War.

In Louisiana, and particularly in New Orleans, this transformation occurred with far less resistance than in other cities in America given the city's prevailing lax attitudes towards what the blue stocking, social elite did and did not constitute as acceptable behavior in New Orleans. Accordingly, their view of things was not always embraced by the rest of the populace. Citizens and visitors alike were able to find some source of amusement at almost any hour of the day, even on Sunday. While other parts of the country observed the Sabbath seriously, Creole Catholics in New Orleans, who were nurtured by the Spanish and French influence on their way of life during the development of New Orleans, felt unconstrained by the Puritan inhibitions of their Anglo-American neighbors found primarily in New England and in the expanding Midwestern United States, and which became even more pervasive in the United States following the Civil War. Such a staunch standpoint would most certainly constrict the sensibilities of an easy going and relaxed populace in New Orleans.

After the war, sports slowly became more inclusive, although any progress made in this regard, however marginal or incremental, did not penetrate society as a whole and thus did not adequately address the lingering problems of racial separation and class division. The involvement of the both upper-class and the upper-middle-class in sports disappeared from those activities where they failed to retain strict control over that sport. Yet having tens of thousands of residents in New Orleans proved to be beneficial to the development of sports in general and baseball in particular. Multiple teams were formed, leagues were organized, savvy promoters brought professional baseball teams from the Northeast to the city to challenge the city's finest amateur teams, and fans by the thousand flocked to baseball games on diamonds scattered throughout the city. Albert Spalding, a famous former baseball pitcher and founder of a sporting goods empire, notably remarked that baseball was a game "too lively for any but Americans to play."

But baseball and other sports appealed to and, as it turned out, were not

– A GAME AT BASE BALL.

An early woodcut from Robin Carver's *Book of Sports* depicting a group of young boys playing "base ball" on Boston Commons in 1834. The accompanying description of the game, however, read more like rounders than baseball. This illustration is typical of the games played in New Orleans as well (from an unknown 19th century publication).

too lively for those new immigrants who soon enough became new Americans. Promoting good health and physical activity, particularly among urban dwellers, was the leading justification for encouraging participation in sports and athletics. Like most things in New Orleans, this approach could not be confined to or framed by a singular point of view. There were numerous complex social relationships between free blacks and whites, between French, Spanish, Creole, American and other immigrant groups such as Germans, Irish, and Italians. For instance, the term "Creole" is perhaps one of the most misunderstood and misused references in New Orleans history. It is derived from the Spanish "*crillo*," referring to all of the children born under Spanish rule in the Louisiana colonies, not, as is often assumed, only the children born to the enslaved peoples brought to Louisiana. To be Creole was to be born in or otherwise have their origin in New Orleans. So by extension anyone or anything could be considered Creole if it was native to New Orleans or South Louisiana. Black people, white people, horses, cattle, tomatoes, or strawberries—if they were indigenous to the city they earned the right to be called Creole.

The interactions between these various groups were each overlaid upon a political environment that was openly corrupt and blatantly dysfunctional and singularly unique to each constituency, making this both a dangerous and exciting time in New Orleans. Each segment of society enjoyed their own spices and cuisine, their own language, and in some cases their own method of dealing with troublemakers. They also had their own forms of leisure and recreation which they played in their preferred neighborhood in the city. Besides, the leisure time activity of an Irish laborer working on the construction of the New Basin Canal was markedly different from an Italian shoemaker who worked in the French Quarter or a German brewer who worked in the Third District. In most cases their paths would never cross. But as New Orleanians discovered more leisure time to engage in sporting events, especially when it involved a competitive sport pitting individuals or teams against one another, the more people were thrown together with a common purpose. Individual sports such as boxing, foot-racing, rowing, or even fencing encouraged participants and spectators alike to find out who was the best, the strongest, and the fastest. It was the same for team sports. New Orleans and indeed all of America was inwardly proud that their country could produce such men of strength, courage and stamina. Irish, German, or Italian, it didn't matter where these athletes came from; almost everyone in New Orleans originally came from somewhere else. America in general, and New Orleans in particular, willingly absorbed immigrants into their vast melting pot, their gumbo, their free-form culture. In a country made up of multiple social, ethnic, racial, and religious groups, in a nation without a monarchy or an entrenched aristocracy, baseball became our common denominator: it became our national game.

As a vital river port and one of the largest cities in the United States during the Antebellum Period, New Orleans successfully absorbed the diverse cultural influences brought by the French, Spanish, English, American, and other immigrants. The waves of immigration between 1791 and 1809 doubled the population of New Orleans and brought new residents of all socio-economic strata to the city, along with their distinct and colorful forms of language, cuisine, and recreation. The city of New Orleans needed to expand its borders. The Faubourg Marigny, for instance, was New Orleans' first suburban neighborhood, developed downriver from the city on land owned by Bernard Xavier Phillippe de Marigny de Mandeville. One look at that name and you can bet that the land grant he received was because of his family's social position back in France, and you would be correct.

A "faubourg" was the French term for a suburb, usually delineated by a large land grant or plantation. Bernard Marigny, as he was most commonly known, was in fact the richest eighteen-year-old in the United States in 1800, having inherited vast land holdings in New Orleans and elsewhere around Louisiana. He was educated in France and England, but he was not a particularly industrious student. Rather, he was a fun loving, free spending rascal who did not learn very much in school, but who managed to learn a dice game called "hazards" in London, which he brought to New Orleans upon his return from school. Having learned only the rudimentary basics of hazards, Bernard improvised the rest and taught everyone he met how to play the new game. Watching the Frenchmen of New Orleans squat and jump about during the game earned the players the derisive term "*crapaud*," or toads, which Americans morphed into "frogs," and which Americans used to refer to Creoles in general. The name of the game was eventually shortened to "craps" and became a local sensation.

The game of craps is actually fairly complicated and not very easy to master with any consistency. The game that Marigny invented used two six-sided dice cubes. A bet was placed before the shooter rolled the dice. If the shooter's first roll was a seven or eleven, players who put their money on the pass line doubled their wager and everyone else lost their money. If the shooter's first roll was a two, three, or twelve this was called "craps" which meant that everyone lost, and a new shooter was chosen. However, if the shooter's first roll was any other number, then this number became "the point." The shooter would then try to roll the point again before he rolled a seven. If he missed his point before he rolled a seven then he would roll again. As you can see, there were a lot of ways for a player to wager and to lose their money and not very many ways that would allow him to win. And all of this was designed by the hapless Bernard Marigny to take his money, or perhaps someone else's. You see as luck would have it, everyone that Bernard Marigny taught to play craps apparently played the game far better than he, resulting in Marigny accruing large gambling debts. With his property already mortgaged to the Citizens Bank, his only recourse was to subdivide his property and sell it off piece by piece, creating the Faubourg Marigny. The resulting term for an undertaking that is dangerous or risky is "dicey."

The "Orleans Laws" were enacted by the Louisiana State Legislature to accommodate Marigny. They were three unrelated acts granting divorces and one specific act authorizing Marigny, a "minor under the age of twenty-five years," and his guardian, Solomon Prevost, to subdivide his plantation adjoining the city of New Orleans into squares and lots. This downriver estate became known as the Faubourg Marigny. Ironically, the street known today as Burgundy Street was originally called Rue de Craps. But Marigny did not have to liquidate all of his property to retire his gambling debts. His land holdings extended upriver into the cities of Lafayette, Jefferson, and Carrollton. Part of his land on the north shore of Lake Pontchatrain became known as the city of Mandeville and was established three years before the city of Carrollton on the old Macarty Plantation upriver from New Orleans. Marigny's 2,800-acre Northshore sugar plantation and hunting preserve was called Fountainbleau after the favorite recreation spot of French kings. It is now part of the Fountainbleau State Park.

Marigny was not always a failed gambler, and his real estate holdings remained significant through the end of his life. He was a well-known and well-respected citizen who was a veteran of the War of 1812 and who became a personal friend of Andrew Jackson. He entered politics and became president of the Louisiana State Senate in 1822 at the age of forty. On Monday, February 3, 1868, Marigny collapsed and died suddenly, probably from a heart attack while walking up Royal Street between Barracks and Ursulines Streets. The grand old man, the revered relic of Louisiana's colonial days, was eighty-nine years old.

Leisure time in New Orleans increased as local society moved from being a rural-agrarian economy to being an urban-industrial economy. Cities planned and built public parks and squares, and New Orleans emerged as a premiere winter resort for visitors in search of a balmy climate and a wide variety of cuisines, amusements, and recreational opportunities. The first of these new public spaces was Jackson Square, originally called Place d'Armes, constructed on the river bank directly in front of St. Louis Cathedral in 1721. Lafayette Square was built as Place Gravier in 1788, and its named was changed in 1825 to commemorate the Marquis de Lafayette's visit to New Orleans that year. Interestingly enough, of the three statues erected in Lafayette Square, none of them are of Lafayette. In 1817 blacks were allowed to congregate in a large area on the outskirts of the French Quarter called Place des Négres, now known as Congo Square, where they could gather for meetings, dancing, and religious events. Washington Square in the Faubourg Marigny and Annunciation Square both appeared by 1854.

During the 1830s there was a third wave of immigration to New Orleans, this time primarily from Europe. These settlers brought with them an even broader array of sports and recreational pursuits, among them the blood sports such as cock fighting and bull-baiting. Animal fighting appeared in New Orleans as early as 1817. For two bits you could gain admission to a fight between a jackass known as the *Great Fighting Jack Rough and Ready* and three large bull dogs in a Gretna venue which advertised the event for April 3, 1854. Cockfighting, dog fights, and bear-baiting were among the more popular blood sports available around the city. Of these, cockfighting proved to be the most prevalent. In the 1830s there was a popular pit in the rear of the Union Hotel in the French Quarter. The *Louisiana Courier* ran an announcement for the opening of a new cockfighting pit at the corner of History and Good Children streets on January 21, 1851.

Mark Twain immortalized cockfighting in New Orleans in his 1883 memoir *Life on the Mississippi* with a vivid account of a match he attended. While humane societies and other civic groups eventually managed to suppress animal fights during the latter half of the 19th century, cockfighting survived in the shadowy underbelly of society until Louisiana became the last state to outlaw the practice 125 years after Twain's published description.

Through economic downturns, political turmoil, natural disasters, and even the Civil War, the citizens of New Orleans eventually turned to more organized sports as a means of making life enjoyable. "The necessity of healthful exercise and out-door sports is important, and the influence on the character of such a nature that it seems strange that arguments are necessary to convince anyone. The people of this country above all others ... give too little attention to athletic sports: they are a brain-working people, forgetting while their lives are ebbing away, and the mental fire consuming them, that a little pure water from the well of wisdom would bring health and long life."[2] Urban residents who may have somehow felt deprived of health resulting from a sedentary lifestyle and general inactivity were now encouraged to engage in some form of physical exercise, if only for their own mental health. The press played a large role in espousing physical activity for adults. "Many a noble soul has been debased and ruined for lack of a few recreation days. Exercise is to the mind what rain is to the flower."[3]

Gymnasiums were among the first purely athletic clubs, and one of the first gymnasiums established in New Orleans was Roper's Gymnasium, Sparring and Fencing Academy which opened on January 22, 1844, at No. 12 St. Charles Street. Extolling the virtues of physical exercise as well as advertising exaggerated claims of medical benefits of exercise such as removing "pains in the breast; also Dyspepsia, and almost any chronic disease." Dyspepsia, in its simplest form, is better known as indigestion. The proprietor, Jim Roper, was an Englishman who came to New Orleans between 1833 and 1838. Despite being quite tall, he initially found work as a jockey, but he was also known for "indulging in the sports of the ring" and for training others to box.

By 1854 Roper moved to larger quarters shared with John Travis' shooting gallery at 9 Perdido Street between Carondelet Street and St. Charles Avenue, on the second floor above *The Shades*, and advertised it as Roper & Travis's Gymnasium. By 1855 the concern was advertised as Roper's Gymnasium, Pistol Gallery and Chess Room. By 1865 it was known as Roper's Gymnasium and School of Arms, still highlighting boxing and fencing lessons. For nearly twenty-five years Roper served generations of New Orleanians worried about being "loose in limb, weak in muscle, and hollow in chest." Athletic development was considered a medical necessity to overcome the impact of urbanization and industrialization on a growing middle and upper-class segment of the population also seeking to offset a lifestyle of "amusement, gaiety and dissipation."

Following Roper's death in 1868 came the formation of several gymnasiums, principally the Clerk's Benevolent Association Gymnasium at 107 St. Charles Street (opposite the St. Charles Theatre) and the American Gymnasium at 103 St. Charles Street in the former home of the Normal Gymnasium founded in 1858. The Young Men's Christian Association (Y.M.C.A.) and the Young Men's Gymnastic Club (Y.M.G.C.) would also emerge between 1869 and 1879.

Gymnasiums were generally operated on a subscription basis or a monthly membership plan. This allowed them to accommodate all levels of society. However, following the trend in business both nationally and locally, private clubs were later chartered and reorganized as stock companies, requiring a member to own at least one share of stock in the venture. The intent was to prevent the lower classes from participating, but also to provide the needed capital to acquire and fully furnish a suitable facility. Among the most successful athletic clubs in New Orleans were the Young Men's Gymnastic Club and the Southern Athletic Club (1888), each boasting in excess of one thousand members at their peak.

This satisfied the need of the upper-class and upper-middle-class who could afford the membership fees and monthly dues. Everyone else was left to their own resources. These people turned to activities such as swimming, rowing, canoeing, footraces, and baseball.

In particular, baseball was portrayed as the "manly sport," giving it an allure not associated with any other participant sports except boxing. That association was part of what tainted baseball's reputation as appealing only to the low-brow element of New Orleans society because of the inherently violent nature of boxing. While sports such as golf, polo, and tennis originated primarily with the upper-class, their very design being based on exclusive, private clubs, and often requiring vast tracts of open land, over time they eventually wound up flourishing in the hands of the common man. Baseball is one such sport.

Yet there is no mention of local baseball in the New Orleans newspapers prior to July 1859. The *Daily Picayune*, the *Times-Democrat*, the *Daily States*, the *City Item*, and the *New Orleans Crescent* were the most popular dailies, with the French paper *L'Abeille* (*The Bee*), the German paper *Deutsche Zeitung* (*German Gazette*), and the black-owned *Louisianian* rounding out the weekly offerings. Nowhere tucked away between the various crime reports, business announcements, and advertisements of all stripes would there be any mention of any baseball game. For one thing, playing baseball was not organized. People of all ages certainly played baseball, but teams were often drawn up spontaneously and games were played wherever and whenever possible. While fun and interesting, there was nothing new and newsworthy about a random group of young men playing baseball. Indeed, these young men might even have been derided for playing a child's game.

With the formation of organized teams and leagues, the city was now presented with something else altogether different and to their credit the newspapers took notice. As baseball became more popular, more teams were formed. Despite the disapproving looks of their elders, young men readily adopted baseball enthusiastically. Early baseball in New Orleans started with an intrepid group of young men trying to reconcile how their efforts to start a new social and athletic club centered around baseball could be taken seriously by others who questioned their reasons for playing a child's game. But by concentrating their appeal on the qualities of strength, skill, agility, and quickness necessary to play baseball at this advanced level, proponents of the game soon claimed a foothold and slowly gained a measure of respectability. In the end, however, playing baseball was simply about a group of friends having fun while providing those playing and watching an equal measure of novelty and excitement.

Beginning in 1859, numerous baseball clubs were established in the city, including the Louisiana Base Ball Club, the Lone Star Base Ball Club, the Empire Base Ball Club, the Magnolia Base Ball Club, the Washington Base Ball Club, the Pelican Base Ball Club, and the Melpomenia Base Ball Club. These clubs were soon joined by the Comet Base Ball Club (1860) and two teams formed by firemen, the Liberty Base Ball Club and the Home Base Ball Club (1860). The R.E. Lee Base Ball Club (1864) and the reorganized Pelican Base Ball Club (1865) both occurred after the Civil War, and with a slow and steady yet significant and deliberate period of expansion following the Civil War. In 1869. After the war, the most active New Orleans clubs were the Lone Stars, Pelicans, Washington, Southern, Comet, R.E. Lee, Fearless, Champion, Hancock, Pickwick, and Atlantic. Rather than struggle to find a large open space in the cramped confines of the city, the original seven teams in the Louisiana Base Ball Association played on the recently established cricket grounds on the lower edge of the Delachaise estate, located in a rural and pastoral setting upriver from New Orleans along the river road on Levee Street (now Tchoupitoulas Street) below the present-day Touro Infirmary.

Founded in 1859, the Louisiana Base Ball Association operated until 1862 and the start of the Civil War. It was not reorganized until after the war in 1867, but once reestablished it continued to operate until 1873. The Crescent City League set up shop in 1880 and operated until 1884, when New Orleans businessman and baseball aficionado Toby Hart's unsuccessful bid to obtain a franchise in the newly formed Southern League led him to form the Gulf League. This new league was the first attempt to establish a professional league in the city. After months of negotiations with other Southern cities, Hart was unable to attract enough interest to form a league in the traditional eight-team format, so when it was finally launched in 1886 the Gulf League consisted of two teams from New Orleans and two teams from Mobile, Alabama. Hart was eventually successful in securing a franchise for New Orleans in the Southern League for the 1887 season and operated off and on with varying degrees of success until the turn of the century, during which the New Orleans Pelicans captured the first of their three Southern League championships.

With the extended month-long visits of the New York Mutuals and the Chicago White Stockings in New Orleans in 1869 and 1870, respectively, not only was the city considered to be the birthplace of spring training, but the city was also a major destination for teams to play baseball during the winter months. They were attracted to the city's mild weather from September through March, as well as for their ample supply of local baseball talent against whom they could scrimmage. Some of the notable professional players from New Orleans who spent their off-season playing baseball in their hometown included Charles Mason of the Philadelphia Centennials; Bill Butler, John Peltz, and George Mundinger of the Indianapolis Hoosiers; Jimmy Woulfe, Harry Spies, and Mike Shea of the Cincinnati Red Stockings; Joe Dowie of the Baltimore Orioles, and Steve Toole of the Brooklyn Grays. For those teams seeking something more adventurous during the winter months, New Orleans was the perfect point of embarkation by steamboat for baseball tours to Havana, Cuba. In 1891, the All-American Team, an aggregation of major league ball players from Detroit, Cleveland, Chicago, Baltimore, St. Louis, and Pittsburgh, gathered in New Orleans to fine tune their skills as a squad before setting off to Havana. Their practice sessions in New Orleans culminated in a brief exhibition game at Sportsman's Park. Playing as the All-American Nine, they met another group of professional ball players from New Orleans on November 22, 1891.

All American Nine versus New Orleans Picked Nine
November 22, 1891[4]

Innings	1	2	3	4	5	6	Total
All American	0	2	2	3	0	0	7
New Orleans	0	0	0	1	2	0	3

From New Orleans, American teams set off for Cuba by steamship to cross bats with either the Club de Béisbol de la Habana (Havana Base Ball Club), the Club de Béisbol de Almendares (Almendares Base Ball Club), or the Club de Béisbol de Matanzas (Matanzas Base Ball Club). Baseball was introduced into Cuba by Nemesio and Ernesto Guillot upon their return from Spring Hill College in Mobile, Alabama, in 1864. They formed the

Havana Base Ball Club four years later. These three teams provided the genesis for the Cuban League which was established in 1878 and operated well into the 20th century. The long-standing rivalry between Havana and the Almendares predates the formation of the Cuban League.

In the years following the Civil War and lasting to the turn of the century, New Orleans was at the very heart of baseball activity in the South,[5] with more than fifteen local teams joining the National Association, the largest contingent from any Southern city. New Orleans also experimented with baseball more than any other team below the Mason-Dixon line before the Civil War. There were the usual nuances made to balls and bats, but also quantum changes such as spring training, winter leagues, covering the infield with a canvas tarpaulin, and adding a detachable rain check stub to tickets. The city and its residents were attracted to baseball as a social binder, with the popularity of the sport being due to its uniqueness rather than its social necessity.[6]

Founded in 1857, the National Association of Base Ball Players (NABBP) was the first nationwide governing body in baseball. They set the rules that regulated the character and content of the game and established the guidelines on permissible equipment and behavior. By the 1860s, New Orleans accounted for nearly 4 percent of the membership in the NABBP. This incredible expansion of amateur baseball clubs in New Orleans represented practically all facets of society. Many teams were formed at their workplace by the workers. For instance, the Lone Star Base Ball Club was established in 1859 by a group of mechanics at the Leeds Foundry on Girod Street. Leeds produced and manufactured everything from steam engines to sugar kettles to iron columns and fronts for buildings. Others were formed to represent their workplace, and by identifying with their workplace, players demonstrated their confidence in their employers and, by extension, with their owner's values and principles, whether or not the employer actually sponsored the team. It was a demonstrable point of pride, a means by which middle and lower-class workers could identify with their upper-middle and upper-class employers.

In New Orleans the firemen had the Screw Guzzles and the Red Hots; the telegraphers had the Morse Base Ball Club; and the postal workers had the Ubiquitous Club. Ethnic groups in the city formed their own teams—the Irish had the Fenian Base Ball Club; the Germans had the Schneider Base Ball Club, the Laners Base Ball Club, and the Landwehr Base Ball Club; and the Italians formed the Tiro al Bersaglio Society, a baseball team comprised of members of their target shooting club. It seemed like only the city's Chinese contingent did not participate in playing baseball, although on occasion the employees of Navra's China Palace restaurant at 167 Canal Street fielded a sponsored team.[7] The city's African American population was well represented by the Orleans Base Ball Club, the A.J. Dumont Base Ball Club, the Aetna Base Ball Club, the A. Fischer Base Ball Club, the Union Base Ball Club of New Orleans, the Pickwick Base Ball Club, and the P.B.S. Pinchback Base Ball Club, among others. Their love of the game was no less fervent than any other ethnic or social segment of New Orleans society.

ONE

The Game They Played

"Baseball is the very symbol, the outward and visible expression of the drive, the push, and rush and struggle of the raging, tearing, booming nineteenth century."
—Mark Twain

Call it what you will, different cities, states, and regions of the United States had their own names for their favorite stick and ball and other safe-haven games. In America they played baste ball, round ball, patch ball, barn ball, feeders, soak ball, and sting ball among many others. The children and young adults of New Orleans played many of these games, but the same game being played in New Orleans might be known by a completely different name in Mobile. It was not intentional, and it was not unusual. Even when playing the same game by the same name, the rules might change from team to team and city to city. And the city's expanding immigrant population had their own names for the games they played, throwing yet another new wrinkle into the process of merging different cultures into the colorful fabric of New Orleans.

The Germans who played "*der Brautball*" would be vaguely familiar with the French who played "*bal nuptiale*" or bridal ball. And both might be able to pick up English or American stoolball quickly enough. The Irish who played "*hurling*," the Welsh who played "*knappan*," and the Scottish who played "*shinty*" would all recognize the French "*la soule*" or the Indians playing lacrosse. The Germans playing "*knucke*" would have no trouble playing cricket with groups of Americans or Britons. New Orleans has always been known for taking the best of something and blending it into the local culture, with the end product generally being better than before.

Poisoned Ball

Although its exact origins are uncertain and unknown before the 19th century, the French played a game called *la balle empoisonée*, or poisoned ball, as early as 1810. There is every reason to believe that children in New Orleans played some rudimentary form of this game or perhaps two similar games called "*thèque*" and "*la balle au bâton*." In poisoned ball, two teams of varying size square off on an open, diamond-shaped field with a designated home base and three other bases. The team in the field defends the bases against a player trying to strike a pitched ball.

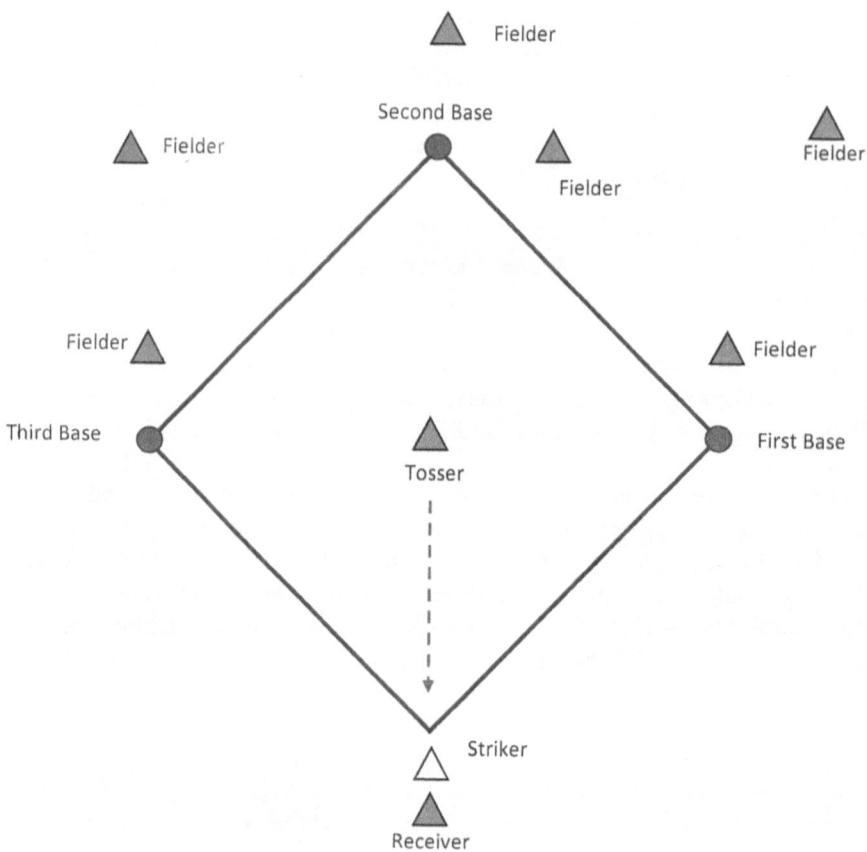

Thus far this sounds almost exactly like baseball, but a further description of poisoned ball reveals that, with a ball in play, the striker or batter must reach base before being touched by the "poisoned" ball, either by another player holding the ball or by a thrown ball. If the batter is successful in reaching base safely, another player comes to the plate to try to reach base safely himself and move the first player on base to the next base or perhaps even further. Once a player is touched by the poisoned ball, his team is out and must take the field. This still sounds remarkably similar to baseball, except that while the fielders may throw the ball to a teammate defending one of the bases, that defender must touch the runner with the ball, not just have their foot on the base before the runner reaches it. Although there is no historical evidence to bolster the claim, poisoned ball might be considered to be the French version of rounders. As you will see, there are many branches in baseball's family tree.

Stoolball

Stoolball was well known in England as early as 1450. There are some who claim that the game listed as *"bittle battle"* in the Doomsday Book, completed in 1086 by the directive of King William the Conqueror, was in fact a form of stoolball. The game enjoyed a popular revival throughout England and France beginning in 1550, where the church encouraged their parishioners, both men and women, to participate in playing the game, particularly during Easter season. It was mentioned in Shakespeare's "Two Noble Kinsmen" in 1634 and was also touched on in "A Little Pretty-Pocket Book" by John Newberry in 1744. Samuel Johnson's 1755 edition of his "Dictionary of the English Language" references "stool ball."

Monastic life in medieval France was not without recreation for monks and nuns, as depicted in this fourteenth century manuscript which shows two figures at left with a ball and bat and three figures on the right as fielders. Perhaps they are playing "poisoned ball" (from an unknown 19th century publication).

Despite their implacable reputation stemming from their overtly somber and stern demeanor, the Puritan community of Plymouth, Massachusetts, was noted for playing "ball" on Christmas Day as early as 1621, more than likely their version of stoolball.[1] It was also popular at Easter. However, the Puritans were also noted for frowning on playing games of any kind, stoolball included, on Sundays, much to the dismay of Governor William Bradford.

Around 1640, John Smyth noted in the Berkeley Manuscripts that "both gentry, yeomandry, rascallity, boyes and children, doe take in a game called Stoball." While some historians throw shade on the relationship between "Stoball" and stoolball, it does provide proof that people were caught up in playing ball, whatever it was called. Its popularity would continue throughout Great Britain until 1927.

Thought to originate in southern England around Sussex, Kent, and Surrey, and is still very popular in these shires (counties) today. Stoolball was one of many games introduced to New Orleans by the English, and indeed seems more like a simplified version of cricket. Like most games, stoolball had multiple versions, a varying number of players, and few rules, but was centered around the use of two three-legged milking stools as bases. Although milking stools are not always used, a wicket serves as the base. The two wickets are shoulder-high and located approximately between thirty and forty-six feet apart. The playing field is so similar to cricket that it is often considered an ancestor and often called "cricket in the air."

The "striker" stood at one of the stools/wickets approximately six feet away and was served a small ball underhanded by the "tosser." Early games saw the striker attempt to hit the ball with his bare hand, but eventually a small bat was introduced. The bat is wooden and is approximately twenty-four inches long and is often made of willow wood, with either a round or rectangular face and a long-sprung handle. The striker may still use their bare hand if they prefer. The striker may swing as often as they like as there are no balls or strikes, no fouls or foul tips. All contact was therefore in play. The striker is protecting a piece of wood called a "wicket" from being hit by the tosser. The striker tries to hit the ball cleanly and run counter-clockwise around the outside of the two stools/wickets. If he hits the ball beyond the boundary he will score either a four or a six. The striker's path must be a round trip in order to score. There is no stopping halfway.

Fielders, who do not use gloves, must be positioned on the stool/wicket side of the striker's line. If the tosser hits either the stool or the advancing striker with the ball, the striker is out. The next player takes his turn as the striker. In its simplest form there were no teams, with the highest individual scoring player winning. As the game grew in popularity, teams grew to consist of as many as eleven players.

A simple variant on stoolball was called One Old Cat. This was a very

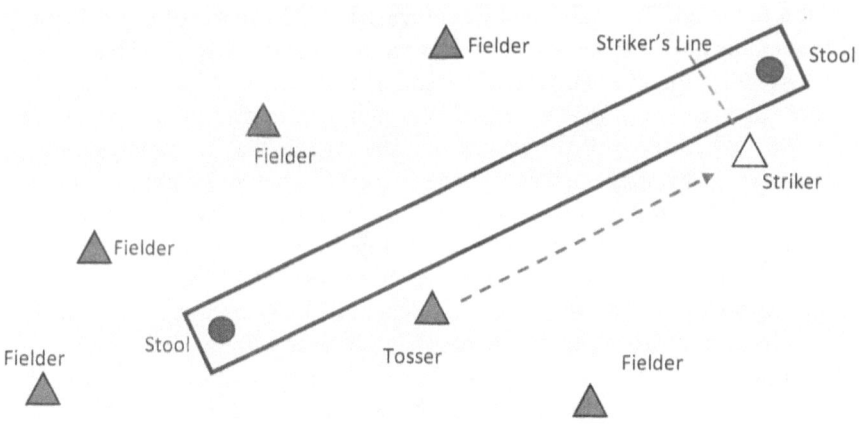

informal game played by at least two players, with infinite variations. Typically, the ball was tossed to and hit by a batter, who attempted to run to a designated point and back. The batter was put out by being hit with or tagged with the ball. More players and more bases constituted Two Old Cat, Three Old Cat, and so on. Once again there were no designated teams and the high scorer won.

Rounders

Although thought to have its origins as early as the 1500s, the earliest printed reference to the game of rounders was in 1744 in "A Little Pretty Pocket-Book" by John Newberry, where it was actually called "baseball."[2] In many places rounders is often called British baseball. Rounders is an old English game that has been played since Tudor times that is still played in the United Kingdom by as many as seven million children. In 1997 the Derby County (UK) Football Club erected Pride Park, their soccer pitch and stadium. Before that the team played at the Baseball Grounds.

Teams in rounders can consist of between six and fifteen players but there may be no more than nine players on the field at one time. Four posts are used for bases, with the goal or home base just off to one side of the batting square. Rules were first published in 1828 by William Clarke in London, and a year later in Boston. Even though the English and Irish governing associations consolidated their rules in 1889, both the English and the Irish have slight variations in the rules under which they play the game today.

The "bowler" or "feeder" must throw the ball in an underhanded motion to the batsman. The ball must be delivered within reach of the batsman between his head and his knees in order to be considered a "good ball." Any ball presented outside of this area is deemed to be a "no-ball" and the batsman is not required to swing at a no-ball although he may do so if he believes he can hit the ball safely. If the bowler delivers a good-ball, the batsman must try to swing at it and must run to the first post whether or not he hits the ball. As in stoolball, there are no strikes and there are no walks.

Using only one hand the batsman swings a short wooden bat no longer than eighteen inches long with a diameter not to exceed 6.7 inches and weighing no more than three ounces. As in cricket, the batsman must run with the bat in hand and as long as he touches the pole/base with his hand or the bat he cannot be tagged out. A batsman is declared to be out if (1) the fielder catches the ball cleanly on the fly, (2) the fielder touches the post before the batsman reaches it, (3) the batsman drops the bat at any time, (4) the batsman leaves the post before the bowler throws the ball, or (5) the batsman/runner is overtaken or passed by another batsman. A runner who reaches the fourth post scores a "rounder," thus the derivation of name of the game. Once a batsman is declared out he cannot bat again in the inning. The inning is over when the entire nine-man side has been declared out. The team with the most rounders or runs after two innings (English rules) or five innings of three outs each (Irish rules) wins the game.

Depending on the length of the stride of the person laying out the field, the posts/bases were located approximately forty-feet apart for the first three posts/bases and approximately twenty-eight feet to the fourth post/base. This gave the playing field a near pentagonal shape with the last leg from the third to the fourth post at a slightly different angle. It is approximately fifty-six feet from the batter's square to the second post. Here again there was no foul territory, but the ball may be put into play in any direction. As in cricket, the ball may be hit in any direction, but if the ball is hit behind the batting square the batsman may only advance to the first post.

A batsman who reaches the second post is credited with a half-rounder. There must be a minimum of six players in the field—one at each post, the bowler, and the backstop. There may be other fielders, but there may not be more than nine defensive players on the field at one time. Variations on rounders are popular throughout the world, particularly in Scandinavia—"*pesäpallo*" in Finland, "*brännboll*" or "*slaball*" in Sweden and Norway, "*palant*" in Poland, "*oina*" in Romania, and "*lapta*" in Russia.

Rounders, as with other stick and ball games, has many similarities to baseball, but to those who contend that rounders was the origin of baseball are mistaken. That is like saying a wheelbarrow was the origin of the carriage because they both have wheels. Rounders was played in America and was probably played in New Orleans, but it was not the origin of baseball. A dis-

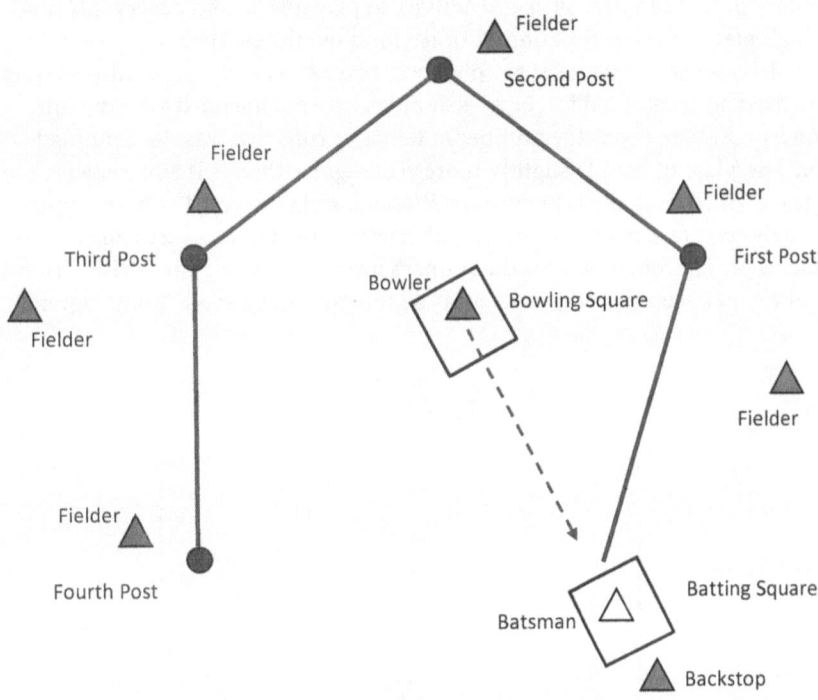

tant relative perhaps, but not a direct relation. Many believe that the closest derivative stick and ball game to baseball in townball.

Townball

Townball was popular throughout New England, New York, and Pennsylvania. Although it is often referred to as "the New England Game" or "the Massachusetts Game," the oldest known organized townball team was the Olympic Base Ball Club of Philadelphia, founded in 1833, although some have put forth the possibility that the team may date from 1831 in nearby Camden, New Jersey. Townball grew in popularity quickly and spread across the United States, even to the western-most states like Louisiana.

New Orleans was familiar with townball and in August of 1859 newspapers compared baseball against cricket and townball to provide their readers with a general idea of the similarities and differences. "[Base ball] preserves the principal and most important characteristics of the old fashion games of 'townball,' 'knockball,' and the other games under other names. But this game, as well as cricket, must be seen by the uninitiated to be properly understood. It requires skill and activity to play it well, and deservedly holds a high place in the estimation of those fond of athletic sports."[3]

In essence, the game of townball was played by two teams of nine players to a fixed number of "tallies" or runs. Innings were not intended as an organizing concept. Rather, it was the number of tallies or runs that was the defining factor. The playing field is slightly more rectangular than it is square, with the "stakes" or bases at the four corners. Wooden stakes were set as bases approximately sixty feet apart and, unless otherwise agreed upon, were run counterclockwise. The fourth stake is the runner's final destination. The "striker" stood midway between the first stake and the fourth stake, called "home bound."

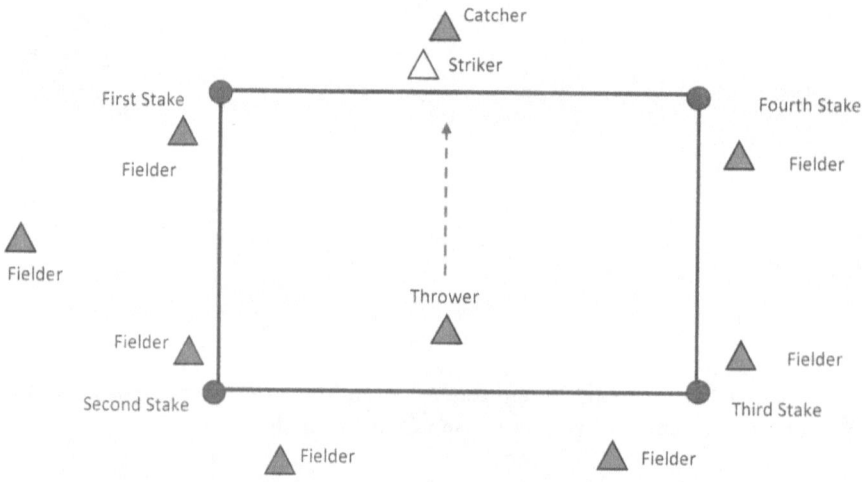

If the striker reaches a stake/base and leaves that position before the thrower releases the ball he will be declared to be out. The "thrower" stood about thirty-five feet away and delivered the ball to the striker in an overhand motion. An out was made by (1) a batter swinging at a thrown ball and missing three times, (2) a fielder catching a batted ball on the fly or on one bounce, or (3) a runner being "plugged" or "soaked" by a thrown ball. This is called one out/all out. The ball is softer than a modern baseball to make plugging more palatable and is only slightly smaller than a modern baseball. As with rounders, there was no foul territory, and a ball may be hit in any direction, so all batted balls were in play.

The number of players per side influences the way the game is played. With fewer than eight players the game reverts to a game of "cat," but with eight or more players the normal game of townball is played. Also, with fewer players there may be an agreement to utilize fewer stakes/bases.

It is well known that Abraham Lincoln played townball as did Ty Cobb, who called it "cow pasture" baseball. It eventually became more commonly known as the Massachusetts game when in 1858 the Massachusetts Association of Base Ball Players adopted rules calling for the bases to be uniformly spaced sixty feet apart, with ten to fourteen players per side, one out per side to an inning, and one hundred "tallies" to win the game. Not unexpectedly, local and regional variations exist, and the players generally enforce the rules themselves, although an umpire may be utilized.

Townball is often called the origin of baseball and there are many similarities with other stick and ball games. The debate will rage on and while there is no doubt that townball contributed to the development of baseball, there are just as many differences as there are similarities. This debate is no different than the Doubleday versus Cartwright controversy, in that there are strong opinions on both sides. Henry Chadwick proclaimed that rounders, not townball, was the inspiration for baseball while some 19th century observers called townball "old fashioned baseball."

Base Ball

In and around New York City, like most American cities, a variety of "ball" games were enjoyed by their citizens—cricket, rounders, and townball being chief among them. The most popular of these during the mid–19th century was townball, which was liberally modified by the teams that played it.

In New York, townball took a different shape, and a set of new rules drawn up by Alexander Cartwright and the Knickerbocker Club in 1845 became widely accepted as the new standard. The distance between the bases was set at ninety feet, and the "striker's point" and "home base" were the same. The ball was pitched underhand from a pitcher's box (not yet a raised mound) fifteen feet from the striker/batter. Batted balls landing outside the first or third baselines were not playable.

Fielders, most notable the short-fielder, were free to position themselves anywhere on the playing field so long as they were in fair territory. From the mid–1860s through the 1880s, additional rules introduced to the National Association of Base Ball Players by sportswriter Henry Chadwick continued to shape the game. For instance, originally in 1845 there were no called strikes. A batter would indicate to the pitcher where he wanted the ball to be thrown and could let the ball go by if he so chose. However, if the batter let the ball go by too many times he would be warned by the umpire for "waiting." Originally, the pitcher was located only fifteen feet away from home base. But as a pitcher's delivery shifted from underhanded to overhand, this was changed

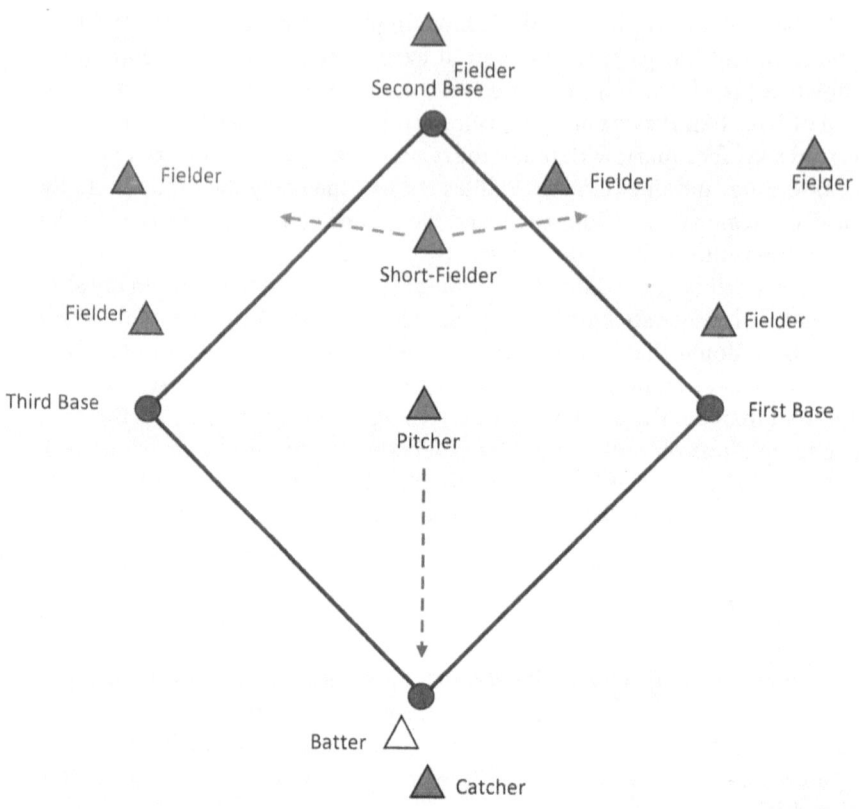

to forty-five feet in 1876, then to fifty feet in 1880, and finally sixty feet in 1893. Runners could be either tagged out or forced out at the base. Batted balls could be caught on the fly or on a single bounce for an out, but by 1858 outs occurred only on the fly. Teams generally had nine players, but rarely more than eleven, and each team had three outs to an inning. Games were originally played until one team reached twenty-one "aces" (runs), but eventually nine players and nine innings became the standard with no limit on the number of runs that could be scored.

Early adopters of the Knickerbocker Rules or the New York Game helped shape the game in the image of their community and their society. In New Orleans this meant playing a game that conformed with and resembled their "modern" sensibilities, meaning a game suitable for gentlemen to engage in. No more chaotic variations of townball or rounders from city to city. In essence, New Orleanians would learn baseball from a rule book, adopting the new, more orderly and rational game as their own. And the game they learned and played would be the same in New Orleans as it was in New York.

But that did not guarantee that players would always interpret these rules uniformly. For that teams would need to engage an impartial arbiter of the rules—an umpire.

For instance, the umpire was originally positioned some twenty feet off to one side from home base, seated at a small table, and initially his role was to interpret the rules. A copy of *The Base Ball Player's Pocket Companion* could be purchased at several local bookstores including Thomas L. White Booksellers at 105 Canal Street.[4] This little book contained all of the rules of the game and also set out the requirements for forming a baseball club. The rule book was indispensable to both the teams and the umpire. After all, baseball was the first game shaped and played from information learned from a book. No one was really sure of the proper distances between bases—forty-two paces. And exactly how long was a "pace"? No one knew if a double play or even a triple play was possible, or if sliding into a base was within the rules. This determination would be made by the umpire after consulting the rule book. With any luck at all, the determination of one umpire would agree with that of a different umpire under the same circumstances in another game at another time. Over time, the umpire's role changed dramatically. The umpire would soon be asked to come off the sidelines and would be stationed behind the pitcher's square in order to call balls and strikes, as well as to make calls at the other bases. However, his role as the arbiter of the rules was gradually diminished as both managers and players became familiar with the rules themselves. But, when called upon, the umpire's interpretation of the rules was still paramount. And as if he didn't already have enough on his plate, so to speak, the umpire was also responsible for controlling player and fan behavior. It was not until later in the 19th century that the umpire moved behind the plate.

In New Orleans, early baseball games were mostly about players enjoying themselves while getting some exercise at the same time, with their practices taking place before they went to work and their games among themselves in the afternoon after work. Their clubs might be named after practically anything—popular places, patriotic figures, flamboyant or classical characters, sponsors and patrons, even admirable qualities. The game was catching on and had already replaced cricket as the most popular sport in New Orleans and many of the city's best athletes would eventually take up the challenge of baseball instead of cricket. However, after the Civil War the popularity of cricket all but disappeared in New Orleans as the conflict had put an abrupt halt on the growth of cricket, not only in New Orleans, but nationwide. Baseball, however, fared much better both during and after the war.

During the Civil War, organized baseball in cities like New Orleans ground to a halt as young men abandoned the ballpark in favor of the battlefield. Young soldiers from New Orleans fought and were captured, fortu-

An engraving from an 1846 baseball game featuring the New York Knickerbocker team which depicts the umpire seated to the right of center beneath an umbrella. The umpire's role was to interpret the rules (from an unknown 19th century publication).

nate to have survived the carnage and resigned to their incarceration in a prisoner of war camp. Once captured they passed the time by playing cards and baseball. Baseball games between guards and prisoners were generally considered to be cordial, at least until 1862 when the war escalated and conditions within prison camps, both Union and Confederate, deteriorated. Despite the all too familiar argument, the Civil War was not responsible for the spread of baseball throughout the South. New Orleans is just about as far away from New York as you can get, but at the outbreak of the war there was already an active and robust baseball community in New Orleans, beginning two years before the Civil War. In fact, baseball had already taken root not only in New Orleans but also was popular in several other major cities throughout the South.

New Orleans was not alone in taking up baseball. As early as 1858, cities across the South from Louisiana, Alabama, North Carolina, South Carolina, Tennessee, Kentucky, and Virginia[5] fielded baseball clubs whose teams wanted nothing more than healthy exercise, spirited competition, and good-hearted fun. These young men followed much the same development path as the clubs in New Orleans. And these are only the teams whose exploits were documented in their local newspaper. To be sure, these games undoubtedly ran the gamut from bedlam and boisterous to the very picture of Victorian proprietary. In the end, however, they shared the common bond of finding baseball to be both electric and addictive. With such a widespread presence in the South it is difficult to defend the claim that baseball was taught to Southerners by Union troops during the Civil War.

For instance, there is a popular art print that was produced from memory by Major Otto Boetticher depicting Union prisoners playing baseball at a Confederate prison camp in Salisbury, North Carolina in 1863. Boetticher was an established commercial artist who enlisted in 1861 in the 68th New York Volunteers at the age of forty-five. Proponents of the theory that the Union forces taught the game to the Confederates often point to this print as proof to bolster their argument. However, Boetticher's own notes regarding the print indicate that the players were Union prisoners formerly held in prison camps in either New Orleans or Tuscaloosa, Alabama, where they were taught to play the game by their Confederate captors. While there is no contemporary newspaper account of the games played in Salisbury, prisoner diaries indicated that the men transferred from New Orleans were more skillful than those from Tuscaloosa and were victorious more often.[6]

Then there was the Union prison camp at Johnson's Island, near Sandusky, Ohio, on the shores of Lake Erie. On August 24, 1864, two teams of Confederate prisoners played in a "championship game," with those below

A popular lithograph by Otto Boetticher illustrating a baseball game between Union soldiers at the Confederate prison camp in Salisbury, North Carolina, in 1863. This piece is often used to argue that Union soldiers taught the Confederates how to play baseball (Library of Congress).

the rank of captain comprising the Southern Nine and those with the rank of captain and above being the Confederate Nine. That this game was billed as a championship game would indicate that there were games played previously, and, indeed, prisoner diaries attest that baseball was a popular pastime. The diary entries of John Dooley stated that on July 26, 1864, there were games nearly every night between the prisoners, and refer to a later championship game between the Southerns and the Confederates on May 12, 1865.

It is interesting to note that at least three members of the Southern Nine at Johnson's Island were also members of the Southern Base Ball Club in New Orleans. Captured as members of the Pelican Regiment and General Harry Hays' Louisiana Tigers Brigade in the Louisiana 7th Infantry at the Battle of Rappahannock Station, Virginia, on November 7, 1863, more than fifty officers were shipped to Johnson's Island. Among them were Lieutenant Edward Ryan of the 7th Louisiana Infantry, Captain William Simms of the 8th Louisiana Infantry, and Captain S.F. Wall of the 9th Louisiana Cavalry.[7] At various times between 1859 and 1861 the New Orleans' Southern Base Ball Club listed Ryan, Simms, and Wall on their pre-war rosters.[8]

The August 1864 championship game was organized by Lieutenant Michael McNamara of the 7th Louisiana Infantry, who was also captured in Virginia on November 7, 1863. Before a crowd estimated to run as large as 3,000 comprised solely of Confederate prisoners, Union soldiers, and a smattering of citizens of Sandusky, the Southern Nine defeated the Confederate Nine by the score of 19 to 11.[9] Also of note is that Lieutenant Charles Hatch Pierce (Pearce) of the 7th Louisiana Infantry, who was a clerk in New Orleans before the war and widely considered the best amateur baseball player the South had ever seen, also participated in the game. Pierce served as captain of the Southern Nine in August of 1864 and returned to New Orleans after he was paroled. He went on to play baseball with the Southern Base Ball Club.[10] The Johnson's Island championship game's organizer, Lieutenant McNamara, moved to New Orleans after the war and he too played for the Southern Base Ball Club, eventually becoming club secretary.[11]

There is more than sufficient evidence that New Orleans' extensive pre-war baseball experience played an influential part in the spread of baseball to both Confederate and Union forces during the Civil War. Following the war, baseball underwent a revival and a rapid expansion in New Orleans that was not always well received. Even before the Civil War, New Orleans openly rejected the constraints of the Puritan Sabbath, from something as simple as having an open-air picnic with beer and dancing to playing competitive sports like baseball. Because the work week was still six days, playing baseball on Sundays became a point of contention, not just in the predominantly Catholic city of New Orleans, but across the country. People who operated their businesses, who played baseball on Sunday, or who did anything that was considered to disregard the Sabbath beyond rest and worship were considered to have violated the Fourth Commandment. By association, baseball became as despicable as excessive drinking and gambling—both of which were openly tolerated and actually flourished in New Orleans. So, the more the New Orleans religious alliance and its silk-stocking fraternity railed against the depravity and licentiousness of baseball, the more they tried to use their bully pulpit to cow their congregation into abandoning the debauchery of playing baseball as falling prey to the wages of sin, the less influence these clerics could actually muster over their flocks in this regard. New Orleans has always been a conundrum, from its deep roots in Catholic moralism to its ready acceptance of prostitution and gambling.

Baseball, as one of the city's most popular and visible sports, drew more than its share of criticism for dragging the city, its children and young men, both middle and upper-class, into the clutches of evil. This would not be the first time that a ball game would come under fire. As early as the 1780s the administration of Princeton College banned their students from playing ball, probably townball, as being "low and unbecoming gentlemen." But the good people of New England could not dampen the spirits of the young men who played townball and rounders. Community elders simply could not come to terms with seeing their fine, upstanding young men having fun and wasting their free time playing a child's game. This disparaging attitude was no different from New England to New Orleans.

But baseball was not the snake in the garden that New Orleans had to guard themselves against. The real struggle would be with the "baneful influence" of gamblers who sought to alter the game for their own profit at the hands of corrupt professional players. On the one hand there were those who felt that baseball was nothing more than a crude pastime unfit for their strata of society and those who aspired to it. It did not matter whether they enjoyed the game as either participant or spectator, both were equally guilty. There were frequent complaints about the noise from the playing fields, making it impossible for decent citizens to enjoy a pastoral stroll through the city without being bombarded by foul language, being unnerved by the unseemly jeering, or being pelted by stray baseballs. The presence of gamblers and liquor only aggravated the situation. Sharps would roam the bleachers looking for, and often finding, an easy mark to fleece.

On the other hand, the game was considered a healthy and invigorating way to get the physical exercise the citizens of New Orleans needed in a pleasant outdoor setting. It fostered spirited, yet friendly competition. It could be played by children and adults from all walks of life and social positions. Clubs and leagues were organized, and uniforms were designed. It was all very forthright and upstanding. The press frequently championed sports as a natural extension of morality and social order, not only intruding on the domain of the religious faction but also forging what opponents felt was an unholy alliance that offered benefits for both camps. It was also a reflection of the national character. For every religious argument against sports as a waste of time and a violation of the social order, the press would counter by arguing for mental and physical health. The scales were more easily tilted to favor the benefit of sports in New Orleans as the citizenry had never been known to pass up an opportunity for a good time.

In a last-ditch effort to exert at least some influence over their sports loving congregations, clerics fought to have baseball prohibited on Sundays. At least if they were successful they could claim some small victory to maintain their relevance in the eyes of church leaders and those members of their congregations who supported them emotionally, philosophically, and financially. They were successful in many areas of the country, but not in New Orleans. For the most part Sunday Blue Laws were ignored with respect to baseball and only selectively enforced in many other parts of the country.

Eventually Louisiana and almost every other state in the country repealed the Sunday Blue Laws that were part of their individual state statutes. As foreign as the concept of Sunday Blue Laws may appear to people in today's society, during the mid–19th century until well into the early 20th century, the move to regulate social behavior based on a specific set of religious standards was a product of its time. In Louisiana, for instance, it is still illegal for an automobile dealership to be open on Sunday. While the people of Louisiana are never at a loss for inane and incomprehensible local laws, there are some that, for whatever reason, have remained on the books as real head-scratchers:

- It is against the law for one to stand on their bicycle handle bars or perform any kind of "fancy" riding (Section 154–1414).
- It is illegal to tie an alligator to a fire hydrant (Section 67–13).

Whether or not it was with a blind eye, New Orleanians played baseball on Sundays for years through decades of unofficial and official Sunday Blue Laws. In the end it was simply a pragmatic decision: players employed outside of baseball worked six days a week, making Sunday the only day available to play. Accordingly, if most players could only play of Sundays, it was only logical that most fans could only attend games on Sunday. With everything else occurring in New Orleans, the police had more important issues to deal with. The unfortunate frequency of robberies, assaults, stabbings, kidnappings, and the murders that occurred on a daily basis was a blight on an otherwise fun-loving and free-wheeling city.

What was Bienville thinking when he laid claim to this paradise for France? The original settlers tasked with clearing land for a new settlement were a sad collection of eighty salt bootleggers, accompanied by an assortment of vagabonds, beggars, thieves, and other casualties of French life fresh from the country's most miserable prisons, with a couple of engineers thrown in to oversee the work. From the time these first beleaguered settlers arrived, New Orleans was by and large a very violent place where an argument over a card game or a woman could escalate to bloodshed in a heartbeat and where rival gangs of immigrants would stage their very public feuds. Their favorite gathering place was usually a sot-hole squarely on the bottom rung of public houses, the *tapis-franc*, an unsavory brothel masquerading as a tavern, usually run by an ex-convict, frequented by felons, and sporting the finest collection of gut-rotting concoctions in and around New Orleans. Visiting merchants traveling to the city by riverboat or railroad were regaled with stories of the exotic and strange pleasures waiting to be discovered in New Orleans. Yet despite its unsavory reputation it was difficult not to love New Orleans, in either its poverty or its glamor, both of which could shock or sadden, but which would eventually capture these visitors, boring beneath their skin and taking up residence in their hearts. However, nothing could prepare them for the city's rampant lawlessness and its dysfunctional law enforcement system.

Between 1820 and the Civil War, a steady stream of flatboats from upriver in Illinois, Kentucky, and Tennessee, and the river pirates who preyed on them, off-loaded whatever cargo they had in New Orleans on the wharves and freight yards from Julia Street upriver to Gaiennie Street. The boatmen eventually found their way to a seedy collection of bars and brothels called The Swamp, an area of approximately six square blocks centered on Girod and Levee (Tchoupitoulas) Streets along the city's waterfront. The Swamp was a real slaughterhouse whose patrons were fresh off the river and could be separated from their money by fist, bludgeon, knife, or pistol after an hour or so of guzzling watered down, cheap whiskey. While the police would rarely set foot in The Swamp to patrol, they were forced to deal with the growing criminal underworld that had expanded their influence into areas beyond the waterfront.

During a single week in 1857 alone the police had to deal with fourteen murders and three hundred and forty cases of assault.[12] Concerned citizens set up vigilance committees to combat what they termed to be the "reign of terror," and so energized the populace that they had a profound impact on the municipal elections in 1858 and 1860. New Orleans Criminal Sherriff E. T. Parker was quoted as describing New Orleans as a "perfect Hell on earth." Only the capture and occupation of New Orleans by April of 1862 Union troops could clamp down on the criminal element and the mayhem they produced.

In 1857 New Orleans was often described as "one perpetual carnival," but it was not Bourbon Street or the French Quarter that was the focus of all the excitement and notoriety. Rather, it was a six block stretch on St. Charles

Avenue between Canal Street and City Hall that developed what was described as a distinct "individuality of character." Indeed, in this six-block stretch there were no fewer than forty-five bars ranging from doggeries to guzzle shops. During the day, the area was generally quiet, with the Bank of New Orleans attracting the most attention from the typical coming and going of its customers. After sunset, however, the scene came alive with its diverse mixture of "eating houses, saloons, shooting galleries, billiard rooms, and bowling alleys alongside music halls and theatres."

That is not to say that during the Civil War criminals disappeared altogether. Rather, they took on an uncharacteristically low profile, staying in the shadows to avoid detection and apprehension. After the war, criminal activity lost no time rearing its head once again. An area downriver on the opposite side of town known simply as Gallatin Street was there to replace The Swamp. As with its predecessor, Gallatin Street was a multi-block area centered around Ursuline Street in the back of the French Quarter. From 1840 through 1870 the neighborhood preyed on the patrons of the bawdy entertainment venues that could be found on every corner at almost any hour of the day. There were often whole city blocks that offered as many as four or five gin mills in one block alone. Numerous "random" shootings were a routine occurrence,[13] not only along Gallatin Street, but throughout the city wherever and whenever ethnic feuds spawned the sort of violence that so often accompanied their nefarious activities. With the degree of serious crime being perpetuated with such savage frequency it was no wonder that the New Orleans police force willingly turned a blind eye to a friendly game of baseball being played on Sunday.

It was not uncommon to see the city's amateur baseball teams holding their practice sessions early in the morning before the start of the workday. Some players might even play catch while on their lunch break. Daylight permitting, teams would return to the field after work for more practice or perhaps a scrimmage. It is difficult to estimate the work habits of the average New Orleanian during the 19th century as the definition of what constituted a full workday is itself full of ambiguities. The traditional "dawn to dusk" theory does not hold true for many businesses, particularly against the background of the conversion from an agricultural-based economy to an industrial-based economy. The Bank Holiday Act was passed in 1871 and this provided a few additional paid holidays to enjoy. In New Orleans, as across America, the burgeoning middle-class sought to come to grips with how to spend their newly found leisure time. While the lower classes generally worked six to seven days per week, businesses with large numbers of middle-class workers in skilled positions found that in most cases a traditional Monday through Friday, five-day work week was often sufficient. However, the typical five-day work week would not be formally adopted nationwide until 1908.

It does not appear that New Orleans held fast and true to the concept of a traditional workday or work week. Many of the earliest baseball games in the city took place during the week toward the end of the workday at three or four o'clock. For instance, the first intra-squad game between two sides of the Louisiana Base Ball Club—Pescay's Side versus Jones' Side—took place on Friday, July 30, 1859, but which was interrupted by nightfall and was concluded on Tuesday, August 2. Both games were scheduled to begin at three o'clock. Allowing for sufficient time for an employee to leave work, change into their uniform, and travel to the ball field—in this case to the Delachaise Grounds in Jefferson City—meant that players had to make arrangements with their employers to take half a day off, presumably to be made up later. However, gauging by the number of mid-week games played, this did not appear to be a serious problem for either the employer or the employee.

But the escalation of organized sports such as baseball had an overwhelming and lasting impact on both the American psyche and on New Orleans. In New Orleans, one could be constantly distracted by a barrage of non-stop entertainment, the ongoing allure of attractive women, the constant aroma and temptation of rich food, and the possibility for commercial prosperity. In short, there was no shortage of pleasurable diversions or competitive challenges. On the extreme other end of the spectrum, the lower-class were consigned to often crushing poverty, meager provisions and subsistence, and the ongoing grind of daily life. The temporary respite offered by simple pursuits like sports provided just enough pleasure to momentarily escape the monotony of their existence.

As baseball grew to become the most popular participant and spectator sport in New Orleans, the game also became one of the most polarizing in the city, with boxing and billiards not far behind. While the game's critics publicly expressed only mild displeasure with the antics and behavior of some of the local teams and players, mostly directed publicly at wayward, hooligan children, they saved their most venomous public condemnation for the teams and players who visited New Orleans to play baseball. Proponents of the game argued that teams from out of town came to New Orleans, stayed in our hotels, ate in our restaurants, and supported our economy. Critics of the game countered that this invasion of rude players from out of town exhibiting what they considered to be awful manners, ranging from their atrocious eating habits in hotels and restaurants to their choice of descriptive language both on and off the field, was an all too frequent occurrence. The newspapers reported on both sides of the controversy. However, it was not lost of the average reader who understood that local ball players were just as likely to exhibit the same social transgressions as their infrequent out-of-town counterparts. Indeed, it was probably more palatable for pundits to ascribe the behavior they found offensive to someone outside of the community than to point the finger at someone they might come into contact with every day.

As one might expect, the objectionable behavior that everyone found so distasteful was exhibited by only a few players in isolated instances that were quickly blown out of proportion in order to support the opposition to baseball. The inflamed rhetoric that found its way into the newspapers did not reflect the true character of baseball. There was, of course, the occasional unsavory character who made the game less palatable for all concerned, but the instances of this type of behavior were quickly dealt with by the members themselves.

Baseball assumed the mantle as the country's National Pastime because of all of the sports available to the upper classes—horse racing, yachting, rowing, baseball, and cricket—only baseball could be readily adopted by the middle and lower classes. Like the upper-class, the middle and lower classes also enjoyed boxing, billiards, bowling and blood-sports, albeit with less of a public presence than their toney cohorts. While baseball and cricket were popular pursuits from their inception in New Orleans in the late 1850s, there was little indication that either would evolve into the National Pastime. It would only be in the years following the Civil War during which, building on the framework created during the Ante-Bellum period, baseball quickly expanded to include even more players who came from a middle-class background and eventually from a lower-class background. Even though, there was still a small but vocal minority who objected to the game of baseball as a whole and to the rowdy people who played such a boisterous and low-brow game.

In the face of such harsh criticism, whether or not it was deserved, proponents and players of the game sought to rehabilitate their image by agreeing to play exhibition games at picnics, fairs and festivals across New Orleans to benefit policemen, firemen, and their charitable or benevolent associations. Fire companies in particular were early proponents of baseball and were frequent sponsors of baseball games at these community fairs and festivals. In so doing baseball teams and their fans benefited from the increased public exposure to a wholesome leisure time activity. The July 1872 festivals under the auspices of the Crescent Steam Fire Engine Company No. 24 and the Louisiana Hose were held at the Fair Grounds, and the featured event was a baseball game between the Mutual Base Ball Club and the Washington Base Ball Club, followed by a series of footraces, then a one-mile trotting challenge between the horses of several fire companies, plus many other games and events.[14] Baseball was also one of the primary drawing card at festivals sponsored by the Clerk's Benevolent Association, the Hibernia Benevolent and Mutual Association of Louisiana, the German-American School, among many others.[15]

The more the general public was exposed to baseball, the more the game grew in popularity and, eventually, in acceptance, even on Sundays. The conversion was gradual, however. The vast majority of businesses in the country were closed on Sunday. Everything from barber shops to bars and saloons were prohibited from conducting business on Sundays. There was a vocal minority in these cities that believed that baseball should also be proscribed from being played on Sundays. From Cleveland to New Orleans, St. Louis to Baltimore, passionate and sensational sermons from the pulpit were delivered by assertive preachers and ministers who attacked baseball on Sunday with the same zeal as anti-slavery.

In New Orleans the entreaties of these honey-tongued preachers and ministers fell on deaf ears. For the working populace, Sunday was generally the only day for recreation as either a participant or a spectator. In most cases, if pressed, the police would arrest a player or two who were taken to the closest precinct and released after paying the obligatory minimum fine of one dollar. However, with the arrest the game was also halted, and the disgruntled cranks went home angry, not with the actions of the police, but with the high-minded righteous reverends and pompous preachers they ultimately held responsible for spoiling their fun. For all the arguments raised by the moral opposition to their congregations, there was not a man among them who honestly wouldn't prefer to spend three hours at the ballpark to spending three hours at the basilica.

Meanwhile, across New Orleans the police had their hands full with what they considered to be real crime while the city fathers were trying to deal with intermittent bouts of yellow fever, cholera, and other maladies that plagued New Orleans. There were simply too many other truly significant concerns for the city leadership to address to bother with baseball. As long as the fans behaved, and the gamblers didn't get out of hand, then baseball was safe on Sundays.

Two

Equipment

"The human hand is made complete by the addition of a baseball."
—Paul Dickson

As one observer once noted, baseball is a combination of memories and facts of discovery.[1] People often apply the realities of today to their impressions of yesterday. For instance, when considering the details of baseball, the assumption is frequently made that the game of the past was not unlike the game today. From 50,000-feet this might hold true: nine men to a team on an open field where a lone batter stares down a pitcher, and the battle between bat and ball takes place as it always has. But under closer examination, the devil can still be found lurking in the details.

Part of the appeal of early baseball was that the game could be played even with a minimum of equipment. With few exceptions, the rudimentary equipment needed was tinkered with from time to time, but by 1872 the basic equipment was agreed upon and codified. Throughout it all these changes have endured the passage of time with a minimum of modification. These minor changes were, however, significant in their contribution to the development of the game, and everything from the bat and the ball to the uniforms and other equipment we are familiar with has undergone a series of subtle and gradual changes over the course of time.

New Orleans baseball clubs could adopt an unconventional uniform such as the "baseball outfit" offered by The Clothier Hein from his emporium on St. Charles Avenue on the corner of Commercial Place. This outfit resembled a young man's matching knickers and double-breasted jacket.[2] More than likely true baseball enthusiasts sought out one of the many sporting goods stores such as P.F. Gogarty's store at 151 Camp Street selling bats, balls, bases, and scorebooks.[3]

Balls

Central to the game of baseball was the ball itself. Just as with the game of baseball itself, and as difficult as it may be to accept, there is no clear evidence pointing to the inventor of the baseball itself. In the early days, those dashing mustachioed men crafted their own balls from whatever materials were available. The first covers were cowhide cut in a "lemon peel" pattern such that all four sides, when stitched, came together at a single point. The number and spacing of the stitches varied from ball to ball. Early balls came in many colors which were all varying shades of brown. It was much later that off-white became the preferred color for a baseball. As the game of baseball evolved so did the ball. The first baseballs were handmade with a soft rubber core wound with yarn or string, sometimes with or sometimes without additional stuffing. A stitched leather cover enclosed the assemblage. The cover of the ball was not always crafted from its now familiar double figure eight figure patterned leather cover sewn together with one hundred and eight precisely spaced and tightly laced double stitched seams. Even the origin of the cover's pattern is shrouded in controversy. Some attribute the design to shoemaker Ellis Drake, while others give the credit to William A. Cutler, who sold this design to baseball manufacturer William Harwood. When it came to the size of the ball there was also little standardization in terms of dimensions and a general lack of consistency as to how balls were constructed.

Equally important as the shape and size of the baseball was what a pitcher did with a baseball, how the ball was thrown. As early as 1845, pitching the ball was required to be in an underhanded pendulum motion from a distance of only fifteen feet from the batter. Far from the role of flamethrower, pitchers were required to exhibit control and to deliver the ball in what we know today as the strike zone, at a height indicated by the batter. There were no called strikes, giving hitters a distinct advantage. Pitchers naturally began looking for ways to gain the upper hand and gradually learned how to throw the ball harder without losing their accuracy. They discovered that they could make it the ball harder to hit by snapping their wrist at the end of their delivery. Of course pitchers knew it was against the rules at the time to attempt to alter the spin on a pitched ball by snapping their wrist during their delivery, but they were hoping to slip one by the umpire. The batters had to find a way to compensate. While there were no called strikes, lethargic batters could be cautioned by the umpire for ignoring too many pitches the umpire deemed to be hittable. Before long pitchers began to throw overhand, with their delivery gaining even more speed. However, trying to induce the hitter to swing at a pitch that wasn't perfect was like trying to catch a snake asleep. Hitters eventually caught up to the increased pitch speed and compensated by swinging the bat faster and with fairly consistent accuracy. It was a crafty hurler

An advertisement for the Official Spalding League Ball from the Spalding 1889 catalog. The price was $1.50 per ball or $15.00 per dozen (Estate of Arthur O. Schott).

who began using the baseball's seams to spin the ball to make it even harder to hit a new pitch called a curve ball. Now it was the pitcher who could break off a real pretzel bender and leave the hitter carving nicks in the weather.

Every time it appeared that the pitcher's increased velocity and control gave him the advantage, the pitcher was moved further away from the batter. From the original fifteen feet in 1854, then to forty-five feet in 1876 and fifty feet in 1880, and finally to the current distance of sixty feet, six inches in 1893, the pitcher had to throw harder to cover the same distance with the same degree of control and efficiency. This back and forth battle between pitchers and hitters would continue through the remainder of the 19th century and learning how to spin and manipulate the trajectory of the ball was paramount to a pitcher's success. To help further alter the trajectory some clever fellow came up with the spitball. Once again no one can definitively say who the architect of this nasty but effective new pitch was. It first appeared in the latter part of the 19th century, leading to freakish deliveries and frustrated batters.

The home teams in New Orleans were generally expected to bring at least three baseballs to a game as they were difficult and costly to come by and, therefore, a prized possession of the club. Should a foul ball be hit into a crowd of spectators, bench players were sent to retrieve the ball before one of the neighborhood boys could run off with it or should a foul ball happen to land in the thick underbrush outside of the ballfield or in a stand of trees nearby the field, the game was halted and both teams were pressed into service to retrieve it. One could only imagine the condition of the ball by the end of the game as being little more than a soggy black beanbag after nine innings of being the recipient of the licorice juice or tobacco juice the players used to keep their leather gloves pliable being transferred from their gloves. Balls also took quite a beating from being pelted around the yard by the hitters.

Early baseball could be an adventure as teams might show up with several different sized balls. With balls being entirely handmade, it was difficult to standardize the construction of the earliest baseballs. Eventually the dimensions of the ball were set in 1858 and were updated in 1861 and again in 1871. From this point forward, every regulation baseball would now start with a molded vulcanized rubber core, not comprised of strip rubber. The core would then be wrapped with woolen yarn. This caused the ball to be less lively. The more durable horsehide became the covering of choice even though it was sometimes harder to obtain. The entire assemblage had to weigh between five and five and one-quarter ounces with a total circumference between nine and nine and one-quarter inches.

One of the first decisions made by baseball owners and managers when starting or joining a new league was to agree upon which ball they would use. Al Spalding, a former major league pitcher who over four years won 241 games in 300 starts (.803) with balls he made himself, made a bold business move by providing the National League with baseballs for free in return for being named the official baseball of the league. When the National League agreed and adopted his ball as the official ball of the league, Spalding's gambit caused hundreds of teams across the country to order Spalding baseballs by the dozen and his baseball empire was launched. Both Spalding and Reach baseballs were popular, but there were dozens of local and regional companies making baseballs at competitive prices. By the time baseball came to New

Orleans, the most popular balls were being manufactured by H.P. Harwood & Sons of Natick, Massachusetts. After the Civil War the ball's familiar figure-eight stitching pattern we know today was designed by Colonel William Cutler, who sold the design to William Harwood in 1858. However, like so many aspects of baseball's early history, there is some question as to who first came up with the design. There are those who believe that a shoemaker named Ellis Drake from Stoughton, Massachusetts, was responsible for the original design. In any event, the figure-eight pattern systematically replaced the lemon peel pattern of early baseballs.

Bats

Children are known to be inventive and imaginative, and they more than proved to be so when playing baseball. The bats they used may have been old whittled-down wooden wagon tongues, wagon wheel spokes, or a shaved down table leg. Of course, none of these were regulation, but then again, who would care? Somewhere along the way they gained access to the necessary tools to shape the square wagon tongue or table leg into a more rounded barrel with a tapered handle as a close approximation to the ones they saw in the catalogs and that the adults using. Early teams who could not afford a professionally made bat relied on the talents of the local cabinet maker or wood turner to shape a "striker's stick" into something that could be used with greater dependability. Length and weight were secondary considerations only in the sense that the batter needed to feel comfortable swinging the bat so that he could make contact with a pitched ball effectively and frequently. Players before the Civil War who had trouble gripping bats with fatter handles began wrapping string or cord around the handle. In general, early bats were manufactured to be longer and heavier and with a more measured, gradual taper to the handle.

Aside from the array of handmade bats, in baseball's earliest days there were as many different types and designs of baseball bats as there were baseballs: long, short, flat, round, or with any combination of features a player could imagine or produce. Originally, bats could be of any length and made from any type of wood. To be accurate, there really was no such thing as a regulation baseball bat until precise dimensions were set forth by the National Association of Base Ball Players (NABBP) in 1859. Regulation bats were described as being round, not more than two and one-half inches around at their thickest part. These standards were amended by the NABBP in 1868, 1885, and finally in 1893. Their now codified standards were for bats to be thirty to forty inches long and forty-eight ounces in weight. The preferred wood was either maple or ash, but rosewood, white pine, pitch pine, and

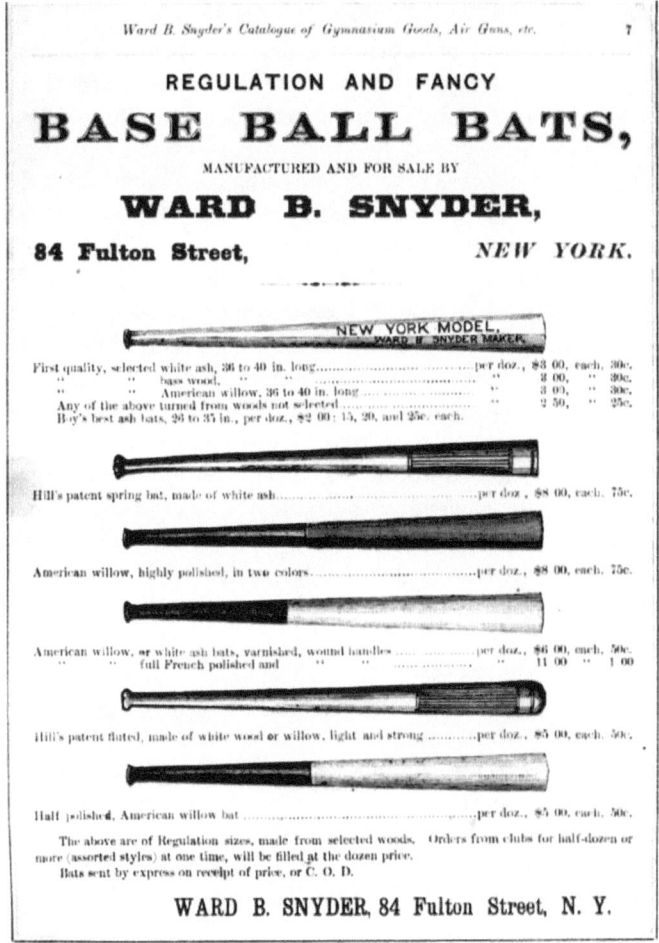

An advertisement from the Ward Snyder catalog for "Regulation and Fancy Base Ball Bats" from 1875. These bats ranged in price from $3.00 to $11.00 and were crafted from either white ash or willow. The shape and taper of these early bats is quite different from the present (Estate of Arthur O. Schott).

hickory were also used. Basically, if you could chop it down, it was fair game for the wood-smith to make into a bat.

Until 1872 players were free to use any bat available, whether it belonged to their team or to their opponents. Utilitarian touches such as fatter knobs at the tapered end of the bat to make it easier to hold onto when swinging and a rounder or flatter bat-head were at the discretion of the bat's owner. In fact, early bats could be made with or without knobs. Players did eventually notice that rounded bats performed better. Decorative touches were optional, but in most instances didn't help the batter hit the ball any more effectively. Occasionally a previously unknown vintage oddity bat surfaces that demonstrates the diversity of design in 19th century bats, with features such as counterweights at the knob or modifications to the handle to improve the player's grip.

When pitchers delivered the ball underhanded there was little need to replace their bat with any frequency, although early bats were prone to splintering. It was not until pitchers began throwing a harder ball overhanded at greater velocity that hitters needed to replace splintered or broken bats more often and a new American industry of professional bat makers came into being.

In 1884, John Hillerich of Louisville, Kentucky, decided to come to the aid of slumping Louisville Eclipse slugger Pete Browning. Legend has it that Browning broke his favorite bat and thereafter his hitting woes began when he tried to use his teammates' bats. Young Hillerich crafted a bat to Browning's specifications in his father's woodworking shop and presented it to him and the very first Louisville Slugger was born. Browning's fortunes turned around with his new bat and before long his teammates and players from other teams all wanted a new Louisville Slugger bat for their own. Hillerich branded his bats, both literally and figuratively, and became the most recognized bat in the country.

Originally considerations such as bat speed or launch angle were not a primary determining factor in the design and selection of a bat or in the analysis of a hitter's swing. Rather, it was universally believed that a forcefully swung heavy bat would allow a hitter to propel the ball further. In the 19th century it was not uncommon for a hitter to use a fifty-two-ounce bat. However, batters using a heavy bat were more likely to swing over the ball and hit a worm burner across the infield than they were to clear the fences on the fly.

Bases

The last basic component to play baseball were the bases. Improvised at first by using a tree stump or a rock, almost anything was used to mark a base, but resulted in their being no set distance between bases. Teams were at the mercy of the terrain. Rounders and townball used upright wooden stakes or posts as bases. Four-foot stakes were tried and proved to be easily portable and could be set to uniform distances, but this tradition did not translate well to baseball. Until 1857 when the NABBP established their regulation for bases to be ninety feet from each other, there was no standard distance between bases. The layout of the available playing field often dictated base location.

Eventually flat bags that could be stepped on became the base of choice.

Cloth bags filled with sand were popular provided you didn't have to carry them for long periods of time from the team's clubhouse to the ballpark. Plain old dirt was just as heavy as sand and other fillings such as old rags and sawdust, were tried. The familiar streamlined square shape we know today would be foreign to the first games played. Bases in the early days might resemble a lumpy pillow that became more misshapen the more it was stepped on or kicked. Canvas proved to be a durable and easily accessible cover for the bases. It was lightweight and long-lasting and could withstand the constant beating from players' spiked shoes. A leather belt or strap was used to secure the bag, a small spike being driven through the belt or strap into the ground to which the bag was then secured in place.

Gloves and Protective Gear

Not initially part of the game because of the softness of early baseballs, players did not see the need to wear gloves in the field. All of this changed as baseballs became harder and pitchers threw with greater velocity. In 1875 Al Spalding claims to have seen Boston's Charles C. Waite wear a neutral-colored glove so as not to stand out. However, Doug Allison, the catcher for the fabled Cincinnati Red Stockings, was believed to use a glove during his tour through New Orleans in 1870. Unfortunately for Waite people did notice and he was ridiculed every-

IRWIN'S GLOVES.
WE HAVE BEEN MADE SOLE AGENTS FOR THESE GLOVES.
No. 25. Irwin's Celebrated Cat ...ers' Gloves........ $5 00
No. 25A.   "   "   Infielder's " 3 50

INFIELDERS' GLOVES.
No. XX. Spalding's Drab Buck Infielders' Gloves.... 2 50
No. X.   "   White "   "   " 2 00

BASE BALL FINGERLESS GLOVES.
———OPEN BACK———

No. 1-0 Glove.

No. 1-0. Spalding's League Cat'hrs Gloves made of extra heavy Indian-tanned buck, and carefully selected with special reference to the hard service required of them, open back, both hands fingerless, well padded, and fully warranted. We especially recommend this glove for catchers........ .... 2 50
No. 1 Spalding's Professional Gloves, made of Indian-tanned buckskin, open back, well padded, but not quite as heavy as the No. 0............................. 2 00

Nos. E. and F.

No. B. Spalding's Amateur Gloves, made of buckskin, open back, well padded and adapted for amateur players. 1 50
No. C. Spalding's Practice Gloves, made of buckskin, open back, well padded............... 1 00
No. D. Open back, a good glove at the price, made of light material............................... 75
No. E. Boy's size, cheap open back glove............. 50
No. F. Youth's size, cheap open back glove........... 25
☞ Any of the above Gloves mailed postpaid on receipt of price. In ordering, please give size of ordinary dress glove usually worn.

CHICAGO. **A. G. SPALDING & BROS.** NEW YORK

A Spalding catalog advertisement for fingerless baseball gloves made of tanned buckskin leather. There was a minimum amount of padding in the palm of the glove, but there was no protection for the fingers and no webbing. Catcher's gloves cost from $2.50 to $5.00 apiece while infielders' gloves cost from $2.00 to $3.50 apiece based on the amount of padding provided (Estate of Arthur O. Schott).

where he played by fans and players. Even then Waite's gloves were little more than leather farm gloves that had most of the finger sleeves removed in order to be able to handle the ball better. If a batter hit a slow ground ball across the infield, fielders could easily handle a daisy cutter like that with or without gloves. A stiff line drive, however, could raise a nasty palm-numbing welt or even break a finger if the fielder did not wear a glove. The harder the ball was hit, the harder it was to handle bare-handed. Despite the idea of softening their virile image by playing the manly game with a glove, the idea caught on. This provided some measure of protection and comfort, or perhaps players were finally fed up with nursing their bruised and broken fingers. But as the ball changed and became harder and livelier, even the manliest players added their own padding for additional protection.

Thus the "kid glove aristocracy" was born and, not surprisingly, Al Spalding was in the forefront of manufacturing baseball gloves, thereby removing the stigma of wearing a glove. First basemen began using a fingerless padded glove as early as 1877. The Decker Safety Catcher's Mitt was introduced in 1890, although there is some evidence that padded gloves were being used during the late 1880s. Shallow webbing between the thumb and first finger was introduced next and in 1895 baseball clubs created restrictions on glove size. By the end of the century, every player in baseball, amateur or professional, used a

This catcher is depicted decked out in the latest in protective gear—a 1889 Gray's Chest Protector. It was available in padded canvas for $1.00 apiece or in padded leather for $5.00 apiece. The catcher is sporting a minimal glove on his left hand and is not wearing any shin guards (Estate of Arthur O. Schott).

glove of some design. Outfielders were the last to embrace gloves, but they too adopted the practice as balls became harder and came at them faster.

Other than a simple mouthpiece, catchers or receivers wore no protective gear until 1877 with the introduction of a modified fencing mask pioneered by Harvard University's Jim Tyng. The padded chest protector came along in the early 1880s when James "Deacon" White introduced a canvas covered rubber bladder that was pumped full of air. Padding eventually replaced the air tubes and by the 1890s Gray's Patent Body Protector became the preferred form of body armor. Shin guards were only introduced in the 20th century.

Uniforms

Uniforms were as diverse as the teams that sported them. The idea of having all of the team members wearing the same shirt and pants, often in the same color, allowed a player to easily distinguish between his team and his opponent. This was a holdover from cricket and was adopted by baseball teams to foster team unity. In the Northeast, flannel was adopted as the preferred fabric. The 1849 New York Knickerbockers wore white flannel shirts and blue trousers. In New Orleans this would suffice during the very active and mild fall and winter seasons but would quickly become uncomfortable during the humid summer heat. The more players began to slide into the bases, teams adopted quilted and padded trousers to minimize the bruising and scrapping on their players. The heavier quilted fabric made the pants hotter, but more durable and effective.

Two close-up images of Spalding's trade-marked catcher's masks. The mask on the left featured Spalding's new patented neck protector beneath the cage which cost $4.00 apiece, $0.50 more than the regular mask on the right. The wire cage was padded with goat hair covered in the "best imported dog skin" (Estate of Arthur O. Schott).

In 1868 many teams adopted knickers because they were not only cooler, and a player could more easily run and field. Almost universally the players of the 20th century would celebrate replacing the baggy flannels with lighter, breathable fabrics.

From there uniforms only got to be more complicated. In the early years of baseball in New Orleans there was no difference between home and road uniforms, and there were no team names or player names or numbers on the tunic or jersey. Having the same color shirts and trousers was sufficient and teams tried to wear their own distinctive combination of colors for their shirts and pants so as not to be confusing. By the 1880s teams sported a logo or the team's initials on the front of their jerseys over the heart. They also had different uniforms for home and away games. There was a move introduced in 1881 to have a player's shirt and hat be a different color to represent the position they played. The idea was that it would be easier for the fans to identify the players, although at a distance it might be difficult to distinguish the catcher (scarlet) from the shortstop (maroon). Their relative position on the field should have been enough, but when running the bases all these colors ran together. It was one of many ideas that never caught on. The color combinations they proposed were:

A variety of lightweight flannel baseball caps. The style, pattern, and color variations helped to identify different teams (Estate of Arthur O. Schott).

- Pitchers: light blue
- Catchers: scarlet
- First Base: scarlet and white vertical stripes
- Second Base: orange and black vertical stripes

- Third base: blue and white vertical stripes
- Shortstop: maroon
- Left Field: white
- Center Field: red and black vertical stripes
- Right Field: grey

Fortunately for the players and the fans this expensive experiment only lasted a single season and was not adopted. But with such a riot of color splashed across the field, teams realized they still needed to devise some mechanism to tell themselves apart. The most expedient means was to wear different color socks. Many teams would change their name to reflect their footwear, such as the Red Stockings or the White Stockings. The multi-colored uniform concept thankfully failed to spark any interest and was set aside. Particularly with infielders running the bases, both teams' second basemen's orange and black hats made it difficult to distinguish between the two players. The use of colored stockings was, however, adopted and remains popular to this day. Not only did players have to pay up to $30 for their uniform, but they had to pay their own laundry bill as well.

Clubs gradually adopted uniformly colored hats and caps, but

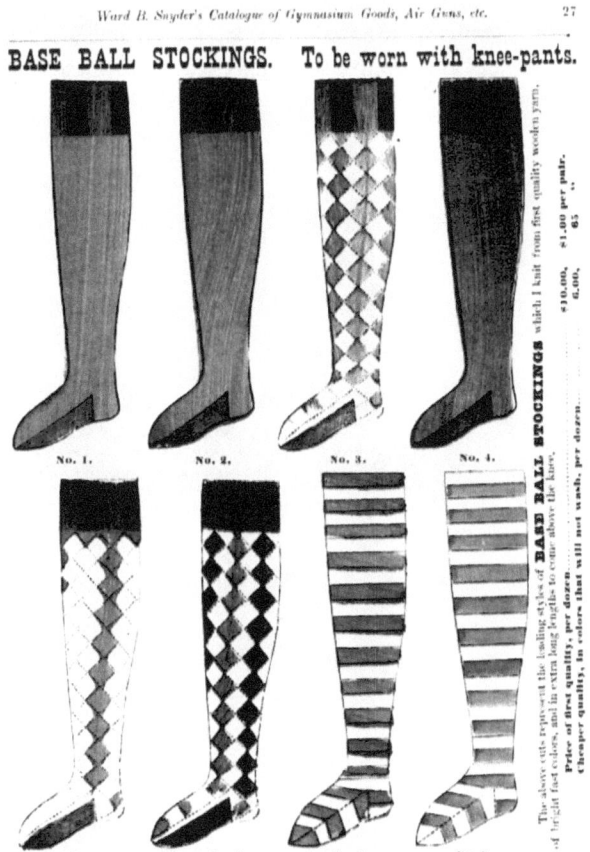

This advertisement features eight varieties of knit wool baseball stockings in a variety of solid, striped, and patterned options that were priced between $6.00 and $10.00 per dozen based on the quality desired. The style and color variations also helped to identify different teams (Estate of Arthur O. Schott).

the rest of the uniform was often brightly colored as an expression of a ball club's personality. For example, the 1893 New Orleans Pelicans in the Southern League had a bright red uniform with black trimming and stockings that they wore on the road and a blue uniform with white trim and stockings that they wore at home. Such distinctive colors were certainly easy to see from the bleachers, but did not necessarily help the players hit, run, or throw any better.

In the years following the Civil War, spiked-sole shoes began showing up as the increased traction made it easier to run the bases in cleats. The familiar round steel shoe plate with cleats found on the toe and the heel of the shoe was adopted in the late 1870s. The original high-top shoe with canvas uppers and leather soles gave way to low-cut leather shoes.

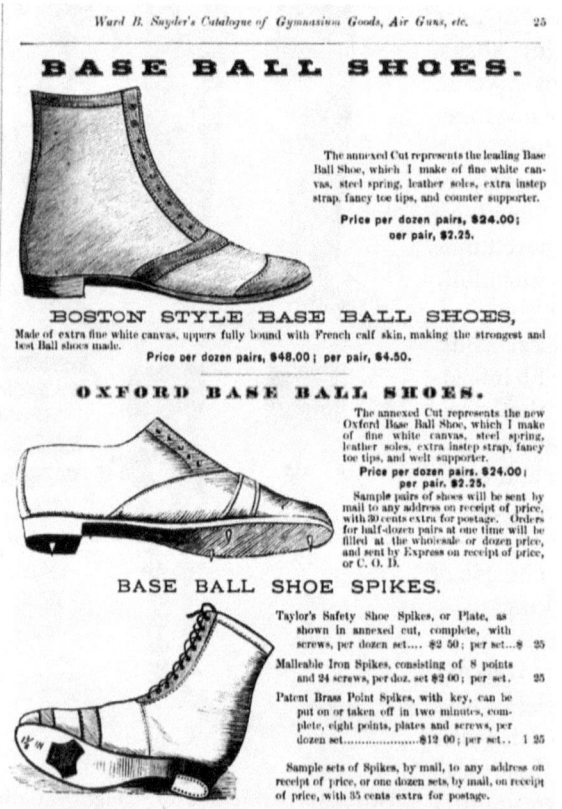

For a mere $2.25 apiece or $24 per dozen a team could be turned out in the finest and most stylish footwear on the diamond. While high-top shoes were the most popular, low-cut shoes were also available. Both versions were crafted with leather soles and canvas uppers (Estate of Arthur O. Schott).

Three

Where They Played

Equally important as the equipment the players used was to the development of the game of baseball was finding a functional playing field. Depending on the game being played, nearly any open area could suffice. For something simple like two-cat or stoolball, a vacant lot with fairly short cropped grass might be pressed into service. But for cricket, townball, or rounders a larger venue was needed. By the time young men began playing baseball, the size of the playing field also had to be much larger than a vacant lot.

Because of the scarcity of open land large enough on which to play baseball, the ballfield was not always neatly-trimmed, smooth grass and raked dirt. The empty lot in the neighborhood might have to suffice in a pinch, and then only for young boys. For young men who could hit the ball harder and farther much more space was needed. Finding an open space on the outskirts of a residential neighborhood in and around New Orleans was easy enough, but only if the site was located far enough away from residential areas. If the land had already been cleared and was at least reasonably dry and level, the permission of the property owner still had to be secured, but this was not always sought or obtained, and did not always deter the newly formed baseball clubs.

Depending on how determined the members of the club were, they might take it upon themselves to clear away any rocks and small bushes that were scattered around the playing field and to keep the grass cut. Ground balls bouncing through the open field like scared rabbits would be slowed by the lumpy and uneven terrain making fielding an adventure and running the bases an ankle-turning undertaking. But as the population of New Orleans continued to rapidly expand through successive waves of immigration, new residential developments and expanding businesses arose to accommodate that growth, clubs were crowded out of the available urban sites and thus were forced to turn to parks or more rural locations. The commercial areas and plantations along the Mississippi River were prime locations.

Travelling upriver from New Orleans, the first suburb one encountered

Detail from a birds' eye view of New Orleans looking upriver at the cities of Jefferson and Carrollton This engraving was drawn from nature on stone by John Bachman circa 1851. Development along the river (*left*) and along St. Charles Avenue (*center*) are quite pronounced, but beyond that there were vast tracts of open land (Bachmann, John, Artist. *Birds' Eye View of New-Orleans / drawn from nature on stone by J. Bachman, i.e., Bachmann*. Louisiana, New Orleans United States, ca. 1851. New York: Published by the agents A. Guerber & Co. Photograph. https://www.loc.gov/item/93500720/).

was Lafayette City, stretching from Felicity Street upriver to Toledano Street, and which was annexed by New Orleans in 1852. This was followed by Jefferson City, beginning at Toledano Street and continuing upriver to Joseph Street, and which was annexed in 1870. Lastly was the City of Carrollton, which ran from Joseph Street upriver to Carrollton Avenue, and which was annexed in 1874. Commercial development in these suburbs was generally along Levee Street (now Tchoupitoulas Street) and residential development was chock-a-block around various plantations and homesteads that remained scattered throughout Lafayette, Jefferson, and Carrollton. The further upriver one travelled, the more open land could be found.

For those New Orleanians who wanted to escape the oppressive summer heat and the choking dust of the city, the resorts and picnic areas located north of the city at West End, Milneburg, and Spanish Fort along the lakefront were popular destinations for water sports and other recreation. All of these locations could be easily reached with a short trip by rail. The blistering summer heat in New Orleans was often accompanied by frequent outbreaks of yellow fever and these epidemics could quickly sweep through the city, often with deadly results. This sent a significant number of its residents to these resorts or even further out of town to the beaches along the Mississippi gulf coast during the summer months. Residents and visitors could still freely enjoy themselves outdoors in New Orleans during the fall through spring, but those who could afford to do so took off for the Gulf Coast during the summer months. There they participated in fishing, swimming, boating, horseback riding, and all manner of water games and sports. In a city that appreciated music of all kinds from opera at the New Orleans Opera House on Bourbon Street, to the raucous dance halls and concert saloons in The Swamp or the Tenderloin District, from the brass bands, minstrel shows and

Baseball was not the only sport played at West End. This engraving shows New Orleanians enjoying rowing, sailing, and boating outside of the West End Hotel while visitors stroll on the wooden boardwalk along the lakefront (from an unknown 19th century publication).

concerts in the theatre, the outdoor garden gazebo, or on the spacious lawns outside of the West End or Spanish Fort resorts, to the city's own beloved home-grown musical style, jazz, it was not unusual to hear passersby humming or whistling a popular tune as they made their way to the race track or to a baseball game under the pavilions of the Delachaise Grounds.

The locations and landmarks mentioned in baseball game advertisements were familiar to the New Orleanians of the day. By providing a rudimentary location such as "Freetown" or "the Beef Lot," most people would know the location. Often mentioned in newspaper announcements were sites described as "greens," probably a holdover from the colonial-era reference to the village green or commons. In New Orleans, however, these greens did not refer to a common gathering area such as Jackson Square, but rather to almost any open patch of land within the city. Some of these had been given colorful names such as Orange Green (1879) which was located on Orange Street near the river, Oil Factory Green (1882), Bee Green (1877), and Pioneer Green (1872). On the other side of the Mississippi River there was Morgan's Green (1877) located alongside the Morgan Railroad Depot in Algiers. Morgan's Green was also known as Algiers Green. Other sites located across the Mississippi River on the West Bank were McDonoghville (1877) and Freetown (1881), both further upriver, which were sites frequented by the city's free people of color and their teams.

In true New Orleans tradition, the area referred to as the West Bank across the Mississippi River is actually east of the city of New Orleans. The twisting path of the river resulted in several sharp twists and turns, with the end result being that property located on that side of the river, the west bank of the river, could actually be reached by travelling due east.

Vacant lots such as the Masonic Lot opposite Tivoli Circle on St. Charles Avenue and Calliope Street, as well as numerous other open lots across the city were often used with or without the owner's permission. Empty rail yards and lumber yards were popular choices as they were easy to get to, offered plenty of open space that was fairly level and were already cleared. But the most common venues were parks and public squares, the open areas and places where people might also picnic. Citizens were quite familiar with City Park, Audubon Park, McDonogh Park, Palmer Park, Clouet Gardens, and Washington Square. Also among the popular sites were the previously mentioned Morgan's Green, the Nashville Station (1866) and the Soniat Station (1867) of the Carrollton Railroad, and the Prytania Streetcar Station (1886). All of these offered large open freight yards which, when vacant, provided more than enough space for the field to be laid out and for a baseball game to be played.

The vast open areas along the wharves downriver in the city's Third District, when not stacked with cotton, timber, or other cargo, were ideal for both practice and club games. Among the most frequently mentioned of these were at the foot of Piety Street (1869), the foot of Clouet Street (1870), or the foot of Montegut Street (1877), all located downriver in the city's blue collar Third District. Further uptown were areas at the foot of Robin Street (1873) or the foot of Girod Street (1877).

One such open space located on Claiborne Street (later Claiborne Avenue) near the corner of Bagatelle Street (now Bourbon Street) in the Third District was the scene of an early baseball game between the Southern Base Ball Club and the Magnolia Base Ball Club on October 3, 1859. The two teams put on quite a show, scoring a total of eighty-two runs—fifty-three for the Southerns and twenty-nine for the Magnolias. Following the Southern victory the two clubs exchanged "badges" as a show of camaraderie before retiring to the United States Hotel to imbibe in a variety of adult beverages and to relive the exciting moments from the game just played.[1]

Public places provided barely enough space for youth baseball and would prove to be wholly inadequate for adults. This, however, did not deter them from trying. Familiar locations such as Annunciation Square (1874), Coliseum Square (1877), Lafayette Square (1874), and Tivoli Circle (1874) were often the site of youth baseball games. Lafayette Square, being directly across the street from City Hall, was an intermittent problem. Even at two and one-half acres, Lafayette Square often had trouble containing a batted ball.

As early as 1866, neighborhood boys ignored the Union soldiers encamped in Lafayette Square and pelted their rubber baseballs all across the camp, much to the displeasure of the camp commander.[2] By 1875, baseball in Lafayette Square was described as "an epidemic" that needed to be dealt with "rigorously and promptly,"[3] as these were no longer just neighborhood boys, but included organized teams of young men using the square as a practice facility and game venue. Because of its location just across St. Charles Avenue from City Hall, the city dutifully issued a prohibition order against playing or practicing baseball in Lafayette Square, which only forced these teams to walk three blocks further up St. Charles Avenue to Tivoli Circle, known today as Lee Circle. Several weeks after the city's prohibition order was announced, there was a near fatal incident at Tivoli Circle involving two ladies trying to cross the street during which one of them was hit in the head with an errant fly ball, crushing her bonnet and shattering one of her hair combs. One witness account claimed that the poor lady had been struck in the head by the batter swinging wildly. While it is highly unlikely that the poor lady in question would be walking so close to a young man swinging a wooden bat, wildly or not, it is only reasonable to assume that she was not struck by the batter. Nevertheless, the printed account sold newspapers and the ensuing uproar called upon the city to extend the baseball prohibition to all public squares.[4]

In 1888, reform-minded Mayor Joseph A. Shakspeare intervened following a flurry of citizen complaints, ordering Police Commissioner David Hennessey to vigorously enforce prohibitions against baseball in both Annunciation and Coliseum Squares.[5] However, it would not be until 1893 before the city issued an ordinance prohibiting the game from being played in Lafayette Square, as much to preserve the city's green space as to safeguard against politicians, visitors, and other pedestrians from being assaulted by an errant baseball or an unpleasant invective.

Part of the early success of cricket and baseball came as a result of having a well-known, designated and accessible playing field. This came about initially with the popularity of cricket, which used a rural location known as the Delachaise Grounds in Jefferson City just upriver from New Orleans.

Delachaise Grounds (1859–1899)

The first neighborhood upriver from the city of New Orleans was the city of Lafayette, followed by Jefferson City, stretching from Toledano Street to the upper boundary of Rickerville, now known as Joseph Street. The first neighborhood one reached in Jefferson City, closest to the city, the Faubourg Delachaise, was first laid out in 1820.

A modest land grant was received and first settled by Jacques Delachaise, who arrived in Louisiana in 1723 as part of Governor Bienville's administration. Jacques carved out a small plantation that was eventually inherited by his grandson, Philippe Pierre August Delachaise (1791–1831). In 1818, Philippe was appointed Justice of the Peace in Orleans Parish (in Louisiana, counties are termed parishes) and began commuting from his plantation to his office in the Cabildo at Jackson Square. With the continued expansion of both the New Orleans and the Carrollton Railroad lines further up St. Charles Avenue, Philippe began acquiring property in the adjoining Faubourg Plaisance in 1820. The land owned by Philippe ran from the river to St. Charles Avenue, from Louisiana Avenue to Antonine Street, named for Marie Antonine Foucher, wife of Philippe August Delachaise.

In partnership with Louisiana Supreme Court Justice Francois Xavier Martin, Philippe established a brick factory on Levee Street (Tchoupitoulas Street) at the river between present-day Amelia and Delachaise Streets. This proved to be a very good investment in a rapidly expanding New Orleans. However, plans to enlarge the business came to an abrupt end with Philippe's untimely death in 1831 at the age of forty-seven. Philippe's sister Aline married her brother-in-law Francoise Dugue Livaudais in 1840 and took over the family brickyard. The business was renamed Degue's Brickyard and remained a family-operated business until 1866 when it was leased to Benjamin Franklin

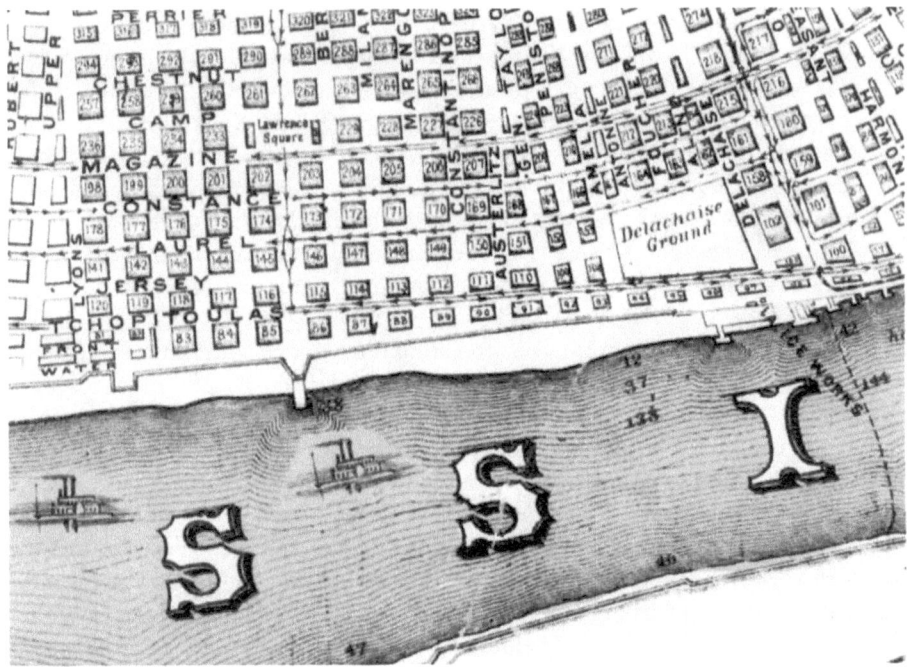

An enlarged area of the 1883 map from the *Atlas of the City of New Orleans* illustrates the location of the Delachaise Grounds. By the time this map was produced the brick factory that would have been located to the left or up river side of the Delachaise Grounds had already been redeveloped into a residential neighborhood (from an unknown 19th century publication).

Smith for three years. In 1855 the heirs of Philippe August Delachaise subdivided the plantation into the Faubourg Delachaise.

Adjoining the brickyard was an open park bounded by Delachaise Street, Laurel Street, Foucher Street, and Levee Street, approximately two city square blocks in size. The brick factory was upriver bounded by Foucher Street, Laurel Street, Amelia Street, and Levee Street, also approximately two square blocks in size.

The summer of 1859 was a welcome respite for New Orleans Mayor Gerald Stith. The city's eighteenth mayor was elected on June 6, 1858, during the height of one of the worst yellow fever outbreaks in recent years, claiming 4,845 lives in the summer of 1858 alone. This was on the heels of a horrific three-year period from 1853 through 1855 during which more than 12,940 souls fell prey to yellow fever, and this did not include deaths from other causes such as consumption, congestive fever, scarlet fever, cholera, typhoid fever, and diarrhea. The grim accounting could be found weekly in the city's newspapers, providing a listing of deaths and burials by the respective cemetery and the known causes of death of those that had been allowed to be buried there.[6] Now, as the mild rains and moderate late spring weather gave way to the promise of a pleasant summer during 1859, it seemed as if the steam had returned from West End and the Mississippi gulf coast to the stride of the citizens of New Orleans. It was certainly evident as people from across the city returned to enjoy the outdoors in New Orleans. As of the beginning of June there had not been a single reported case of yellow fever.[7] The city's social clubs also felt more confident in presenting their spring festivals and the picnics which abounded at the city's popular parks and leisure areas.

Among the new groups congregating for outdoor sport and recreation activities were the newly formed cricket clubs and baseball clubs. In the spring of 1859, the Crescent City Cricket Club secured the permission of the heirs of the Delachaise estate to hold their matches on their property adjoining their brick factory in Jefferson City, and this became known as the Delachaise Grounds. In mid–May, the Crescent City Cricket Club held an intra-squad match between Coppell's Side and Hanlon's Side on the Delachaise Grounds, with wickets pitched at ten o'clock for the two eleven-man sides. The match was slated to run from "one o'clock to three o'clock, when a recess will be taken, and the game finished before sunset."[8] Great pains were taken to ensure the comfort of the members' female guests, with three large canvas tents erected to provide shade, but with the side panels rolled up to facilitate cross ventilation and to provide a proper view of the game. A break in play to serve refreshments from three smaller tents nearby provided a welcome respite from the heat. For all of the gentility observed, the game was described as 'the manly game."

In late June of 1859 a second cricket club was formed, the Pelican Cricket Club.[9] With approximately thirty members in this new organization they certainly had adequate members to hold multiple intra-squad matches. They scheduled their practices on Tuesday, Thursday, and Saturday afternoons at the Delachaise Grounds. It would not take long before this new team would be ready for a challenge match with the Crescent City Cricket Club.

It was only a matter of time before the city's baseball teams found their way to the Delachaise Grounds. The first baseball game recorded and mentioned in the newspapers of New Orleans took place on Friday, July 29, 1859. "There was a large and interesting gathering, yesterday afternoon, at the Delachaise ground, near Louisiana Avenue, to witness a match at base ball between two parties of the Louisiana B.B. Club. The day was fine, and everything was propitious for the play. Messrs. Pascay [sic] and Jones threw up for first choice, as heads of the sides, and nine were chosen on each side. The rules require that a match shall consist of nine innings on each side. The play commenced at four o'clock, and continued until sunset. Four innings were played on each side, Pascay's [sic] making fifty-five and Jones's fourteen runs. The match is to be concluded on Tuesday afternoon."[10]

Louisiana Base Ball Club
Pescay's Side versus Jones' Side
July 29 and August 2, 1859

Pescay's Side	Runs	Jones' Side	Runs
Charles Pescay	11	J.H. Jones	3
H.B. Jones	11	Verlander	0
J.B. Collie	11	Holiday	2
T.R. Higginbotham	11	Grinnell	2
Stagg	10	Born	4
Stanislaus Guillett	10	Selleck	1
Barstow	5	Scott	3
Ferris	3	Forshee	3
Beauvais	3	Allen	1
Bell	3	Bidwell	2
TOTAL	78	TOTAL	21

The first four innings took place on Friday, July 29, beginning at four o'clock and continuing until being halted because of darkness. By agreement the game was continued on Tuesday, August 2, with the remaining five innings played and Pescay's side victorious with 78 runs to Jones' 21 runs.[11]

The second game of the match took place on Friday, August 12.[12]

Louisiana Base Ball Club
Pescay's Side versus Jones' Side
August 12, 1859

Pescay's Side	Runs	Jones' Side	Runs
Charles Pescay	3	J.H. Jones	4
J.P. Stagg	4	Verlander	6
H.B. Jones	4	Selleck	6
T.R. Higginbotham	4	Forshee	7
J.B. Collie	4	Young	4
Stanislaus Guillett	5	Oliver Burdett	2
Ferris	1	Scott	3
Bell	1	Allen	3
Barstow	2	Southyard	3
Folger	3	Bidwell	3
TOTAL	31	TOTAL	41

Jones' side played much better in the second game, outscoring Pescay's side by ten runs, with the final score being 41 to 31. A third and deciding game would determine the winner of the series and the match.

While there was newspaper coverage of the first game of the match on July 29, the report of the second game was sandwiched between stories on the weekly report on the number of patient admits, discharges, and deaths at Charity Hospital, including those from yellow fever, and that of the sad demise of an elderly Irish widow. The third game played on Friday, August 19, however, was well covered and was prominently placed on the front page.[13]

> The Louisiana Base Ball Club had a fine day, yesterday, for closing their grand match between Pascay's [sic] and Jones's side. There was the usual large attendance of lookers-on, of both sexes, the ladies' tent being particularly well filled, and the characteristic hospitality of the club was most munificently displayed.
>
> It will be seen that Jones's side, which, in the first game, was beaten 82 to 24, and which won the second game by a few runs, came out the victor in the "conquering game," by a majority of 6. This was very close, and a review of the whole match will show that the sides were very evenly matched. We may look upon this match as virtually the inauguration of this noble and manly game among us; and we hope it will be kept up with the same spirit in which it has been commenced and so far maintained. Before giving the score of this game, we would remark that, after the fifth inning had been played, it was agreed between the parties that seven innings, instead of nine, should decide it.

Louisiana Base Ball Club
Pescay's Side versus Jones' Side
August 19, 1859

Pescay's Side	Runs	Jones' Side	Runs
Charles Pescay	3	J.W. Jones	7
J.P. Stagg	5	Verlander	4
J.B. Collie	4	Holiday	2
T.R. Higginbotham	5	Forshee	1
Stanislaus Guillett	2	Allen	1
Barstow	3	Grinnell	2
Young	2	Bidwell	4
Bell	2	Oliver Burdett	5
H.B. Jones	2	Charles Southyard	6
Folger	2	Scott	4
Total	**30**	**Total**	**36**

Recapitulation of the Match

Pescay		Jones	
First game	78 runs	First game	21 runs
Second game	31 runs	Second game	41 runs
Third game	30 runs	Third game	36 runs
Total	**139 runs**	**Total**	**98 runs**

A quick glance at the primitive box score of the three games will demonstrate that while the Louisiana Base Ball Club was playing according to the Knickerbocker Rules or the New York Game, they were doing so with a tenth man, an additional short fielder between first and second base. While the use of a tenth man was typical of the Massachusetts Game, it was also permissible under the Knickerbocker Rules at the time. Also typical in early baseball were the high scores. Pitchers served up an easy cock-shot that the hitters slapped all over the field.

Pescay's Side saw the greatest run production from the top six hitters in the batting order, accounting for seventeen of their thirty runs. Jones' Side saw six players, mostly from the bottom of their batting order, accounting for thirty of their thirty-six runs. But this only tells us which players scored the runs, not who drove the runs in or how. Nor was it customary in those days for the scorer to track hits or any of the other statistics we are accustomed to seeing in a box score or line score. The only thing that mattered was the total number of aces (runs) scored during nine innings.

Even if an interested editor at the newspaper sent a reporter to the games, press coverage generally relied on the club's secretary or another designated member, probably in concert with the club's official scorer, to provide a handwritten list with the names of the players for the roster. With any luck at all the newspaper copy room could decipher the reporter's handwriting. A case in point is that throughout all three games, Charles W. Pescay's name is misspelled as "Pascay." Another deficiency in the reporting of the day is the general lack of use of first names in the reporting. While not expected in the box score, the accompanying article makes no mention of the player's first names either beyond a first initial if at all.

Pescay's Side

	Game One	Game Two	Game Three	TOTAL
Pescay	11	3	3	17
H.B. Jones	11	4	2	17
Collie	11	4	4	19
Higgenbotham	11	4	5	20
Stagg	10	4	5	19
Guillett	10	5	2	17
Barstow	5	2	3	10
Ferris	3	1	0	4
Beauvais	3	0	0	3
Bell	3	1	2	6
Folger	0	3	2	5
Young	0	0	2	2
TOTAL	78	31	30	139

Jones' Side

	Game One	Game Two	Game Three	TOTAL
J. Jones	3	4	7	14
Verlander	0	6	4	10
Holiday	2	0	2	4
Grinnel	2	0	2	4
Born	4	0	0	4
Selleck	1	6	0	7
Scott	3	3	4	10
Forshee	3	7	1	11
Allen	1	3	1	5
Bidwell	2	3	4	9
Young	0	4	0	4
Burdett	0	2	5	7
Southyard	0	3	6	9
TOTAL	21	41	36	98

Pescay's Side was led by T.R. Higginbotham with twenty runs scored, followed by J.B. Collie and J.P. Stagg with nineteen runs scored apiece. With no further details provided by the newspaper reports, we have no idea how these fellows achieved their run production. The nature of the game at the time would suggest that both sides used a soft-core baseball thrown underhanded, leading to multiple hits. The scoring would further suggest that these hits came strung together in bunches. Beyond that any further attempt at analysis would be pure conjecture. There is no way of knowing what type of hits were being pounded out. After all, a bug bruiser or a duck-snort both result in a man on base, but there was no thought to tally the number of singles, doubles, triples, or home runs. One might assume from the scores that there were a fair number of extra base hits, but that too is conjecture. Outs may have been the result of a fly ball, an out on bounds or a ball caught on one bounce, a ground out, or a strikeout. Here is an instance where we run into an absence of information that limits our understanding of how the game was played.

As the only determining factor in winning these match games was the same as in cricket, thus the only statistic tracked was the only one that mattered at the time: the total number of runs scored. It would be several years before the influence of New York writer Henry Chadwick's penchant for recording the basic statistics of the game would introduce America to the baseball box score. Among Chadwick's innovations were the calculation of batting average and earned run average, defensive attempts, errors, putouts, at-bats, and hits. On the scorecard he devised the abbreviation "K" to designate a strikeout and assigned numbers for the defensive positions. The first box score appeared in an 1859 issue of the *Clipper*. His original box score looks remarkably like those we see today. The rise of statistics also contributed to the competitive fervor between the players to see who among them was the best hitter (batting average), the best pitcher (earned run average), the best fielder, and so on. An unfortunate by-product of tabulating individual statistics was the shift in emphasis from the team's performance to the player's individual performance.

The members of the Louisiana Base Ball Club, whose two sides faced each other, were comprised of young middle-class and upper middle-class gentlemen from a wide variety of backgrounds—merchants, grocers, store clerks, a steamboat pilot, a seed store owner, and a revenue inspector.[14] Among them was thirty-one-year-old Charles W. Pescay, a native of Florida who had relocated to New Orleans and who in July of 1859 was employed as a grocer. By virtue of having won the coin toss, he was the captain of the Louisiana Base Ball Club's first nine.

In addition to his baseball playing, Pescay is noted for participating in a citywide grand parade to commemorate the dedication of a massive new bronze statue of Henry Clay on Thursday, April 12, 1860, set to be installed in the neutral ground (street median) on Canal Street near Royal Street. Being an avid sailor, Pescay's entry in the parade was a large wagon decorated to resemble a sailing ship compete with four miniature cannons that delighted the crowd when they were fired. The rig was drawn by six large draught horses and his crew consisted of four men and ten boys who monitored the height of the two flag-filled masts and their rigging so as not to run afoul of the strings of telegraph lines overhead.[15] In the years that followed, the Clay statue would become the most popular and prominent central meeting place for the citizens of New Orleans.

Commissioned in 1856 and completed on April 12, 1860, by sculptor Joel T. Hart, the Clay statue was a larger than life-size rendering of the famous orator and politician from Kentucky who just barely lost the presidential election of 1844 to James Knox Polk. The immense bronze figure rose above an equally large granite base. Although Henry Clay was well known in New Orleans, he had no ties to the city save that his brother Martin had relocated to New Orleans in the 1850s. The statue was relocated to the center of Lafayette Square in 1900 and is one of three statues in the square, the others being of a bronze bust of Benjamin Franklin from 1860 and a bronze bust of John McDonough from 1898. Among the many idiosyncrasies in New Orleans is that there is no statue of the Marquis de Lafayette in Lafayette Square.

Pescay was also involved in local civilian military organizations, serving at the sergeant for Company C of the Louisiana Guards,[16] which was later assigned to the 24th Regimental Infantry of the Crescent Regiment, in the 2nd Corps of the Army of the Mississippi in the Confederate Army. Among other battles, his outfit participated in the Battle of Shiloh in 1862. After the war, Pescay returned to New Orleans and, at the age of thirty-eight, entered into the employ of local jeweler E.A. Tyler, first making a name for himself as a silversmith, and eventually garnering regional accolades for his artistic craftsmanship in various exhibitions throughout the state.[17] He later relocated to Houston to help Tyler expand his business there, but before long went into the jewelry business on his own. Pescay died in Houston in 1887 at the age of fifty-nine and was buried in Lafayette Cemetery Number One in New Orleans.

However, the talk of New Orleans throughout the majority of 1859 was not about baseball or cricket. It was about opera. For years, the cultured citizens of the city had enjoyed opera at the Orleans Theatre, a venue better suited to traditional theater than to grand opera. So when the opera company's director Charles Boudousquié proposed the construction of a grand opera house for French opera, the city's French and Creole elite willingly opened their pocketbooks. The Théatre de l'Opéra, designed by renowned New Orleans architect James Gallier, was erected on the northwest corner of Bourbon and Toulouse Streets in the French Quarter. The building quickly took shape within a year at a cost of $118,000 (approximately $3.1 million today). The Greek revival style building opened its doors on Friday, December 2, 1859, with a production of "William Tell." The Théatre de l'Opéra was the first opera house in the United States and it quickly became the most fashionable establishment in New Orleans and the most important fixture in New Orleans social life with its own rituals and traditions. It became the center of Creole society, with discrete screened boxes for pregnant ladies, for *les pleurants* (ladies in mourning draped in multiple folds of black fabric), and years later, of course, for the working ladies from Storyville.

The opera house was a point of pride for New Orleanians who could boast that their grand opera house had staged the American premieres of fourteen operas—including five by Jules Massenet, three by Charles Gounoud, and one by Camille Saint-Saëns. Even though the city did not have a proper sewerage system until 1899, it had a magnificent opera house that could seat 1,600 for operatic performances and as many as 2,500 for orchestral concerts. The city burned to the ground in 1788 and again in 1794 even as more than 300 billion gallons of water per day from the Mississippi River flowed past the city. But with no municipal water system to collect and direct the water, the city continued its unfortunate relationship with fire. In the end, the opera house itself fell victim to fire in 1919 after staging hundreds of operatic productions, Mardi Gras balls, debuts, concerts, and other functions over its sixty-year history.

While the opera house would draw thousands to a single performance, early baseball games at the Delachaise Grounds were only attended by as many as one hundred invited guests of the club and other club members. Newspaper coverage of baseball was still something fresh and new to New Orleans, and descriptions of the games spread mostly by word of mouth, with the general public very quickly taking more of an active interest. While far less grand a social event than the opera, the Delachaise Grounds offered three large canvas pavilions erected originally by the cricket clubs which were there to provide shade for those attending the cricket and baseball games, serving as a makeshift grandstand. Shortly thereafter new terraced wooden "bleacher" seating was erected to accommodate more spectators. They were called bleachers because over time the wooden planks used in their construction would become bleached out and faded from constant exposure to the sun.

With the great stir caused by the Louisiana Base Ball Club's grand three-game intra-squad series, two of the other new baseball clubs now had their games reported in the press. For many spectators the battle between Pescay and Jones was their first glimpse of a baseball game. On Thursday, August 25, 1859, the Empire Base Ball Club fielded two eleven-man teams for a single game match, Smith's Side tallying 44 runs against McManus' Side scoring 35 runs. Four days later, on Sunday, August 29, the playing fields in New Orleans were full. The Southern Base Ball Club played in Algiers; the Magnolia Base Ball Club played on a lot near the old paper mill, with Sambola's Side tallying 35 runs proving victorious against Bradbury's Side at 30 runs[18]; and the "darkeys" played at an old field at Claiborne Circle.[19]

The Louisiana Base Ball Club played their first match against another club when they accepted the public challenge of the Empire Base Ball Club. In fact, this would mark the first game between two different clubs in New Orleans. This game took place on Wednesday, September 14, 1859, and was as much a novelty spectacle as it was a baseball game. Spectators were only familiar with the basics of the game, if at all, but this did not dampen their enthusiasm in the least. In addition to watching the game, the invited guests seated under the canvas tent pavilions were catered to by the club stewards, who saw to their every need, comfortably located beneath the burgeoning canopy of live oaks along the edge of the Delachaise Grounds. A master of ceremonies introduced the players from both teams. There were a variety of refreshments served to make the afternoon even more festive. Every consideration was given, and elaborate preparations were made for the comfort of their guests. The clubs provided baskets full of food and cases of wine, along with other refreshments. In its own unique way this was their attempt to associate themselves with the aristocracy and gentility of those clubs whose members enjoyed high social standing.

The game itself had to be suspended because of darkness after the conclusion of six innings, the Empires holding a twelve-run lead. The teams of course agreed to resume the contest the following week. The entire event that afternoon was every bit the upstanding, although casual, outdoor social function befitting the cadre of young gentlemen who were now part of the emerging baseball fraternity.

As expected, the two clubs reassembled at the Delachaise Grounds on Thursday the 22nd. Despite being one man short, the Empire club played the final three innings at a disadvantage with only nine players on their side, yet they managed to extend their lead to win the game by thirteen runs. At the end of the game the umpire, George Bond, presented the game ball to H.M. McManus, the captain of the Empire club, who graciously called for three cheers for the Louisiana club.[20]

As was the custom, a return match was promptly agreed upon and took place on Thursday, October 6 at the Delachaise Grounds, with the Empire club proving once again to be too much for the Louisiana club, winning by the score of 56 to 26.[21] A non-roster member of the Empire Base Ball Club named Toby Hart served as the official scorer for the match. Although not well known as a player, Hart would eventually take on an influential and prominent place in the history of New Orleans baseball.

The Delachaise Grounds would remain a popular ball park for several years, even as other larger and more ornate ballparks came into fashion. To this day, the Lyons Playground and Recreation Center on the corner of Louisiana Avenue and Tchoupitoulas Street abuts the old Delachaise Grounds.

The Louisiana Base Ball Park (1869–1874)

The last of the uptown Faubourgs or neighborhoods to be subdivided and laid out for development in the city of Jefferson was Burthville. It was the former plantation of Dominique Francois Burthe, acquired for $38,000 in 1831 (roughly $1,025,000 today) from the perpetually cash strapped Bernard Marigny. The area was subdivided in 1854 but was slow to see any meaningful progress. Burthville, as well as the neighboring areas of Bloomingdale and Hurstville, had once been the sprawling plantation of Jean Etienne Bore, who in 1803 became the first mayor of New Orleans and who operated a granulated sugar business on the property beginning in 1795. He acquired the property in October of 1781 from the widow of Juan Paseros. It extended from the lower line of the L.F. Foucher plantation, now known as Audubon Park in Uptown New Orleans. The property once reached from the Mississippi River to the large canal that would later define the boundaries of Claiborne Avenue.

In 1869 it was announced that a new baseball park would be constructed in Burthville on four squares of ground bounded by Henry Clay Avenue (now Palmer Avenue), Long Street (now Freret Street), Victor Street (now Magnolia Street), and the L.F. Foucher property (now Tulane University). The land was leased for five years by the Louisiana Base Ball Park Association, who planned to construct a quarter-mile race track with a baseball field in the center. Formal groundbreaking took place on February 23, 1870, with a ceremonial gilded baseball being thrown out by J.N. Howard, the oldest active baseball player in the South, accompanied by several rounds of champagne. A box with the ball and an empty champagne bottle containing the names of the officers and stockholders was buried beneath the first post set to define the property. It took approximately six weeks to clear the property and prepare the field. The association was headed by David Schwartz (president), G.W. Doll (vice-president), D.M. Kelly (secretary), and J.N. Howard (treasurer). Local businessman Toby Hart, baseball figure William F. Tracey, and W.H. Beanham (Benham) were named directors of the association. The association was capitalized at $3,750 through the issuance of one hundred and fifty shares of stock at $25 per share.

At the lower end of the complex was a dancing platform with raised seats at each corner. On the upper end was a grandstand to accommodate ladies, but which was open for all fans. The main entrance and ticket office was located on the Henry Clay Avenue (now Palmer Avenue) side. Upon entrance, fans were free to roam through the ballpark, with more than 4,000 available seats to choose from. It was the largest facility of its kind in the city, if not the South.

The new baseball park could be reached from the city center by street rail up St. Charles Avenue to the Burthville depot near Henry Clay Street. Fans would then enjoy a short walk of five squares or blocks through a pastoral setting to the new stadium. The area from the rail stop to the ballpark had been partially cleared but was far from the gentle promenade beneath a glorious canopy of live oaks that line the street today. There were no paved sidewalks and the street was not even cobble-paved. There were only about a dozen rather unimportant buildings along Henry Clay, but these were on the river side of St. Charles Avenue. The new ballpark was the first construction on the lake side of St. Charles Avenue of any significance.

The location was rural, and the neighboring buildings were not much more than shanties. Prior to the delineation of the area into squares and lots, the upper portion of Henry Clay Avenue housed stables and stalls for the operation of an unsanctioned abattoir for horses. All of this had to be cleared away before anyone would even consider walking the five blocks from the rail terminal to the ballpark. Even then, the land was still isolated and somewhat undesirable given the amount of available land closer to the city. In June of 1870 J.J. Alston offered one hundred and fifty lots on Henry Clay Avenue to "colored people" for two hundred dollars, payable at twenty dollars down and five dollars a month for thirty-six months.[22] These lots were located in the rear of the ballpark, being the north side or the farthest side of the property closer to the Claiborne Avenue side.

Being situated in a rural setting midway between downtown and the suburb of Carrollton, approximately four and one-half miles from the city center, the new ballpark needed to make an immediate favorable impression to convince patrons to make the trip. While the edifice itself was remarkable, the investors wisely decided to schedule a test run, a dress rehearsal if you will, to ensure that everything was in readiness. On Sunday, November 28, 1869, the R.E. Lees took the field against the Lone Stars. The field was level and quick and the dirt was smooth. Fans had no problem making their way to the ballpark, they had their choice of abundant seating to choose from, they enjoyed a fine selection of concessions, and watched a lively baseball game between two popular local amateur clubs. The teams proved that the ballpark should indeed open its gates to the public.

The next event at the ballpark was between the Mutual Base Ball Club of New York, better known simply as the New York Mutuals, and the R.E. Lee Base Ball Club.[23] This marked the very first time a professional baseball team would visit New Orleans. "The Mutuals, of New York, having deferred their departure, arranged a game with the champion R.E. Lees, which came off at the Park, yesterday, in the presence of an audience which was select if not numerous. The contest was the very best of the Mutual series in this city, and eclipsed the famous game of the Stars played last Sunday. To the close of the eighth inning the score was small and the game evenly contested, the total figures at that point being 8 to 8, and decidedly interesting. In the ninth inning, however, the New-Yorkers rallied to the tune of seven runs, and putting the Lees out for a blank, scored the victory. The following is the score."

The Mutuals of New York versus the R.E. Lees
November 30, 1869

Mutuals	1B	TB	*Lees*	1B	TB
Hatfield, ss	3	3	Hennessy	2	5
Eggler, c	1	1	Burt	2	2
Patterson, lf	2	3	Levi	0	0
Nelson, 3b	1	1	Tilton	0	0
E. Mills, 1b	2	5	Eastin	1	1
Martin, p	3	5	Bertel	1	2
C. Mills, cf	1	2	Bond	2	4
Wolters, rf	2	2	Landon	2	2
Higham, 2b	3	4	Laner	0	0
TOTAL	18	23	TOTAL	10	16

Innings

	1st	2nd	3rd	4th	5th	6th	7th	8th	9th	TOTAL
Mutuals	3	2	1	1	0	0	0	1	7	15
Lees	0	0	1	0	3	0	2	1	0	8

Time of game—One hour and forty minutes.
Umpire—T.D. Williams

The local lads performed reasonably well against the first professional team they encountered. Eight of the Lees' ten hits came from Hennessy, Bond, Burt, and Landon, each with two hits. The Lees nearly matched the Mutuals' hit total and the score was knotted at eight runs apiece headed into the final frame. It was the seven runs surrendered to the visitors in the ninth inning that made all the difference in the outcome. Unable to rally in the bottom of the ninth inning, the Lees fell to the Mutuals 15 to 8. The sparse crowd, described as "select if not numerous," was treated to an exciting contest and word of mouth about the game and the new ballpark would soon circulate throughout the city. This was only the second game at the new ballpark, so the small crowd was understandable.

There is some disagreement as to whether the Mutuals were actually a professional team. One camp will argue that they were not, in fact, a professional team given that their players had other employment. The other camp will debunk that position, saying the Mutuals, in fact, truly did nothing other than play baseball. As it turns out, the Mutuals were not the first clandestine professional baseball team. That distinction goes to the 1867 Washington Nationals, comprised of clerks employed by the United States Treasury Department who were some of the best recruits in the East.[24] The Mutual Base Ball Club of New York was formed in Brooklyn, New York, in 1857 during the first baseball convention, although they were not a founding member of the National Association of Base Ball Players (NABBP). They toured the country selectively, arriving in New Orleans in December of 1869 by way of exhibition games played in Cincinnati and Louisville on their way to New Orleans via the Jackson and Great Northern Railroad, accompanied by an entourage of prominent New York politicians, most noticeably William Marcy "Boss" Tweed.[25] Although the Mutuals were members of the National Amateur Association from 1858 through 1870, it was well known that the players only held perfunctory positions in the corrupt Tammany Hall administration of politician Boss Tweed. The team gained a measure of respectability when they emerged from the shadow of being closeted professionals and joined the National Association of Professional Base Ball Players (1871–1875). Without the financial backing of Boss Tweed, however, their meager finances caused them to be expelled from the league in 1875 for refusing to honor their schedule against Western teams, principally teams from Chicago and St. Louis. They affiliated with the National League in 1876 but were once again expelled from the league when their perpetually shallow treasury again precluded them from travelling west. The team became inactive in December of 1876.

The Mutuals extended their stay in New Orleans through the new year, playing in a series of exhibition games that drew between 1,700 and 1,800 paying customers for each game. On December 28, 1869, the Mutuals downed the Pelicans 34 to 5 at the Fair Grounds, then defeated the Lone Stars by the score of 16 to 10 the following day.[26] Whether the crowds continued to be "select if not numerous" is unknown, but the average gameday turnout was respectable in any case. At twenty-five cents per ticket, these games grossed between $425 and $450 per game. They began on New Year's Eve 1869 against a picked nine comprised of ball players from the Lees, the Lone Stars, and other local amateur teams that the Mutuals handily won 31 to 15. They also played multiple games against the Lone Stars and the Southerns that they won in equally impressive fashion. The new ballpark was off to a rousing start and was happily embraced by New Orleans fans.

Organized with thirty members on August 1, 1864, by John Kaiser, A.B. Johnson, and G.W. Young, the R.E. Lee Base Ball Club was very active, fielding both regular and junior teams, and frequently taking and issuing challenges from teams across the city and occasionally from out of town teams. Junior teams were comprised of the younger members of the club who found themselves somewhere between hay and grass, older than seventeen years old but younger than twenty. The team also travelled out of town as early as 1870,[27] setting out to Missouri to meet the Palm Grove Base Ball Club in Cape Girardeau, winning by the score of 44 to 37. They quickly established themselves as a force to be reckoned with in the upper echelon of amateur teams in New Orleans. They joined the Gulf League in 1885 to play professional baseball, with the hope that their club would eventually be selected as the New Orleans franchise in the Southern League. This was not an unreasonable assumption on the part of owner and manager Conrad Leithman given his close association with Toby Hart, the man who was leading the investor group trying to secure that franchise.

Unfortunately for Leithman and the Lees, their strategy did not work out in their favor and the Lees returned to the ranks of the city's most talented amateur teams. After foundering for several years in the shadows of their past glories, the club finally reorganized in 1887 with E.K. Skinner as president, G.K. Stockton as vice-president, and W.L. Saxon as secretary/treasurer. Directors were Skinner, Stockton, and Saxon as well as F.M. McKeough, Gus Lauer, Jas. J. Woulfe, Adam Lorch, Henry Powers, and Conrad Leithman.[28] The club would continue to enjoy a successful record in amateur circles in New Orleans and the Gulf Coast region for the remainder of the century.

The Louisiana Base Ball Park would host the Louisiana State Championship series between the Southerns and the Lone Stars. The Lone Stars captured the first game by the score of 36 to 21 on April 21, 1870, only to fall to the Southerns in the second game 27 to 18. This second game drew 2,500 fans and the ballpark association and their investors were quietly celebrating their new venture, but the third and deciding game in the series would have to wait.

Fresh on the heels of the productive trial run with the Mutuals and the Lees, and the state amateur championship series, the next team to visit the Louisiana Base Ball Park was the fabled Cincinnati Red Stockings. The country's premiere professional ballclub was slated to square off against five of the best amateur clubs in New Orleans. The Carrollton Railroad agreed to run extra cars before and after the game to ensure all patrons could be accommodated. Although only the second public event to be promoted, the success of this series would ultimately determine the success of the new ballpark.

On Wednesday, April 25, 1870, the first game of the exhibition series took place with Asa Brainard on the mound for Cincinnati and Bell for the Pelicans. The umpire for this momentous event was none other than David Schwartz, President of the Louisiana Base Ball Park Association, who was also a member of the Lone Star Base Ball Club. When Red Stockings leadoff hitter and team captain George Wright came to the plate the Pelican pitcher Bell must have felt a bit like an early Christian in the Coliseum about to be introduced to his first Roman lion.

Cincinnati Red Stockings versus New Orleans Pelicans
April 25, 1870[29]

Innings	1	2	3	4	5	6	7	8	9	Total
Cincinnati	12	3	0	6	10	9	0	8	3	51
Pelicans	0	0	1	0	0	0	0	0	0	1

Unfortunately or fortunately, depending on your point of view, the suffering was short and one-sided. Cincinnati easily defeated the Pelican Base Ball Club by the score of 51 to 1 before a crowd again described as "select, if not large in number." The rainy weather that had threatened all day finally arrived close to game-time and this had more to do with the poor turnout of only two hundred people than the prospect of a lambasting by the "Knights of the Crimson Hose." The lone Pelican score was made by the leftfielder Everett.

The fans turned out in the thousands the following day to see the second game of the series, eager to catch an eyeful of the vaunted Red Stockings. This time it was the Southern Base Ball Club who stepped up to face the Cincinnati team. The umpire was the well-respected owner-manager-player William F. Tracey of the Lone Star Base Ball Club.

Cincinnati Red Stockings versus Southern Base Ball Club
April 26, 1870[30]

Innings	1	2	3	4	5	6	7	8	9	Total
Cincinnati	13	9	27	2	2	2	10	4	40	79
Southern	0	1	2	0	0	3	0	0	0	6

The Red Stockings proceeded to embarrass the Southerns 79 to 6. Southern pitcher C.A. O'Keefe gave up eighty-three hits, most of them in the third and ninth innings when Cincinnati scored twenty-seven runs and forty runs, respectively. Although no one as yet kept statistics on such things, one cannot help but wonder what the pitch count was for the beleaguered O'Keefe. This was actually the second meeting between these two teams, having first faced each other back in August 25, 1869, in Cincinnati. The Southerns held the Red Stockings to 35 runs in that game, falling 35 to 3.

Taking a well-deserved day off on Thursday, aided by a seasonal torrential rain storm that made the field unplayable, the Red Stockings next played the Atlantic Base Ball Club of Algiers, a suburb across the river from New Orleans, on April 28. The weather was still dubious, but the two clubs were determined to give it their best for the 1,500 assembled. The umpire for the third game was J.N. Howard of the Lone Star Base Ball Club who had tossed out the ceremonial gilded baseball back in February to dedicate the groundbreaking for the new ballpark.

Cincinnati Red Stockings versus Atlantic Base Ball Club
April 28, 1870[31]

Innings	1	2	3	4	5	6	7	8	Total
Cincinnati	2	9	3	4	3	8	9	1	39
Atlantic	0	1	1	0	3	0	1	0	6

The field was still sloppy, having only partially drained from the prior day's rain, and the game started later than originally scheduled because of the continued bad weather. The game was called after eight innings because of darkness. The fans of the Atlantics who endured the inclement weather had to further endure a long ride home by rail and ferry that evening.

The Lone Star Base Ball Club, who had postponed their state championship series against the Southerns knotted at one game apiece, was Cincinnati's next opponent on April 29. A crowd that was described as "immense" was in the ballpark to witness the fourth game of the series, which got under-

The celebrated Cincinnati Red Stockings' First Nine pictured in this lithograph produced in 1869, the year before they travelled to New Orleans (Library of Congress).

way just after three o'clock in the afternoon. Hopes were high for the Lone Stars who, as one of the best teams in the city, were expected to give the champion Red Stockings a real run for their money. James Gilthorpe of the Crescent Base Ball Club served as the umpire.

Cincinnati Red Stockings versus Lone Star Base Ball Club
April 29, 1870[32]

Innings	1	2	3	4	5	6	7	8	9	TOTAL
Cincinnati	3	1	3	0	0	5	4	1	9	26
Lone Star	0	0	0	0	4	2	0	1	0	7

The Lone Stars held the Red Stockings to the lowest run total thus far, but still succumbed 26 to 7. Thus far the Red Stockings had taken on the best amateur teams in the city and had run through them like a hot knife through butter. New Orleans had one final chance to pull off an upset, but only if the R.E. Lees were up to the task.

Cincinnati Red Stockings versus R.E. Lee Base Ball Club
April 30, 1870[33]

Innings	1	2	3	4	5	6	7	8	9	TOTAL
Cincinnati	9	0	1	0	3	1	4	5	1	24
Lees	0	0	3	0	0	0	1	0	0	4

The Red Stockings finished their series in New Orleans by beating the R.E. Lees 24 to 4 on April 30 in a game that lasted two hours. A return match against the Lone Stars was announced but could not be scheduled before the Red Stockings headed north to Memphis for their next series. The local clubs played their best and gave their all, but in the end were simply outclassed by a talented professional club.

Despite the outcome of the games, the New Orleans contingent had no reason to hang their heads. The amazing Cincinnati Red Stockings, led by brothers George and Harry Wright, cranked out sixty-four consecutive wins during 1869 and twenty-four consecutive wins in 1870 before suffering their first defeat at the hands of the Brooklyn Atlantics in eleven innings on June 14, 1870. During that same time period they won over seventy barnstorming games such as the exhibition series played in New Orleans. Their remarkable streak of one hundred and fifty-eight consecutive victories may never be broken, primarily because professional teams no longer engage in barnstorming tours in the off-season, but those games only account for seventy wins. Their complete and total dominance of their competition was so extraordinary that no modern team could achieve eighty-eight consecutive wins over their professional peer group.

Pitching for the Red Stockings while in New Orleans was twenty-nine-year-old Asa Brainard, a former member of the New York Knickerbockers. He was a one-man pitching staff, tossing more than 70 percent of the team's games. His prowess as a hurler helped the Red Stockings achieve their remarkable string of victories, but he was a constant source of aggravation for his teammates. Given to heavy drinking, Brainard once tried to pelt a rabbit running across the ball field, but propelled the wayward baseball into the outfield, allowing two runs to score on a "wild pitch." His distinctive delivery and command rarely allowed his opponents to make solid contact with the ball. Brainard combined ball speed with a subtle wrist snap to confound his opponents, including the five teams from New Orleans.

Meanwhile, back in Chicago, manager Tom Foley of the White Stockings decided to bring his team down to New Orleans in April of 1870 to challenge the Red Stockings. Unfortunately for Chicago, by the time they arrived in the city in early May, the Cincinnati team had already moved on to Memphis. However, impressed by the city's mild tropical climate and a large, enthusiastic fan base, Foley kept his players in New Orleans to help his fleshy fielders work off their winter weight and to get ready for the 1870 season. The White Stockings played multiple exhibition games at the Louisiana Base Ball Park against the Atlantic Base Ball Club, the Lone Star Base Ball Club, the R.E. Lee Base Ball Club, and the Southern Base Ball Club. Over this one-month period, during which the New York Mutuals and the Chicago White Stockings were in town, it may be said that the first "spring training" season was established in New Orleans.

A gentleman with the unlikely name of John Barleycorn was employed as a scout by the Chicago White Stockings and accompanied them on their trip to New Orleans. While he was there he was impressed with the skill and overall play of the local players. As the spring training experience of Cincinnati and Chicago became known, other major league teams traveled to New Orleans and before long amateur players in the city found positions on major league teams in Louisville, Buffalo, Cincinnati, St. Louis, and Indianapolis.

The White Stockings were so satisfied with the facilities in New Orleans and the Louisiana Base Ball Park, which they called "the finest arranged base ball park in America,"[34] they would return to New Orleans nearly every spring. The word soon spread and New Orleans would play host to the Boston Beaneaters, the Chicago White Stockings, the Cincinnati Red Stockings, and the New York Giants for their spring training. Exhibition games were not only a steady draw, but the local teams improved the caliber of their play by facing professional teams.

However, one of the most intriguing side-notes to the Cincinnati–New Orleans Pelicans game occurred off the field sixteen years later.

Irish-born Patrick Ford played second base for the New Orleans Pelicans against the Cincinnati Red Stockings in April of 1870 at the Louisiana Base Ball Park during their swing through New Orleans. The Pelicans were crushed behind the pitching of Asa Brainard, whose six-hitter for the Red Stockings puzzled the Pelicans. His brother, Thomas J. Ford, was a man of considerable influence in the Democratic Party in New Orleans and was a sitting judge for the Second Recorder's Court. He was also a police magistrate. With his brother's assistance, Patrick Ford was given several city jobs when not playing baseball and at one time was the Acting Chief Engineer for the New Orleans Fire Department.

Over the years Thomas Ford developed a bitter personal rivalry with Andrew H. "Cap" Murphy, himself a well-connected Democratic politician and a deputy at the city jail. The feud began when Murphy was arrested for being drunk and disorderly and was brought before Judge Thomas Ford. Murphy was fined, and Ford wrote in the official record that Murphy was "a hoodlum, a dead beat, and a city official." Murphy paid his fine but took umbrage at Thomas Ford's comments that were now part of his permanent record. He began circulating flyers which characterized Ford as "a coward, a liar, a thief, and a perjurer." Ford responded by having Murphy arrested for libel. The case was still awaiting trial when, on December 1, 1884, Thomas Ford gathered his brother Patrick and several policemen, a group which could best be described as mean-spirited thugs, to seek out Murphy with the clear intent of doing serious bodily harm. Among the men assembled was Ford's cousin John Murphy (no relation to Andrew Murphy).

The men found Andrew Murphy around two-thirty in the afternoon as he was overseeing a chain gang at the corner of Claiborne and St. Philip Streets. Instead of the pummeling the Judge had intended, Patrick Ford and his crew drew their pistols and started shooting. Andrew Murphy returned fire, emptying his revolver before taking off on foot down Claiborne. Ford then fired the shot that felled Murphy.

The incident occurred in the presence of between seventy to eighty witnesses. With a dozen fatal wounds, Murphy died on Dumaine Street between Claiborne and Robertson Streets. Patrick Ford and his cohorts were quickly arrested. Judge Ford's cronies intimidated witnesses against testifying at the trial. Nevertheless, the prisoners were brought to trial on Tuesday, January 27, 1885, amid political pressure, bribery, influence peddling, intimidation, and threats that were blatantly present during every step of the trial.

After a ten-day trial the case was handed to the jury, who deliberated for three days. Before a verdict could be reached, Judge Baker declared a new trial with a new jury due to several reported incidents of witness tampering that could not be ignored. The second trial began on February 18, 1885, and went to the jury ten days later. After only thirty minutes of deliberations the new jury found Patrick Ford and John Murphy guilty of first degree murder since it was determined that the fatal shots had come from their weapons. The other three members of the group were also found guilty of manslaughter and sentenced to twenty years in prison. Patrick Ford and John Murphy were sentenced to death by hanging.

After a number of exhaustive and ultimately unsuccessful appeals, Governor Samuel D. McEnery issued the death warrants on September 9, 1885, and the executions were scheduled for November 13th. Ongoing political pressure in an effort to commute their sentences prolonged the process and the executions were rescheduled for Friday, March 12, 1886. That morning the prisoners were found unresponsive in their cells. Ford and Murphy had somehow gotten hold of atropine, a poison that is a derivative of belladonna. Murphy was eventually revived but Ford remained unconscious.

Unsure of how to proceed, prison officials were in a quandary until the governor reaffirmed that the execution be conducted as ordered. Deputies then dressed the prisoners, bound them, and hoisted then into chairs which several stalwart deputies used to carry the limp prisoners down a corridor for about fifty feet from the jailhouse to the gallows. The pair was then laid side by side on the scaffold with their heads against the prison wall in the pelting rain.

At 12:50 that afternoon the signal was given, and the trap door flew open with a terrible clang that could be heard by the crowd of four hundred people who were holding vigil on the street outside the prison. The unconscious condemned men fell a distance of roughly eight feet, sufficient to dislocate their necks and end their lives quickly. The newspaper noted, "It cannot longer be said in reproach that no white man can be hanged for murder in Louisiana."[35]

Former New Orleans Pelican Patrick Ford is believed to be the first professional baseball player to be executed.[36]

Over the years, the Louisiana Base Ball Park was the scene of many memorable baseball games and historic events, as well as a great many unusual and unconventional events. One of these unconventional events took place in the early morning hours of Saturday, January 11, 1873, when "two well-known gentlemen" entered the grounds to "repair damage done to wounded honor." Apparently one of the gentlemen took exception to the abusive language used by his antagonist and the duel was arranged. Double-barrel shotguns loaded with ball-sized shot were the weapon of choice which were made ready and fired from a distance of twenty paces, putting the shooters approximately eighty feet apart. Each man unloaded both barrels of his weapon in the direction of his opponent. The only damage done was a single hole that had been bored by the ball shot through one of the participant's trousers.[37] Grateful to have survived the incident, the two gentlemen and their seconds quickly and amicably agreed to dismiss the matter and repaired to the city for breakfast.

Having hosted hundreds of amateur and professional games during its

Three—Where They Played

The enlarged image is of a map showing the location of the Louisiana Base Ball Park. The oval in the center of the image indicates the location of the ballpark with undeveloped wooded area at the top right of the image (detail from 1880 Hardee Topographical and Drainage Map of New Orleans).

five-year lease, the Louisiana Base Ball Park was deemed to have "outlived [its] usefulness,"[38] and the property was once again designated for redevelopment into thirty squares consisting of 607 lots.[39] One of those lots, on the corner of Freret Street and Palmer Avenue, was purchased by Louisiana Base Ball Association Director Toby Hart, who constructed a unique Gothic-Victorian cottage at 2108 Palmer Avenue that served as his country home. This magnificent building still stands today and is on the National Register of Historic Places.

Crescent City Base Ball Park (1880–1884)

Like so many of the ballparks in New Orleans, the new Crescent City Base Ball Park was situated in close proximity to a street rail line for easy access, but almost always near the end of the line. The decision to locate the facility on the outskirts of the city was made with the public encouragement of and frequently with the financial support from the rail lines and utility companies in order to encourage future transportation and real estate development. Located at the foot of Canal Street was an open plot of land across the street from the Greenwood Cemetery, in the vast open gardens behind the very well-known Half-Way House and abutting the New Basin Canal.

The Half-Way House served as the border between Orleans and Jefferson Parish (county) in the 19th century, although that dividing line is now a little over a mile further west at the 17th Street Canal and Metairie Road. A rather ordinary looking building located on the southeast corner of the intersection quickly became known as the Half-Way House, because it was almost exactly halfway from Gallier Hall, New Orleans City Hall in 1831.

But its original notoriety was as something of a local landmark. A newspaper advertisement by Alfred Bonnabel instructed prospective buyers interested in purchasing one or more of his twenty-five dairy cows that his farm could be found at "Metairie Ridge, just 1½ miles from the Halfway House."[40] Whether it was the discovery of a body floating in the canal or of a crime report involving one of the boathouses or shipyards that lined the New Basin Canal, the location of the incident was usually given in relation to its distance from the Half-Way House. Flower shops clustered near the numerous cemeteries in the area advertised their proximity to the Half-Way House, and rail and street car lines published their routes and transit times in relation to the Half-Way House.

The Half-Way House was erected in 1849 shortly after the completion of the New Basin Canal and its draw bridge was operated by a gentleman known simply as Old Jounneau as a popular tavern. The interior was marked by a black and white terrazzo tile floor in a checkerboard pattern throughout, beneath simple chandeliers and ceiling fans. Its wide-pitched roof with scalloped edges projected out over large windows extending from the floor to beneath the eaves which, when opened, would allow the evening breeze to cool the scores of tourists and locals who were en route from New Orleans to the recreational area known as New Lake End on Lake Pontchatrain north of the city. The far end of the building's interior featured a small stage barely large enough to accommodate a dozen musicians and their instruments.

Travelers would take the Canal Street rail line to the Half-Way House before transferring to a second rail line that ran along the side of the New Basin Canal, ending up at New Lake End. The area would be renamed West End in 1880. With the modest speed of rail at the time, this was pretty much of an all-afternoon excursion. W.W. Walker operated an omnibus service that offered a coach every thirty minutes from 6:00 a.m. through 10:00 a.m. and again from 2:00 p.m. through 9:00 p.m. An omnibus coach could accommodate approximately twenty riders with light baggage, so the Half-Way House served as a way station as travelers awaited the next coach or rail car.

A local reporter remarked that every streetcar headed to the Half-Way House was packed with "crinoline, screaming babies, little folks and big folks ... like sardines." Once there, the reporter commented on the twelve-piece orchestra "thundering on brass instruments, gambling tables well patronized, and the votaries of Bacchus, male and female, enjoying good things."[41]

During Reconstruction New Orleans, owner Gus Richards welcomed between 5,000 and 6,000 visitors to the Half-Way House every weekend in the spring and summer months making their way to New Lake Basin. Once ensconced in either the Light House Hotel, Elkin's Hotel, Bishop's Hotel, or another of the smaller resorts that lined the lakefront between West End and Spanish Fort, patrons could engage in swimming, sailing, rowing and other amusements at the West End Rowing Club, the Riverside Boxing Club, or the St. John Boat House. Although certainly not organized, groups of friends and resort guests no doubt played baseball on the large open areas that surrounded the hotels. Afterwards they might stroll along the boardwalk before gathering at one of the many restaurants in the area. Bruning's Restaurant opened in New Lake Basin in 1849 and operated at the same location continuously for 156 years until it was demolished by Hurricane Katrina in 2005. On Sundays, open-air concerts were given in the midst of the elegant and elaborate gardens in the area we now know as Bucktown.

But there was a very different side to the Half-Way House than that of the carefree way station.

At one time, in St. Anthony's Garden behind the St. Louis Cathedral, duels were conducted until 1855 when pressure from Mayor John L. Lewis caused the City Council to enact ordinances against dueling which were to be strictly enforced by the police. Although the *Dueling Oaks* in City Park were well known as the scene where a matter of honor was often settled, the grounds behind the Half-Way House were also notorious as an alternative dueling ground. Prospective duelists would nervously steel their courage and resolve with one or more strong alcoholic beverages at the Half-Way House before walking out to the field of honor on the grounds behind the building.

New Orleans being the sporting town that it was, large sums of money were often wagered by non-combatants on the outcome of these duels, drawing scores of incidental spectators who were also customers of the Half-Way House.

One typical duel at the Half-Way House occurred between Joseph T. Howell of New Orleans and Colonel Henry, "formerly of the United States Army but more recently of the Nicaraguan Army." Approximately one hundred and fifty bystanders witnessed the combatants and their seconds agree to terms: a brace of Navy pistols was provided by Colonel Henry which were to be fired at will from a distance of ten paces. Although neither of these gentlemen was of particular renown in New Orleans at the time, the story was picked up and reported as far away as New York.[42] As with many such encounters, neither gentleman was injured.

There is a well-known engraving by renowned artist Albert R. Waud entitled "Sunday Amusements at New Orleans—Duel at the Half-Way House" which appeared in the July 14, 1866, issue of *Harper's Weekly*. The piece depicts the aftermath of a duel before several spectators. One man is pictured on the ground, obviously wounded in some manner, while the other is reaching for his forehead, reeling backward as if struck by his opponent's bullet.

In reality, few duels resulted in fatal wounds. Contests involving swords were usually satisfied when one participant drew a bit of their opponent's blood, and dueling pistols which were notoriously inaccurate and ineffective at any distance beyond two to three feet. During one duel between two merchants, several shots were fired, but the errant gunfire only resulted in killing a horse grazing nearby.

In the latter part of the 19th century, the area surrounding the Half-Way House was also something of a sporting Mecca. The Metairie Course was a popular horse racing venue located on the Jefferson Parish (county) side of the New Basin Canal. Built in 1838, racing aficionados would travel down Canal Street by either omnibus or street rail, walking to the Half-Way House to partake in a festive luncheon or to enjoy a libation or two before crossing the drawbridge to attend the races. The Metairie Course operated until 1861. Oakland Park, a popular trotting track, was adjacent to the Metairie Course across Metairie Road, and is presently part of the New Orleans Country Club golf course. The close of the 19th century saw activity move away from the area. Dueling finally fell out of favor, the last documented dispute having taken place in 1890. The Metairie Course closed at the beginning of the Civil

War, reopened briefly after the war, but in 1872 was converted into Metairie Cemetery.

With the expiration of their lease, the Louisiana Base Ball Park Association now turned their attention to constructing a new baseball park which they called the Crescent City Base Ball Park on land leased from the city for a six-year term. For the cost of a five-cent rail fare and a twenty-five-cent ballpark ticket, spectators were treated to baseball in a wonderful new facility. In 1880, the Crescent City Base Ball Park was erected on the open area behind the Half-Way House. Opening Day saw the Lone Star Base Ball Club vie with the Hop Bitters of New York before a scant 200 fans. The small crowd was nonetheless treated to a close game as the teams battled to a 1–1 tie after ten innings when the game had to be called because of darkness.[43]

It was a short distance from the baseball park to the Half-Way House. Baseball games and boxing matches were among the most popular sporting events of the day and drew fans from New Orleans and the surrounding areas on a regular basis. Between 1887 and 1900, Abner Powell, celebrated player-manager of the New Orleans Pelicans baseball club, was a regular customer of the Half-Way House for post-game celebrations. Among the notable amateur championship teams to play at the Crescent City Base Ball Park were the J.S. Wright Base Ball Club in 1880 and the Thomas Brennan Base Ball Club in 1883.

The Crescent City Base Ball League operated from the ballpark, with the Lone Star Base Ball Club, the Eckford Base Ball Club, the Washington Base Ball Club, and the C.T. Howard Base Ball Club serving as mainstays of the league.[44] However, a combination of seemingly ever-present concerns over a series of economic recessions pinching the pocketbooks of New Orleanians and national outrage following the assassination of President James Garfield, the unsettling situation weighed on most New Orleanians in one way or another, and the ballpark was closed in 1884. The Crescent City Base Ball Park was renovated and renamed Sportsman's Park in 1884 and was, in turn, replaced in 1898 by Athletic Park across town at the corner of Tulane and South Carrollton Avenues.

New Orleans Base Ball Park (1884–1889)

With the decline of the Crescent City Base Ball Park, the seemingly ever-present Toby Hart announced the formation of the New Orleans Base Ball Park Association with himself as president and Maurice Kauffman as secretary/treasurer. Directors included Thomas C. Brennan, Jonathan T. Fitzgerald (clerk of First City Court), Charles H. Genslinger (president of Hunter & Genslinger), and D.A. Mayer (Mayer & Seeskund).

On February 28, 1884, the New Orleans City Council granted Toby Hart and the New Orleans Base Ball Park Association a five-year lease for what amounted to a tax sale for $24.49 that secured a large block of land in the 4500 block of Canal Street bounded by Olympia Street, Murat Street, and Customhouse Street (now Iberville Street).[45] Opening Day at the new ballpark came on Sunday, September 28, 1884, with a game between the R.E. Lees and the Faranta Base Ball Club, won by the Lees 10 to 9.

Hart was an established businessman in New Orleans who seemed to be involved in nearly every aspect of New Orleans baseball. Born on August 29, 1835, in Newberry, South Carolina, Hart and his family moved to New Orleans around 1847 when he was twelve years old. Although little is known about his education, it is well documented that Hart was engaged in the business of painting houses and signs in and around New Orleans.

It was not long after he established his painting business that he became active as an amateur baseball player and enthusiast. During August of 1859, along with H.M. McManus, J.B. Rareshide and others, the twenty-four-year-old Hart helped to establish the Empire Base Ball Club, one of the first organized baseball clubs in New Orleans. Although the Louisiana Base Ball Club was the first to have its intra-squad games covered in the local press, we have no record of the date that the Louisiana Base Ball Club was established. Suffice it to say that the Louisiana club and the Empire club were both formed in mid–1859.

Hart was also a charter member of the Louisiana Base Ball Association. The practices and games of the Empire club were held on the Delachaise Grounds, located in Jefferson City, in the present-day Garden District of New Orleans and just a little over a mile away from Hart's home at the time on Camp Street and Jackson Avenue. Hart was soon elected treasurer of the club and often served as the official scorer for their matches with other clubs.

Off the field Hart gained national attention in 1860 when he designed a flag for an independent Louisiana[46] almost a year before Louisiana native General Pierre Gustave Toutant Beauregard fired on Fort Sumter to begin the Civil War. The banner was quite striking, crafted of rich blue silk and bordered with gold gilt fringe, with a large red star bearing the state's coat of arms. In keeping with the rhetoric sweeping through the Southern states at the time, the inscription above and below the star read "Equality in the Union" and "Or Independence Out of It." Hart was an ardent participant in local military organizations, joining the "Minute Men of '60" and the Mississippi Rifles.[47]

With Louisiana's secession in January of 1861, Hart quickly enlisted in the Confederate Army and served briefly with the forces tasked with the defense of New Orleans. However, after the surprisingly and embarrassingly easy capture of New Orleans by Admiral David Farragut and the Union naval forces, Hart sought his release to form his own command. He organized Company E of the Eighth Battalion, Louisiana Heavy Artillery, and served as its captain. His unit placed the very first battery upriver at Vicksburg, Mississippi, on March 29, 1863, even as Union General Ulysses Grant's army was slowly encircling the city. His principal duty was to command a ten-inch Columbiad battery—a massive seven and one-half ton cannon mounted on rails and swivels, capable of firing a sixty-five-pound projectile approximately 4,400 yards (two and one-half miles) in almost any direction. He and his company were captured on July 4, 1863, and eventually Hart was paroled on May 8, 1865, in Meridian, Mississippi. In 1913, his son, W.O. Hart, erected the first monument by a private individual in the Vicksburg Military Park in honor of his father.

Hart made his way back to New Orleans and resumed his life as a painting contractor. Even though New Orleans escaped any serious battle damage during the war, there was still plenty of work to be done courtesy of the benign neglect of the war years. The painting business was brisk, and Hart became financially secure. In 1873 he designed and built a Gothic Revival home in Uptown New Orleans on land he had acquired three years earlier after the closure of the Louisiana Base Ball Park. The Hart House is located at 2108 Palmer Avenue on the corner of Freret Street and has been on the National Register of Historic Places since 1984.

His return to New Orleans in 1865 also meant his return to the local baseball scene. Hart joined the Lone Star Base Ball Club as an officer, not a player, and was instrumental in arranging the club's successful 1870 Midwestern tour. In 1877, he became one of the founders of the Phunny Phorty Phellows, a Mardi Gras krewe that followed the Krewe of Rex parade for the first time on March 5, 1878, and grew in prominence over the next twenty years. Hart was also involved with several other Mardi Gras-related groups.

In 1883 Hart was selected to organize a committee to present an exhibition of the burgeoning new national pastime sport of "base ball" during the 1884 World Industrial and Cotton Centennial Exposition in New Orleans. The architectural plans for the Exposition included a baseball field to be located in the infield of the agricultural show track. Hart was the principal shareholder of the New Orleans Base Ball Park which catered to amateur and semi-professional teams, both black and white, while professional teams would play at the old Crescent City Base Ball Park, now renamed Sportsman's Park, located near the foot of Canal Street and abutting the New Basin Canal. The New Orleans Base Ball Park facility was eventually developed into home sites. Interestingly enough, one of the first homeowners to purchase and build there would be Abner Powell, the first captain of the New Orleans Pelicans and later owner-manager of the club, whose home was located at 4579 Canal Street.

Hart also led the effort to obtain a professional baseball franchise in the recently organized Southern League that had been formed in 1885, but he could not muster enough financial support. In the interim he formed the New Orleans Base Ball Association and sponsored two professional teams in the Gulf League to play two professional teams from Mobile, Alabama. By late 1886, however, Hart and his friends had garnered the necessary financial support to secure a franchise in the Southern League. In 1887, the New Orleans Pelicans became the city's Southern League franchise. This was an entirely new team built from scratch, for lack of a better description, who simply appropriated the amateur club's name.

To give you some idea of the rural nature of the New Orleans Base Ball Park's location at the time, in 1885 it was the site of an international clay pigeon tournament, with team shooting competition taking place in the morning and individual shooting competition in the afternoon. Spectators could gain general admission for twenty-five cents or shaded grandstand seating for fifty cents.[48] The sound of shotguns blasting away nearly non-stop from nine o'clock in the morning until six o'clock in the evening might have caused anyone living nearby almost as much concern as the final destination of any errant buckshot. The truth is that there simply were not that many residents in the area to be concerned. Ballparks were commonly erected on the outskirts of the city, often with the public encouragement and private funding of the railroads and utilities. These companies could justify their expenditure in extending service further out of town for the ballpark, knowing that the area was likely to be redeveloped into residential sites within a few years, particularly given the short-term leases granted to the ballpark associations, usually for only a three to five-year term.

Hart had to be aware that the ballpark future was in jeopardy when the city refused to renew his lease. Hoping for an agreement at the last minute, he was surprised to learn in July of 1890 that the city of New Orleans had given him a mere three days' notice to clear the land of all fencing and other obstructions. Like so many other large tracts of land within the city, the site was to be auctioned and redeveloped into residential lots. When Hart withdrew from baseball he continued his painting business, but also became involved in tourism, organizing and sponsoring excursions by private rail cars and by steamboats. However, he never really lost his interest in baseball and toward the turn of the century combined his interests in baseball and travel by organizing baseball barnstorming tours to Cuba. He died in December of 1907 at the age of 72 years.

Sportsman's Park (1884–1900)

Even though teams and fans seemed to prefer the newer New Orleans Base Ball Park as being closer to the city, there was more demand for residential property that there was supply and the ballpark was razed. The New Orleans Base Ball Park was originally intended to serve the scores of amateur and semi-professional teams while the Crescent City Base Ball Park was intended to serve professional baseball clubs. When Toby Hart first began negotiating for a franchise in the newly formed Southern League in 1884, it was immediately assumed that the team would play at his facility, not the Crescent City Base Ball Park. But the city had only granted Hart a five-year lease and if history was consistent, the ballpark site would soon be redeveloped into residential lots. In August of 1884 plans were announced to renovate the neglected Crescent City Base Ball Park.[49] The Fireman's Charitable Association that owned the land where the Crescent City Base Ball Park was built now had the opportunity to enter into a new lease.

In what at first appeared to be an unusual move, the printing firm of Hunter & Genslinger assumed control of the ballpark's lease,[50] and they quickly revealed their ambitious plans to install a quarter-mile bicycle track and a one hundred yard running track along with a regulation football field on the site. Those familiar with Hunter & Genslinger president Charles Genslinger knew him as a respected sporting man. He was a member of the New Orleans Bicycle Club and was at one time president of two internationally renowned boxing and athletic clubs, the Olympic Club and the Metropolitan Club. He was also a founding member of the Lone Star Base Ball Club. He would eventually become one of the principal shareholders and president of both the New Orleans Pelicans and the Southern League.

Fresh off his recent experience with Toby Hart and the New Orleans Base Ball Park, Genslinger wasted no time is refurbishing the old ballpark, and he renamed the old Crescent City facility. The new venture would be called Sportsman's Park. While not all of the extensive renovations he envisioned took place, those related to baseball took priority and the facility quickly became the city's preeminent baseball park until close the emergence of Athletic Park in 1898.

The ballpark played host to the first Southern League game on Monday, April 18, 1887, the first of hundreds of Pelican games New Orleanians would enjoy over the next thirteen years until the turn of the century. Not only professional baseball but amateur baseball and other sporting events found a welcome home in the new Sportsman's Park. The great boxing champion Jack Dempsey, the "Nonpareil," fought Charles Bixamos there on Thursday, March 19, 1885, winning in a fifth-round knockout. But the park's principal tenant was the New Orleans Pelicans, so when the Southern League suspended operations at the end of the 1889 season there would be a brief pause in professional baseball in New Orleans.

With no professional baseball to look forward to in the spring of 1890 as the Southern League remaining shuttered, New Orleanians turned their eyes skyward, not in fervent prayer for the return of baseball, but to monitor the spring rainfall. Throughout the Mississippi River valley, the seasonal rainfall was heavier and more frequent than usual. The city's attention, along with most residents, immediately turned toward the fragile levee system. The river had already reached flood stage and numerous crevasses—deep fissures or breaches in the levee embankment—were showing up between Vicksburg and New Orleans. Although the state had spent more on levee construction and maintenance in the prior year than ever before, there was an immediate need for additional funds to bolster and shore up the levees. An unexpected windfall came when the Louisiana State Lottery Company offered Governor Nicholls $100,000 to use as he saw fit to address the problem. This posed quite a conundrum for the reform-minded, anti-lottery governor who ultimately was forced to decline the lottery company's offer. His decision was fraught with political peril, especially if the river over-topped or broke through the levee at any one of the scores of crevasses already threatening the state from Ferriday in northeast Louisiana to Belle Chasse just south of New Orleans.

Chartered by the Louisiana State Assembly in 1868, the Louisiana State Lottery Company sponsored daily and monthly drawings for prizes ranging from $100 to $300,000. There were also semi-annual drawings for a $600,000 grand prize which drew national and international players. Former Confederate generals P.G.T. Beauregard and Jubal Early presided over the monthly drawings and provided an air of respectability and the promise of fair play to the proceedings, in exchange for $30,000 per year in remuneration for less than two days' work per month. In exchange for their exclusive right to conduct the lottery statewide, the privately-held company agreed to contribute a relatively minor annual sum of $40,000 per year through 1893 for the upkeep of Charity Hospital in New Orleans, with the lottery corporation keeping the remainder of their revenues. The company, owned by John Morris and Charles T. Howard, was suspected of paying substantial bribes to state legislators for the lucrative lottery franchise. It is estimated that the Louisiana State Lottery Company returned 48 percent of its revenues to the company. In the spring of 1890, the end of their twenty-five-year agreement was drawing near and a well-organized anti-lottery faction was gaining traction statewide. Even though it was "the most powerful gambling syndicate in the country" at the time, it was in their best interest for the Louisiana State Lottery Company to position itself as an engaged and philanthropic member of the community.

Although Governor Nicholls declined the lottery's offer, Mayor Shakspeare, who was also a reformer and anti-lottery advocate, could not afford to stand on principle and begrudgingly accepted a $50,000 donation from the lottery to be used for the levees around New Orleans. Fortunately, the levees held, and the city was spared from flooding.

During the Southern League's hiatus fans had to be content with watching amateur teams play, running the gamut from female baseball teams playing against both male and female teams to employee games such as those from the Keller Soap Works, the Treme Market butchers, the city's letter carriers, and the day shift versus the night shift of Western Union. These contests took place away from Sportsman's Park at many of the city's smaller facilities such as Loeper's Park and Valence Green. Quite a letdown both in terms of the quality of play and the level of competition. Unless you were a friend or family member of one of the butchers at the Treme Market there was no driving reason for the public as a whole to be excited about showing up for a game. It was not all cold coffee for baseball fans as there were first-tier amateur teams such as the Theard Base Ball Club, the J.C. Bach Base Ball Club, the Crescent City Base Ball Club, as well as some of the old standbys such as the R.E. Lee Base Ball Club and the Remy Clarke Base Ball Club, who played the occasional game.

Initially the city was not completely devoid of professional baseball during the start of 1890. Local baseball figure Henry Powers arranged for several exhibitions games to be held in the city during the 1890 spring training season between the Chicago White Stockings and the Cleveland Indians, but any further interest by professional teams was minimal. Professional baseball would return to Sportsman's Park for the 1893 season, but the park was showing signs of neglect and the inevitable calls to either renovate the ballpark or find a suitable replacement could be heard. These demands fell on deaf ears as there was no money in the city's coffers to do anything other than basic maintenance. As the city approached the end of the century Sportsman's Park was abandoned in favor of Athletic Park.

Athletic Park (1898–1906)

The first facility in New Orleans known as Athletic Park was actually named Southern Athletic Park and was located near Canal Street on Gravier Street, bounded by Broad Street, St. Patrick Street, and Tulane Avenue. In 1895, in an all too familiar scenario, the property was subdivided and auctioned by Curtis & Walmsley to make room for seventy-five residential lots.

In 1898 a new park facility was constructed on Carrollton Avenue, Tulane Avenue, and the New Basin Canal. As was the custom of the day, most sporting facilities were designed to serve multiple purposes and multiple sports. The principal feature of Athletic Park would be a large oval track that could be used for footraces and bicycle races. From the earliest boneshakers that appeared between the 1820s and the 1850s, bicycles underwent rapid improvement in design and construction, resulting in the very popular high wheel models

Athletic Park was packed for a holiday baseball game, probably on the Fourth of July judging from the flags and bunting that covers the top of the grandstand. The left side of the grandstand is covered with a canvas awning for additional shade. (Historic New Orleans Collection).

that promised greater speed. Bicycle races were not for the faint of heart, for with greater speed came the possibility of tossing its rider over the front wheel causing serious injury. It was exciting to watch. Bicycle races were known to attract thousands of spectators every weekend. The interior of the course was large enough to be laid out to play rugby, football, or baseball. Over time, Athletic Park became best known for football and baseball. To make the park accessible, it was only seven minutes away from the Clay statue by street rail.

The New Orleans Pelicans played several exhibition games in 1898 against the Houston Buffalos and the Galveston Sand Crabs from the Texas League. Their first game was against Houston on Saturday, March 26, 1898.

New Orleans Pelicans versus Houston Buffalos
March 26, 1898[51]

Innings	*1*	*2*	*3*	*4*	*5*	*6*	*7*	*8*	*9*	*10*	*11*	*12*	*13*	Total
Houston	3	1	1	1	1	0	0	0	1	0	0	0	0	**8**
New Orleans	2	1	2	2	0	0	0	0	1	0	0	0	0	**8**

New Orleans was still waiting for several of their players to report and even though they were fighting with the little end of the horn, they held their own against Houston. In the early innings each Houston score was answered in turn by the Pelicans and after the fourth inning New Orleans held a 7 to

6 lead. The small crowd described as "a few hundred," tried to rally their club and cheered until they were hoarse. Houston came back with the tying run in the top of the fifth inning. An unfortunate error in the top of the ninth inning by Pelicans second baseman Goldie allowed the Houston batter to reach base safely and eventually score the go ahead run on a long line drive to the outfield. This was one of nine errors committed by the Pelicans and proved to be the costliest. Abner Powell rallied his boys and they responded in the bottom of the ninth inning when Pelican catcher Fred Abbott scored to once again even the score at eight runs apiece. After four more scoreless innings the game had to be called because of darkness. New Orleans dropped the second game of the abbreviated series before welcoming Galveston to the new ballpark for a four-game series, after which they turned their attention to the Chicago White Stockings before starting league play.

The Pelicans formally opened the new park for baseball on Wednesday, April 13, 1898, hosting Mobile before 1,000 fans. The Blackbirds outlasted the Pelicans in another extra innings battle, gamely going ten innings only to see the Pelicans fall by the score of 5 to 4.[52]

The local newspapers described Athletic Park by saying, "No baseball grounds in the South is half as pretty as those of Athletic Park." Given that "pretty" was not really a priority in a ballpark, the playing field was larger than most—427 feet down the left field line, 405 feet in center field, and 418 feet down the right field line. And while it was not uncommon for newspapers to periodically engage in hyperbole or to wax poetic in order to amplify the tone of their written articles, and no doubt such was the intent of the unnamed reporter covering the Opening Day festivities at Athletic Park. "Baseball is the cleanest sport of the day, and is fraught with brilliancy, activity, skill, and daring. Unlike the coarser sports, there is no fear of dishonesty, and the teams cannot help battle their best in a contest. There is hardly a game or sport that has not been tainted by deception and fraud, but baseball has been so purified that in years there has been no accusation against a player for dishonest work."[53] Much to the dismay of the New Orleans community, and the consternation of *The Daily Picayune's* reporter, baseball in New Orleans was not any more immune to the impact of gamblers than any other professional or amateur sport.

Athletic Park remained in use until 1907 when it was replaced by Pelican Park, located further up Carrollton Avenue at Banks Street across from present-day Jesuit High School.

Lesser Known Ball Parks

There were a number of lesser known neighborhood ballparks scattered throughout the city. Most of these lasted anywhere from three to five years before the inevitable encroachment of real estate or commercial development displaced them.

Racetracks (1860–1899)

During the mid-19th century and lasting until the end of the century, the city of New Orleans was the epicenter of horse racing in the United States, with four race tracks scattered around the city: the Eclipse Course (1833–1849), the Metairie Course (1838–1872), the Bingaman Course (1847–1862), and the Union Course/Creole Course/Fair Grounds (1852—present). During Reconstruction the owners needed to use their horse racing venues for other purposes. The large interior field on the infield of the race course had more than enough space to accommodate picnics, fairs, and, of course, baseball. One such game at the Bingaman Course was scheduled to take place on June 24, 1860, between two sides from the Magnolia Base Ball Club,[54] but which was not played until July 1, 1860.

Magnolia Base Ball Club
Stinson's Side versus Delamore's Side
July 1, 1860[55]

Stinson's Side	R	Delamore's Side	R
Stinson, 3b	2	G. Delamore, p	2
Smith, p	1	C. Meister, c	3
Kelly, c	2	R. Allen, 1b	4
Swanson, 2b	5	Chandler, lf	4
G. Meister, 1b	2	Capprice, 2b	3
Fisher, cf	4	Kingman, cf	2
Strong, lf	4	A. Wallace, rf	1
A. Delamore, rf	2	Magnon, ss	3
W.T. Smith, ss	1	Brown, 3b	2
Lucie, f	3	Tracy, f	2
TOTAL RUNS	25	TOTAL RUNS	24

Of interest in this intra-squad game was that even in mid-1860 each side played with ten men, each having an extra fielder—Lucie for Stinson's Side and Tracy for Delamore's Side. It would also appear that the Magnolia Base Ball Club was very much a family affair with at least two sets of brothers on the field: A. Delamore (Stinson's Side) and G. Delamore (Delamore's Side) joined by G. Meister (Stinson's Side) and C. Meister (Delamore's Side). The inclusion of initials in players' names was unusual and not without purpose—W.T. Smith, R. Allen, and A. Wallace—which might infer that they too had relatives in the club who were not playing on this particular day.

The Union Course was originally opened in 1852 and operated until

1857. It was reorganized and reopened as the Creole Course in 1858 and remained in operation until the Civil War. It was renamed the Fair Grounds in 1863 and is the third oldest continuously operated thoroughbred racetrack after Saratoga and Pimlico. The 400-acre complex saw its first baseball game in 1868 during the Odd Fellows picnic on April 26, 1868, when the Southern Base Ball Club faced off against the Crusader Base Ball Club.[56] The Southerns prevailed by the score of 32 to 24 against the Crusaders, after which the spectators were treated to a free concert by Jaeger's Silver Coronet Band.

That same year the Metairie Course, located on the west side of the New Basin Canal from the Half-Way House, also hosted their first baseball games. As with other race tracks, the Metairie Course, was an ideal location for fairs and picnics which featured baseball as one of the main attractions. The Metairie Course ceased operations in 1872 and was converted into a cemetery. An aerial view of the property reveals the outline of the original oval racetrack.

Just across the road from the Metairie Course was a trotting track called Oakland Park. Established in 1872, it was not as popular as the Metairie Course but nonetheless played host to picnics, fairs, and concerts. On June 16, 1872, there was quite an eclectic "Dolly Varden" picnic that featured not only baseball, but a promenade, dancing, and old English sports and pastimes.[57] Dolly Varden was a fashionable women's outfit named after a character in Charles Dickens' "Barnaby Rudge." Because the facility had less demand than the Fair Grounds and the Metairie Course, it became very popular with black charitable groups to hold their functions and for black teams to play baseball. Oakland Park is now part of the New Orleans Country Club golf course.

Oakland Park was the site of a baseball match between the Pickwick Base Ball Club, a black team, and a picked nine comprised of junior white players.

Pickwicks versus Picked Nine
September 17, 1882[58]

Innings	1	2	3	4	5	6	7	8	9	Total
Picked Nine	1	0	4	0	1	0	0	0	1	7
Pickwicks	1	3	1	0	0	0	0	5	0	10

Although not the first baseball game between black and white teams in New Orleans, the line score above illustrates that the younger white players, all aged under twenty years old, held their own against the older and more experienced black players. They were tied at five runs apiece through four innings and were actually leading by one run going into the eighth inning. At this point the Pickwick hitters exploded for five runs to take a three-run lead in the bottom of the eighth inning which the Picked Nine could not answer, losing by the score of 10 to 7.

Ogden Park (1877–1881)

Prospects for "a genuine revival of the game of baseball" occasioned the opening of Ogden Park in 1877,[59] with some of the older clubs reorganizing into new, stronger teams. The popularity of baseball as a spectator sport was nearly in direct correlation to the health of the national and local economy. What this meant for New Orleans was that the long depression that began in 1873 was still weighing heavily on the city, resulted in deflation and wage cuts, leaving the average worker with less discretionary income for things like baseball games. Yet by 1877, after five years of relatively austerity, New Orleanians were more than ready to return to the ballpark.

Located two blocks upriver from Louisiana Avenue on Prytania Street in the city's Garden District, Ogden Park was built just a stone's throw from the original Delachaise family home, located just a block away from the present day Touro Infirmary. The grounds were surrounded by an eight-foot high wooden fence and terraced bleacher-style seating and was erected to accommodate as many as five hundred fans, which in itself provides a telling commentary about the popularity of baseball at the time. Just two years prior to the construction of Ogden Park the Louisiana Base Ball Park, which could accommodate 4,000 fans, was closed. The first game was scheduled for Sunday, December 2, 1877, between the R.E. Lee Base Ball Club and the Howard Base Ball Club, the first of many amateur games to be played over the next four years. The park also played host to a variety of other types of entertainment, such as the circus.

With the expiration of their lease, the property was developed to suit the growing hospital complex next door. Touro Infirmary had relocating into the area in 1882 on Prytania and Aline Streets and began expanding almost immediately thereafter.

Loeper's Park/Stonewall Green (1878)

A "cozy little nook"[60] when compared to other ballparks or to the open resort areas of West End, Milneburg, or Spanish Fort, Loeper's Park was actually nothing more than a popular neighborhood beer garden with an adjacent open field often called Stonewall Green.[61] At the time, this ballpark was located, like most, on the outskirts of the city which today would now be considered to be in the center of the city. It was situated on Bienville Street and was bounded by Conti Street, Napoleon Street (now Hennessey Street), and Alexander Street and was easily reached in minutes via the Spanish Fort steam car or on the Bienville Street Lake Railroad. Loeper's Park was a favorite site for picnics and small gatherings for the smaller social clubs and benevolent associations who leased their park. Baseball was often one of the main attractions at these events catering almost exclusively to second-tier amateur groups. Before long the park gained wide acceptance as a baseball site in its own right. With the expansion of baseball in the 1880s, amateur teams and leagues often used Loeper's Park as one of their many available venues.

Exposition Park (1884–1885)

Mayor William J. Behan and the city's civic and business leaders were gambling that 1883 would be a pivotal year for the city of New Orleans. The populace was still recovering from the massive flooding that swept through more than two hundred and sixty crevasses along the levees from Memphis to New Orleans in 1882, washing away whole sections of rail lines and roads as well as a significant number of homes in the low-lying areas of New Orleans. Parts of the city were underwater for over ninety days.[62] At the same time the city was dealing with flood control they were also preparing to host the 1884 World Industrial and Cotton Centennial Exposition. The event was proposed by the National Cotton Planters Association the preceding year to celebrate the 100th anniversary of the nation's cotton industry's first export to England in 1784. By 1884, over one-third of the cotton grown in the United States passed through the port of New Orleans. The port also handled the majority of the nation's sugar exports following the discovery by a Creole black man, Norbert Rillieux, of the process of boiling sugar cane to produce refined sugar. His 1843 breakthrough added significantly to the overall tonnage of cargo passing through the port, which necessitated importing more and more slaves to harvest the labor-intensive sugar cane crop in Louisiana while exporting the refined sugar all over the world.

The site that Behan and the City Council had selected for the exposition was upriver from the city, in the former town of Carrollton, where the cattle had been relocated from the bucolic lower City Park, the area closest to the river, and the swamp and weeds that covered upper City Park, the area closest to St. Charles Avenue, were filled in. Nearly every available inch of the 425-acre tract of the new exposition grounds was swarming with construction workers erecting everything from the massive three-story Main Building that, at 1,247,100 square feet, was one of the largest buildings in the world at the time, to the 500,000 square foot United States Pavilion, to the 117,000 square foot Horticultural Hall—the largest conservatory in the world at the time of its construction—to the dozens of exhibition pavilions representing the numerous states and countries[63] that dotted the landscape now known as Audubon Park. Overcoming an unexpected financial shortfall that occurred when Louisiana State Treasurer Edward Burke absconded with nearly $1.8

million of the exposition's construction funds before making his way to some foreign shore, as well as the typical corruption and scandals that always seem to accompany any public project in Louisiana, the exposition was surprisingly only two weeks behind schedule when it finally opened in December of 1884. By the time the celebration ended in May 1885 the city had hosted more than one million visitors, but the event ended deeply in debt. The city kept the Exposition open well past its scheduled end date in an effort to recover some of its investment, now calling itself the American Exposition.

Toby Hart was appointed as the Baseball Commissioner for the 1884 World Industrial and Cotton Centennial Exposition. Among the many buildings at the exposition was a sprawling two hundred and forty-nine-acre facility that boasted a livestock arena and a bicycle race track. The interior of the race track was used as a baseball field in the very same way that had been done in other parts of the city such as the Metairie Course (1868), the Fair Grounds (1869), and Oakland Park (1872).

Hart used his numerous contacts with the professional baseball teams who had visited the city for spring training to try to convince them to return to New Orleans during the Exposition, enticing them with the prospect of grandstands and bleachers packed with paying visitors. Teams were, of course, interested in Hart's offer, but the constant delays in completion of the project and the prospect of playing winter baseball was not necessarily a part of the recipe for success. Even with those objections Hart was successful in scheduling several professional baseball teams to travel to New Orleans to play exhibition games.

These would not be the first baseball games in New Orleans to feature professional clubs as there had been numerous exhibition games played between a professional team and one or more of the city's elite amateur teams, starting with the Mutuals of New York in 1869 and the Cincinnati Red Stockings in 1870. Exposition Park was, however, the site of the first known game in the city between two major league teams—the St. Louis Browns and the New York Giants—on November 16, 1885.[64] Indeed it was the first time either team had played each other since at that time there was no such thing as inter-league play. St. Louis was in the American Association and had finished the 1885 season in first place, sixteen games ahead of the Cincinnati Red Stockings. The New York Giants were in the National League and finished the 1885 season in second place behind the Chicago White Stockings.

A large and enthusiastic crowd estimated to be 3,000 of which 800 filled the grandstands and 2,200 were strung out all along and around the fences that surrounded the race track. They were treated to a beautiful, sunny afternoon expecting the inaugural game at Exposition Park to be memorable. It would be, but for all the wrong reasons. The diamond was strange to the teams whose players by their own admission were "rusty," having not played in several weeks. The field was "sandy and absolutely dead," making for poor fielding and base-running conditions. New York was out of the gate quickly, scoring two runs in the first inning, and New York pitcher Keefe was a terror for the first two innings until he split open the index finger of his pitching hand. St. Louis fielders fared better on the foreign field, with only two errors against six by the Giants, two each by Tim Keefe and shortstop Ewing. But St. Louis was the more consistent team that day. Browns pitcher Dave Foutz puzzled the vaunted New York hitters, sawing the air more often than they made contact with the ball. He shut out the Giants for the remaining eight innings of the game while his teammates outscored New York 8 to 2 to emerge victorious.[65]

On the left is New York Giants pitcher Tim Keefe depicted on the Allen & Ginter's 1887 N28 tobacco card. On the right is St. Louis Browns pitcher Dave Foutz on the Buchner Gold Coin 1887 N284 tobacco card (Tim Keefe card: collection of the author. Dave Foutz card: Library of Congress).

New York Giants versus St. Louis Browns
November 16, 1885

Innings	1	2	3	4	5	6	7	8	9	Total
New York	2	0	0	0	0	0	0	0	0	2
St. Louis	0	0	4	1	2	0	1	0	x	8

In support of the American Exposition, the community not only attended baseball games, but also participated when circumstances dictated. On the afternoon of Saturday, December 5, 1885, two teams drawn from two if the city's preeminent social clubs—the Louisiana Club and the Pickwick Club—agreed to battle each other for five innings at the ballpark at the Exposition.

At a quarter past two o'clock an eager group of lawyers, merchants, cotton brokers, and other well-heeled professionals took the field. The Louisiana Club team wore baseball knickers and stockings, swallow-tail coats, and silk hats while the Pickwick Club team wore red shirts and white plantation pants with caps with sunflower peaks. Apparently, the uniforms were considered to be so garish that the press commented that "society men in such costumes before their lady friends were certainly a novelty." The crowd of more than 3,000 packed the Exposition Park to witness the spectacle that was staged in good natured fun as most of the participants had not actively played baseball in several years.

To the contemporary reader the following box score read like a Who's Who of New Orleans society, listing more than a smattering of well-known and well-respected business and society figures whose family names remain prominent to this day. The object of their participation was to draw a huge crowd of their friends and other interested onlookers to the Exposition Park, and in that regard, they were successful, although the two clubs expected a far larger crowd.

The Louisiana Club versus The Pickwick Club
December 5, 1885[66]

Pickwicks	AB	R	1B	PO	A	E
F.W. Baker, 2b	3	2	1	0	0	1
Peter Labouisse, rf	3	1	2	0	0	0
James Legendre, lf	2	2	0	0	0	0
Walter Denegre, p and c	3	3	3	1	6	2
L.W. Fairchild, rss	2	3	0	0	2	0
E.H. Farrar, cf	4	1	1	0	0	0
E. Van Benthuysen, c and p	3	2	1	2	3	0
W.S. Dudley, 3b	2	2	0	0	0	1
W.P. Curtis, lss	3	2	1	0	0	3
Charles M. Hunt, 1b	2	3	1	9	0	0
Totals	27	21	10	12	11	7

Louisianas	AB	R	1B	PO	A	E
J.A. Lafitte, rf	3	1	0	0	0	0
A.S. Smith, cf	3	3	1	0	0	2
J.S. Boullemet, rss	3	4	1	0	1	0
H. Carter, lss	3	4	1	0	0	2
E.R. Violett, c	3	3	2	4	4	2
Thomas Sully, 2b	3	3	0	0	0	0
Frank Gordon, p	3	1	2	0	3	0
A.J. Murray, 1b	3	2	2	7	0	1
James Flower, 3b	3	0	0	1	0	1
L. Lyons, lf	3	0	0	0	0	0
TOTALS	30	21	9	12	8	8

By Innings	1	2	3	4	5	TOTAL
Pickwicks	4	8	1	8	x	21
Louisianas	8	6	5	2	x	21

Umpires: T.L. Airey and M.J. Kelly

The game was played with ten men to a side, and the box score shows that the two middle fielders were designated at "lss" and "rss" to denote the left-side shortstop and the right-side shortstop.

Players of note include noted cotton factor John Peter Labouisse, attorney and businessman Walter Denegre, and celebrated architect Thomas Sully.

At the rate the two teams were capable of scoring runs a full nine inning game would have taken all day which was why the original plan was to play five innings in the interest of time. However, the original five innings were halted at the completion of four innings as darkness had begun to fall. There was the usual discussion about either continuing the game or scheduling a rematch at some later date. Reading of the success of the two social clubs in drawing a crowd to the ballpark there was tremendous interest expressed by other social and athletic clubs in playing baseball at the Exposition.

Despite the numerous challenges experienced by the Exposition as a whole, baseball was one of the few bright spots both critically and, to a lesser extent, financially. In the end, all of the magnificent buildings that made up the Exposition, including the ballpark, were auctioned off for a fraction of their cost, dismantled and the building materials and architectural elements dispersed for resale. The land was cleared to create Audubon Park.

Carrollton Park/Ferran's Park (1893–1913)

In early 1893, the directors of the St. Charles Railroad were actively and vocally endorsing the idea of a new baseball park to replace the declining Sportsman's Park.[67] The location they were promoting was the site of their old streetcar stables at the corner of St. Charles Avenue and Napoleon Avenue.

However, having just lost two seasons during which the Southern League did not operate, baseball was still a hit-or-miss proposition due to declining attendance. As a result, the proposed new ballpark found little financial backing outside of the railroad, who stood to profit from the sale of the land.

Instead of replacing Sportsman's Park, planners began looking for a sight to replace the former New Orleans Base Ball Park on Canal Street, now a residential community. Given the pace of development along Canal Street, many people felt that Canal Street was no longer a viable location for a ballpark and all eyes turned back toward the river in Carrollton where there was still ample land for such a project. Instead, a more modest project was proposed for the far upriver end of St. Charles Avenue where it turned into Carrollton Avenue, bounded by Dublin and Nelson Streets, not far from the old Carrollton Gardens Resort. The new facility would cater to a full gamut of baseball activity, from neighborhood teams to low amateur leagues to exhibition games between semi-professional and professional players and was popular well into the 20th century.

One such semi-professional versus professional match occurred between the Leo Base Ball Club and the Gatti Base Ball Club in the fall of 1899. The Leos were formed in 1898 to compete in the newly formed City League while the Gattis were only formed in 1899 to provide local and visiting professional players a team to play on. The two teams scheduled a three-game championship series that was billed as the Championship of the South in order to garner fan interest, but was really about the $50 purse, actually just a side bet between the two teams.

The first game took place on Sunday, October 29, 1899, which was won by the Gattis by the score of 7 to 6 behind the excellent pitching of former New Orleans Pelican pitcher Jim Delaney. The second game went to the Leos 12 to 7 two weeks later. The third and deciding game was scheduled for the following week but had to be rescheduled for Sunday, December 10.

Carrollton Park/Ferran's Park was perfect for a neighborhood field but not nearly large enough for the city's top echelon amateur teams or professional teams. That would fall to Athletic Park to fill the void.

Many of these ballparks and recreational facilities remained in operation for only a few years as the usual residential development became a more profitable use of the land. There were literally scores of places across New Orleans that became impromptu ballgame sites being used with or without the owner's permission for as long as the team could get away with it.

Four

Teams and Leagues

"Well—it's our game; America's Game; has the snap, go, fling of the American atmosphere; it belongs as much to our institutions, fits into them as significantly, as our constitution's laws; is just as important as the sum total of our historic life."

—Walt Whitman

The early baseball clubs of New Orleans took their lead from the other social and fraternal organizations in the city by adhering to the formalities of drafting a constitution and by-laws, electing officers and directors, and arranging for a clubhouse. The organizational documents were easily available in template form in *The Base Ball Player's Companion*. The clubhouse could be anything from a rented banquet room at a popular restaurant to a small building with a side lot large enough to hold practice and intra-squad games.

The Louisiana Base Ball Club held their monthly meetings at the Iron Horse, a bar room at 209 Tchoupitoulas Street opposite St. Mary's Market.[1] In 1859 a group of the largest of these new baseball clubs formed an association, the Louisiana Base Ball Association, and engaged in spirited competition. Initially after a number of informal practices, and if a club was large enough, they would not only select their best nine, but also their second nine, and perhaps even a junior nine made up of their youngest players. When baseball first became organized in New Orleans, teams or sides could, according to the Knickerbocker Rules, be made up of between nine and eleven players. Of the twenty original rules adopted by the Knickerbocker Base Ball Club on September 23, 1845, the only guidance provided in this regard is Rule Three, which states that both sides on the field must have the same number of players. This structure worked well but was interrupted by the Civil War.

The renewal of interest in baseball that followed the Civil War was both prolific and pervasive. Between 1859 and 1869 there were approximately forty-four active and organized amateur baseball clubs operating in the city. From 1870 through 1879 a rash of teams exploded that number to two hundred and eighty-eight teams, and from 1880 through 1889 that number grew again to more than six hundred and ninety-nine teams. These figures only include those teams that took the time to organize, find a sponsor, arrange for and schedule a game, and report the results of their games to the newspaper.[2] In addition to the well-known and better-established teams such as the R.E. Lees, the Lone Stars, the Empires, the Southerns, and the Pelicans, were teams such as the employees of the mercantile companies Meyer, Weis who were challenged by the employees of Freidman Brothers to play a game for the benefit of the Young Men's Hebrew Association,[3] or the Custer Busters versus the Buster Custers.[4] Many of these teams were only formed for the purpose of playing a single benefit game or occasionally a best of three series. Teams such as the Morse Nine and the Picayune Base Ball Club,[5] which featured telegraph operators challenging their newspaper counterparts, may have provided the spark to reorganize the team at a later date to take part in a commercial league. The Morse Nine, for example, had been organized in 1870 strictly with employees of the Western Union Telegraph Company, but a later incarnation of the Morse Nine was made up of telegraphers from different companies expressly for the game against the newspaper.

Matches consisted of two sets of picked sides of nine, ten, or eleven players in an arranged, intra-squad match. The winning side would earn bragging rights within the club, but once a match was over, it was really over. There were no standings, no rankings, and no statistics beyond the total number of runs scored kept. Each match stood on its own. Yesterday's first nine might be made up of one or more different players next week or yet again next month. Every side had a team captain who selected the best players to represent his side. While this fostered a certain degree of competitiveness within the club, it was all good natured, healthy competition. It was openly encouraged and was ultimately for the benefit of the team. The formation of a league was a bold move. It was one thing to organize a baseball club and play games between members of your own team, but quite another thing altogether to attempt to coordinate the schedules of eight or more teams and to mediate the inevitable disputes that arose in such a competitive environment. They were still learning the rules of baseball and running a league only added a layer of complexity to the situation and their interactions with each other.

Despite those concerns, and as would be expected, league games were still played purely for fun. While the rules provided order, it was the familiar customs and rituals of the club format that provided structure. This held sway even as the curiosity of competition had clubs wondering which of them was the best. In such an instance a challenge would be formally issued by one club to another club in writing, which challenge would also be printed in one or more of the city's daily newspapers.[6] The challenged club would respond in kind and the match would be scheduled. On both sides, the pride the players felt in belonging to a spirited, driven baseball club meant that the players competed more for the honor of victory. After all, in accepting the challenge the reputation of the club was at stake. Irrespective of the team preference of the fans, poor sportsmanship of any kind was to be greeted with boos and hisses from spectators who were expected, as a matter of courtesy, to applaud good play from either team. Winning and losing was kept in its proper perspective. It really was all about how the game was played, but for those playing the game it was also about bringing credit to one's club.

The losing club frequently treated the winners to a festive dinner at one of the city's popular restaurants, perhaps at Galpin's Chop House at No. 9 Exchange Place or McDonnell's Restaurant at 149 Common Street. During the festivities speeches and dramatic and comedic recitations by players from both teams provided the evening's entertainment. The winning team was often presented with a gilded ball or a prized bat to commemorate the match.

The club structure was defined by matches between individual teams who determined when and if they played each other. There were no set schedules, no standings between the teams, no rankings between the players, and no statistics. It was simply one-on-one competition in the moment. After the Civil War the club structure was gradually replaced by the league structure. Under the league structure, teams tallied their wins and losses to determine the best team in the league. Eventually, individual offen-

> The following correspondence between the Lone Star and Southern Base Ball Club, will explain itself:
>
> LONE STAR BASE BALL CLUB,
> Club Room 93 St. Charles street,
> New Orleans, April 12, 1870.
>
> To Southern Base Ball Club:
>
> *Gentlemen*—If agreeable to you, we will play the first game of the series on Saturday, April 16, 1870, on the Louisiana Base Ball Park, weather permitting, as the draining machine went to work this morning. The game to commence at 3 P. M. If the above proposition suits, please answer immediately, so that the necessary arrangements can be made.
>
> Yours respectfully,
> W. F. TRACY,
> Captain 1st Nine L. S. B. B. C.
>
> ---
>
> HALL OF SOUTHERN BASE BALL CLUB,
> New Orleans, April 12, 1870.
>
> W. F. Tracy, Esq., Captain 1st Nine, Lone Star Base Ball Club:
>
> *Dear Sir*—Your proposition of this day is accepted. Let us make arrangements for Saturday next, April 16, at 3 P. M., on the Louisiana Base Ball Park.
>
> Very respectfully,
> J. J. WALL,
> R. K. PITKIN,
> L. L. SIMMES,
> Board of Directors.
> J. T. HOLTZMAN,
> Captain 1st Nine. S. B. B. C.

The challenge system illustrated here was initiated by W.F. Tracy (Tracey) of the Lone Star Base Ball Club challenging the Southern Base Ball Club to a match starting on April 16, 1870, followed by the Southerns' acceptance later that same day, made public in the newspaper (*The Daily Picayune*, April 13, 1870).

sive statistics were tracked to determine the best hitter, and defensive statistics to determine the best pitcher and the best fielder.

The club structure actually began under the auspices of the Louisiana Base Ball Association which was organized in 1859 with seven teams: the Louisiana Base Ball Club, the Lone Star Base Ball Club, the Magnolia Base Ball Club, the Empire Base Ball Club, the Pelican Base Ball Club, the Washington Base Ball Club, and the Melpomenia Base Ball Club. The following year two volunteer fire companies formed baseball clubs—the Liberty Base Ball Club and the Home Base Ball Club—bringing the total pool of competitors to nine teams. Their initial games were intra-club, but before long competitive curiosity took root and clubs began challenging each other to a three-game series. This was not a best of three games series or the best two games out of three game series. All three games were played. The Louisiana Base Ball Association would operate until 1873.

There was also the New Orleans Baseball Association (1879), the Crescent City League (1880–1886), the Louisiana Base Ball League (1882–1886), the Louisiana Amateur Association (1884), the New Orleans Amateur League (1884, 1888–1889, 1894), the Gulf League (1884–1886), and the Southern League (1887–1899). The black community organized their own teams and leagues, with the Southern League of Colored Baseballists (1885) and the Colored Amateur League (1886) being the most prominent. There were dozens of other active leagues on all skill levels active in New Orleans such as the Catholic League, the Commercial League, the Rowing Club League, the Bankers League, the Athletic Club League, and the Association of Gymnastic Clubs.

Even with the unconscious transition from the club structure to the league structure, the pride a player felt in his club was easily transformed into pride in one's city as the most accomplished local clubs began accepting challenges from clubs in other cities. Newspapers from cities along the Mississippi River and its tributaries were shipped downriver to New Orleans by riverboat from Memphis, St. Louis, Louisville, and Chicago, among others, to allow visitors from these cities to stay abreast of the news at home. Similarly, New Orleans newspapers also found their way upriver. All along the Mississippi, amateur baseball clubs soon became aware of the top teams in other cities and inevitably challenges were issued. Visiting teams were hosted as honored guests even as intercity rivalries developed. This tradition of team challenges did not change after the Civil War even with the formalization of baseball leagues and league competition.

The Louisiana Base Ball Association (1859–1873)

Teams in New Orleans were still getting the feel of the club structure and challenge system that developed in 1859 between the newly formed baseball clubs. In the interim, the clubs played intra-squad games between their best nines. There were dozens of these games played at the Delachaise Grounds during the early days of baseball in New Orleans, but none more striking that the first doubleheader played in the city between two picked sides from the Melpomenia Base Ball Club.[7]

Game One
Wooden's Side versus F. Coburn's Side
October 21, 1859

Wooden's Side	Runs	F. Coburn's Side	Runs
Wooden, p	6	Pope, p	2
Strondbach, c	5	Cram, c	1
Steel, ss	6	Coburn, ss	1
A.L. Plattsmier, 1b	3	Minch, 1b	2
McCardy, 2b	5	Sherry, 2b	4
Gouville, 3b	4	Bumetz, 3b	4
Parker, cf	6	Higgins, cf	1
C. McCoy, rf	3	Barrett, rf	1
A. McCoy, lf	6	Ernest, lf	2
		Norton	2
		A.A. Plattsmier	2
TOTAL	44	TOTAL	22

Game Two
Wooden's Side versus Norton's Side
October 21, 1859

Wooden's Side	Runs	Norton's Side	Runs
Wooden, p	1	Norton, p	5
Coughlin, c	2	Pope, c	3
Steel, ss	3	Cram, ss	3
A.A. Plattsmier, 1b	2	Minch, 1b	2
A.L. Plattsmier, 2b	2	Sherry, 2b	4
Phillips, 3b	3	Richtor, 3b	1
Strondbach, cf	1	Higgins, cf	1
A. McCoy, rf	2	Ernest, lf	2
Kennedy, lf	0	Bumetz	2
TOTAL	16	TOTAL	24

The Melpomenia Base Ball Club was one of the seven original members of the Louisiana Base Ball Association, and they appeared to have a very active and engaged membership, especially for a newly formed club. On Friday, October 21, 1859, Wooden's Side played the first game in the morning against Coburn's Side and the second game in the afternoon against Norton's Side. The second game was played in the rain and on a slippery field which would account for the relatively low scores. Both Coburn's Side and Norton's Side were essentially the same players with only a few changes in position and revisions in the batting order.

From an informal group of seven clubs playing intra-squad games to the city's first league, the Louisiana Base Ball Association had taken its first unsure steps in 1859 and was headed to more sure footing in 1860 when the clouds of war began to gather across the South. The teams in the Association continued to grow more confident and adventurous in their playing until Louisiana's secession finally put baseball in New Orleans on the back burner. But after the war a familiar renewal of an old justification appeared in the *Daily Picayune*: "An hour or two on the green sod, participating in one of those manly matches, will give a person so much healthful vitality that a week's work can be performed with twice the ease and cheerfulness."[8] That certainly encouraged new players to take up the game and veteran baseball players to pick up the game again, but what about the spectators? Would they embrace the game as they had before the war?

Baseball in New Orleans emerged from the Civil War as a sport able to be played by everyone, not just the middle-class gentlemen of New Orleans. It was more democratic, a game that could hopefully help to heal the wounds that divided the country. The first reported baseball game in New Orleans following the Civil War took place on Sunday, January 9, 1866, on the Delachaise Grounds between the Empire Base Ball Club and the Crescent Base Ball Club. This renewal of an old rivalry was heartily welcomed by the fans and applauded in the press for cultivating "a spirit of courteous and generous rivalry that promises well for the enjoyment during the coming season of not only the players, but the hundreds of ladies and gentlemen who witness these sports."[9] The two clubs neither gave nor received any quarter on the field, playing vigorously even as daylight was departing. The Empire club had the better of the "manly match," narrowly winning by the score of 26 to 25.

Crescent Base Ball Club versus Empire Base Ball Club
January 9, 1866

Crescent Club	*Runs*	*Empire Club*	*Runs*
Conners, p	4	Conlon, p	3
Fox, c	2	Doyle, c	4
Bertell, 1b	3	Cain, 1b	2
Maley, 2b	3	Voyard, 2b	1
Grace, 3b	5	Grahm, 3b	2
Martinez, ss	2	Gray, ss	3
Dunn, lf	0	McClusky, lf	4
Depassan, rf	4	Hanefy, rf	4
Williams, cf	2	Ward, cf	3
TOTAL	25	TOTAL	26

It is interesting to note that both the Crescents' side and the Empires' side of the box score as listed in the newspapers read more like a position roster than an actual batting order as each of the players are listed in identical order by their position. It is highly unlikely that both teams duplicated their batting order or that this was an actual batting order. Rather, it is more than likely that it was the submission of their club's secretary or scorer rather than the work of a reporter.

Other teams that competed for and captured the Louisiana Base Ball Association's championship trophy over the years include the Lone Star Base Ball Club (1870, 1872), the R.E. Lee Base Ball Club (1870), and the Southern Base Ball Club (1869), among others. Sometimes the championship was not easily determined. It was a rule of the association that whichever team won the most games against their opponent could claim the right to be city champion. However, the 1870 championship was disputed by both the Southerns and the Lone Stars.

The Lone Stars took the first game of the series on Thursday, April 21, 1870, by the score of 36 to 21. The second game took place the following Sunday, April 28, and was won by the Southerns 27 to 18. The third and final game in the championship series was played several weeks later and was won by the Southerns 25 to 20, but the game was protested by the Lone Stars because one of their players, Frank Benton, had joined the team from Memphis and had played in the third game without waiting the mandatory sixty days after transferring teams.

The protest filed by William F. Tracey of the Lone Stars was heard by the Louisiana Base Ball Association which sided with the Lone Stars, forfeiting the Southern victory in game three and awarding the City Championship to the Lone Stars. In an uncharacteristic show of defiance and poor sportsmanship, however, the Southerns never publicly recognized the league's decision and steadfastly maintained that their team was the one true City Champion. Following the Lone Stars' 1870 tour they were challenged for the city championship, this time by the R.E. Lees, who won the first and third games of the series to claim the city championship for their team. The Southerns never recognized the Lees' championship either, claiming that the Lone Stars had not legitimately won the City Championship from the Southerns in the first place.

The following spring the Southerns and the Lees played a championship series which the Lees won, once again capturing the first and third games. The Southerns were finally forced to admit that the Lees were indeed the 1871 city champions, but they continued to deny the Lone Star's protest victory in 1870. Following this controversy the challenge system was replaced by using each team's winning percentage during the season to determine the City Championship. Under this method the Lone Stars won the championship for the next several years.

The Louisiana Base Ball Association disbanded with the outbreak of the

Civil War and struggled to revive league play during peacetime, and by 1873 realized the costs to operate proved to be insurmountable.

The New Orleans Base Ball Association (1879)

Six years after the closure of the Louisiana Base Ball Association there was still a considerable amount of interest among the city's amateur clubs in the formation of a new league—the New Orleans Base Ball Association. Make no mistake, the teams and players that made up the old disbanded Louisiana Base Ball League continued to play baseball and were even joined by new teams. They simply did not play under the auspices of an organized league. At the new league's initial meeting on August 5, 1879, in the meeting hall of the Washington Fire Company No. 20, a full slate of officers was elected. T.H. Lawrence, representing the Wash Marks Base Ball Club, was elected chairman. Other officers included F.M. McKeough from the Crescent Base Ball Club, Gus Alexander from the Wash Marks Base Ball Club, Conrad C. Julier from the Paul Waterman Base Ball Club, Joseph Barthe from the William Fagan Base Ball Club, S. Philbin from the P. Philbin Base Ball Club, A. Aixler from the Edward Maber Base Ball Club, and Ed Scully from the Pat Glennon Base Ball Club.[10] These gentlemen were tasked with drawing up the rules to govern the league. Five other team delegates were assigned with acquiring suitable meeting and headquarters space.

Indeed, many of the players were veterans of other teams and many of the teams were newly formed in order to submit an application for membership to the new league. By late August, the original group of twelve clubs had grown to twenty-nine clubs being admitted to the league. Most of these clubs were truly amateur outfits being sponsored by and named for physicians and business owners.[11] In truth, most of these new teams were only trying to ride the coattails of the older, more prominent teams like the Washington Base Ball Club and the Crescent Base Ball Club. However, with so many moving pieces, formulating a viable schedule[12] and arranging for playing grounds proved to be like nailing soup to a tree. The September 8 deadline for clubs to submit the roster of their playing nines came and went. There were a handful of games played in the hope of energizing those teams who were serious about participating in league play, but in the end, there were just too many voices all trying to be heard over the others, all jockeying for the prime playing fields, the most favorable playing dates and times, and the most challenging opponents. By mid–September most teams abandoned the New Orleans Base Ball Association,[13] but as in other league collapses, the teams continued to find opponents on their own and to schedule their own games. However, even with the failure of the league to take root it did sow the seeds to future growth.

The Crescent City League (1880–1884 and 1886)

Not to be confused with the local political organization of a similar name, the Crescent City League had a brief five-year tenure during 1880 which gradually faded away due to cost considerations. The league was reorganized in mid-May 1886 by Toby Hart and other baseball men who agreed to serve as interim officers until a more complete slate of financially stable teams could be decided upon.[14] On May 19 the formal organizational meeting was held to elect permanent officers from among the assembled delegates. Toby Hart (honorary president), S.M. Kauffman (president), J.A. Reinecke (vice-president), P.A. Donnelly (treasurer), and Clem Flanders (secretary). Two umpires were appointed, J. Wedig and J. Hogan, and Walter Emerson was tapped to serve as the official scorer for the league.[15]

Among the teams of note during the 1880 season were the R.E. Lee Base Ball Club, the J.S. Wright Base Ball Club, the Crescent Base Ball Club, the Thomas Brennan Base Ball Club, and the Remy Clarke Base Ball Club. The Lees and the Crescents were established teams, while the J.S. Wrights had been formed in 1877. The Thomas Brennans were formed in 1879 and the Remy Clarkes were also formed in 1879 from former players of the Pat Glennon Base Ball Club. By year-end 1880 the R.E. Lees, having won the most games, were declared the city champion and awarded the pennant.

Between 1880 and 1884 teams came and went from the league with predictable regularity, leaving the league itself on rather unstable footing. By 1884 none of the league's original clubs remained. The eight teams that competed during the 1884 season finished as follows:

The Crescent City League
Standings as of September 23, 1884[16]

Team	Won	Lost	Pct
Bernards	11	2	.846
Hunter & Genslinger	11	3	.786
Hunters	10	4	.714
Landwehrs	10	4	.714
Ponsettis	7	6	.538
Bachs	6	7	.462
Farantas	6	9	.400
Fagets	3	8	.272

With the exception of the Fagets (1879) and the Landwehrs (1881), all of the other teams were established in 1884 expressly to play in the Crescent City League. Try as they might, the league folded at the conclusion of the 1884 season.

In reviving the league in 1886 and looking for teams to play at his new ballpark, the New Orleans Base Balk Park on Canal Street, Toby Hart stepped up to reorganize the Crescent City League in May of that year. During the 1886 campaign there were seven teams slated to compete—the Bob Lamson Base Ball Club, the Seymour Base Ball Club, the Bernard Base Ball Club, the Borges Base Ball Club, the Flanders Base Ball Club, and the Thomas Pye Base Ball Club, with several other teams rumored to be jockeying for the coveted eighth spot in the league. At the head of the list were the H&G Base Ball Club and the McCarthy Base Ball Club, with the McCarthys eventually getting the nod. As expected, all games were scheduled to be played at Hart's New Orleans Base Ball Park.[17] Opening Day consisted of a lively double header on Saturday, May 22, 1886, that began with a pitcher's duel from the Pyes, holding the Seymours to two hits against eight hits from the Pyes in an abbreviated, seven-inning contest marked by a disappointing fifteen errors split between the ham-handed fielders from both teams. The Pyes prevailed 8 to 2.

Seymours versus Pyes
May 22, 1886[18]

Innings	1	2	3	4	5	6	7	TOTAL
Seymours	0	0	0	0	1	1	0	**2**
Pyes	2	0	2	0	4	0	0	**8**

The second game that day was also marked by more errors than hits, twelve for the Lamsons and six for the McCarthys, and the hitting was nearly even, with the McCarthys doing a better job of bunching their hits to produce runs, winning the game 10 to 7.

McCarthy versus Lamson
May 22, 1886

Innings	1	2	3	4	5	6	7	8	9	TOTAL
McCarthy	0	0	0	3	0	0	4	0	3	**10**
Lamsons	0	0	0	0	0	0	2	1	4	**7**

Attendance was sparse, and Toby Hart discovered that he finally realized that he was not drawing any greater number of fans but was actually cannibalizing his own fan base. This was because the 1886 edition of the Crescent City League was forced to compete with Hart's own Gulf League at Sportsman's Park on many of the same afternoons.[19] Although Hart had not applied for any formal classifications for either of his two leagues, the Crescent City League would have been the equivalent of a Class C outfit when compared to the Gulf League which might have been designated as Class A. The fledgling Crescent City League lasted less than a month, disbanding on June 18.[20]

There was an attempt to resurrect the Crescent City League in September of 1888,[21] but the group was made up of even smaller teams than it had been in 1886, although among the rosters were several prominent players such as

Abner Powell, Jules Pujol, and Joe Dowie. The brief winter league operation ceased operation on October 11 after just over thirty days.[22]

The Louisiana Amateur Base Ball Association (1884); The New Orleans Amateur League (1884, 1888–1889, 1894)

In February of 1884 there was a meeting of the Louisiana Amateur Base Ball Association at Dan Owen's on the corner of St. Charles Avenue and Perdido Street.[23] Gathered together were representatives of four of the city's preeminent amateur baseball clubs—the Thomas Brennan Base Ball Club, the Lone Star Base Ball Club, the R.E. Lee Base Ball Club, and the Remy Clarke Base Ball Club. Their intent was to establish a league that would be appropriately suitable for their caliber of play and to be able to vie for a state championship title in the league. To get things started the group nominated and elected officers: R.H. Mooney from the Brennans as president, Dan Owens from the Lone Stars as vice-president, William F. Tracey of the Lone Stars as secretary, and William Moneal of the Remy Clarkes as treasurer.

The first game in the Louisiana Amateur Base Ball Association took place between the Brennans and the Lone Stars on Sunday, April 27, 1884, at the New Orleans Base Ball Park. In a closely fought contest, the Lone Stars plated the winning run in the bottom of the ninth inning to defeat the Brennans 7 to 6 before a poor turnout. The disenchantment of the few fans who paid to see the game was shared by the equally unhappy observer from the *Times-Democrat* who aptly summed up the Lone Stars—Brennans game by stating that "the present condition of the game is certainly disappointing."[24] It might be said that the game itself was well played, with the only blemish being the stone-cold hands of the Lone Stars' fielders who accounted for twelve errors, four on the first baseman Maginnis and four on the pitcher Childs. Maginnis helped redeem himself by collecting four hits, matched by Lone Stars shortstop Stevenson.

Lone Stars versus Thomas Brennans
April 27, 1884

Lone Stars	AB	R	1B	PO	A	E
Porter, c	4	2	0	8	2	2
Maginnis, 1b	5	1	4	9	0	4
Stevenson, ss	4	1	4	1	2	0
Pommeroux, 2b	4	1	1	2	1	1
Shea, cf	4	1	1	1	1	1
Weydig, 3b	4	0	1	3	4	0
Childs, p	4	1	1	1	4	4

Lone Stars	AB	R	1B	PO	A	E
Bothner, lf	4	0	2	2	0	0
Bomberry, rf	3	0	0	0	0	0
TOTALS	36	7	14	27	14	12
Thomas Brennans	AB	R	1B	PO	A	E
Lambeau, 1b	5	1	1	9	15	0
Farrel, 3b & ss	4	1	1	1	0	0
McCormick, 2b	4	1	2	4	11	0
Lorsch, p & rf	4	1	2	1	0	1
Berkery, rf & 3b	4	0	0	1	1	0
Landry, ss & p	4	0	0	2	0	2
Mundinger, c	4	0	1	7	0	0
Pujol, cf	3	2	1	8	0	0
Cruso, lf	3	0	0	0	0	0
TOTALS	35	6	8	25	27	3

By innings:	1	2	3	4	5	6	7	8	9	TOTAL
Thos. Brennans	1	1	2	0	1	0	0	0	1	6
Lone Stars	0	0	0	0	0	3	1	0	1	7

Umpire: James Dunn
Time of game: 2 hours

The detail provided in this 1884 box score, while not the first such example in New Orleans, illustrates the expanded level of statistical detail that baseball had adopted thanks to the influence of Henry Chadwick, which would better satisfy the fan's interest in the game.

Tom Brennan and ballpark co-owner/manager Bob Brown met following the game, during which Brown informed Brennan that the Lone Stars, the winning team, would only receive $2.70 from the gate receipts. There was nothing left over for the Brennans as the losing team. With the imminent departure of catcher George Mundinger and first baseman Mike Lambour (Lambeau) to the majors, there was talk of disbanding the Brennans.

Two players from the Brennans who were in the lineup that day are worth noting. The first was centerfielder Jules Pujol. He came to the attention of the New Orleans baseball scene while playing on the 1883 championship Brennans squad and in 1884 would catch the eye of R.E. Lees manager Conrad Leithman and businessman Toby Hart, who were putting together the Gulf League after failing in 1885 to secure a franchise for New Orleans in the newly formed Southern League. In an unusual compromise arrangement Hart and Leithman scheduled for two teams from New Orleans to face off against two teams from Mobile in the Gulf League—New Orleans, Mobile, the Acid Iron Earths, and the Robert E. Lees.

In 1887 New Orleans was admitted to the Southern League and Pujol became a member of the New Orleans Pelicans. He played fifty-one games in center field, twenty-nine games at third base, three games in right field, and one game at shortstop. He even appeared as pitcher in a single game, giving up five hits and two earned runs in the single inning in which he appeared. His offensive production was better than average, compiling a .314 batting average for the pennant winning Pelicans in their inaugural season in the Southern League. But after the 1889 season, when the Southern League decided to take a two-year break, Pujol's heart was no longer in the game and he felt a higher calling.

For several years Pujol had been a non-paid member (volunteer) of the New Orleans Fire Department while playing baseball. Along with his brother Louis, he joined Pelican Hook & Ladder Company No. 4 on April 3, 1883, first as a Ladderman and later as a Tillerman. In the early morning hours of October 31, 1892, Pelican Hook & Ladder No. 4 responded to a tremendous fire at the corner of Baronne and Canal Streets which was consuming a building known as Grunwald Hall. The ground floor of the building served as a piano warehouse while the upper floors were occupied by the families of Louis Hess and Joseph Mutz.

Cut off from escape by the smoke and flames, there were nine people from the combined Hess and Mutz families who seemed destined to perish in the blaze. Realizing that their ladders were too short to affect a rescue by conventional means, Pujol and four other firemen ascended the fire escape on the adjoining Chess, Checkers and Whist Club building. From that vantage point they swung by rope to the adjoining roof of the burning building, hauling a ladder over to bridge from one building to the other and passing the nine endangered persons across the makeshift ladder bridge one-by-one to safety. For their courage and resourcefulness, Pujol and the four other firefighters, including his brother Louis, were awarded the department's highest honor and were feted with a parade through downtown New Orleans.

Pujol rose through the ranks of the department and was an Assistant Chief on February 23, 1924, when he responded to an early morning fire at the Marks-Isaacs warehouse on Canal Street. The fifty-nine-year-old Pujol died after being trapped in the building when the upper floors and walls collapsed. Five other firefighters were seriously injured.

The other Brennan player of note was their backstop George Mundinger. Born in New Orleans on November 20, 1854, Mundinger broke into baseball with the Thomas Brennan Base Ball Club in 1884 and was noticed by the Indianapolis Hoosiers of the American Association. The twenty-nine-year-old rookie played a scant three games for the lowly Hoosiers during 1884 but caught on with the Minneapolis Millers of the Northwestern League later that same season, playing in five games. Mundinger returned to New Orleans at the end of the 1884 season to play winter ball with the Brennans.

He was signed by Macon in the newly formed Southern League to catch such flamethrowers as Cyclone Miller and Peek-a-Boo Veach but was released after six games because of an anemic bat. Once again Mundinger returned to New Orleans to play with the Brennans and other amateur teams. His work behind the plate caught the eye of Toby Hart and Conrad Leithman, who signed Mundinger in 1886 to play alongside former teammate Jules Pujol with the R.E. Lees in the Gulf League. He enjoyed a full season with the R.E. Lees before hanging up his professional spikes at the conclusion of the 1886 campaign. Mundinger died in Covington, Louisiana, on October 12, 1910, at the age of fifty-three.

The whirlwind of activity surrounding the Louisiana Amateur Base Ball League found every local amateur team of any caliber trying to challenge and schedule games with the four teams in the league. In May of 1884, the Brennans reorganized as the G&P Base Ball Club and challenged the Lees, supposedly for a cash prize instead of being part of league play. The newly formed G&P squad thoroughly licked the Lees 8 to 4.[25] With all of the other sources for baseball available in New Orleans, attendance at the Louisiana Amateur Base Ball League games was being played before nearly empty bleachers. This was of little concern to teams like the Brennans and the Lees who knew they would see only pennies from the gate receipts but preferred instead to play for a side bet between the teams that would range from twenty-five to fifty dollars.

The New Orleans Amateur League was a junior circuit, a league specifically for younger players. It was comprised of ten teams and was the brainchild of Charles H. Genslinger, proprietor of Hunter & Genslinger (H&G) and second in command to Toby Hart. In May Genslinger was involved in every aspect of the formation of the new league[26] and by late June had finalized and published the league's constitution and by-laws.[27] Genslinger's printing company had a very profitable sideline printing the organizational documents, contracts, schedules, and programs for almost all of the city's baseball leagues and teams.

The ten teams in the New Orleans Amateur League consisted of the Hunters, the Gardners, the Poinsettias, the O'Learys, the Currys, the Alf. Dupres, the McGeehans, the Bernards, the Landwehrs, and the Hunter & Genslingers. The scheme was to schedule five games every Sunday which would allow everyone in New Orleans the opportunity to see a baseball game at ballparks across the city.[28] In essence, Genslinger was intentionally flooding the market with cheap goods in order to capture market share for his junior circuit. Many of the junior teams were strong enough to give their older brothers a run for their money.[29] With attendance and gate receipts falling well behind expectations, it did not take long for the four teams of the Louisiana Amateur Base Ball League to seek greener pastures. Between the ten teams in the New Orleans Amateur League and the four teams in the Louisiana Amateur Base Ball League there would be anywhere from seven to nine baseball games every weekend between the two leagues. Die-hard baseball fans had their choice of games to watch and teams to root for.

In July, the Remy Clarkes set off for Shreveport to play a three-game series against a picked nine[30] before heading south to play a series of games in Alexandria, Lecompte, and Cheneyville in central Louisiana.[31] By September, the Louisiana Amateur Base Ball Association tried to reorganize,[32] but to no avail. It was becoming increasingly apparent that fan interest had been diluted without any one team or league capturing the public's fancy as Genslinger intended. Naturally he had hoped to capture the lion's share of gate receipts, but his miscalculation only served to alienate the other leagues and the teams. From this point forward, the four teams of the Louisiana Amateur abandoned the league and played their games for cash prizes, usually $25, and admission was free. The end result was to cripple both leagues.

The Louisiana Amateur Base Ball League did not reorganize and did not return for another season. After an absence of four years, a determined group of baseball men reorganized the New Orleans Amateur League. On May 18, 1888, three teams—the Atlantic Base Ball Club, the Louisiana Base Ball Club, and the West End Boat Club—announced their intention to join the league.[33] There was a rumor that several gymnasium clubs were also interested in joining the league. Membership notwithstanding, the league pressed ahead, scheduling games to begin on May 20. An abbreviated schedule kicked off and, in the hopes of attracting new members, the league announced that teams would be competing for gold and silver medals for the best averages at the end of the season. The gymnastic clubs fielded two teams, the Athletics and the Somersaults. The composition of this league made it a very different type of amateur league, perhaps more along the lines of a commercial league. There was a feeling among spectators that the caliber of play was not up to the level of prior teams from four years ago. League organizers were initially optimistic, but their enthusiasm proved to be short-lived and the league was shuttered.

In his weekly address, Mayor Joseph A. Shakspeare announced a reinvigorated effort from the New Orleans police force to curb baseball games from being played in public squares and parks. He also informed the city that he was revisiting prohibitions against playing baseball on Sundays,[34] having received several letters from concerned citizens about hooligans crowding the street rail and other objectionable behavior at or in the vicinity of the ballpark. How much of this was simply political rhetoric designed to satisfy his supporters would yet to be seen.

In the wake of the mayor's announcement, and just as the New Orleans Amateur League was gaining some traction, baseball was used as a metaphor for political discord when the newspaper reported a "base ball riot," described as being a "general free fight" taking place at the corner of Claiborne Avenue and Common Street between two "baseball teams," the Y.M.D.A. and the Regulars. In reality, the event was unrelated to and had nothing whatsoever to do with baseball. It was simply a self-serving depiction of baseball being dominated by thugs. The Y.M.D.A. stood for the reform-minded Young Men's Democratic Association which was supported by the mayor and the governor while the Regulars represented the entrenched and corrupt Republican faction known as The Ring. These two groups had been squabbling in the weeks leading up to the mayoral elections in May and this was nothing more than a release for the pent-up anger of the Regulars, who lost the election, quite literally taking a poke at their rivals. A number of blows were struck with baseball bats, none with any consequence, and no arrests were made.[35] In the eyes of many New Orleanians, however, baseball was dealt another black eye: guilt by association.

Nevertheless, the 1889 season of the New Orleans Amateur League resumed operations in earnest, although later in the year, on September 22, 1889, with the Taylor Brothers Base Ball Club besting the Atlantic Base Ball Club by the score of 4 to 0 and the Somersaults beating the Atlantics 5 to 3.[36]

A break of four years ensued before the New Orleans Amateur League would undergo another attempt at reorganization in 1894 with the now all too familiar initial four team format and the hope of more to follow. This iteration of the league was no more successful than any of its predecessors, folding within a short period.

Female Baseball (1879, 1886)

The earliest mention of baseball being played in New Orleans strictly by a female team comes from an incident in late May of 1879 when the Society for the Prevention of Cruelty to Children, through its Ladies' Athletic Association, were cited for leading "girls under sixteen to take part in immoral performances"[37] for playing baseball. However, it was another incident that occurred around the same time that caused a citywide sensation when an all-female baseball team was organized in New Orleans to play for gate receipts.[38]

The novelty of an all-female baseball came to a head when a modest banner advertisement appeared under the Amusements section of the newspaper announcing the First Grand Female Base Ball Festival to be held at the Fair Grounds on Sunday, June 15, 1879, between the Lady Nine of Baltimore and the Lady Nine of Boston.[39] As it turned out, both teams had been organized in New Orleans, not in either of the out of town namesake locations. The firm of Hezekiah & Company was hired to organize the festivities which included the usual assortment of amusements: mule and pony races, foot races, blind man's bluff, as well as prizes for the best male and female waltzers. The foot race and blind man's bluff events were specifically designated for "fat Men, 200 pounds or over," for which the winner would interestingly enough be awarded a box of cigars and a keg of lager beer, respectively. But clearly the prospect of seeing two female baseball teams crossing bats was the highlight of the program as indicated its prominent and oversized headline in the newspaper advertisement. With a portion of the proceeds designated to benefit the Auxiliary Sanitary Association, the clear intent was to use the novelty of two all-female baseball teams to draw a large crowd willing to pay fifty cents for admission to the day-long event.

Female baseball remained nothing more than a novelty attraction, with the occasional game between a female team and some other opponent, male or female. Over the years there were several all-female teams playing in New Orleans: the Boston Nine (1874), the Baltimore Base Ball Club (1874), the Gangers Base Ball Club (1874), the Rice & Hayes Base Ball Club (1885), the T.S. Weber Base Ball Club (1889), and the Lasses (1890). In 1884 a female nine from Philadelphia journeyed to New Orleans to play the J.C. Bach Base Ball, one of the city's crack amateur male teams, at Sportsman's Park.[40] Even Toby Hart promoted a "Great Female Base Ball Club" in 1885 at his New Orleans Base Ball Park. How many fans were willing to pay the twenty-five cents admission is unknown, but it is likely that attendance was sufficient for Hart to continue to periodically promote female baseball games through 1886.

The most notorious incident involving female baseball arose from the detention of two young girls from Cincinnati upon their arrival by train in New Orleans. Ella Burke and Fannie Crambert were apprehended at the Press Street Station of the Queen and Crescent Line by detectives Gaster and Cain. They were subsequently transported to the Central Police Station where the two young ladies told the detectives that they had come to New Orleans from Cincinnati to play baseball for Harry H. Freeman's Female Base Ball Club. Apparently, Freeman had auditioned the two girls during one of the team's trips through Cincinnati, but who declined to add the young ladies to his teams due to their age and because of the protests from their parents. The two determined young ladies nonetheless corresponded with Freeman through a mail drop at a New York sporting journal, informing him that all opposition from their parents had been resolved and that they intended to leave their employment at the spice factory in Cincinnati to join him in New Orleans. Freeman wired them the rail fare to New Orleans and was at the station to meet them when they were arrested by the police. Little did he know what awaited him.

Freeman was actively recruiting female players in an effort to rebuild his team, once twenty-nine ladies strong but now diminished to only four players due to financial concerns. He once recruited a blind man's daughters and several others. It was just over a week before the arrest of Burke and Crambert that, during a game at the lakefront resort of Spanish Fort, the young lady playing third base was "captured" by her brother with the assistance of the crowd, further diminishing the strength of Freeman's squad. With the arrest of Burke and Crambert, Freeman decided that New Orleans was no longer a profitable base of operations and began to make preparations to depart for Mobile. However, before he could make good his escape, Freeman was arrested for vagrancy and his trial dominated the headlines for several weeks. He was sentenced by Judge Davey to the municipal workhouse and in mid–May appealed to the mayor directly to allow he and his team to leave New Orleans for Pensacola. It was discovered that Freeman's real name was Sylvester Franklin Wilson and he kept his players cooped up in a house on Broad Street near Customhouse (Iberville) Street with no furniture. These young girls slept on the floor and relied on the neighbors to provide them with food. It was also learned that Freeman/Wilson had another young girl secreted away in a house on Magazine Street between Thalia and Erato Streets who was eventually rescued by her brother-in-law. The police complied with the Judge Buisson's orders to rid the city of this suspected Lothario and escorted the whole menagerie to the train station.

For the remainder of the 19th century female baseball was played infrequently in school programs and even less frequently elsewhere. While occasionally a female team would play against a well-known male amateur team, it remained nothing more than a novelty attraction at charitable picnics and church fairs. In the latter part of the century and well into the 20th century female baseball would finally come into its own because of its inclusion in high school and college programs.

The Southern League of Colored Baseballists (1885)

Among the earliest recorded games involving two black teams in the United States was an October 1867 game in Harrisburg, Pennsylvania, between the Monrovia Base Ball Club and the Philadelphia Pythians. The city of Philadelphia had at least two black clubs, the Excelsiors and the Pythians.[41] Black clubs were admitted to the National Association of Base Ball Players (NABBP) in 1875[42] and New Orleans teams held a local organizing convention in 1875 to facilitate NABBP membership by black teams.[43]

Black citizens of New Orleans took to baseball with the same fervor as white citizens, despite the significant disparity in resources, access, and social acceptance. Following the Civil War there were increased opportunities for blacks to enjoy baseball more so than most other sporting activities. Even so, in 1885 New Orleans was by and large still a very segregated society. Black citizens did almost everything white citizens did but were forced to do so separately. But baseball was more inclusive than other sports. In April of 1880 there was a picnic held at Oakland Park by the black baseball clubs of New Orleans to benefit the Howard Base Ball Club.[44] Although the event was described as a "Grand Colored Base Ball Picnic," it was to benefit a white club, Howard Base Ball Club, who would be playing a picked nine from the city's black clubs.

Local black teams also hosted traveling black baseball teams. One such series took place on Wednesday, June 16, 1886, between the Union Base Ball Club of New Orleans and the Eclipse Base Ball Club of Memphis before 500 spectators. The first game was an ugly pitchers' duel between Arnold of the Unions and Renfroe of the Eclipse as to which of them could be the wildest. Arnold threw ninety-four pitches, sixty-four were balls and thirty were strikes. He managed only seven strikeouts but somehow held the Eclipse squad to only three hits. For the visiting Eclipse, Renfroe fanned thirteen Union batters and held the rest to five hits. However, he also let four Union batters on base through errors.

The difference in the game, other than the propensity of both pitchers to throw wildly at inopportune moments in the game, turned out to be the three runs scored by the Eclipse in the top of the first inning. Two batters reached base on missed third strikes, scoring on wild pitches and passed balls. The Unions scored their lone run in the sixth inning with a hit and a stolen base, followed by a sacrifice fly to move the runner to third who then scored on a passed ball. Even though the game was neither handsome nor efficient, the Eclipse prevailed by the score of 3 to 1.[45]

The second game was played the following day with the Unions notching up with five runs in a late inning rally to prevail against the Eclipse by the score of 11 to 7. The newspaper reporter covering the game was understated in his comment that "the game was not brilliant in fielding...." With twenty-four errors between the two teams, fourteen for the Eclipse and ten for the Unions, this was certainly not a display of fielding prowess. Pitching was once again something of a challenge for both batteries with seven passed balls and a wild pitch for the Eclipse and two for the Unions. However, both teams redeemed themselves when it came to swinging the willow with sixteen total hits tallied in the game, eleven for the Unions and only five for the Eclipse. The Union hitters were led by the pitcher Arnold and the second baseman Recasner with three hits each.[46]

After taking Saturday off to rest and regroup, the rubber game of the match was played on Sunday, June 20, and went to the Eclipse club 8 to 7. Unfortunately for the 450 fans at the New Orleans Base Ball Park that afternoon the fielding was just as unseemly as it was in the previous games in the field with thirteen errors for the Eclipse and twelve errors for the Unions. But on the positive side, once again both teams had their hitting shoes on, stroking out twenty-three hits between them, thirteen for the Eclipse and ten for the Unions. In the end, the crowd watched the Union club triumph with three unanswered runs in the ninth frame to win by the score of 12 to 11.[47]

The Eclipse played the W.L. Cohen Base Ball Club on Tuesday, June 22, 1886, after a challenge from the local club. The Cohen's gauntlet was as much as a challenge to the Unions as it was to the Eclipse to show "that there was more than one first class colored club in New Orleans." The visitors played slightly better ball that afternoon, limiting themselves to only three errors, two passed balls, and one wild pitch. However, they had no answer for Cohen hurler Price who held them to two hits, a single and a double, both by Newman. The game was cut short due to the travel schedule of the Eclipse club, so only six innings were played, the Cohens winning by the score of 7 to 2.[48]

Over and above the "Grand Colored Base Ball Picnic," there is additional evidence that blacks and whites openly played each other. Among the first proponents of white teams competing against black teams was William F. Tracey, manager of the Lone Star Base Ball Club. One of their earliest games took place on Sunday, December 19, 1869, at the Delachaise Grounds.[49]

Pickwicks versus Lone Stars
December 19, 1869

Pickwicks	O	R	Lone Stars	O	R
Rainey, p	2	2	Tracey, p	2	6
Feytel, rf	1	2	Amar, 3b	2	6
Klein, 1b	3	0	Scott, lf	4	3
Ferry, 2b	5	0	Thebault, c	2	5
Solomon, 3b	3	1	Waterman, rf	5	3
Reynolds, c	5	0	Levy, ss	2	5
Morgan, ss	2	1	Young, 1b	4	2
Rainey, lf	4	0	Johnson, 2b	3	3
Jamison, cf	2	1	Carson, cf	3	4
TOTAL	27	7	TOTAL	27	37

Innings	1	2	3	4	5	6	7	8	9	TOTAL
Pickwicks	3	0	0	1	3	0	0	0	0	7
Lone Stars	8	3	1	4	6	8	2	1	4	37

The Pickwicks were bolstered by the play of Klein, Feytel, and Reynolds and were so noted by the *Daily Picayune* reporter covering the game. The team itself was deserving of "high praise for their pluck in facing so strong a club." Obviously punching above their weight, the Pickwicks nevertheless gained valuable experience by playing a better team and pushing their players to improve their game. While scoring eight runs in the bottom of the first inning would prove enough to win the game, the Lone Stars continued to belt out hits and runs against the Pickwick moundsman Rainey, scoring at least one run in each of the remaining eight innings.

The Lone Star's lead-off hitter and pitcher listed in the box score above was player-manager William F. Tracey, who organized the match between the Pickwicks and the Lone Stars. While extremely civil, such games were infrequent, and given the times, were organized at the behest of and under the terms and conditions dictated by the white teams. Every element of the match down to the smallest detail was controlled by the white clubs. Despite such heavy-handed tactics in setting up games, the interracial matches were usually viewed as being both competitive and collegial on the playing field. More often than not these games were promoted as the white champion of New Orleans versus the black champion of New Orleans, or some other similar hyperbole guaranteed to boost ticket sales. This, of course, is where the common connection between the players generally ended. There would be no communal supper, no dramatic recitations for entertainment, no trophy presentation over toasts and free flowing libations. In short, there was no social interaction off the field.

Yet black baseball had no bigger advocate than William F. Tracey. So admired was Tracey in the black baseball community that the Pickwick Base Ball Club played a picked nine comprised of players from other black clubs on February 10, 1878, in a benefit game for Tracey at Ogden Park in the Garden District of New Orleans.

In New Orleans, blacks had been active in baseball since the late 1860s and early 1870s, with the most noted early adopters being the employees of the Boston Club and the Pickwick Club. These teams were not always organized in the general sense of the word, with a black captain picking out his best nine to play another black captain's best nine, acting in very much the same fashion as the white baseball clubs would. The Pickwick Base Ball Club was considered to be the "colored champion" of New Orleans for many years and was active from 1869 through the turn of the century. During this time there were several other black teams coming to prominence: the Pickwick Base Ball Club (1869), the Aetna Base Ball Club (1872), the Democrats Base Ball Club (1872), the Franklin Base Ball Club (1872), the A.J. Dumont Base Ball Club (1881), the Poets Base Ball Club (1881), the Boston Base Ball Club (1881), the Orleans Base Ball Club (1884), the Union Base Ball Club (1884), the A. Fischer Base Ball Club (1885), the Walter L. Cohen Base Ball Club (1885), the Athletic Base Ball Club (1885), the Blue Stocking Base Ball Club (1886), the H. Brown Base Ball Club (1886), the Bordel Base Ball Club (1886), the Jackson Base Ball Club (1886), the Louisiana Base Ball Club (1886), the Shannon Base Ball Club (1886), the M. Sullivan Base Ball Club (1886), the Wilson Base Ball Club (1886), and the P.B.S. Pinchback Baseball Club (1888).

These teams, like others in New Orleans, played at different times with and against one another. Formed in 1885, several members of the Walter L. Cohen Base Ball Club, including of course Walter Cohen, were former members of the Pickwick Base Ball Club. The Aetna Base Ball Club was formed in 1872 from former players of the Franklin Base Ball Club. Like their white counterparts, black baseball teams were periodically joined by other teams formed from the ranks of different companies or organizations.

Even with the lack of support for the Southern League of Colored Baseballists, the teams continued to arrange games and play baseball on their own whenever possible. The Pickwicks continued to play white teams whenever they were asked. There was a noteworthy game played between the Pickwicks and the Thomas Brennan Base Ball Club, a prominent white club, on Sunday, August 28, 1881, at Oakland Park near the old Metairie Course in Jefferson Parish.

Pickwicks versus Brennans
August 28, 1881[50]

Thomas Brennans	R	O	*Pickwicks*	R	O
Mundinger, c	0	4	Williams, ss	2	3
Farrell, 3b	1	3	Turner, 2b	1	3
Dowd, p	1	3	Kennedy p	1	2
Butler, ss	1	3	Robinson, rf	1	3
H. Hannon, 2b	2	2	W. Cohen, 1b	2	1
Hennesy, 1b	2	2	Francis, c	1	3
Rick, rf	2	2	E. Cohen, cf	1	3
J. Hannon, cf	3	1	Canfield, 3b	1	1
Hanley, lf	1	1	Boisseau, lf	0	2
TOTALS	13	21	TOTALS	10	21

Innings	1	2	3	4	5	6	7	8	9	TOTAL
Brennans	1	0	2	3	3	1	3	x	x	13
Pickwicks	3	0	0	4	0	0	3	x	x	10

A sold-out crown of over 2,000 spectators overflowed the bleachers of Oakland Park and were forced to stand wherever there was available room, some even ascending to the nearby fences or to the surrounding treetops for a better view of the action. Local defense attorney Lionel Adams was the umpire, and it was he who stipulated that curve balls would not be permitted during the game. Although an unusual request, both teams agreed, with the Brennans substituting Dowd for their ace hurler Lally. The Pickwicks went with Kennedy, their regular pitcher. Both teams also agreed that any balls passing the catcher, whether it be a wild pitch or a passed ball, be declared "dead" and the baserunners allowed to advance only one base. The intent was that these two game rule modifications would cut down on the number of errors in the game, but several Brennan baserunners did in fact score on such a "dead" ball.

The game was evenly matched with each team demonstrating admirable hitting and fielding skills. The two teams were tied at three runs apiece after three innings, but the Brennans had the better of the middle innings, leading ten to seven at the end of the sixth inning. Both teams tallied three runs in the seventh inning before the game had to be called because of darkness. After the game those who witnessed the goings-on engaged in enthusiastic and friendly debate as to which team might have prevailed had the final two innings been played. One thing everyone agreed on was that these were two crack teams and talk of a return match was on everyone's minds. It was said that "as a money-making affair the game was certainly a success." With 2,000 fans and estimated gross gate receipts of $500, a return match was not out of the question.

Later that year another black team, the A. J. Dumont Base Ball Club, squared off against the A.S. Badgers Base Ball Club, a white team, before a small crowd of only 200 at Oakland Park on Sunday, September 12, 1881.

A.J. Dumont versus A.S. Badgers
September 11, 1881[51]

Innings	1	2	3	4	5	6	7	8	9	Total
Dumonts	7	5	4	6	2	1	0	2	x	27
Badgers	0	0	1	0	3	0	0	0	x	4

The Badgers were clearly no match for the Dumonts who seemed to hit Badger pitcher Sullivan almost at will, scoring seven runs in the first innings and additional runs in every inning except the seventh. The game was called at the end of the eighth inning because of darkness, but there was clearly no chance for the out-classed Badgers to stage a comeback.

Like their white counterparts in other leagues, the Southern League of Colored Baseballists was organized in 1885 in the height of baseball fever but could only manage to remain afloat for a very short time as a formal entity. There were simply too many teams playing across New Orleans at any point in time for lesser known league teams to gain any type of competitive advantage. The teams themselves continued to organize and play matches against each other as well as other black teams from Natchez, Mississippi, to Mobile, Alabama.

The Colored Amateur League (1886)

An entirely new slate of black teams banded together in 1886 to form the Colored Amateur League. Among those rising to prominence were the Walter L. Cohen Base Ball Club, the Blue Stocking Base Ball Club, the Union Base Ball Club, and the A.J. Dumont Base Ball Club. They played their games at the New Orleans Base Ball Park and at Loeper's Park. In reviewing the press of the day, the league appeared to operate more like a loosely associated group of journeymen ball players than as an organized league. Nonetheless, numerous games were played in a random fashion with frequent breaks for teams to pursue other opportunities or challenges both in and outside of New Orleans. Winning a $25 challenge match had a much higher probability of financial success than splitting the gate receipts with another team from a crowd of less than 200 fans. The end result was a very fluid league schedule that the four-member teams willingly accepted.

One of the first games played outside of the league schedule was a match between the Union Base Ball Club and the white Petrie Base Ball Club on May 28, 1885, at the New Orleans Base Ball Park. The Petries out-played the Unions and won the contest 4 to 2.

The Walter L. Cohen Base Ball Club was reorganized in 1885 from the remnants of the former Pickwick Base Ball Club by their second baseman, Walter L. Cohen. The twenty-five-year-old Cohen was a free man of color at his birth in 1860 and was well on his way to a successful business career when he became involved in baseball. He would later become immersed in statewide Republican politics, becoming one of the few blacks to hold appointed office in Louisiana during the early 20th century.

The Cohen Base Ball Club was known to travel in order to play professional teams from Memphis, Nashville, and Montgomery[52] in the Southern League, as well as other black and white amateur teams from Mobile and Memphis. In September of 1885, Walter Cohen put up $300 for a game between an all-white team from Columbus, Georgia, to be played on Sunday, September 27, at Sportsman's Park. Noted New Orleans odds-maker Marsh Redon put up $500 on the Columbus team. The Columbus team travelled to New Orleans for the game but was thwarted by the weather with a rain out. Before the game could be rescheduled four Columbus players returned home, but the Cohen players agreed to allow the Georgians to recruit local players in order to have enough players to be able to field a team. The game eventually was scheduled for October 10 and a crowd of 3,000 fans saw the Columbus team prevail over the Cohens by the score of 11 to 6.

The prior week the Cohens squared off against another white team, the George N. Dauer (Daner) Base Ball Club at the New Orleans Base Ball Park, which the Cohens won 8 to 2. The Daners replaced the A.A. Bohne Base Ball Club who had originally be set to play the Cohens.

However, by the end of October of 1886, the "league" championship was decided by the last men standing. The Cohens and the Union Base Ball Club took part in a traditional best-of-three championship set to begin in mid–October at the New Orleans Base Ball Park.

In a contest marked by the sloppy play of both teams, these players to a man must have had the slippery hands of a butcher as together they committed twenty-six errors between them—sixteen for the Unions and ten for the Cohens. Price, the Cohen pitcher, held the Unions to five scattered hits while there were four Cohen players who tallied two hits apiece. Scoring in the first three innings and then again in the last three innings, the Cohen squad was victorious 13 to 4 in the first game.

Cohens versus Unions
October 17, 1886[53]

Innings	1	2	3	4	5	6	7	8	9	Total
Cohen	1	4	1	0	0	0	4	1	2	13
Union	0	0	0	2	2	0	0	0	0	4

The second game in the series took place a week later. The Unions started a pitcher named Fowler who had recently been acquired from St. Louis. He held the Cohens to five spread out hits. The Cohens again sent Price to the mound only to be roughed up for eight hits. Although still error-prone with eleven errors between the two clubs, the game was tied after ten innings with two runs apiece before the umpire called the game because of darkness.

Cohens versus Unions
October 24, 1886[54]

Innings	1	2	3	4	5	6	7	8	9	10	Total
Cohens	0	1	1	0	0	0	0	0	0	0	2
Union	0	0	0	2	0	0	0	0	0	0	2

The third game in the series could only go eight innings before the umpire declared the game to be over in the favor of the Unions. The Cohens fell behind early but chipped away with no impact.

Cohens versus Unions
November 7, 1886[55]

Innings	1	2	3	4	5	6	7	8	Total
Union	0	0	0	4	0	0	3	0	7
Cohen	0	1	0	0	1	1	1	0	4

With the series still tied at one game apiece and with one tie game, the fourth and deciding game of the series saw the Cohens pitcher Ferren fare badly as the Unions pulled away starting in the fifth inning from that point there was no looking back, with the Unions winning the game 14 to 5 and the series in four games.

Cohens versus Unions
November 14, 1886[56]

Innings	1	2	3	4	5	6	7	8	9	Total
Union	0	1	0	3	2	3	0	5	0	14
Cohen	0	1	3	0	1	0	0	0	0	5

After nearly a month of competition, the Union Base Ball Club could finally claim local bragging rights over the Cohens for the 1886 Colored Amateur League championship of New Orleans. In that the league did not operate much like a league in the traditional sense during the 1886 season, no real effort was made to operate the league in 1887. In truth these teams fared better operating independently.

Black baseball would continue to thrive with equal passion as it would across New Orleans as a whole. The most prominent black teams would periodically meet against white teams,[57] but by 1890 all vestige of amicable competition was gone.

The Louisiana Base Ball League (1886)

Amateur baseball enthusiasts the Thomm Brothers and the Donnelly Base Ball Club tried to organize the Louisiana Base Ball League,[58] but with all of the activity surrounding the Crescent City League and the Gulf League, as well as the Southern League, there was just too much competition to make the Louisiana Base Ball League a practicable enterprise. The enterprise folded after only a few games.

College Baseball

Originally established in 1834, Tulane University became a comprehensive educational institution in 1847 as the Medical College of Louisiana as part of the University of Louisiana system. In 1884, a wealthy merchant named Paul Tulane donated more than one million dollars to establish Tulane University as a private institution. As in other institutions, it was only a matter of time before the students at Tulane University organized a baseball team. The sport began to grow steadily on campus, with intramural teams being formed at each of the university's colleges (departments) and among the school's fraternities. Eventually an established pattern emerged. Each spring a series of games were played between the teams from the school's different colleges to determine the undergraduate championship while the best players from the intramural and fraternity teams came together to form the varsity team. The team's manager would arrange for games with other universities. The team's manager and Captain were elected at the end of the campaign to serve for the following season.

Even the women of Newcomb College took an avid interest in the game, as reported in the *Tulane Collegian*: "With our fair friends nearby we are inspired to be heroes in the base ball strife; particularly when said friends are in delightful ignorance of all rules and applaud heartily with their daintily gloved hands bad and good plays alike." Clearly such an overtly patronizing attitude, while probably typical of the day, did little to promote baseball at Newcomb College.

There were periodic teams organized in the 1880s, but they did not play more than a few sporadic games. Students at Tulane University began to express their desire for athletic teams in the late 1880s, leading to the formation of a baseball team in the spring of 1887. In the fall of that year, Tulane University President William Preston Johnston approved the petition of a group of students led by Erasmus Darwin Fenner to formerly establish the Tulane Athletic Association.

On Monday, May 30, 1887, the university fielded a team to face the Crescent Light Guards, upon which the *Daily Picayune* reported: "The Tulane varsity nine played its first game at the New Orleans Park against a nine from the Crescent Light Guards. The score was 20 to 4 in favor of Tulane. The Light Guards failed to get a man as far as first base until the fourth inning.

A team photograph of the Tulane University baseball team circa 1899 (Tulane University Athletic Department).

Frank, captain of the Tulane nine, distinguished himself by knocking the ball over the fence at the first delivery by the pitcher. The Tulanes made but three errors."[59]

Apparently, the fellows took the summer and the fall semester off without any other games and were idle outside of intramural competition until 1888. They began the new year off by traveling to Baton Rouge. On the afternoon of Friday, January 6, 1888, eleven young men from Tulane University in New Orleans boarded a train for a six-hour journey to Baton Rouge to play a hand-picked nine from the state university there. Although unsanctioned by either university, this could be considered the first intercollegiate sporting event in Louisiana's history. Following a convivial dinner during which the spirits were free-flowing, the two teams met the next morning to play baseball. The Tulane squad defeated the boys from Baton Rouge by the score of 22 to 8.

Tulane versus Louisiana State University
January 7, 1888[60]

Innings	1	2	3	4	5	6	7	8	9	Total
Tulane	1	2	2	3	3	1	1	6	3	**22**
LSU	0	0	1	3	2	0	0	0	2	**8**

That six-hour train ride to Baton Rouge would have the train moving at approximately ten miles per hour with no stops along the way. There was plenty of time on the return trip to celebrate their victory. With this game one of the great sports rivalries in the state's history was born. Games between the two universities are still being contested after more than one hundred and thirty years.

Baseball thrived on the campus of Tulane University and the sport's popularity grew among the male and female students alike. The game developed into a university-wide competition, with a series of games to determine the undergraduate championship. Following the intramural season, the best players from the class and fraternity teams, as well as from the law and medical colleges, formed a varsity nine for intercollegiate competition. Led by baseball, the campus-wide popularity of all sports was evident by the mid–1890s. Indeed, when the university moved from its downtown campus approximately five miles further uptown via the street rail line to its present location on St. Charles Avenue across from Audubon Park, the Tulane Athletic Association marked off playing fields on the vast open area behind the main building. These fields stretched for two miles between St. Charles and Claiborne, much of it still wooded at the time. They would accommodate baseball, track and field, and football. Prior to this move, most baseball games were held at the city's Fair Grounds.

On January 8, 1893, the university announced that they would be joining the Intercollegiate Athletic Association and it did not take long before Louisiana State University issued a challenge, once again inviting Tulane up to Baton Rouge. The gauntlet had been thrown and the challenge was quickly accepted. Making the trip for Tulane coach J.P. Clinton would be J.D. Britton (catcher), A. Gates (pitcher), C.W. Butler (first base), W. Johnson (second base), J.J. Potts (third base), J.R. Conniff (shortstop), L.E. Maubret (left field), J.P. Chilton (right field), and J.E. Lombard (center field and team captain). Substitutes J.D. Houston and C.C. Waterman rounded out the team.

The Tulane team was greeted at the Baton Rouge train station with near ceremonial honor and then conveyed to a reception on the university grounds hosted by Governor Murphy J. Foster's wife and the wives of several prominent politicians and citizens. A large pavilion had been erected on the edge of the campus' parade grounds and was festively decorated with flags and bunting. A band provided music for entertainment and dancing that lasted well into the night.

The next morning the Tulane team was invited to attend a field day exhibition on the Louisiana State University campus hosted by Governor Foster. The festivities began with a military dress parade followed by a mock battle between the university's cadet troops. When the field of battle was cleared, baseball became the object of interest for the assembled politicians, students, and faculty. In a hard-fought contest, the Louisiana State University team defeated the Tulane club by the score of 10 to 8. Both teams were then whisked away to the home of William Garig for a celebratory reception.[61] Upon later reflection, the Tulane players commented that they thoroughly enjoyed their weekend in Baton Rouge, although the quality of their play on Saturday afternoon may have been diminished by the volume of libations they had consumed the night before.

The school's entire 1893 season consisted of just two games: a 10 to 2 victory over the Southern Athletic Club in New Orleans and the 10 to 8 loss to Louisiana State University in Baton Rouge.

Tulane University Varsity Baseball Record
1893–1899

Year	Won	Loss	Tied	PCT
1893	1	1	0	.500
1894	3	0	0	1.00
1895	No varsity team was fielded			NA
1896	No varsity team was fielded			NA
1897	0	4	0	.000
1898	7	2	0	.778
1899	5	3	2	.625
TOTAL	16	10	2	.615

From 1893 through 1899, Tulane's baseball program continued to grow. The team's first coaches were J.P. Clinton (1893), Jack Dowling and T.L. Byrne (1894–1895), F.B. Morris (1896–1897), and H.T. Summersgill (1899–1900). Their record during these five years was 16–10–2. The 1899 campaign saw Tulane face off against five opponents: Louisiana State University, the University of Alabama, the University of Mississippi, the University of Texas, and the New Orleans Press. By 1899, the school had become a member of the Southern Intercollegiate Athletic Association, an organization made up of nineteen colleges and universities.

Baseball at other New Orleans universities had to wait until those institutions were established in the 20th century, principally Loyola University of New Orleans (1912), Xavier University (1915), Delgado Community College (1921), Southern University (1959), and the University of New Orleans (1962). Dillard University was established in 1869, but it is uncertain if the institution offered organized sports in the 19th century. Not all colleges had varsity-level baseball programs, but their students played baseball on intramural or club teams as well as informally as most young men would—just for the fun of it.

The Gulf League (1886–1887)

Representatives from Mobile, Montgomery, and Birmingham in Alabama, Pensacola in Florida, Jackson and Vicksburg in Mississippi, and New Orleans arranged to meet in New Orleans in early March to discuss the formation of a new league to be called the Gulf League.[62] Many of these cities had previously applied for admission to the Southern League, but like New Orleans were unsuccessful. Birmingham was the only city who played in the Southern League in 1885, but they were unable to complete their schedule and disbanded just two weeks before the end of the season. They elected not to reapply to the Southern League in 1886 and were considering the proposed Gulf League.

Toby Hart gathered together a group of baseball men from New Orleans in mid-February of 1886[63] for the purpose of starting a subscription list to raise the necessary capital. By Mardi Gras, the local contingent included "Governor" Conrad Leithman of the R.E. Lees, Billy Miller, W.L. Saxon, and Henry Peters in addition to Toby Hart. Meanwhile, in Mobile, John F. Kelly was trying to coordinate the various cities in Alabama who had indicated an interest and who were out also beating the bushes themselves trying to raise money to finance a franchise for their city in the new league.

On March 8, delegations from six cities met in New Orleans to formally establish the Gulf League. Representatives from Mobile, Pensacola, Columbus, Montgomery, Selma, and New Orleans were invited to attend. Officers were elected, and a charter was to be drawn up by the time the group reconvened on March 22. However, only Mobile, New Orleans, and Columbus were represented at the meeting on March 22. Letters from Selma, Pensacola, and Montgomery attempting to explain their absence should have been a telltale sign and did not bode well for the three cities who were on hand, but the new league optimistically pressed ahead with new business. An exhibition match game between the R.E. Lees of New Orleans and the Acid Iron Earth Base Ball Club of Mobile was scheduled to coincide with the formal launch of the new league in Mobile on the 22nd,[64] but this game was cancelled, and the discouraged representatives returned home with the absence of the representatives from Selma, Pensacola, and Montgomery weighing heavily on their minds. They were still hopeful in the long-term prospects for the new league. A new committee was established to devise a viable schedule that would begin on April 24 and end on October 15.

By the time officers were finally elected in June of 1886 there were only two cities committed to the Gulf League—New Orleans and Mobile. The new officers were the Honorable J.G. Brien from New Orleans (president), Richard Sheridan from Mobile (vice-president), Charles Shaffer from Mobile (treasurer), and F. McKeough from New Orleans (secretary).[65] Sensing that the other cities in the new league were having far more difficulty raising money than was originally anticipated, the Mobile delegation brought forth the suggestion that the Waters Base Ball Club of New Orleans[66] be assigned to represent Selma as the Gulf League franchisee. There was a local rivalry between the Lees and the Waters clubs and this suggestion was thought to stimulate interest in the new league. Negotiations with the Waters club and the city of Selma began but quickly fell through, with neither side willing to shoulder what they considered to be a disproportionate portion of the financial responsibility on their respective organizations. Just as hope springs eternal, Toby Hart and John Kelly were quietly optimistic that more teams and cities would join the Gulf League in the coming weeks.

In an effort to keep the ball rolling, another game was scheduled between the Acid Iron Earths and the R.E. Lees to kick off the new league—an exhibition game that took place on Sunday, April 25, 1886, at Frascati Park in Mobile. More than 2,000 fans witnessed a well-played game that was dominated by the Lees,[67] although in all fairness the Mobile squad had only just been signed and barely had any time to practice as a team before the game. The first Lees' run came on a home run by Behan in the fourth inning, and the errorless contest lasted two hours and ten minutes. Despite their team's goose egg, the Mobile fans continued to support their team and their patience would be rewarded.

R.E. Lees versus Acid Iron Earths
April 25, 1886

Innings	1	2	3	4	5	6	7	8	9	Total
R.E. Lees	0	0	0	1	1	1	4	0	0	7
Acid Iron Earths	0	0	0	0	0	0	0	0	0	0

However, after months of meetings and countless hours of discussions, planning and preparation, only two cities, New Orleans and Mobile, were left standing by June 16. Each city agreed to provide two teams. Mobile provided the Acid Iron Earth Base Ball Club and the Mobile Base Ball Club. New Orleans offered the R.E. Lee Base Ball Club and the New Orleans Base Ball Club.[68] The unusual four-team format was finally launched in late June, still hopeful of attracting other teams down the line.

The first official game of the new Gulf League took place under threatening skies and inclement weather at Sportsman's Park in New Orleans on Sunday, June 20, 1886, between the R.E. Lees from New Orleans and Acid Iron Earths of Mobile. At game time there was a cooling breeze that made the pensive crowd a bit more comfortable. Timely hitting by both teams overcame a game plagued with twenty-five errors—twelve by New Orleans and thirteen by Mobile. "A poorer game among clubs of any pretension was perhaps never seen in New Orleans." Despite their challenges in the field, the New Orleans nine rallied in the bottom of the ninth inning, plating four runs to come from behind 11 to 10.[69]

Mobile versus New Orleans
June 20, 1886

Innings	1	2	3	4	5	6	7	8	9	Total
Mobile	0	0	0	2	0	2	1	4	1	10
New Orleans	1	0	0	2	1	1	2	0	4	11

Two thousand weather weary fans were disappointed with the quality of the play, sitting through a game plagued with errors between the two "professional" sets of what turned out to be hard hands. Lees pitcher William Bokenfohr gave up five hits while the Mobile hurler surrendered nine hits, three of them to the New Orleans right fielder Bill Butler and two by the catcher Hanlon.

Meanwhile over in Mobile, the Acid Iron Earths dispatched the R.E. Lees by the score of 5 to 3 at Frascati Park. Apparently ball control was a problem for the Acid pitcher who hit several Lee batters, most notably J. Cruso who was grazed on the forehead and eye hard enough to remove him from the game. Even the umpire was hit twice, once in the head and once on the foot.

By August the two Mobile clubs held a substantial lead over the two

New Orleans teams, with the Mobile Base Ball Club in front with 14 wins against 5 losses (.737) and the Acid Iron Earths with 12 wins against 6 losses (.667).[70] Despite a limited slate of opponents, the public's support did not wane as the season wore on. The average attendance hovered around 2,000 per game. The Mobile Base Ball Club held on to capture the inaugural Gulf League pennant for 1886.

This was a vibrant and freewheeling time in the evolution of baseball. Teams began to adopt colorful names like the Acid Iron Earths and the Swamp Angels, both teams from Mobile. Elsewhere in the country were the Brooklyn Bridegrooms, the Boston Beaneaters, the Worcester Ruby Legs, and the Cleveland Spiders. Their whimsy and imagination was not limited to team names. The most personable and colorful players were also given nicknames such as Noodles Hahn, Egyptian Healy, Old Hoss Radbourn, Cyclone Miller, Peek-a-Boo Veach, Pretzels Geitzen, and Buttercup Dickerson. It was all part of making baseball more entertaining.

The unlikely success of the four-team league format spurred a renewal of interest from teams in Pensacola, Vicksburg, Birmingham, and Shreveport. Yet even as plans were being made for the 1887 Gulf League season, New Orleans turned its eyes once again to the Southern League.

The Southern League (1887–1899)

Rumors of a new professional baseball league being organized in the South began circulating as early as 1881.[71] The New Orleans baseball community was seeking "public spirited gentlemen, favorably inclined to such sport" who would collectively provide the necessary financial backing to bring a professional team to New Orleans. Across the city, baseball fans were certain that such a professional team could be formed, pulling together the best players in the Louisiana Base Ball League and the Gulf League. While there was a great deal of interest expressed, unfortunately nothing would ever come of it. The spark was reignited in 1883 when Thomas Brennan, owner/manager/captain of the Brennan Base Ball Club began talking to baseball men along the Gulf Coast about forming a new league.[72] Interest was high, but in a new venture of this magnitude most cities were waiting for New Orleans to make the first move. They would not have to wait for long. Having spent two years putting together an investor group to back the Gulf League, Toby Hart knew the people who would be predisposed to taking the next step to invest in a Southern circuit.

When the call went out for delegates from other Southern cities to take up the mantle and, after hours of preliminary talks, a meeting was called to finalize the new Southern League. New Orleans was represented by Charles

H. Genslinger and J.C. Bach. The city's envoys met at the Windsor Hotel in Montgomery, Alabama, on November 25, 1884.[73] The eight cities represented were Nashville, Chattanooga, Atlanta, New Orleans, Columbus, Montgomery, Augusta, and Memphis. The Southern League of Professional Base Ball Clubs was formally established, officers and directors were elected, and an eighty-game schedule was proposed and approved.

Enthusiasm for the new league was widespread in New Orleans, that is until it came time to write the check. New Orleans was largely distracted from participating in ongoing discussions regarding the establishment of a professional baseball circuit by the city's involvement in and preoccupation with the 1884 World Industrial & Cotton Centennial Exposition which was running behind schedule and over budget. It was a huge financial gamble and everyone in city leadership and the business community was committed to making the Exposition both a critical and financial success. As a result, New Orleans would have to forego a Southern League franchise in 1885.

As fall turned into winter, New Orleans and Montgomery dropped out of the running for a Southern League spot and were replaced by Birmingham and Macon. In time for spring training there was a stable slate of eight teams and the 1885 Southern League was up and running. In an abundance of optimism, the previously approved eighty-game schedule was expanded to a very ambitious one hundred games,[74] an unheard of and incredibly largescale schedule for an established league much less one just getting started. To the surprise of observers throughout the South, five of the eight teams managed to complete ninety-eight games of their one hundred game schedule, with Atlanta claiming the inaugural Southern League pennant and a winter's worth of bragging rights with a record of 66 wins against 32 losses, a .673 winning percentage, finishing just one game ahead of the Augusta Browns.

Toby Hart and Charles Genslinger were quietly using the exhibition games scheduled during 1885 as part of the city's ongoing World Industrial and Cotton Centennial Exposition, now called the American Exposition, to evaluate potential players. There were more than a dozen games contested by the Exposition Nine, an ever-changing roster of local and regional talent assembled by Hart, Genslinger, and Thomas Brennan. The Exposition Nine's opponents ranged from local teams such as the J.C. Bach Base Ball Club to visiting professional teams from Dayton, Ohio, St. Louis, and Birmingham. All in all, however, baseball at the exposition, like the exposition itself, was a critical success, but in most respects a commercial flop. Between the American Exposition and the Gulf League, Hart reluctantly sat out the 1886 Southern League season.

However, Hart was eventually successful in attracting a large enough group of enthusiastic investors with both deep pockets and open checkbooks, thus ensuring a franchise for New Orleans in the Southern League for the

1887 season. He began signing ballplayers in earnest during early December of 1886, beginning with Harry Eldred, Joe Dowie, and Ed Cartwright.[75] The sixth player he signed in December was a wiry former major league pitcher and outfielder named Abner Powell.[76] Slowly building the city's Southern League team, the New Orleans Pelicans, Hart and company still had an arduous task in front of them. With a total payroll of $1,740 per month for fourteen players, less than $125 per month per player, the New Orleans Pelicans had the lowest overhead in the league.[77] This decision was by design as Hart and his associates, all experienced baseball men, were well aware of the financial gamble they were taking. The New Orleans teams in the Gulf League were credibly supported by the fans, but the burning question was whether or not they would turn out to see the Pelicans. After its first two years the Southern League was restructuring—out were Atlanta, Augusta, Macon, and Chattanooga while Mobile and New Orleans were newcomers for 1887. The smaller league was no less tenuous.

The question of fan support would be answered soon enough. Opening Day for the New Orleans Pelicans came on Sunday afternoon, April 17, 1887, drawing approximately 4,700 paying customers. Among them was New Orleans Mayor Joseph Valsin (J.V.) Guillotte, a well-known sporting man and prominent member of the Olympic Club, the city's premiere boxing venue. However, he was not there to throw out the first pitch. That tradition did not take root until 1890 and really became popular in 1892 when newly-elected Governor William McKinley of Ohio did so in Cleveland. Instead, Mayor Guillotte and his friends would be treated to a crackerjack of a ballgame and would witness the next phase in the long-standing rivalry between New Orleans and Mobile baseball teams. It was only fitting that the Pelicans faced off against the Swamp Angels in their debut in the Southern League. The game was described for the *Daily Picayune* by an uncredited reporter.

> It was a new sensation to the old baseball admirers who visited Sportsman's Park yesterday. This is the first time that New Orleans has been regularly represented in a league under the national agreement. It is the first time it has had a real baseball park, a real New Orleans club and real league games. The first taste was delicious. There were no delays in going to the bat or into the field, there were no long waits for balls, there was no talking back to the umpire, there was only one captain to each team, each side had its time for practice, and everything worked with the regularity and smoothness of clock work.
>
> Returning to the subject of the park, it was hardly recognizable in its new dress. The only thing unchanged about it is the cemetery fence. The field stretched high and level to the stands against the fences, and the stands have the seating capacity for about 6,000 people. It was somewhat cloudy yesterday and the management at one time dreaded the coming of the rain. The clouds did not disappear, but the weather remained dry. Even with this unfavorable circumstance the stands were almost called upon to hold their full capacity. It was said that there were 4,700 paid

admissions, making the attendance about 5,000. It was a patriotic crowd that stood by the New Orleans team from first to last, applauded every good play, and almost went wild when the nine took a decided lead. There is something in a name after all, especially when the name happens to be New Orleans.

It is not claimed that New Orleans has a team that will easily walk away with the Southern championship. It is not even claimed that New Orleans has as good a nine as it ought to have. But it has so lively, hard-working, capable set of youngsters who will make it lively for all comers. The nine only got down to work in earnest a few days ago and the change is already apparent. They showed considerable improvement in team work, and there was an earnestness about their play all the time which did them credit. It was well that they made a good impression, for they had a new organization to popularize, local pride to uphold, and an overwhelming defeat at Mobile the Sunday previous to wipe out.

If the New Orleans nine showed a change the Mobile team was hardly knowable alongside of the raw set that came here two weeks ago. It has been strengthened up, the men all played in proper positions, and it looked like a ball team. Looks spoke truly, for the Alabamians made a fine showing. Kelly, their pitcher, made his first appearance here and created an excellent impression. His only fault was his tendency to nervousness at critical points. McVey gave him fair support behind the bat. The rest of the nine started off to give him perfect co-operation, but all of them got rattled with him in the latter part of the game and assisted in giving the "home team" the victory.

Flynn and Bright, the new men, showed up very well. Of the old favorites, Behan did a little ragged work in his anxiety to do too well in front of home folks, and Duffee made the catch of the day. It was a long, backward running fly catch of a ball hit from Cartwright's bat, which ought to have been good for three bases.

Aydelotte got his revenge. The Mobilians who judged of their ability to hit him by the preceding Sunday's work judged without their reckoning. He pitched a great game, striking thirteen men out and holding the opposing side down to a matter of five scattered hits. Brennan gave him fine backing up behind the bat. Outside of a bad and needless throw by Brennan and a muff by Harry Fuller the team p0layed an errorless game in the field. It failed to get on to Kelly safely, but showed the Mobiles how to get around the bases once having reached first. Mention has already been made of the team work improvement. Each player was backed up and several errors saved by someone else being around to assist the fielder called for. There was, however, a lack of good coaching. New Orleans has not yet developed a Latham or Comiskey, and several runs were lost yesterday because the men on bases did not have cooler heads on the outside to guide them. Powell did some of the best work for the home team. He ran bases with daring and judgment and picked a shot fly off the ground in right field in a manner which set the crowd wild.

The game was a very interesting one and the result was very doubtful for six innings at least. Cartwright got in the first run of the game upon his first time at bat, getting his base on balls and coming all the way around on passed balls. Mobile tied the score in the fourth inning, Klusman hit safe to left, stole second, went to third on Flynn's drive to right, and scored on Brennan's foolish throw to second, which turned out an overthrow. In the sixth Mobile was on top. Duffee hit to center for a single, but Fuller let the ball go through him and Duffee reached third, scoring on a passed ball.

There was blood in the eyes of the New Orleans team as they came to the bat in the seventh inning. Harry Fuller hit a hot grounder through Behan and stole second. Shorty Fuller then hit to Klusman who let the ball go, and Harry Fuller scored on Duffee's throw home. McVey threw the ball back to second to catch Shorty but the latter secured the bag by a desperate slide. A passed ball advanced him to third where he stopped to see Aydelotte get to second on a hit by pitcher and a steal. Cartwright then hit a hot liner to Kelly who stopped it and played the ball to first, Behan catching Aydelotte at second while Shorty Fuller scored.

New Orleans fastened its grip on the lead in the eighth. Powell's fly was muffed by Duffee, who followed up the error with a foolish throw which let the Captain to second. He made a pretty steal to third and when McVey threw the ball a little wild to Flynn, Powell came home. Henry Murphy hit safe to right field, stole second and scored on Shorty Fuller's timely single to right field.

Mobile during this time did not get beyond first. In the last inning Aydelotte struck Klusman and McVey out. Flynn then came in and rapped a single to right. He tried to make two bases, but Powell got the ball to Geiss and Flynn retired the side and ended the game, which was an exciting one throughout.[78]

Mobile Swamp Angels versus New Orleans Pelicans
April 17, 1887

Mobile	AB	R	1B	BS	PO	A	E
Duffee, cf	4	1	1	0	3	0	2
Klusman, 2b	4	1	1	1	5	2	1
McVey, c	4	0	1	0	4	1	1
Flynn, 3b	4	0	2	0	2	6	1
Behan, 1b	3	0	1	0	12	1	2
Bright, ss	3	0	0	0	0	1	2
Neihoff, rf	3	0	0	0	0	0	0
Hays, lf	3	0	0	0	1	0	1
Kelly, p	3	0	0	0	0	7	0
TOTALS	31	2	6	1	27	18	10
New Orleans	AB	R	1B	BS	PO	A	E
Cartwright, 1b	5	1	1	0	15	0	0
Geiss, 2b	5	0	1	1	0	3	0
Brennan, c	4	0	0	0	11	2	1
Pujol, 3b	4	0	0	1	0	3	0
Powell, rf	4	1	0	1	1	1	0
Murphy, lf	4	1	1	1	0	0	0
H. Fuller, cf	4	1	0	1	0	0	1
W. Fuller, ss	4	1	2	1	0	3	0
Aydelotte, p	3	0	0	1	0	13	0
TOTALS	37	5	5	7	27	25	2

By Innings:	1	2	3	4	5	6	7	8	9	TOTAL
New Orleans	1	0	0	0	0	0	2	2	0	5
Mobiles	0	0	0	1	0	1	0	0	0	2

Earned runs—New Orleans 3. Total bases on hits—Mobile 6, New Orleans 5. Bases on hit by pitcher—Kelly 1. First base by errors—New Orleans 9, Mobile 6. Left on bases—New Orleans 6, Mobile 5. Struck out—by Aydelotte 13, by Kelly 4. Passed balls—McVey 4, Brennan 6. Wild pitches—by Aydelotte 1. Balls called—on Aydelotte 58, by Kelly 58. Strikes called—off Aydelotte 63, off Kelly56. Double plays—Kelly, Behan, and Klusman. First base on balls—by Aydelotte 1, by Kelly 2.

Umpire: Atkinson.

Time of game: 2 hours

Nearly five thousand fans braved an overcast and windy afternoon, huddled together in the grandstand and bleachers. The grandstand was festooned with the flags of several nations, each of which had a representative from their country in the ballpark that afternoon. The Newsboys' Band provided the entertainment and the overall mood was decidedly cheerful. Marsh Redon was on hand to accommodate those gentlemen wishing to place a wager on the outcome of the game and the betting was brisk. There was even a telegraph operator standing by ready to relay all of the game action by wire direct to Lamothe's Turf Exchange in downtown New Orleans.

Although there was a wicked wind gusting through the stadium, it was not really a factor. Instead, it was Mobile's fielders who committed ten errors, allowing nine Pelican hitters to reach base, four of them on passed balls. The Pelicans also ran wild on the base paths, pilfering seven bases to stretch their five hits into additional scoring opportunities. On the mound, Pelican pitcher Jacob Aydelotte threw one hundred and twenty-one pitches—sixty-three for strikes and fifty-eight for balls. He was not known as a fireballer, but that afternoon he struck out thirteen of the thirty-one Swamp Angels he faced and held the remaining batters to six scattered hits. He would finish the season with a record of fourteen wins against ten losses for a .583 winning percentage, with two shutouts, seventy-seven strikeouts, and a 2.36 ERA.

Often listed as "Aydelott" in some box scores and game summaries, the native of Marion, Indiana, came to New Orleans as a twenty-five-year-old in 1887 with two seasons in the major leagues under his belt. In 1884 he appeared in 12 games with Indianapolis Hoosiers, posting a record of 5 wins against 7 losses (.417). Bill Butler, John Peltz, and George Mundinger from New Orleans were his teammates that season. In 1886 he played in only two games for the Philadelphia Athletics, losing both games.

Among the other notable players taking part in this historic game were Abner Powell and Ed Cartwright.

Powell was born in Shenandoah, Pennsylvania, in 1860 and was discovered while playing semi-professional baseball in Philadelphia for fifty cents a day in 1881. He was a twenty-six-year-old veteran of two major league seasons—the 1885 Washington Nationals and both the Baltimore Orioles and the Cincinnati Red Stockings during 1886—when his contract was purchased in December of 1886 by Toby Hart to play for the Pelicans. It did not take long for Powell to be tapped as the team's captain in their inaugural 1887 season. His enthusiasm was infectious, his hustle was inspiring, and his skill as a field general in managing the game made him the logical choice. During the season he played in 116 games as an outfielder and he occasionally played as a utility infielder, batting .314 with ninety-two stolen bases. But it was as a pitcher that Powell truly excelled, starting and completing twenty-eight games, winning twenty against only nine losses (.690 winning percentage) while making an additional four appearances in relief. As a player, his competitive fire was a match for the devil himself. As a manager he could always convince his players to show a little extra ginger when

Abner Powell was the first team captain of the New Orleans Pelicans in the Southern League. He would become the team's second manager in 1888. He is credited with devising the practice of covering the infield with a canvas tarpaulin to protect against rain and the invention of rain check on tickets (collection of the author).

the chips were down, and they needed to rally. He was a fierce competitor who hated to lose. That Powell served as the Pelicans' player-manager for most of his career makes his achievements all the more impressive.

Powell was also an imaginative baseball force, little appreciated or remembered today. For instance, when he realized that the frequent rainfall in New Orleans could sometimes make field conditions unplayable, thus causing games to be cancelled if they could not be rescheduled. He needed a solution. As the story goes, Powell was standing on the New Orleans waterfront waiting to meet a new player from St. Louis due to arrive by riverboat when a heavy rain storm sent everyone running for cover. Everyone that is except the crews working with the cargo along the dockside. Powell noticed that when the rain started, the stevedores and longshoremen hauled out several large waxed canvas tarpaulins in order to cover the stacks of cotton bales to prevent them from absorbing the rainwater. The wetter the cotton bales became, the heavier they would become, thereby making them harder and slower to load onto the riverboats. Powell reasoned that if he covered the infield and pitching mound at the ballpark with these types of canvas tarpaulins, the game might be delayed, but it would not be cancelled. This ultimately meant that if the game was played, the players got paid; if the game was cancelled, the players would not be paid. The practice of covering the infield with a waxed canvas tarpaulin was soon noticed by major league clubs during their spring training camps in New Orleans and was eventually adopted throughout every major league and minor league ballpark.

Rain also played a role in another of Powell's innovative ideas. It was standard procedure that on those days when prolonged rain forced the postponement of a game, the team would issue the fans leaving the ballpark a thick cardboard ticket good for admission to another game, not just the game that had been rained out. This cardboard ticket was known as a "rain check," and was good for any future game. Powell soon recognized that he was handing out more replacement tickets than he had sold from the box office, courtesy of fence jumpers and other freeloaders. He contracted with a local printer that could add a perforated end on each ticket sold. The new appendage was also labeled the "rain check" to replace the thick cardboard ticket, but this version was detachable and only good for admission to the rescheduled game with the same team. This practice was also adopted throughout major league baseball, as well as in the entertainment industry.

Powell never patented either of his innovations and never profited from them. But for all of the innovations that Powell introduced into baseball, he is most often remembered for being involved in one of those plays that earns a ball player a permanent footnote in baseball history, or at least in that section that details baseball oddities. On Sunday, August 22, 1886, Powell was playing centerfield for the Cincinnati Red Stockings on the road against the Louisville Colonels at Eclipse Park in Louisville.

The game was tied at 3 to 3 in the bottom of the eleventh inning when Jimmy "Chicken" Wolf (real name: William Van Winkle) stepped up to the plate. The Cincinnati pitcher served up a ball that Wolf sent flying into the far reaches of center field. Patrolling the garden in center was Abner Powell, who immediately gave chase as the ball rolled all the way to the fence in centerfield. Wolf took off around the bases and six thousand fans were on their feet, alternating their gaze between watching Powell and watching Wolf, wondering which man would win the race. Depending on whose version of the story was told, events at this point took a strange turn. A dog, some claimed it was a simple stray dog while others said it was the groundskeeper's dog, supposedly sleeping in the outfield, and that the hound took off after Powell and the ball. Powell always claimed that the groundskeeper deliberately unleashed his dog on Powell. In either event the dog, sensing that Powell was winning the race to the ball, bit into Powell's leg and refused to let go. Wolf rounded the bases for a game winning two-run inside-the-park home run, his second home run of the game. Powell left the field without the ball or the dog.[79] The incident is frequently memorialized as part of baseball's more unusual plays for that date in history and thus Powell's more noteworthy contributions to baseball are often overlooked.

Abner Powell's Playing Career
1883–1899

Year	Team	League	Games	BA
1882	Pottsville Maroons	Anthracite League		
1883	Peoria Reds	Northwestern League		
1884	Chicago Unions	Union League (outlaw league)		
	Peoria Reds	Northwestern League	58	.202
	Washington Nationals	Union Association	48	
1885	Washington Nationals	Eastern League	86	.284
1886	Baltimore Orioles	American Association	11	.179
	Cincinnati Red Stockings	American Association	4	.230
1887	New Orleans Pelicans	Southern League	116	.335
1888	New Orleans Pelicans	Southern League	55	.279
	New Orleans Pelicans	Texas-Southern League	29	.274
1889	New Orleans Pelicans	Southern League	51	.289
	Hamilton Hams	International League	40	.322
1890	Spokane Bunchgrassers	Pacific Northwest League	46	.320
	Hamilton/Montreal	International League	47	.249
1891	Seattle	Pacific Northwest League	99	.281
1892	New Orleans Pelicans	Southern League	59	.236
	Seattle Hustlers	Pacific Northwest League	44	.233
1893	New Orleans Pelicans	Southern League	81	.266
1894	New Orleans Pelicans	Southern League	13	
	Nashville Tigers	Southern League	18	
1895	New Orleans Pelicans	Southern League		
1896	New Orleans Pelicans	Southern League	102	.318
1897	New Castle Quakers	Interstate League		
	Wilkes-Barre Coal Barons	Eastern League	27	.218
1898	New Orleans Pelicans	Southern League	21	.316
1899	New Orleans Pelicans	Southern League	12	.235
	Paterson Giants	Atlantic League	8	.143
	Newark Colts	Atlantic League	1	.333

Abner Powell's Managerial Career
1884–1904

Year	Team	League	Record	Finish
1883	Richmond Virginians	Eastern League		
1888	New Orleans Pelicans	Southern League	25–32	3rd
	New Orleans Pelicans	Texas-Southern League	18–9	
1889	New Orleans Pelicans	Southern League	46–9	1st
	Hamilton Hams	International League		
1890	New Orleans Pelicans	Southern League		

Year	Team	League	Record	Finish
	Hamilton Hams/Montreal	Pacific Northwest League	25–26	
1891	Seattle	Pacific Northwest League	45–51	
1892	Seattle Hustlers	Pacific Northwest League		
	New Orleans Pelicans	Southern League	66–57	3rd
1893	New Orleans Pelicans	Southern League	40–51	8th
1894	New Orleans Pelicans	Southern League	34–35	3rd
1895	New Orleans Pelicans	Southern League	46–55	4th
1896	New Orleans Pelicans	Southern League	68–33	1st
1897	Wilkes-Barre Coal Barons	Eastern League		
1898	New Orleans Pelicans	Southern League	10–15	6th
1899	New Orleans Pelicans	Southern League	19–23	3rd
	Paterson Giants	Atlantic League		
	Newark Colts	Atlantic League		
1900	Elmira/Oswego Pioneers	New York State League	32–74	8th
1901	New Orleans Pelicans	Southern Association	68–56	4th
1902	New Orleans Pelicans	Southern Association	73–48	3rd
1903	Atlanta Crackers	Southern Association	59–59	4th
1904	Atlanta Crackers	Southern Association	78–57	2nd

Powell, along with Newt Fisher from Nashville and Charles Frank from Memphis, established the Southern Association in 1901 from the ashes of the Southern League that folded for the final time in 1899. He would serve as the owner-manager for the New Orleans Pelicans in 1901 and 1902 before moving to Atlanta. There he was also the owner-manager in 1903 and 1904 before being forced to sell his interest to a contentious political faction led by the city's fire chief. Powell was forty when he co-founded the Southern Association and during his tenure he retained an ownership interest in three different teams—the New Orleans Pelicans, the Atlanta Crackers, the Nashville Volunteers, and the Selma Christians.

In 1902, when he was the manager in Atlanta, Powell hired an aspiring young reporter named Grantland Rice to be his publicity writer, giving him his first start in baseball. Although he retired from baseball in 1904, he divested all of his ownership interests in 1908 in order to go into the automobile business. He established Powell's Garage at 1317 Canal Street as a dealer for the White Motor Company, selling a steam powered automobile that in its day outsold the better-known Stanley Steamer. His automobile dealership and garage were located one block away from Krauss Department Store, erected in 1903. Powell also built and operated the first miniature golf course in New Orleans near City Park.

Powell remained close to the game he loved by visiting spring training camps in New Orleans during the twenties and thirties, and later by travelled to spring training camps in Florida. In 1950 the great Connie Mack wrote to Powell, saying that he had "contributed more to the game of baseball than any man alive."[80]

The other notable Pelican player from their first Opening Day was Ed Cartwright, a native of Johnstown, Pennsylvania, who broke into baseball with Youngstown in the Western Interstate League in 1883. Three years later he was playing first base for the Mobile Acid Iron Earths in the Gulf League where he caught the eye of Toby Hart, who signed him as one of the first three players for the Pelicans for the inaugural 1887 season. Cartwright peppered the opposition with his .373 batting average while swiping one hundred and eight bases and scoring one hundred runs during the one hundred and fourteen games in which he played. He was a standout on a team chock full of talent and was considered the team's first power hitter, alongside Charles "Count" Campau.

Cartwright enjoyed five seasons in the major leagues, first with the St. Louis Brown in 1890 where he played in 75 games, batting .300 with 90 hits and 8 home runs. He returned for four seasons with the Washington Senators from 1894 through 1897, compiling a .295 batting average with 472 hits, 278 runs, and 16 home runs. After fifteen seasons in organized baseball, Cartwright retired to St. Petersburg, Florida, where he died from pneumonia on September 3, 1933, at the age of 74.

Managed by Toby Hart's long-time business associate Thomas Brennan (no relation to catcher Jack Brennan), the New Orleans Pelicans not only won their inaugural game in the Southern League, but they continued winning for most of the 1887 season, capturing their first pennant with a record of seventy-four wins against forty losses, a .649 winning percentage, and a four and one-half game lead over the Charleston Seagulls. Team captain Abner Powell assumed the additional role of manager of the club in 1888 and remained in the player/manager role through 1899. He led the Pelicans to two additional Southern League pennants. In 1889 the club compiled a record of forty-six wins and nine losses, a .836 winning percentage, and finished fifteen games ahead of the Charleston/Atlanta aggregation. In 1896 the Pelicans finished with seventy-four wins and twenty-three losses, a .763 winning percentage, fourteen games ahead of the Montgomery Gladiators.

The City League (1898–1899)

When the Southern League closed in June of 1898 Abner Powell and several other baseball backers established the City League in mid-June.[81] It started as a four-team league made up of the J.C. Bach Base Ball Club, the George W. Foster Base Ball Club, the Levy Base Ball Club, and the Athletic Base Ball Club. They were soon joined by the Archinard Base Ball Club. In the league schedule, the Levys were referred to as the "Upper District" and the Archinards as the "Lower District." The league intended to fill in the gap left by the Southern League and the circuit started off well-financed, but eventually suffered the same fate as the Southern League—lack of attendance. Like most amateur and semi-professional efforts at this time there was just too much headwind for baseball teams to make any financial headway.

Five

The Business of Baseball

"Baseball is becoming more of a paying business ... and the gatekeeper is kept busy handling the tickets of admission."[1]

For amateur clubs, getting enough money to purchase bats, balls, bases, and uniforms was a straight forward proposition: members paid their weekly or monthly dues, usually along the lines of ten cents per person per week, which allowed the paid-up members to attend and participate in that week's practice. When accumulated in sufficient quantity, these dues were then available to purchase the necessary equipment, the best of which was held in reserve for game day. That is not to say that this everyday equipment was taken for granted. Quite the opposite, the rudiments of the game were highly prized, especially balls and bats. As baseball clubs were also social in nature, with periodic suppers, picnics, and perhaps even an annual grand ball staged during the off-season which was a popular fundraising event to which the club sold tickets to their friends, family, and co-workers.

Clubs held their practices whenever it was practically possible, often in the early morning hours before work. Daylight permitting, after business hours might afford an opportunity for additional practice as well. Some employers were more than accommodating when an employee asked for the afternoon off to play in a baseball game, but as games during the work week became more common, many business owners became less tolerant of their employees and baseball. Conversely, some aspiring young men embraced the game as long as it didn't interfere with their work, their standing with their employers, and their careers. Of course, this was not a problem for company sponsored teams or teams on which employers themselves or their children played. As with so many things in New Orleans, participation in sports fell loosely along class lines, with the upper crust easily accepting activities such as yachting, horse racing, polo, and tennis. Baseball, in their eyes, was a much more difficult sell and was not generally seen as an appropriate use of their time. In some cases it was frowned upon as a leisure time activity, much less an acceptable accommodation to allow employees to leave work to indulge in baseball games. Lower class, unskilled, or day laborers often lacked the money needed to join a baseball club. They spent their leisure time at cards, dice, or blood sports such as cockfighting or rat-baiting. They may have played two-cat or another rudimentary form of stick and ball game provided a ball and a bat could be acquired. Thus, early baseball in New Orleans largely owes its initial success to the flexibility in the working environment of the upper-middle class and middle-class, who found in baseball whatever they lacked in their employment or their careers.

Baseball clubs, like any other social organization, offered their members a fraternal support system and network, and it was the social aspect of baseball that was integral to its early acceptance. Baseball was a brand-new sport trying to capture the public's imagination and acceptance. Kindred spirits played baseball with and against their clubmates. The excitement of playing baseball was no doubt discussed after the game as the key hits and the clutch fielding chances were reviewed over and over in great detail. Players would regal each other with game highlights, particularly those in which they themselves were involved. It was a celebration of competition and camaraderie that was both electric and addictive.

However, as soon as one club challenged another club, the social fabric of belonging to a baseball club began to slowly unravel. It was inevitable that the additional excitement of playing against another team instead of one's own clubmates would fuel the competitive curiosity of the best players. It was one thing to have bragging rights within your own club, as long as you were consistently a member of the club's first nine at the discretion of being selected by the team captain. The underlying problem was that the group of players who made up a club's first nine was constantly changing. In order to get bragging rights citywide, team captains had to take steps to ensure their club had the best players at each position as members of their club, thus being available to play on their first nine. The lofty lure of earning extra money from a share of the gate receipts, of receiving citywide and perhaps even statewide publicity for their team, and the elusive glory that accompanied winning a championship changed the complexion of how a club picked their first nine. This infatuation with team selection left the casual, less proficient ball playing members sitting in the grandstands. Still, even for the perpetual bench jockeys there was an ever-present sense of pride, albeit vicarious, in the success of one's club and one's club mates. But make no mistake, while the club's first nine battled another club, the remaining members still participated in intra-squad games on a regular basis.

For those clubs who wanted to test their mettle and challenge the best teams outside of the city or state, they would have to go on tour. In order to do so these clubs needed to raise additional funds over and above their normal dues. Most members were generally not in the financial position of being able to self-fund such an endeavor from dues alone, so the club needed to raise the additional funds by participating in match games for prize money or through other fundraising activities. This became a weekly or monthly occurrence among local teams, either by direct challenge between two clubs or arranged by one or more of the numerous social, fraternal, or benevolent associations as a feature attraction at their periodic holiday picnics and festivals. Generally, a $20 gold piece would go home with the winning team. In this fashion, the top echelon amateur clubs such as the Southern Base Ball Club, the R.E. Lee Base Ball Club, or the Lone Star Base Ball Club might be able to bring in as much a $240 during the summer months alone if they were consistently successful. If a club was industrious they might be able to raise $1,500 during the course of a year between their share of gate receipts, prize money from fairs and festivals, and ticket sales for the club's annual ball. With sufficient funds in their coffers, clubs were then free to make arrangements for a tour.

1869 Southern Base Ball Club Tour

Fresh off of their defeat of the R.E. Lee Base Ball Club for the Louisiana state championship on June 7, 1869,[2] the Southern Base Ball Club believed they had accumulated sufficient funds, and confidence, to become the first team from New Orleans to take to the road on an extended tour, scheduling games in Memphis, St. Louis, Louisville, and Cincinnati during the month of August. The Southern team was comprised of John Holtzman (left field and team captain), Fred Fay (center field), J.S. Twomey (third base), Nick Larkin (second base), James Hennessey (first base), Phil Donovan (catcher), Gallagher (right field), Joseph C. Buddendorf (short stop), and C.A. O'Keefe (pitcher). Substitute players included M.K. Chandler, George Didilake, John Hanefy, and E.I. Thebault.

Several Southern officers accompanied the team on the tour: Michael McNamara, J.J. Wall, and R.E. Warren. You may recall that McNamara was one of the organizers of the August 1864 championship games between Southern prisoners being held at the Union prison camp at Johnson's Island, Ohio. William F. Tracey of the Lone Stars went along as a friend and advisor to the team, as did C.D. Brandenburg and G.T. Crawford. Thirteen players, the manager, three officers, and three observers made a full complement of twenty people in all representing the Southerns.

For baseball men, the proliferation railroads across the country provided an affordable and far-reaching network for their teams to travel. At roughly two cents per mile for rail versus twenty-five cents per mile for a small room on a steamboat, teams could afford to travel almost anywhere as it was cheaper and faster. The Southerns arrival in Memphis on the Jackson Railroad was delayed, causing the game to be postponed by a day. On Friday, August 13, 1869, the Southerns and the Bluff City Base Ball Club took to the field, with the Southerns victorious by the score of 25 to 19 before "a large concourse of people."[3] The team continued on to St. Louis where they had arranged for a four-game series against four of the best amateur clubs in that city.

On Monday, August 16, the Southerns squared off against the Atlantic Base Ball Club of St. Louis. The New Orleans boys were victorious, besting the Atlantics 10 to 4.[4] They next faced the Empire Base Ball Club of St. Louis winning by the score of 23 to 10. The following day they played the Union Base Ball Club of St. Louis, taking the high scoring contest 35 to 33. Thus far, with four consecutive victories under their belt, the Southerns had every reason to be pleased with their performance on the tour.

The Southerns played their final game in Missouri at Cedar Hill, located just southwest of St. Louis, crossing bats with the Eagle Base Ball Club on August 21 in a closely matched game. A respectably large crowd watched anxiously as the Southerns overcame a two-run deficit after the first three innings and a seven-run eighth inning from the Eagles, finally outlasting the Missouri men, winning 25 to 22.[5] The team received an impromptu invitation to play in Indianapolis by the Marion Base Ball Club of that city, but their travel schedule would not permit the detour. They also lost the services of right fielder M.K. Chandler in the win over the Eagles, and Chandler returned to New Orleans on the steamboat *Lizzie Gill*. Gallagher replaced him in the field.

Making their way to Cincinnati, the Southerns stopped in Louisville, Kentucky, and played the Kentucky Base Ball Club on August 23, winning their sixth game of the tour by the score of 43 to 25.[6] The Southerns touched up the Kentucky pitcher Crooks for at least one run in each inning, most notably tallying seven runs in the second inning, fifteen runs in the eighth inning, and another eight runs in the ninth inning.

Finally arriving in Cincinnati, they met the vaunted Cincinnati Red Stockings. With no realistic expectation of winning, and with a sky threatening rain which may have brought some comfort for those fans sweltering with the temperature reaching ninety-eight degrees in the shade, the Southerns were nonetheless excited to test their pluck against a professional team. They met on Monday, August 25. Southern pitcher C.A. O'Keefe surrendered twenty-one runs to Cincinnati before the Southerns finally scored two runs in the fourth inning. That was, unfortunately, the high point of the game for the boys from New Orleans, whose bats went uncharacteristically cold against the Cincinnati hurler Asa Brainard. In the end, the Red Stockings out-classed and out-scored the New Orleans amateurs 35 to 3.[7] The end result did not diminish their excitement in playing a well-known and respected professional club that few teams, amateur or professional, had beaten.

The following is a summary of the Southern Base Ball Club's twelve-day, seven-city tour.

Date	Location	Opponent	Score
August 13	Memphis, TN	Bluff City Base Ball Club	Southerns 25–19
August 16	St. Louis, MO	Atlantic Base Ball Club	Southerns 10–4
August 17	St. Louis, MO	Empire Base Ball Club	Southerns 23–10
August 18	St. Louis, MO	Union Base Ball Club	Southerns 35–33
August 21	Cedar Hill, MO	Eagle Base Ball Club	Southerns 25–22
August 23	Louisville, KY	Kentucky Base Ball Club	Southerns 43–25
August 25	Cincinnati, OH	Cincinnati Red Stockings	Cincinnati 35–3

Headed back home, the Southerns returned to New Orleans on Saturday, August 28, 1869, to a hero's welcome. Having followed the Southerns every move in the daily reports published in the newspapers, arrangements were made by officials of the Louisiana Base Ball Association to gather their baseball clubs at the Clay statue on Canal Street at seven-thirty that evening. The Southerns arrived in New Orleans just before seven-thirty the evening and were taken by carriage from the Jackson Railroad depot to their clubrooms at Turner's Hall on St. Charles and Girod Street. They were met at eight o'clock by a torch-lit parade, complete with a brass band, which wound its way up St. Charles Avenue from the Clay statue to Turner's Hall. The Southerns' carriages were followed by their fellow players from the Lone Star Base Ball Club, the R.E. Lee Base Ball Club, the Pelican Base Ball Club, the Comet Base Ball Club, the Hope Base Ball Club, and the Hancock Base Ball Club, as well as a sizable throng of enthusiastic onlookers they gathered along the way. Their route ran up St. Charles Avenue to Calliope Street, then to Prytania Street and then down Felicity Street to Magazine Street. They continued up Magazine Street to Race Street, then Annunciation Street and back to Calliope, up to Camp Street as far as Chartres Street, through the French Quarter along St. Louis Street, then a left turn on Royal Street back to the Clay statue.

The route of the Southerns' celebratory parade was not unlike that of a Mardi Gras parade, covering more than ten miles to acknowledge and applaud the accomplishments of the Southern Base Ball Club.

To gauge the financial success of the Southerns' tour is difficult and requires a number of broad reaching assumptions to be applied. For instance, the following assumptions were utilized in preparing this analysis:

Item	Description and Assumption	Estimated Cost
Railroad Tickets	New Orleans to Memphis— 395 miles @ $0.02/mile	$7.90 per person
	Memphis to St. Louis— 285 miles @ $0.02/mile	$5.70 per person

Item	Description and Assumption	Estimated Cost
	St. Louis to Louisville—260 miles @ $0.02/mile	$5.20 per person
	Louisville to Cincinnati—100 miles @ $0.02/mile	$2.00 per person
	Cincinnati to New Orleans—1,040 miles @ $0.02/mile	$20.80 per person
TOTAL		**$41.60 per person**
Hotel Rooms	Memphis—three days @ $1.00/night	$3.00 per person
	St. Louis—six days @ $2.00/night	$12.00 per person
	Louisville—two days @ $1.00/night	$2.00 per person
	Cincinnati—two days @ $2.00/night	$4.00 per person
TOTAL		**$21.00 per person**
Meals	16 breakfasts @ $0.15	$2.40 per person
	32 lunches and dinners @ $0.25	$8.00 per person
TOTAL		**$10.40 per person**
Estimated Travel Expenses per Person		**$73.00 per person**

The table above provides an estimate for the travel expenses the Southerns might have incurred during their 1869 tour, assuming they ate three meals per day from August 12 through August 28, stayed in a modest hotel, and traveled on a second-class train ticket from city to city. No other incidental expenses such as laundry, haircut and shave, and so on were included. The estimated expense per person totals $73.00 per person for the trip.

Once again assuming that the Southerns negotiated a 50 percent split of the gross gate receipts with the host team for each of the seven ballgames they played, and that only the seventeen people directly related to the team—the thirteen players, the manager, and the three club officers—would have their expenses covered by the team, the estimated expenses for the Southerns would have been $1,241 in total. If we can further assume that each game drew 500 people who paid an average ticket price of $0.25 per ticket, then the individual game receipts would have been $125 per game. The Southerns' share would amount to $62.50 per game which, over seven games would amount to $437.50 in total income to the Southerns, resulting in a loss of $803.50 on the tour. If we accept the estimated expenses of $1,241 for the team, their breakeven point would have been just over 1,400 paying fans per game. While not impossible, none of the dispatches received from the local press covering the game cited any specific attendance figures. The description of the crowd was usually given in the most general terms such as "a large concourse of people," or as "another large crowd," but nothing that would lead one to believe that the ballpark was teeming with 1,500 or more fans at any one game. Thus the final assumption in this analysis is that the Southern Base Ball Club itself absorbed the estimated shortfall, paid for out of an unknown amount of financial reserves raised for the tour.

The success of the Southerns' tour is even more striking given the fact that it took place during a brief yet painful recession which came about because of ongoing financial difficulties following the Civil War. In this environment, among other things, businesses were discouraged from building their inventories. As sales dropped, inventories rose and could not be sold to customers quickly enough to turn a profit. This meant that prices would have to fall in order to off-load excess inventory at lower profit margins. To make things worse, several months into the recession there was also a major financial panic. That the Southerns were able to self-finance their tour explains their ability to participate on their tour as long as they did. That fans could afford to shell out discretionary income to make the tour even partially successful financially at the ballpark, even if the team only broke even, is testament to the drawing power of the Southerns outside the city of New Orleans. The baseball community was certainly aware of the best teams in New Orleans just as the city's baseball clubs were aware of the best clubs in Memphis, Louisville, St. Louis, and Cincinnati.

1870 Lone Star Base Ball Club Tour

Having accompanied the Southerns on their successful 1869 tour, William F. Tracey relayed the details of the trip back to his colleagues with the Lone Star management. His report only served to whet the appetite of the Lone Star club to set up a tour of their own. On July 17, 1870, team president Toby Hart announced the first annual tour of the Lone Star Base Ball Club, ambitiously scheduling seventeen games with sixteen teams over a twenty-six-day period.[8] The team and its officers departed at seven o'clock in the morning on Wednesday, July 20, from the Jackson and Great Northern Railroad terminal with their arrival in Memphis scheduled for later that evening.

As the contemporary traveler is painfully aware, travel schedules can often go terribly awry. Now try to imagine travelling by train from city to city with the schedule shown below. In some instances, the distance travelled, and the frequency and availability of train cars was quite manageable. For instance, the Lone Stars' tour began by covering quite a bit of ground, starting with a three hundred and ninety-five-mile haul from New Orleans to Memphis, for which they had allocated ample time to travel and rest. The next leg of the trip was from Memphis to St. Louis and covered another two hundred and eighty-five miles. Here the team once again allotted enough time for travel and also scheduled a layover in St. Louis to break up the strain of travel. And so it was for the Lone Stars throughout the entire twenty-six-day tour.

The following is a summary of the Lone Star Base Ball Club's 1870 tour.

Date	Location	Opponent	Score
July 21	Memphis, TN	Bluff City	Bluff City 54–12
July 24	St. Louis, MO	Union	Lone Stars 35–34
July 25	St. Louis, MO	Empire	Lone Stars 29–16
July 26	Springfield, MO	Liberty	Liberty 33–23
July 27	Bloomington, IL	Bloomington	*Cancelled*
July 29	Chicago, IL	Liberty	Liberty 24–21
July 30	Rockford, IL	Forest City	Forest City 44–8
August 1	Chicago, IL	Athletics	Lone Stars 24–19
August 3	Kankakee, IL	Grove City	Lone Stars 23–7
August 4	Chicago, IL	White Stockings	White Stockings 42–8
August 5	Chicago, IL	Garden City	Lone Stars 21–11
August 6	Chicago, IL	White Stockings	*Cancelled*
August 9	Indianapolis, IN	Indianapolis	Lone Stars 19–4
August 12	Cincinnati, OH	Red Stockings	Red Stockings 49–11
August 13	Louisville, KY	Eagle	*Declined to guarantee expenses*
August 15	Nashville, TN	Nashville	Lone Stars 18–14

The Lone Stars won seven of the thirteen games they actually played on their tour, for a respectable .538 winning percentage.[9] Considering the caliber of their opposition, which ranged from amateur clubs like themselves to professional teams like the Chicago White Stockings and the Cincinnati Red Stockings, one would have to opine that the New Orleanians acquitted themselves admirably and would have been greeted triumphantly with the same exuberance as the Southerns in 1869 upon their return had Toby Hart not wired ahead expressly requesting that no public reception be arranged.[10]

Item	Description and Assumption	Estimated Cost
Railroad Tickets	New Orleans to Memphis— 395 miles @ $0.02/mile	$7.90 per person
	Memphis to St. Louis— 285 miles @ $0.02/mile	$5.70 per person
	St. Louis to Springfield— 216 miles @ $0.02/mile	$4.32 per person
	Springfield to Chicago— 511 miles @ $0.02/mile	$10.22 per person
	Chicago to Indianapolis— 185 miles @ $0.02/mile	$3.70 per person
	Indianapolis to Cincinnati— 112 miles @ $0.02/mile	$2.24 per person
	Cincinnati to Louisville— 100 miles @ $0.02/mile	$2.00 per person
	Louisville to Nashville— 174 miles @ $0.02/mile	$3.48 per person
	Nashville to New Orleans— 533 miles @ $0.02/mile	$10.66 per person
TOTAL		**$50.22 per person**

Item	Description and Assumption	Estimated Cost
Hotel Rooms	Memphis—three days @ $1.00/night	$3.00 per person
	St. Louis—three days @ $2.00/night	$6.00 per person
	Springfield—one day @ $1.00/night	$1.00 per person
	Chicago—six days @ $2.00/night	$12.00 per person
	Indianapolis—	
	one day @ $1.00/night	$1.00 per person
	Cincinnati—	
	three days @ $2.00/night	$6.00 per person
	Nashville—two nights @ $1.00/night	$2.00 per person
TOTAL		$31.00 per person
Meals	26 breakfasts @ $0.15	$3.90 per person
	52 lunches and dinners @ $0.25	$13.00 per person
TOTAL		$16.90 per person
Estimated Travel Expenses per Person		$98.12 per person

Although press accounts indicate nothing exceptional with respect to attendance, and therefore the gate receipts to be shared, it is highly unlikely that the tour was even a modest moneymaker. Toby Hart and the Lone Stars had raised the money to launch the tour in the months prior to the event. Gate receipts might have covered their meal money, but there is no indication that Hart and the Lone Stars made money on the tour.

The Lone Stars' tour was far more extensive and expensive that the Southerns' tour the prior year. For one thing, they played thirteen games in twenty-six days versus the seven games played in sixteen days by the Southerns. Yet the Lone Stars only covered 2,080 miles versus the Southerns who covered 2,511 miles on their tour. All in, the Lone Stars compiled estimated expenses of $98.12 per person for the 1870 tour. Assuming that their group numbered at least fifteen people, their estimated expenses were approximately $1,471.80 in total. However, in terms of being a moneymaker, the Lone Stars were more likely to have covered their expenses than the Southerns.

Assuming that the Lone Stars drew 900 paying fans to each of their thirteen games, and further assuming they reached the same 50 percent revenue split with their host teams, the Lone Stars would have pocketed $112.50 per game which would total $1,462.50 over thirteen games. Compare this to the hurdle of 1,400 paying fans needed for each Southerns game and it is entirely feasible that the Lone Stars could have hit their breakeven mark. They were still fighting the same economic headwinds that the Southerns had the year before, but it is possible that the Lone Stars could have made money on the endeavor.

Lone Stars had no expectations for the tour over and above the joy of pure competition and the enhancement of their club's reputation. The Lone Stars did not have the same winning percentage as the Southerns—.538 versus

.858, respectively. They also played twice as many games as the Southerns and travelled farther afield than the Southerns. By all accounts it could be said that the Lone Stars' tour was a success despite the lack of a homecoming celebration. Not every tour would result in the critical success of the Southerns tour in 1869 or the critical and financial success of the Lone Star's tour in 1870.

1872 R.E. Lee Base Ball Club Tour

Periodically a tour by the Lees in 1872 is mentioned during which the club is reputed to have toured through Texas by stagecoach, playing games against teams from Dallas, Waco, and Austin. Press coverage of such a tour is absent from the New Orleans newspapers as well as those in Texas, although the tour is referenced only in passing.[11]

There is, however, a documented record of a similar swing through the Midwest in 1872 where the R.E. Lee Base Ball Club set out to replicate the success of the Lone Stars.

An engraving depicting the post-game celebration at the June 1871 Base Ball Festival of the Lone Star Base Ball Club at the New Orleans Base Ball Park. The three gentlemen on the left are all wearing their baseball uniforms, and the figure third from the left is wearing a star insignia on his jersey. The festival was held as a fundraiser for the club for their planned 1872 tour (from an unknown 19th century publication).

Five—The Business of Baseball 159

Date	Location	Opponent	Score
07-21	St. Louis (MO)	Empire	7-24 game listed as "return game"
07-24	St. Louis (MO)	Empire	Lees lose 14-7
07-30	Kansas City (MO)	Mutuals	Lees 37-11

There is a record of their game on Wednesday, July 24, against the Empire Base Ball Club of St. Louis which the Lees lost by the score of 14 to 7, and the news reports of this game reference that this game was a "return game," meaning that the two teams had already faced off on Sunday of the prior week. That would make the date of that game July 21, 1872, but there is no record in either the St. Louis or New Orleans papers of that game's score, so we cannot determine if they won or if they lost. It was also reported that the Lees were headed west to face the Mutual Base Ball Club in Kansas City, who they defeated easily 37 to 11. Although not noted as such in the press, the date of this game would have been Tuesday, July 30.[12] For whatever reason, this appears to be the extent of their tour, whether by choice or by circumstances. We know that the team was back in New Orleans with sufficient time to conclude a three-game championship series against the Crescent Base Ball Club on August 25.[13] It is therefore reasonable to assume that the Lees arrived back in New Orleans in early August.

Obviously, the Lees were disappointed in the aborted three-game tour, a poor return on the time and money spent. Is it possible that financial constraints forced the Lees to return to New Orleans by travelling south through Texas by stagecoach through Waco, Dallas, and Austin before winding up in New Orleans? It could be possible, but lack of reporting casts doubt on the premise.

1872 Lone Star Base Ball Club Tour

At nearly the same time as the Lees were travelling through Missouri, the Lone Stars had already embarked upon their second tour of the Midwest. After a pleasant and relaxing trip up the Mississippi on the packet ship *The Potomac*, the Lone Stars arrived in Evansville, Indiana, on July 17, 1872. The length of the first leg of the trip to Evansville made the choice of traveling by riverboat for an overnight trip necessary.

Date	Location	Opponent	Score
07-18	Evansville (IN)	Riverside Base Ball Club	Riverside 20-5
07-20	St. Louis (MO)	Varieties Base Ball Club	Called in 3rd (rain) tied 11-11
07-21	St. Louis (MO)	Empire Base Ball Club	Lone Stars 17-13
07-26	Chicago (IL)	Active Base Ball Club	Lone Stars 17-6

Date	Location	Opponent	Score
07–28	St. Louis (MO)	Empire Base Ball Club	*Unable to schedule*
07–30	Evansville (IN)	Riverside Base Ball Club	*Unable to schedule*

Perhaps it was due to the long confinement on a succession of riverboat trips in covering the 685 miles to Evansville, or perhaps it was a too much of the cold local beer during a stop in Cairo, but it was obvious that the Lone Stars appeared "stiff" during their game on Thursday, July 18, 1872, against the Riverside club. There was a sizeable turnout estimated to be several thousand with standing room only in the outfield. The Lone Star's pitcher Leonard may have also suffered from anxiety as he gave up home runs to second baseman Miller and third baseman Baker. The game was plagued by thirteen errors, eight for the Riverside club and five for the Lone Stars, who dropped the game 20 to 5.[14]

They traveled to St. Louis to meet the Varieties club on Saturday, July 20, 1872, and battled for three innings before the game was called due to heavy rain. Both teams yielded eleven runs to their opponent and it was noted that the Lone Stars "batted heavy but fielded poorly."[15] The Varieties wanted a return game and were trying to negotiate a series while the Lone Stars were still in St. Louis.

The Lone Stars remained in St. Louis the following day and fared better against the Empire Base Ball Club. A crowd of 2,000 turned out for the game which the *St. Louis Globe* credited to the "fine reputation" of the Lone Stars. Behind the bats of Richard M. Thibault (Thebault), Tennison (Tennyson), and Marsh Redon, the Lone Stars still had to withstand a late-game surge of five runs in the final three innings from the Empire club to win the game 17 to 13.[16] It was noted that the Empire club was nervous and played below their abilities.

The Lone Stars landed in Chicago on July 25 and were reasonably rested to meet the Active Base Ball Club the following day. The Lone Stars prevailed 17 to 6, but at a cost. Their crack center fielder, Marsh Redon, was injured following a collision with Scott of the Actives while catcher, Richard Thibault was punished at the plate. These two fellows were pivotal to the Lone Stars offense.

Licking their wounds, the Lone Stars were unable to finalize arrangements for a return game with either the Empire club in St. Louis or the Riverside club in Evansville, and wisely decided to turn south on Tuesday, July 30th and return home on the steamboat *J. Harry Johnson*, stopping at Memphis before landing in New Orleans.

One of the more colorful characters playing for the Lone Stars was Marsh Redon, injured during the July 26 game against the Actives in Chicago. During his baseball career he would also play for both the R.E. Lees and the Remy Clarke Base Ball Club. But Redon was so much more than a ballplayer. Born in France in 1852, Martial J. "Marsh" Redon emigrated with his parents to New Orleans in 1857 and was still in his teens when he became involved in politics. In 1878 he was elected to the Louisiana House of Representatives at the age of twenty-six and was a delegate to the state's Constitutional Convention. For a number of years he was the chief clerk in the Tax and Mortgage office under Mayor J.V. Guillotte. With his political days behind him, Redon became a sporting man, acquiring a reputation as a horse racing and boxing aficionado, and earning a favorable reputation not only in New Orleans, but nationwide and in Europe as well. He was often referred to as "the squarest gambler in the country." Redon operated his popular betting parlor from his poolroom located beneath the St. Charles Hotel. It was here that New Orleans' sporting men learned the results of prizefights, horse races, and other major sporting events courtesy of Redon's telegraph.

Redon was one of the founding members of the Crescent City Jockey Club and also instigated winter racing in New Orleans. He was one of the foremost turfmen in both the United States and Europe, particularly in Great Britain, France, and Germany. Next to his love of horse racing was his expertise in pugilism. Even though Redon was a personal friend of boxing legend John L. Sullivan, the outspoken and unflappable Redon was one of the first professional odds-makers to lay the longest odds against Sullivan in his fight in New Orleans against challenger James Corbett in 1892. As a result, he was inundated with wagers from all over the country and realized a fortune when Corbett won the fight in New Orleans at the Olympic Club during the Fistic Carnival. Redon was involved with or witnessed all of the major bouts in the United States and England, winning and losing several fortunes on their results.

Redon was also an actor and a theatrical magnate, operating both the Olympic Theatre and the West End Theatre in New Orleans, noted for the many Baker and Ferran produced shows that toured the country for a number of years.

All in all, both of the 1872 tours would have to be considered a disappointment for both the Lees and the Lone Stars. True, the Lone Stars did win two of the three games they played, but for all of their effort they played only three complete games over fifteen days,[17] so it would have to be characterized as a waste of time and, more importantly, financial resources for both teams. Chief among the factors contributing to the discouraging tour would include the Panic of 1873 and the Long Depression which caused deflation and wage cuts, leading to very disruptive labor turmoil, and culminating in the great railroad strike in 1877. To help stabilize the country's fiscal health, the United States returned to the gold standard in 1879. In all, the Long Depression was true to its name, lasting twenty-three years from 1873 through 1896.

Redon was also involved in a nasty and divisive baseball rivalry involving

Toby Hart and Frank Waters. In 1885 the senior amateur clubs were split over which clubs had the right of first refusal when scheduling games at either the New Orleans Base Ball Park or Sportsman's Park. On one side was the J.C. Bach Base Ball Club and the Petrie Base Ball Club at Sportsman's Park, and on the other was the R.E. Lee Base Ball Club and the Waters Base Ball Club at the New Orleans Base Ball Park. After weeks of bitter bickering, Frank Waters brought forth the idea that the four teams should form a league, acquire the strongest players they could—as long as they weren't from one of the other three teams—and play each other at alternate parks. The winning team was to receive 50 of the gate, the losing team to receive 25 percent of the gate with the remaining 25 percent to be held in reserve to go to the winner of the league championship. With all of the teams and baseball park associations now in agreement, the three men shook hands and the rivalry was settled, to the delight of the thousands of fans who were torn between wanting to see different teams at the two parks.

The final ten years of Redon's life sadly saw his fortunes reverse and slowly slip through his fingers. He died at his home in New Orleans on October 5, 1908, aged 56 years old.[18]

1883 Brennan Base Ball Club Tour

Tom Brennan had been a fixture on the New Orleans baseball landscape since the early 1870s, so when he sponsored his own baseball club in 1879, the Thomas Brennan Base Ball Club, it came as no surprise to anyone used to hanging around the ballpark.

In the summer of 1883, leaving on the Louisville and Nashville Railroad, the Brennans embarked upon an ambitious eighteen-day tour through the Southeast beginning in Montgomery on Wednesday, August 1, 1883.

Date	*Location*	*Opponent*	*Score*
08–01	Montgomery (AL)	Montgomery	Brennans 15–6
08–02	Selma (AL)	Selma	Brennans 12–0
08–03	Meridian (MS)	Meridian	Brennans 14–1
08–04	Pensacola (FL)	Our Boys Base Ball Club	Brennans 19–6
08–07	Pensacola (FL)	Pensacola Mallorys	Pensacola 1–0
08–08	Augusta (GA)	Augusta Browns	Brennans 10–0
08–09	Savannah (GA)	Savannah Dixies	*Assumed victory by the Brennans*
08–10	Savannah (GA)	Savannah Dixies	*Assumed victory by the Brennans*
08–11	Savannah (GA)	Savannah Dixies	*Assumed victory by the Brennans*
08–13	Savannah (GA)	Savannah Dixies	Brennans 10–0

Date	Location	Opponent	Score
08-14	Savannah (GA)	Savannah Forest Citys	Brennans 7-1
08-15	Savannah (GA)	Picked Nine	Brennans 15-3
08-16	Jacksonville (FL)	Florida Mallorys	Brennans 9-2
08-17	Jacksonville (FL)	Florida Mallorys	Brennans 3-0 (Called in 7th inning for rain)
08-18	Savannah (GA)	Savannah Oglethorpes	Brennans 5-1

The Brennan squad consisted of some of the best ballplayers in the region: James J. Woulffe (Woulfe) (captain and centerfielder), William A. Landry (pitcher), Adam Lorsch (right fielder and pitcher), Mike Lambeau (first base), Nick Brennan (second base and catcher), George Mundinger (catcher and second base), William J. Butler (left fielder), Jonathan J. Irvin (shortstop), and Jonathan T. Farrell (third base). Two players from the Lone Star Base Ball Club, William McCormick and C.P. Drohler, went along as substitutes.

Four of the Brennan's starting nine would go on to play baseball in the major leagues. Jimmy Woulfe was with the Cincinnati Red Stockings and the Pittsburgh Alleghenys in 1884; George Mundinger, John Peltz, and Bill Butler were with the Indianapolis Hoosiers in 1884; Bill Smith was with the Detroit Wolverines in 1886; and John Farrell played with the Washington Senators and the St. Louis Cardinals between 1901 and 1905.

Manager Tom Brennan's boys earned their pay, playing fifteen games in eighteen days and covering over 3,100 miles on the rails between seven cities. Games originally scheduled for Gainesville, Florida, Columbus, Georgia, and Atlanta, Georgia, were cancelled and replaced on the tour with games in Pensacola, Florida. There are three games absent from the tour summary, all of which were set to be played in Savannah, but for which there are no newspaper accounts. However, it is known that the Brennans record on the tour was fourteen wins and one loss, so the Brennans must have swept those three games, doing so by a combined score of 31 to 6. The Brennans most assuredly had packed their hitting clothes for the tour as they scored 150 runs to their opponents 27 runs, which is how we can extrapolate the combined score for the three missing games.[19]

The Brennans 1883 tour was by all accounts both a critical and financial success. Although by the time of their return to New Orleans they were four games behind in their Louisiana Amateur Base Ball Association schedule, putting them in third place behind the Lone Stars and the Remy Clarkes. Their time on tour caused them to miss four games, but the league granted the Brennans a waiver so they would not have to forfeit those games.

Even by the time the Brennans embarked upon their 1883 tour, baseball as a money-making venture was still a dicey proposition on an everyday basis.

In a challenge match between two clubs, the host team or the challenger had to arrange for the ballpark and select a suitable stakeholder to hold the prize money, typically a set amount ranging from ten dollars to twenty dollars for a three-day series. If the clubs were well known to the public, they might even sell tickets to the event and the host team would be in charge of selling tickets and collecting gate receipts. After paying for the ballpark rental, the net receipts were then split between the two clubs according to a prearranged formula. In most cases the gate receipts would be evenly split unless otherwise stipulated and agreed to by both clubs in advance. On a good day, a match between two rival clubs might draw as many as 1,000 fans who would shell out ten-cents for a single ticket, thereby providing $100 to be split between at least eighteen men (a minimum of nine players to a side) but most certainly more. After deducting the ballpark rental, usually between $10 and $20 per game, and using the minimum numbers of shares, $93.35 to $96.70 would provide each man with between $5.20 to $5.35 for their trouble. This is a very optimistic example. More often than not, players would see anywhere between $1 to $2 for a game, still more than the average American worker, but not enough to elevate a baseball player securely into the middle-class.

By comparison, a well-known team might command a twenty-five-cent ticket price. Assuming they draw at least 1,000 fans the gross gate would reach $250 to be split in similar fashion, resulting in $12.78 to $13.33 per man. This is a vastly different outcome for the players and teams.

The more successful amateur clubs that had accumulated sufficient excess funds from their endeavors might take the next step of setting up a home field—leasing the grounds, clearing, leveling, and building the field, constructing the bleachers and a fence to surround the facility. This was rare. More often than not the required teams to join together to form a ballpark association or to pool their resources, which inevitably led to the informal development of leagues of six to eight teams whose combined funds might prove adequate to the task. Each team would be assigned a specific day and time to practice during the week and games were played during the weekend. Team owners could supplement their ticket sales by selling concessions and premium seating. They could also lease the ballpark to other teams or leagues at prices ranging from $5 to $10 per game based on the day and time requested and, of course, demand.

New Orleans would soon discover that professional baseball teams such as the New York Mutuals or the Cincinnati Red Stockings were able to engage in their successful barnstorming tours across the country because the high caliber of play they offered would attract large numbers of paying fans to the ballpark. The higher turnout, and therefore the higher net pay, was a direct result of these teams having professional players on their rosters. These salaried players earned between $400 and $1,200 per year, meaning that they would not necessarily need to have a traditional daytime job to pay the bills. They could, therefore, devote their full time and energy to practicing and playing baseball. With this improved quality of play came larger paying crowds. The gamble for the local clubs was that their team might not be financially solid and therefore would be less competitive. To combat that drawback, teams often "borrowed" the best players from local amateur teams to play in a limited league series.

Post-Bellum New Orleans found an undeterred cadre of returning military veterans who, undeterred by the South's loss to the Union, longed for a return to the past, a futile exercise in nostalgia designed to assuage the sting of their defeat. New Orleans was one of the largest cities in the United States and was the largest and wealthiest city in the Confederacy. Its importance as the gateway to the Mississippi River should have merited more than the cursory military defense mounted by the Confederacy. Their concentration on protecting the front door to the Confederacy through Virginia proved one-sided, leaving the back door wide open for the Union to walk through virtually untouched, and which in the end proved to be wholly inadequate. Because of New Orleans' embarrassing fall to Union forces so early in the war, many of the returning soldiers were greeted by a populace who did not share their recidivist attitude and who no longer felt the same sting of defeat. The city they came back to was far more familiar with and therefore accepting of Federal control. With respect to baseball, this only fueled their animosity towards professionalism, which many saw as an extension of Northern influence. Like many, they longed for the good old days, unable to reconcile their Ante-Bellum and Post-Bellum lives in New Orleans. Thus organized baseball languished following the war until emotions could be soothed sufficiently for there to be a return to normalcy. Not an easy task with all they had to deal with.

The city's prominent businessmen who rode out the war in New Orleans could see the city's once preeminent position in the country slowly slipping away. Disillusioned veterans simply wanted things to return to the way they were before the war. It was not to be. Alternative methods of transportation developed and expanded during the Civil War, particularly the railroads, slowly eroded the city's importance as a commercial center. In 1840 New Orleans was the third largest city in the United States, behind only New York and Baltimore. By the outbreak of the Civil War the city had slipped into sixth place, having been surpassed by Philadelphia, Brooklyn, and Boston. By 1870, New Orleans was clinging to ninth place, just ahead of San Francisco.[20] Tons of cotton and timber were still being shipped out of New Orleans, but more frequently by rail, not on the river. As a result, by the late 19th century freight and passenger traffic, including New Orleans baseball teams, would no longer travel by riverboat, opting instead for the much faster and less expensive rail passage.

Those who paid attention to the game were well aware that professional players were already involved in every aspect of baseball. The death knell for amateur baseball was the slow decline of the club/challenge system in favor of the league system. This was an inevitable and natural progression in New Orleans and the rest of the country and amateur baseball died a natural death. Devoted amateurs emphatically rejected the path to professionalism and continued to play baseball purely for the joy of playing the game. They further rejected those things they felt distracted players and fans from the purity of the game: ungentlemanly conduct and foul language on the field and, most of all, the scourge of gambling. For once this divide did not fall along class lines, with those staunchly remaining amateurs and those who quickly embraced the potential windfall of professionalism nearly equally divided. This is not to say that the upper-class and upper-middle-class did not appreciate the quality of play offered by professional players, but they did so as sometimes spectators, sometimes as participants. The response of New Orleans fans to watching professional teams like the Cincinnati Red Stockings and the New York Mutuals was proof of their acceptance of professional baseball. And there is some evidence that the city's monied citizens sponsored and invested in baseball clubs and related ventures, but there was more at stake than winning and losing. The presence of gamblers along with pickpockets, thieves, and louts was a constant source of concern and disorder. Gambling threatened the stability and integrity of the game itself and, even more seriously, a loss of control.

New Orleans offered professional gamblers an attractive alternative to life on the Mississippi River or on the stagecoach trail from town to town out west, allowing them to operate openly in the city. Small gambling houses eventually came out of the shadows to offer opulent, well-appointed facilities that provided dozens of ways for someone to lose their money. Faro, poker, blackjack, and roulette were among the most popular table games. It was all very elegant, with croupiers and dealers in evening dress, skillfully separating most visitors from their bankroll during the course of the evening.

But these were not the types of gamblers that threatened baseball. It was a seedy collection of morally corrupt sharps and guttersnipes who flocked to New Orleans from all parts of the country to prey on the average citizen. The ballpark was just another location, but it was no place for gamblers to try to use card tricks and skimming to cheat someone. Rather, it might be something as basic as wagering on balls and strikes, the number of runs scored, or some seemingly basic element of the game where they could use their knowledge of the players and teams to take advantage of the inexperienced and unknowledgeable spectator. Knowing whether the pitcher was an arsonist who would fall prey to a good hitter or whether he was a flamethrower who would leave the hitter taking devastating swipes through the empty air was

Five—The Business of Baseball

information the gambler could use to shift the odds in his favor. Dozens of individual gamblers would haunt the bleachers to pick out their marks, ply them with liquor from a hip flask, and systematically work their worst on their unsuspecting victims. Eventually the fans became more game savvy, so the gamblers needed to develop more elaborate and clandestine methods of gaining their advantage. This is where the gamblers colluded with one or more ball players to affect the outcome of the game.

Although paid more than the average worker, for enough money baseball players, like almost anyone, could be tempted to do something that would steer the advantage the gambler's way. It was only human nature. Particularly if they thought no one would notice what they were doing. A pitcher might walk a batter at an inopportune time during the game. Just a bad break. A usually reliable flycatcher might tank a fly ball to allow a base runner to advance or score. Just another bad break lost in the sun. These were generally small, seemingly unrelated actions that might appear nothing more than bad luck. But it was just the advantage the gamblers needed. The influence of these predators threatened the integrity of baseball.

After gambling, one of the most distasteful aspects of professionalism was "revolving," players who jumped from one team to another for higher wages. While players signed a contract to play for a team for an agreed upon salary, there was little to stop a player from signing with a different team for a higher salary. His only downside was the bridges he burned with his former team. With the increase in the number of professional teams came the opportunity for a manager to poach players from another team or in an effort to bolster his team so that they would not only win, but that they would fill the bleachers at the same time because it was the competitive nature of the game itself that filled the grandstands and engendered team loyalty. The natural extension of this was the development of rivalries—first intra-city and then between neighboring cities and states. Inevitably, matches were arranged for city and state championships. Of course, the freewheeling nature of baseball at the time was that you might have multiple teams from multiple cities all claiming a state championship. None of these were necessarily sanctioned or recognized, and different teams might boast rival claims until a match between them could be arranged to settle the matter. These rivalries provided the fans with the chance to witness some top-notch play, and for team owners to finally see a profit.

For players, the prospect of playing for a meager share of the gate receipts only made the influence of gamblers more probable. Newspapers hinted that games might have been fixed, and it was not uncommon for teams to split the first two games of a three game championship series in order to profit from the large crowd drawn to the third and deciding game. For players who relied on receiving a cut of their team's percentage of the gate receipts, this occurred more often than anyone would like to believe. A cut of the gate receipts from three games was always better than the gate receipts from only two games. The third game might even draw more fans to the ballpark to see how the series ended. While most fans would have preferred their team to win the first two games of a series outright, one has to believe that they also enjoyed the added excitement of a third and final game.

There were even unscrupulous players who when contacted by telegraph would agree to sign a contract with a team, take the money sent to them for a train ticket before a physical contract could actually be signed and then turn around and sign with another team somewhere else. These unseemly tactics only served to drain the reserves of the owners and their clubs. Eventually baseball clubs, like other businesses, sold stock in their organization in order to raise the funds necessary to field a professional team and gain some measure of financial security with additional working capital.

Unable to pull matters together in time to become one of the eight teams in the newly formed Southern League in 1885, businessman Toby Hart and others organized the Gulf League which consisted of only four teams—two from New Orleans and two from Mobile. Lurking on the horizon was the ever-present possibility that either city could be adversely impacted by one of the periodic recessions to plague the economy during the latter part of the 19th century. It was also likely that an actual plague such as yellow fever could ruin a team's ability to play when one or more cities were shuttered by such a quarantine. A larger city like New Orleans was less likely to collapse under financial pressure, but a smaller city like Mobile might not have sufficient capital to withstand a recession. During a recession, individuals saw their disposable income shrink, leaving less money for leisure time pursuits such as baseball. At the same time as he was forming the Gulf League, Hart spearheaded a group to form the Crescent City League with eight teams, chiefly high caliber amateur clubs, but designed so as it was not likely to compete with the Gulf League. Hart had seen first-hand how Charles Genslinger and the New Orleans Amateur League had worked against itself, leading to its collapse in 1884. Hart's aim was to have the teams of the Crescent City League play when the teams of the Gulf League were off or on the road.

After years of deliberations, the Southern League was finally organized on February 11, 1885, in Atlanta with an initial slate of eight teams: the Atlanta Atlantas, the Augusta Browns, the Nashville Americans, the Memphis Browns, the Columbus Stars, the Chattanooga Lookouts, and teams from Birmingham and Macon. The league schedule totaled a hefty one hundred games, a feat never before attempted by a minor league where eighty-five games schedules were the norm. And it nearly worked, but there three teams that dropped out with only two weeks remaining in the season. Although three teams failed, five teams succeeded, and Atlanta won a hard-fought battle with Augusta to win the inaugural Southern League pennant.

Final Results of the 1885 Southern League Season

Team	Won	Lost	Pct	GB
Atlanta Atlantas	66	32	.673	
Augusta Browns	68	36	.654	-1
Nashville Americans	62	39	.614	-5.5
Macon	55	47	.539	-13
Memphis Browns	38	54	.413	-25
Columbus Stars	49	47	.510	NA
Chattanooga Lookouts	33	61	.351	NA
Birmingham	18	76	.191	NA

The 1886 season saw Birmingham and Columbus decline the invitation to rejoin the Southern League. Birmingham played a full ninety-four games in 1885 although with little success, winning only eighteen games. Columbus played ninety-six games with slightly better results, but preferred a less rigorous travel schedule. Toby Hart once again received assurances from the league that New Orleans' application for membership would be approved upon receipt of their $2,000 fee, but Hart once again came up short. He could personally afford to pay the $2,000 fee, but he lacked the necessary working capital needed for payroll and other operating expenses. Hart found himself spread too thin as he was supporting his main facility, the New Orleans Bae Ball Park, as well as the Gulf League and the Crescent City League. For the second straight year New Orleans came up lemons.

Savannah and Charleston stepped in to replace Birmingham and Columbus for the 1886 season. The league eased the schedule from one hundred games back to eighty-five games in hopes of having all eight teams complete their schedule. Unfortunately, Augusta and Chattanooga both withdrew in July. Far from a hollow victory, the league had six of its eight teams, 75 percent of the league, complete their schedule. Atlanta repeated as league champion with a record of 64 wins and 28 losses (.696), five games ahead of Savannah.

Final Results of the 1886 Southern League Season

Team	Won	Lost	Pct	GB
Atlanta Atlantas	64	28	.696	
Savannah	59	35	.641	-5
Nashville Americans	46	43	.571	-16.5
Memphis Grays	43	46	.483	-19.5
Charleston Seagulls	44	49	.473	-20.5
Macon	32	59	.352	-31.5
Augusta Browns	21	31	.404	NA
Chattanooga Lookouts	20	40	.333	NA

In 1887, two-time champion Atlanta did not return to the Southern League, and Augusta, Macon, and Chattanooga decided to play elsewhere. New Orleans was finally able to snag one of the vacancies, Mobile secured another, and Birmingham returned to the league, leaving the league with only seven teams at Opening Day. Hart, along with Tom Brennan and Conrad Leithman, secured the signed contracts from the Southern League that granted New Orleans a professional baseball franchise.[21] The new stock company was called the Southern League Base Ball Club, which was soon renamed the New Orleans Base Ball Company. The board was made up of several familiar names: Toby Hart, Thomas Brennan, John T. Fitzgerald, Charles H. Genslinger, and D.A. Mayer. Each of these gentlemen were involved with Hart in one or more of Harts' prior or current baseball endeavors. Hart was elected president of the club and Maurice Kauffman named club secretary.[22]

The team would be called the New Orleans Pelicans. The former amateur team, the Pelican Base Ball Club, established in 1859, was currently inactive, allowing Hart to scoop up the name without opposition. A mad scramble to sign players for the new franchise began even before Hart and company had transmitted the required $2,000 deposit with the Southern League. In the first week of January 1887, New Orleans signed four players" Jacob Wells, W.B. Fuller, Al Tebeau (Thibau), and Abner Powell.[23] By the middle of January the club had signed a total of thirteen players.[24] Tom Brennan was tapped to be the team's first manager and Abner Powell was named team captain.

Beginning on Opening Day, the Pelicans were recognized as a force to be reckoned with. Only days after their historic Opening Day, Abner Powell and the Pelicans made history once again with the introduction of their first Ladies' Day on Thursday, April 28, 1887, in a game against the Charleston Seagulls at Sportsman's Park.

> It was the first regular ladies' day in New Orleans and was certainly a success, several hundred ladies attending. They came in carriages, in buggies, in street cars and on trains, charming in their spring attire, and made the cozy grand stand a bower of beauty. Of course, in their ignorance of the American game, they amused their escorts by their questions. One of them said Umpire Sack couldn't play ball at all because he let all of the balls go by him, jumping out of the way. When Powell hit a double, one of them said she was glad he had made two runs—would it had been so. After an inning or two, however, they entered fully into the spirit of the contest and were as staunch partisans of the home team as anybody on the grounds. They forgot themselves and yelled right out when the excitement was intense, applauded every good play, and thought the Charlestons were awful mean to beat New Orleans. They were the life of the grand stand.
>
> It was a great game to see. It was the quickest, prettiest, and most exciting game of the year. Charleston's "rugged little team" braced up and played great ball and the locals were not a bit behind. Both pitchers did great work. Drouby was hit the hardest, but the hits were not bunched.

He has speed and curves and can put the ball over the plate when necessary. Powell is not his equal in the matters of swiftness and curving but has considerable more strategy and worked the big batters in fine style. Both pitchers were on their mettle and both received magnificent support.

Neither catcher has a passed ball, but Wells carried off the honors because of his superior guard of the bases. He and Powell watched the bases as cats do their prey. Glenn, who is considered Charleston's greatest base runner, was caught twice. In the first inning he stole second. Powell faced the batter, but when Glenn got a little way off, Wells gave the pitcher a sign, the latter whirled around and let the ball go and Glenn was caught dead to rights. The fielding on both sides was well-nigh perfect. The outfield work on both sides was superb. Murphy was again around when wanted, but Glenn was the king pin of the fly catchers. He not only got everything in reach, but when a ball did go safe he picked up the ball and got it into the diamond with lightning speed. Had it not been for this sort of work, New Orleans would certainly have got in a run or two.

New Orleans worked hard for a run. In the first inning Powell opened up with a two-bagger to left field. Brennan's sacrifice advanced him to third, where he was left on Cartwright's fly to third, and Geiss' hit to second, McLaughlin throwing him out at first. In the next inning Pujol hit through Corcoran. Fuller also hit to Cochran and the latter threw over second and Pujol reached third, Fuller getting second. Pujol tried to come home on the play and Carl threw him out at the plate. Murphy was thrown out by Cochran, Fuller getting third, where he stepped out on Harry Fuller's fly to Glenn. In the fourth Pujol got a rattling double to left, but McLaughlin made a pretty catch of a fly from Shorty Fuller's bat, going to center field and left the runner on second. Murphy led off the fifth with another double. It was a long hit, just inside the foul line in left field, and might have let the runner home had Glenn had not fielded the ball so quickly. Harry Fuller and Wells popped up easy flies and Powell was thrown out at first, leaving the slugger on second. In the sixth, with two men out, Geiss hit safe and Pujol followed with another single, Geiss going to third on Glenn's throw into short, Pujol stealing in to second in the meantime. Shorty Fuller then flew out to right field, leaving both on bases. In the eighth, with two men out, Cartwright got a base on balls, the only one of the game, and stole second. The ball thrown by Grady struck Cartwright and bounded away, the big first baseman getting third. Geiss then hit a foul fly and Cochran made a fine catch, again retiring the side with a man in sight of home.

The ninth inning and the local's best chance showed them weakest at the bat, Pujol and Murphy striking out, through over-anxiety to hit, and Shorty Fuller getting the ball no further than Williams.

Charleston did not even fare as well as New Orleans for six innings. Glenn got as far as second on a single and a steal and was thrown out by Powell. Not another man got to second until the seventh inning and then the visitors came in and won the game. Powell was first to bat and hit safe to center. Williams was given a life by Wells letting a foul fly go and hit to third. Either Pujol's throw to second was a little wild, or Geiss made a failure of a one-handed grand stand catch, but anyhow both runners were safe, Powell going to third and Williams to second as the ball rolled into the outfield. Carl hit to the pitcher and was thrown out at first. Cartwright put the ball into home in a hurry and Powell slid in. Suck decided the run was good and it was a close decision. It was Charleston's only run and it won the game. Drouby hit to short and was thrown out at first, and Williams tried to steal in. This time Wells got the ball in plenty of time, and the runner and the side were out. Charleston did not see second in the eighth, but did not mind that, as New Orleans got no further than third, and the game was won.

Charleston versus New Orleans
April 28, 1887[25]

Innings	1	2	3	4	5	6	7	8	9	Total
Charleston	0	0	0	0	0	0	1	0	0	1
New Orleans	0	0	0	0	0	0	0	0	0	0

This was also the first Ladies' Day in the history of minor league baseball.

It was a bright and festive Thursday afternoon at the ballpark. The Pelicans were feeling confident in facing the Charleston boys again, having pounded out a 7 to 1 victory the prior day. The day had been set aside as Ladies' Day and about three hundred of the 6,500 in attendance were women. The Newsboys' Band provided a delightful musical background to the entire scene. However, this was to be the high point of the afternoon for the Pelicans.

Despite being fairly evenly matched with Charleston, the Pelican batters could not manage more than six hits off of Druby (Drouby). Abner Powell was on the mound for the Pelicans and he held Charleston scoreless for six innings. Poor fielding and an untimely error proved to be the Pelican's undoing in the seventh inning as the Seagulls' first baseman James Powell scored the game's only run. With the final out in the ninth inning, a collective groan from thousands of throats both male and female was audible outside the ballpark. It only took eighty-five minutes for the Seagulls to apply a thick coat of kalsomine on the Pelicans. Although the ladies' day event was a success, the series against the Seagulls would set the stage for a heated rivalry during the season.

To be accurate, this was not the first time women were invited to attend a baseball game. In 1867 the New York Knickerbockers began designating the last Thursday of the month for members to bring an invited female guest to the games. Both Cincinnati and Philadelphia held a Ladies' Day in 1876. Nor was this the first time such an event was advertised. In 1883 no fewer than four teams—New York, Philadelphia, Baltimore, and St. Louis—sponsored a Ladies' Day event. With the exception of the New York Knickerbockers, which was a members-only function, all of the other claimants were for a single game event, or at best an infrequent or periodic event. It was Abner Powell who had the idea to make Ladies' Day a regularly recurring event as part of the standard season schedule. His thought was not only to make the game more familiar to the wives whose husbands regularly attended Pelican games, but at the same time he hoped the presence of ladies in the grandstand would tone down the language from the more tempestuous fans, hold down the drinking from the more intemperate fans, and discourage gambling from the more hapless fans.

It should be mentioned that while the grandstand was a model of propriety. Many of the ladies in the bleachers that afternoon were "working girls" who were comfortable with the language, the drinking, and the gambling. Nonetheless, Powell convinced Toby Hart and his investors to continue holding Ladies' Day games on a regular basis.

The Pelicans were in pennant contention from the outset and the other teams were determined to bring New Orleans down a peg. But in mid–May, after Memphis scored 119 runs in four games against Mobile, and after only twenty-six games, Mobile felt compelled to retire from the league. They were followed by Savannah on May 31. Nashville lasted until August 2, but their exit left only four teams to carry on. As the season was coming to an end, New Orleans was still in first place when they once again faced off against Charleston Seagulls on the road in South Carolina on Thursday, September 29, 1887.

The Pelicans were losing badly to the Seagulls by the score of 15 to 3 when team captain Abner Powell took exception to a call by an umpire by the name of Simonin. Apparently, it was just one of many calls during the game that he believed to be biased towards Charleston. Many of the Pelican players believed that Simonin's stance behind the catcher at home plate made it impossible to consistently and precisely call balls and strikes accurately. Having had enough, Powell began to remove his team from the field when Pelicans manager Tom Brennan came rushing onto the field to advise Powell to keep his team on the field and to continue playing. It was at this point that Charleston player-manager, James Powell, threatened to have Brennan ejected from the ballpark if he didn't immediately leave the field. As the Pelicans' manager, Brennan had every right to be on the field and referred Powell to Section 49 of the Southern League constitution. There was such a ballyhoo that the Pelicans left the field, and the game was called in Charleston's favor.

Depending on whose version of events one chooses to believe, later that evening Abner Powell encountered the umpire Simonin in the bar or restaurant of the Waverly House Hotel. Words were exchanged. Powell expressed his low opinion of Simonin's qualifications as an umpire and serious questions were apparently raised concerning the marital status of Simonin's parents at the time of his birth. According to Powell, Simonin was already in a fine pucker when he somehow got the bulge on him and applied a hearty drubbing to the irate and prostrate Powell, including kicking him when he was down. Several of the Charleston club's fans and players, some brandishing knives, prevented any of the Pelican players from intervening on Powell's behalf.

According to Simonin, he felt that since he could not fine Powell because they were not on the ballfield, he simply had no other alternative other than to engage Powell, which he claims he did on his own without anyone else's involvement, whereupon he throttled Powell and left the hotel.

Regardless of the preliminaries, Powell was, in fact, assaulted by Simonin and he promptly telegraphed Toby Hart to inform him that Charleston's blatant, home-cooking umpire had repeatedly treated the Pelicans badly and had sought him out and assaulted him at his hotel. His refusal to call men out when put out, to allow men on base on foul balls, and discriminating against the New Orleans pitchers who felt bulldozed and threatened was simply shameful. That Simonin and others followed Powell to his hotel and had beaten him physically following the game, and that the team was not safe playing in Charleston was more than a passing disagreement with the umpire. Hart then promptly telegraphed Charleston president Thomas Young to say that he would remove the team from Charleston if his club could not be protected on the field, and that even his friends in Charleston had advised him to remove the team. Despite Young's assurances, Powell refused to play the Friday game and insisted on returning to New Orleans with his players. When the players informed Brennan that they too felt threatened, he acquiesced, and Hart agreed that the team should return to New Orleans.

The headline in the Saturday morning Charleston newspaper read "Moonlight Excursion of the Great Crescent City Menagerie," and the accompanying story was conveniently already typeset since the decision to return to New Orleans had only been finalized at four o'clock in the morning on Saturday. The Pelicans reported the incident to the league office, renewing their objection to allowing teams to hire their own umpires instead of arranging for a league-paid umpire, which practice prevented impartial oversight. Simonin was hired by Charleston to umpire home games and his string of biased calls during this and other games put the outcome of the game in question.

At the league meetings in Nashville on November 1, 1887, there was a rumor circulating that New Orleans would be forced to forfeit the Friday game with Charleston and that they would also be forced to vacate three wins against the Mobile Swamp Angels. If this scenario went through, New Orleans would no longer be in first place and the pennant would be awarded to the Charleston Seagulls. Charleston's gambit was transparent to everyone and, in the end, the league only required New Orleans to pay Charleston the standard $500 for forfeiting the Friday game and set aside any argument regarding vacating the three New Orleans victories over Mobile. As a result, New Orleans ended the 1887 season with a record of 74 wins against 40 losses (.649), four and one-half games ahead of Charleston.[26]

There was a certain degree of animosity directed toward Toby Hart and the New Orleans franchise by many of the other teams in the Southern League. Some resented that New Orleans was not only the biggest toad in the puddle but was also bigger and richer than the other cities. This made it much easier for New Orleans to raise capital, which in turn allowed them to withstand the financial stress of recessions and depressions. While there is no verifiable means of determining the financial stability of any of these cities, there is no doubt as to the size of these cities.[27]

City	1880 Population	City	1890 Population
New Orleans	216,090	New Orleans	242,039
Charleston	49,984	Nashville	76,168
Nashville	43,350	Atlanta	65,533
Atlanta	37,409	Memphis	64,495
Memphis	33,592	Charleston	54,955
Savannah	30,709	Savannah	43,189
Mobile	29,132	Mobile	31,076
Birmingham	3,086	Birmingham	26,178

There were those teams, namely Birmingham, Chattanooga, Nashville, that were genuinely grateful that the New Orleans Pelicans freely offered financial assistance to their teams. For instance, Toby Hart routinely had New Orleans pay the travel expenses of a struggling team so that the team could afford to travel to play another team. But there were other teams, being Mobile and Savannah, that resented that New Orleans appeared to turn a blind eye to their teams by refusing to help bail them out and forcing them to collapse. There were rumblings that New Orleans was stacking their roster with ringers designed to steamroll the rest of the league, ignoring the fact that New Orleans had the lowest overhead of any team in the league. There were also rumors that Toby Hart and his baseball cohort wanted to snap up the failing franchises for pennies on the dollar. Because of its proximity to New Orleans, there were persistent rumors that Hart wanted to buy the Mobile club, and in the years to come his preferential treatment of Mobile gave legs to this line of thinking. This sort of animosity and hostility usually resulted in the formation of a bitter rivalry based on competitive fire. This current attitude can best be attributed to a David versus Goliath mentality, the struggles of smaller cities trying to compete with the much larger New Orleans. However, absent from the analysis of the vocal critics was the deficit that New Orleans accrued following the 1887 season, estimated in the league financial reports to be ($1,500), which may well have been higher. Hart and New Orleans were unfairly vilified by those owners who did not see the full picture and were only angry that they did not receive any assistance from Hart.

There were three teams that were unable to complete their 1887 schedules. Mobile, with a disappointing 5–21 start, went toes up after only thirty days. Two weeks later, on May 31, Savannah determined that they could not overcome their 9–26 record and folded as well. The Nashville Blues held on until August 2, but finally threw in the towel when their record stood at 32–92. Birmingham held out longer than most, finally going out with only four games remaining on the schedule, having played eighty-one of their eighty-five games.

Final Results of the 1887 Southern League Season

Team	Won	Lost	Pct	GB
New Orleans Pelicans	*74*	*40*	*.640*	
Charleston Seagulls	66	41	.617	-4.5
Memphis Browns	65	46	.386	-7.5
Nashville Blues	32	32	.500	NA
Savannah	9	26	.257	NA
Birmingham Ironmakers	18	63	.222	NA
Mobile Swamp Angels	5	21	.192	NA

Feeling very confident of his team's initial success in winning the Southern League pennant in their first season, Abner Powell agreed to an exhibition series with the New York Giants during the winter. New Orleans not only attracted major league teams for spring training, but the city was also a popular destination for professional barnstorming teams during the off-season. This type of freelance tour was an unsanctioned event that allowed players to earn money during the off-season. It kept the team from lying idle and growing fat and lazy. New Orleans typically enjoyed a mild winter, especially when compared to the Midwest and Northeast. Powell and his Pelicans were looking forward to meeting the New York Giants in late October of 1887. For Powell it was also a way to keep his men in fighting trim by going up against a much better professional team. At the same time he could showcase his players with the hope that he might be able to sell one or more of his players to a major league team such as the New York Giants.

John Montgomery Ward, the popular pitcher, shortstop, and second baseman for the New York Giants, was celebrating his marriage to Helen Dauvray, one of the most popular actresses of the day, by touring the South playing exhibition games with a professional team made up primarily of New York players, but which also included players from the Boston Beaneaters and the Indianapolis Hoosiers. Many of the other players brought their wives on the tour.

The team arrived in New Orleans on Saturday, October 29, 1887, and was greeted at the St. Charles Hotel with a brief reception in their honor. Ward's new bride did not comment in public how she felt about having all of her husband's baseball friends with them on this rather unconventional honeymoon. Then again, as an actress she was probably used to an unusual lifestyle.

The New Orleans segment of the tour began on Sunday, October 30,

John Montgomery Ward and several of his teammates from the New York Giants played in an exhibition series in New Orleans as part of the American Exposition, the continuation of the 1883 World Cotton & Industrial Exposition. He is depicted in the field on the Allen & Ginter's 1887 N28 tobacco card (Library of Congress).

1887, against the Pelicans at Sportsman's Park in front of 6,000 fervent fans. The weather was far from the expected mild winter that Ward and the Giants were expecting, and it was far from an ideal day for baseball. The temperature was near freezing and a stiff wind blew across the field in cutting blasts. Nonetheless the Pelicans and their loyal fans were undeterred. New York hurler Tim Keefe held the Pelicans to only two ninth inning runs to claim victory for the Giants by the score of 7 to 2. The following day the two squads were in a 4-to-4 deadlock after eight innings when all hell broke loose.

The Pelicans reported to their manager, Abner Powell, that several members of the New York team were already intoxicated when they took the field and that their conduct was disgraceful. The Pelicans' club secretary, Maurice Kauffman, summoned the police to eject these players from the ballpark. Three of the players singled out for drunkenness were Buck Ewing, Jerry Denny, and King Kelly. So disgraceful was their behavior during the game that Ward escorted his wife from the ballpark and arranged for a carriage to take her back to the St. Charles Hotel. In New York, there was such a hue and cry over the incident that the Giants discussed cancelling the tour and returning to New York.

With the remaining games in the series on the line, the New Orleans newspapers attempted to downplay the incident, alluding to the players having spent too much time with "too many friends with tempting ways" when they reached the field. After several days tempers had cooled and Abner Powell proposed that the series continue. They met again on Friday, November 4, and again in a doubleheader on Sunday, November 6, to end the series. While the Friday game only drew 500 spectators, the doubleheader once again brought out 6,000 to witness the Giants' swan song.[28] While the Pelicans lost all four games they played against the New York Giants, in the end they were not put off by the ugly incident on Halloween. Abner Powell reminded his players that every man jack among them had been in his cups on occasion, just not on the field.

For all of his pluck and bluster, team captain Abner Powell was no blind monkey. He was a talented pitcher and outfielder and a natural leader both on and off the field. He played 113 games for the Pelicans in 1887 during which he compiled a .335 batting average. From the mound he won 20 games against only nine losses for a .690 winning percentage. His relationship with Toby Hart was such that Hart named Powell to be manager of the Pelicans for the 1888 season.

There was an expected backlash against New Orleans that cast aspersions on their pennant victory, that they forced out all but three other teams, that they paid their players under the table, and so on. All of this was nothing more than sour grapes. After three years of scrapping and struggling to become established, the Southern League hit its first really rough patch in 1888. The league started its first two seasons with eight teams and only lost three teams in 1885 and two in 1886. After they lost four of the starting seven in 1887, the league was bloodied, not beaten. The 1888 season started with only four teams—New Orleans, Birmingham, Charleston, and Memphis. There were ongoing discussions aimed at taking in Chattanooga, Atlanta, and Mobile into the league, but nothing ever materialized. Early in the season New Orleans was in third place with a disappointing record of 11-14 (.440) and the fear was that most teams would be forced to sell their best players to teams in other leagues in order to stay alive. It was a fear not without a basis in history. In the past, whenever a team held a fire sale, owners knew that the season was basically over for the fans, leading to the inevitable downward spiral in attendance that would end in either selling the franchise to another city or disbanding altogether.

As expected, the three teams who had been unable to finish their 1887 schedule, Mobile, Savannah, and Nashville opted not to participate in the Southern League for the 1888 season. The league then unwisely, or desperately, chose to go forward with only four teams—the Birmingham Maroons, the Memphis Greys, the New Orleans Pelicans, and the Charleston Seagulls. The league slashed expenses where they could, but they still had to pay for umpires and for their dues to the National Association, so there was not much more room to trim expenses except for player salaries. The Pelicans, already with the lowest overhead in the league, trimmed their monthly payroll from $1,740 in 1887 to $1,500 in 1888.[29] Based on having eighteen players on the roster, this means that the average monthly player salary dropped nearly 14 percent from $96.67 in 1887 to $83.33 in 1888.

Memphis played fifty games but disbanded on June 30, 1888. Their final game was a 3-1 loss to Birmingham after which Memphis unconditionally released all of their players. Toby Hart tried to have the league transfer the Memphis franchise to Mobile, but the league could not find any financial support coming out of Alabama. There was no way that the league could remain viable with only three teams and they were forced to shut down the next day. Despite the league's situation, New Orleans went forward against Charleston on July 1 in front of 800 hearty souls who braved the rain to watch the Pelicans beat the Seagulls 9 to 5. The weather and the fan's gloomy mood seemed to match the disposition of the league. Charleston and Birmingham both declined to continue playing either in the Southern League or, when approached, in the Texas League. Birmingham was offered a $1,500 bonus to be paid from the Southern League's reserves, but team officials revealed that their team had lost ($7,000) during the past two seasons. During their last home game with New Orleans they could not even raise the visitor's guarantee, which New Orleans of course waived. Charleston was offered the same $1,500 bonus but told league officials that the bonus proposed would not even cover one month's losses. Hart and Powell turned their eyes to the Texas League who was undergoing a reorganization of its own.

As part of the many restructuring options under consideration, Texas League officials preferred to combine their remaining four teams with New Orleans and Birmingham into a six-team league, even as representatives from Austin and San Antonio were actively trying to raise money to reorganize their teams. This would give the Texas League either a six-team league to stand on its own or an eight-team league if the merger moved forward. The Texas League representatives who met at the Tremont Hotel in Galveston to determine the future of the Texas League were Robert Adair from Houston, J.J. McCloskey from San Antonio, S.H. Levis from Dallas, and C.H. Dorsey and Alexander Easton from Galveston.

But rather than disband, as was widely reported, Hart and the New Orleans Pelicans took their team to the faltering Texas League that was also reorganizing after its own collapse on July 9. There was still a glimmer of life in the two new leagues yet. Renamed the Texas–Southern League and attracting five other teams, the league crawled and then stumbled through the next two months to complete twenty-eight games. With Abner Powell at the helm, New Orleans finished 18-9, good enough for second place in the cobbled together Texas–Southern League. Their combined record for 1888 was 43 wins against 41 losses, a respectable enough showing given all of their challenges, not the least of which was playing all of their Texas–Southern League games on the road to save on travel expenses. However, from the outset Powell was having trouble signing his players to new Texas–Southern League contracts as the new league minimum of $150 per month was far lower than they were being paid in New Orleans under the old Southern League contract. In early September, the Houston Red Stockings and the Galveston Giants dropped out of the new league and the last teams standing, the New Orleans Pelicans, the San Antonio Cowboys, and the Dallas Hams, decided to pack it in as well.

New Orleans closed out the 1888 Southern League season in third place with a record of 25 wins and 32 losses, a disappointing .439 winning percentage.

Final Results of the 1888 Southern League Season

Team	Won	Lost	Pct	GB
Birmingham Maroons	32	19	.627	
Memphis Grays	26	24	.520	-5.5
New Orleans Pelicans	*25*	*37*	*.438*	*-10*
Charleston Seagulls	20	28	.416	-10.5

Try as they might to save money, the 1888 season was a complete financial boondoggle, not just for New Orleans, but for the other three teams across the Southern League. The allegation that the New Orleans Pelicans had disbanded the team following the closure of the Southern League on July 1 resulted in many players believing that their contracts had been voided when the team surrendered its franchise to the league. In point of fact, New Orleans never surrendered their franchise. They proactively approached the remnants of the Texas League to form a new league. There were the same arguments made when the Texas–Southern League eventually fell apart.[30]

Final Results of the 1888 Texas–Southern League Season

Team	Won	Lost	Pct	GB
Dallas Hams	20	8	.714	
New Orleans Pelicans	*18*	*9*	*.667*	*-1.5*
San Antonio Cowboys	11	9	.550	-5.0
Galveston Giants	9	18	.333	-10.5
Houston Red Stockings	6	19	.240	-11.0

The Texas–Southern League was only in existence for less than half of a single season. When play was stopped, the Dallas Hams were firmly in control despite being only a game and a half ahead of the Pelicans. They had dominated the Texas League before it folded, with a winning percentage over .800 and their competition losing money by the boatload. Additionally, most players in the Texas League were often going weeks without a paycheck. New Orleans more than held their own on the diamond against Dallas and may have had the best chance to challenge Dallas in the truncated season for a pennant. They simply ran out of time.

Struggling franchise owners breathed a sigh of relief when they hung on to complete their schedule but were still waiting for their anticipated financial payoff. As a result of a season plagued by instability and uncertainty, ongoing player disputes over the validity of contracts, and a fan base weary of frequent rain delays and postponements. In early October, Toby Hart was forced to report another losing season financially, with receipts of $32,340 and expenses of $36,875 resulting in a loss of ($4,535).[31] This poor financial performance eroded the confidence of the other shareholders and the accumulated criticism of Hart led to his ouster as president in late October. Hart was replaced by Phillip Reilly, but remained on the board along with Joseph Oteri, Augustus Lehman, and Henry Powers.[32]

Still smarting from its abrupt failure in 1888, the owners and management in the Southern League somehow managed to stitch together six teams to start the 1889 season. Such was the commitment of businessmen across the South, to continue to pour money into a losing venture simply for the love of the game, holding out for the possibility of seeing a profit at some point in time. New Orleans roared off to an early 9–2 start, but within weeks Birmingham was in the soup and disbanded when their fans grew "tired of rotten ball."[33] They were replaced by Mobile, but it was clear that the five-team format was doomed to failure. On June 12 Memphis and Atlanta folded, and Charleston followed three days later. The Charleston franchise was moved to an all new owner group in Atlanta. On the field New Orleans continued to pile on the agony and was steadily moving away from the pack behind the hitting of Mark Polhemus, whose .369

Mark Polhemus was a standout hitter for the New Orleans Pelicans, hitting .369 with ninety hits and eight home runs in the 1889 season and helping the Pelicans capture their second Southern League pennant. He is depicted on the 1887 Buchner Gold Coin N284 tobacco card (collection of the author).

batting average and sixty-three runs, ninety hits, and five home runs led all Southern League hitters. He also led the league in visits to the keystone sack with eighteen doubles, just five more than his teammate Tom McGuirk. The Pelicans were backed by the pitching of Jack Huston with a record of 20-4 (.833) with 139 strikeouts over his league leading twenty-four complete games. His twenty victories over twenty-four complete games and led all Southern League hurlers.

However, with such disparity between the teams the inevitable end result was that the league was shuttered two weeks later. The Pelicans finished the truncated fifty-five-game season with forty-six wins and nine losses (.836), fifteen games ahead of the Charleston/Atlanta combination, and nailing down their second pennant in three seasons. Newspapers throughout the South quipped that it was getting such that lasting until the 4th of July was almost the equivalent to winning the Southern League pennant itself. As a result, Hart and the board called for a shareholder assessment of ten dollars per share which would raise $14,000 to retire accumulated debt.[34] New Orleans, with the deepest pockets in the league, had the luxury of a shareholder assessment to wipe out the team's losses and replenish the working capital for the next season. No matter how much financial backers and shareholders loved baseball, it was still a bitter pill to swallow. For teams without the resources to prolong their participation for another season it was a constant scramble to raise money.

Final Results of the 1889 Southern League Season

Team	Won	Lost	Pct	GB
New Orleans Pelicans	46	9	.836	
Charleston/Atlanta	26	19	,578	-15
Chattanooga	25	25	.500	-18.5
Birmingham/Mobile	12	36	.250	-30.5
Atlanta	14	22	.389	NA
Memphis	12	24	.333	NA

The 1889 winter meetings were interrupted by the funeral for Jefferson Davis in New Orleans on Wednesday, December 11, 1889. Thousands of New Orleanians were joined by prominent public figures and people from across the Gulf region who paid their respects to the former president of the Confederacy. Davis' body lay in state at City Hall in New Orleans for five days before being interred in Metairie Cemetery.

The 1890 season began with discussions revolving around alternatives to the dormant Southern League. Toby Hart was in favor of moving New Orleans to the Texas League,[35] an opinion that Hart would continue to champion even as his reputation in Southern League circles slowly began to dissolve altogether. The Southern League was not the only professional baseball league that was under pressure. Other notable collapses included the Brotherhood, the American Association, the Player's League, plus a failed revival of the Gulf League. Even though by 1890 the United States had become the world's most productive economy, doubling the industrial output of England, baseball itself still remained a shaky proposition. The campaign to industrialize the South had failed as only 5 percent of the Southern labor force worked in non-agricultural trade or a factory or industrial installation, resulting in the average income in New Orleans lagging well behind industrialized cities in the Northeast.

New Orleans attended a meeting with other Texas League team representatives and the Pelican's application was accepted. This meeting reaffirmed Toby Hart's shift in preference for the Texas League over the Southern League, at least from his perspective. At this point in the season New Orleans planned to join Galveston, Houston, Dallas, and Fort Worth. With only five teams, however, New Orleans was still on the bubble unless the league could add at least one more team. They would, of course, prefer to have eight teams in the league, but would settle for six. Towards the end of February Hart began pushing in earnest to have Mobile admitted to the league alongside New Orleans, a proposal that most Texas League owners did not favor. Hart's affinity for Mobile dated back to 1884 when Mobile was the only Southern city to support his effort to establish the Gulf League. Mobile fielded two teams alongside two teams from New Orleans allowing the Gulf League to be able to launch and survive until Hart and New Orleans were able to join the Southern League in 1887. Mobile also joined the Southern League later that same year.

The Texas League owners, however, saw Mobile as an outlier, a small city located too far away from the customary circuit. They were willing to consider New Orleans because of their size and potential drawing power. But Hart was so insistent on having Mobile in the Texas League that he made New Orleans' participation conditional upon admitting Mobile. This was a terrible miscalculation on Hart's part. At the same time, in an unusual turn of events, Hart offered the manager's position to Dick Phelan instead of Abner Powell which may have signaled a loss of confidence in Powell or have been the result of a falling out between Hart and Powell. When Phelan declined the offer, Hart approached two other candidates about managing the Pelicans. Smarting from Hart's very public rebuke, Abner Powell and several of his teammates headed to the Pacific Northwest to join a team in Spokane, Washington, in the Pacific Northwest League. Along with Powell were pitcher Jack Huston, pitcher Thomas McGuirk, second baseman Frank "Piggy" Ward, and outfielder Mark Polhemus—making five of the nine players from the 1889 New Orleans Pelicans. The remaining players caught on quickly elsewhere. Third baseman Joe Dowie went to the Hamilton Hams/Montreal in the International Association; outfielder Henry Fabian played for Dallas Tigers in the

Texas League as did shortstop Willard Holland who also played with the Kansas City Blues in the Western Association; catcher/outfielder Joseph Schachern played with the Portland club in the Pacific Northwest League and the Austin Senators in the Texas League. Texas League officials took notice of Powell's departure and, fed up with Hart's demands, pressed ahead with a four-team schedule without either New Orleans or Mobile.

After two consecutive mid-season failures in 1888 and 1889, the Southern League decided not to operate in 1890 and 1891. For all intents and purposes, the New Orleans franchise, despite having tremendous success on the field, was a casualty of the Southern League's overall weakness and Toby Hart's bull-headedness. His former ballpark, the New Orleans Base Ball Park, had been torn down and was scheduled to go on the auction block for residential development. As an inducement the local ferry company offered to build a brand-new ballpark in Algiers for Hart and the Pelicans to use.[36] This, of course, would mean more paying customers on game day for the ferry company. But with no team, there was no need for a new ballpark.

Hart's baseball empire was eroding right before his eyes. He had lost the New Orleans Base Ball Park, shuttered the Gulf League and the Crescent City League, alienated both the Texas League and Southern League owners as well as his own shareholders in New Orleans. With the Pelican players scattered across the country with other teams New Orleanians still had a handful of exhibition baseball games to watch during the start of 1890 with teams from Chicago, Cleveland, and Brooklyn all camped out in the city for spring training. The Pelicans' relative success in the Southern League and the Texas-Southern League over three seasons had not resulted in the financial return their shareholders were looking for. And, as a result of his failed gambit to force the Texas League to admit New Orleans and Mobile together, Toby Hart was replaced as club president by Phillip Reilly who unfortunately fared no better than his predecessor. After two years without Pelican baseball in New Orleans, control of the New Orleans franchise came under the control of Charles H. Genslinger and Henry Powers in 1891. Both were long time baseball men and, by coincidence, both were in the commercial printing business.

Charles Genslinger was a successful businessman, having established the printing firm of Hunter & Genslinger in 1883. He was a member of the Louisiana Sugar Exchange, the New Orleans Bicycle Club, and was also involved with the Lone Star Base Ball Club as a player and manager. Genslinger eventually became a principal shareholder and Treasurer of the New Orleans Pelican Base Ball Club, President of the Sportsman's Park Association, and President of the Southern League. He was also the president of the Olympic Club in New Orleans until November 1889, after which he established the rival Metropolitan Club.

The Olympic Club was the preeminent boxing venue in the United States between 1890 and 1896 and Genslinger was one of the primary proponents of staging high profile, world championship prizefights by expanding the club's facilities to accommodate as many as 5,000 spectators in their arena to witness these world championship prizefights. Under Genslinger's business model, the club would fill their arena at $10 per ticket, raising $50,000 in gross receipts. The customary ticket price of $3.00 to $5.00 for a regular boxing match was raised for a marquee bout that featured a world championship on the line. With a purse of as much as $12,000, an unheard-of payday at the time, the club would have $38,000 remaining from gate receipts to retire the debt assumed to expand their arena, with the remainder available to pad the club's coffers for the next event. This was exactly the formula that the Olympic Club used in staging the title match between Jack Dempsey and Bob Fitzsimmons in 1890 and to generate approximately $31,000 in net income in 1891 (approximately $787,750 today) and $95,000 in net income in 1892 (approximately $2,415,000 today). While boxing was flourishing and producing wagon loads full of money for its shareholders, baseball was struggling to keep its head above water.

Down but not out, the Southern League struggled to regain its feet and organized once again on January 27, 1892, in Atlanta. While no longer the team president, Hart was still a director and shareholder in the company that owned the Pelicans and therefore still had the ability to express his opinion. Following his earlier course of action, in January of 1892 Hart was still pushing for New Orleans to join the Texas League. Atlanta was in favor of adding New Orleans and Memphis to the Southern circuit, magnanimously agreeing to erase their prior disputes concerning New Orleans' alleged business practices. Despite this subtle swipe at Hart and New Orleans, the majority of the other Pelicans shareholders preferred to play in the Southern League over the Texas League. With all of this ongoing upheaval, it was not until the first week of March that the Southern League was complete, and managers could begin signing players for the 1892 season.

Opening Day was on April 10 with the Pelicans facing off against their perennial Opening Day opponent, the Mobile Blackbirds.

Mobile versus New Orleans
April 10, 1892[37]

Innings	1	2	3	4	5	6	7	8	9	Total
Mobile	3	1	0	0	0	0	0	0	0	4
New Orleans	4	0	0	0	0	1	3	0	0	8

The Pelicans took the first step on the road to recovery by defeating Mobile by the score of 8 to 4. Abner Powell was back at the helm as manager and there was a tone of cautious optimism that began to creep into the denizens of the ballpark.

To stimulate fan interest during the 1892 season, the league set up a split season. This would result in a pennant winner in each half of the season with the potential of a post-season playoff. The idea was to keep the season relevant in the event that a team fell way behind during the first half of the season. They had a new chance to turn the tables during the second half of the season. Southern League officers had seen this format work in other leagues, and their decision paid off from the outset, with the league realizing its most profitable season since its inception.

After a quick start, New Orleans slid into fourth place in early May at 8 wins and 5 losses (.615) behind a strong Chattanooga squad with 12 wins and 3 losses (.800). But it was still early in the first half of the season. A month later, however, Chattanooga still led the pack, and New Orleans was mired in a tie for fourth place with Atlanta. In the second half of the split season, with the won—lost rankings reset, the Pelicans improved to 14 wins and 10 losses (.583) and were tied for third place with Mobile by the end of August. In an altogether uninspiring season, all eight teams managed to complete their schedule. New Orleans improved their performance in the second half and ended the 1892 season tied for second place with Mobile, each with a record of 66 wins and 57 losses (.537). Chattanooga captured the first half of the season but faded in the second half. Birmingham took the second half. This was just the sort of outcome the league had envisioned.

As intended, the winners of each half faced off in an eight-game playoff series, but it was not without controversy. With an eight-game series the league ran the risk of a deadlock should the two teams each win four games. Most observers expected either an odd-number of games for the playoff or a provision for a tie-breaker. They got neither. And as if on cue, Chattanooga and Birmingham were tied at four games apiece when the first hullabaloo arose. Chattanooga claimed that they had won the pennant due to Birmingham's disbandment.[38] At the same time, Mobile manager John Kelly accused Birmingham of throwing the last game in Chattanooga in order to milk the gate receipts. Chattanooga manager Ted Sullivan quickly came to Birmingham's defense, disputing Mobile's claims. Since Birmingham and Chattanooga had completed the eight-game playoff and were knotted at four games each, with no provision for a ninth and deciding game, Birmingham let their players return home, believing the season was over. It was now up to the league to resolve the matter during their October 31 meeting in Atlanta. Since Birmingham had the highest overall winning percentage for the two combined seasons they were awarded the 1892 pennant.[39]

Final Results of the 1892 Southern League Season

Team	Won	Lost	Pct	GB
Birmingham Grays	73	50	.593	
Mobile Blackbirds	66	57	.537	-7

Team	Won	Lost	Pct	GB
New Orleans Pelicans	*66*	*57*	*.537*	*-7*
Montgomery Lambs	66	58	.532	-7.5
Chattanooga Chatts	63	57	.525	-8.5
Atlanta Firecrackers	58	65	.472	-15
Macon Central City	51	69	.425	-20.5
Memphis Giants	46	76	.377	-26.5

All eight teams finished their 1892 schedules, and the split season format was ultimately declared a success, giving owners a growing sense of security. The league announced at the winter meetings that the league would come back with eight teams in 1893. Abner Powell spent much of January crisscrossing the country recruiting and signing players, a difficult task with a $1,000 per month salary limit. Nevertheless, he signed Mark Polhemus in Pennsylvania, Thomas Thorp in Illinois, and other players across Ohio, Wisconsin, and Indiana. The league unexpectedly found their slate of teams complete and stable in early February and the season schedule was finalized by mid–February. As was their practice, the Pelicans played a full slate of spring training games against visiting major league teams, including the Louisville Colonels and the Pittsburg Pirates.

However, the 1893 season proved to be as difficult and dismal as the national economy. Spurred on by the usually aggressive league president Genslinger, and inspired by the prior season's success, the league, moved forward with an ill-conceived decision to expand the lineup to twelve teams. In this case bigger was not better, only more ambitious. But with the first profitable season for some owners still fresh in their memories, most were anxious to capitalize on the momentum of 1892. Returning were the Birmingham Grays, the Atlanta Windjammers, the Macon Central City, the Memphis Giants, the Chattanooga Warriors, the Montgomery Colts, the Mobile Blackbirds, the Nashville Tigers, and the New Orleans Pelicans. Added shortly thereafter to that group of nine teams were the Charleston Seagulls, the Savannah Electrics, and the Augusta Electricians.

At home, Genslinger and Peters reorganized the New Orleans franchise, changing the company name from the New Orleans Base Ball Company to the Southern Amusement Company. Genslinger served as president, Abner Powell as vice-president, and Henry Peters as secretary/treasurer.[40] As part of the overall change, new uniforms were introduced: bright red with black trim and stockings for road games and blue with white trim and stockings for home games.

The Mobile Blackbirds were clearly not intimidated by the new red uniforms and the Pelicans dropped their Opening Day game against Mobile 12 to 2. Sadly, the season did not get any better for New Orleans from there. By mid–May New Orleans was in fifth place (out of twelve teams) at 17 wins and

15 losses (.531). By June the cranks were roasting Abner Powell and his players from the bleachers for the team's apparent lethargic play and were just about ready to haul the lot of them off in the chip wagon. Perhaps to keep the fan's minds off of what was happening on the field, there was talk of constructing a new ballpark to replace the neglected Sportsman's Park,[41] but not even this distraction could spark people to come to the ballpark. Powell and the hapless Pelicans spiraled down into eighth place with a mark of 40 wins against 51 losses (.440). This was on par with their dismal performance in the 1888 Southern League and now everyone was forced to reexamine and reevaluate the road ahead.

Not even the split-season format could satisfy Southern fans, and for some inexplicable reason the fans would not be satisfied with an exciting pennant race. The first half was won by Augusta, followed by Charleston and Savannah. In the second half, however, things began to unravel. Not wishing to see any club fold and thereby cast doubt on the league's expanded twelve-man format, Genslinger directed the league to step in to operate the franchises for the Chattanooga Warriors and the Nashville Tigers in the second half due to financial constraints. The second half was won by Macon, followed by Memphis and Mobile. When Birmingham was close to packing it in they found a willing partner in a group from Pensacola. Their relief would be short lived as Pensacola was quarantined on August 12, 1892, due to an outbreak of yellow fever. When all was said and done, Charleston claimed the flag, finishing just one game ahead of Macon and Atlanta, and one and one-half games up on Memphis and Savannah.

Final Results of the 1893 Southern League Season

Team	Won	Lost	Pct	GB
Charleston Seagulls	51	33	.607	
Macon Central City	54	38	.587	-1
Atlanta Windjammers	55	39	.585	-1
Memphis Giants	53	38	.582	-1.5
Savannah Electrics	53	38	.582	-1.5
Augusta Electricians	51	39	.567	-3
Chattanooga Warriors	49	45	.521	-7
New Orleans Pelicans	**40**	**51**	**.440**	**-14.5**
Mobile Blackbirds	38	53	.418	-16.5
Montgomery Colts	38	57	.400	-18.5
Birmingham/Pensacola	34	58	.370	-21
Nashville Tigers	33	60	.355	-22.5

To the surprise of the nay-sayers who believed the twelve-team format would collapse under its own weight, seven teams were in the pennant race while the remaining five teams were out of the hunt. The important point was that all twelve teams completed nearly all of their 1893 schedule, the best playing ninety-four out of one hundred games.

Genslinger's gamble on a twelve-team format was too ambitious bit it almost succeeded. Now, with the season was behind him, he was focused on the future as he sat in his office pondering his fortunes and comparing the return on investment of two of his different sporting interests—boxing and baseball. In September of 1892 the Olympic Club staged a prizefighting spectacle never before seen anywhere in the world of boxing—the Fistic Carnival. Three world championship prizefights scheduled on three consecutive days, culminating in the heavyweight championship fight between world champion John L. Sullivan and challenger James J. Corbett. All told during 1892, the Olympic Club experienced its most successful year of operation in its brief history, with five major fight events drawing unprecedented crowds, estimated to be between thirty-five thousand and thirty-eight thousand to their now 10,000-seat arena, garnering critical acclaim for their facilities and arrangements from both national and international observers, and in the process ensuring the financial security of their athletic club. It is estimated that the Olympic Club brought in gross income of approximately $159,300 against which they had $65,000 in estimated expenses, leaving an astonishing $94,300 in net income worth somewhere near $2.3 million today.

Meanwhile, the New Orleans Pelicans had been in the Southern League since 1887 and were enjoying a moderate degree of success on the field, capturing pennants in 1887 and 1889. However, they were still struggling at the ticket office and the league did not operate in 1890 and 1891. As Genslinger assessed his team's time in the Southern League, he determined that the Pelicans had played in five out of seven years and, with the exception of 1892, had yet to turn a profit. In fact, he was unaware of any club in the Southern League that could boast of being consistently profitable. When compared against what was happening in boxing circles it became clear to Genslinger how he wanted to devote his energies in the future, and it was not in baseball. Disillusioned by the inability of the Pelicans to produce a profit, much less the type of financial windfall that the Olympic Club was capable of, Genslinger approached Henry Powers about buying Genslinger's interest in the ball club.

At first Powers was understandably reluctant to buy out Genslinger but agreed to consider his proposal in the off-season. As Powers was contemplating his options during the first week of October, New Orleans was frequented by *Jupiter Pluvius* nearly every day almost continuously, inundating the city and battering both buildings and citizens with torrential rain and stiff tropical winds. Such weather was commonplace during the height of hurricane season from June through August. But by October, hurricane season was nearly over. So to many this current wave of weather, while inconvenient, was nothing to fear as it was thought to be far too late in the season for a tropical storm or hurricane. As the days rolled on, the city's fledgling drainage system was taxed to the limit handling the near constant rainfall. However, despite the date, experienced residents of New Orleans knew instinctively from the duration of the rain that somewhere out in the Gulf of Mexico there was a storm lurking and braced themselves just in case that storm was headed their way. On Thursday morning, October 5, 1893, New Orleanians opened their morning newspaper to read with horror about the disaster this most recent storm had caused just south of the city. The unnamed hurricane struck the barrier islands and settlements along the Gulf Coast with frightful ferocity, moving from southeast due west across Louisiana's southern coast. The greatest loss of life came in the small community of Cheniere Caminada, a stretch of scrubby oak groves (*cheniere* in French) cultivated during the period of Spanish rule by a sugar planter named Francisco Caminada. It was here that the shrieking winds pushed the storm surge ashore, sweeping away over 1,100 of the town's 1,200 residents, destroying every structure in the town and washing away most of the surrounding landmass. Another eight hundred and fifty lives were lost in Grand Isle, the Chandeleur Islands, and neighboring coastal communities. New Orleans was sparred the brunt of the storm.[42]

In early 1894 Powers relented and purchased Genslinger's interest in the Pelicans. Genslinger left New Orleans not long thereafter following the collapse of the Metropolitan Club, an athletic/boxing club he had established to compete with the Olympic Club. Powers was now the sole owner of the New Orleans franchise[43] and went from being referred to as "Treasurer Powers" to the lofty "Magnate Powers." Along with relinquishing his positions with the Southern Amusement Company, the New Orleans Pelicans Base Ball Club, and the Southern League, Genslinger also left New Orleans for New York to establish the Manhattan Athletic Club. He attempted to repeat the success of the Olympic Club by opening athletic clubs in New York, Illinois, and Missouri, but none of these ventures, while successful, ever achieved the level of success he had achieved in New Orleans and that he so desperately desired to replicate elsewhere.

Powers frequently spoke to the press about his vision for the Pelicans franchise and one of his favorite topics was replacing Abner Powell as the team's manager. Powers preferred Charles "Count" Campau, an experienced outfielder who was one of the team's first fence-busters and who hit seventeen home runs in 1887, ten in 1893 and another twenty round trippers in 1894.

Charles C. "Count" Campau earned his nickname because his teammates admired his stately appearance and because he had been educated at the University of Notre Dame. A native of Detroit, Michigan, Campau was also regarded as one of the brightest baseball minds of his day. While his major league career was only 147 games over three seasons, he spent twenty years in the minor leagues between 1885 and 1905. He was a prolific base stealer, nabbing sixty-three bases in one hundred and forty-seven major league games and six hundred and sixty during his twenty-year professional career. He stole one hundred bases as a twenty-three-year-old playing for Savannah and New Orleans in 1887. Not slowing down a step, he stole twenty-five bases when he was thirty-six playing for the Rochester Bronchos in 1900.

Campau was noted for extolling the virtues of baseball. "Baseball is a great exercise, for it is played with [the] brain and every muscle, and daily practice will make any person become strong quick, for every muscle is brought into play and is developed." He was especially popular in New Orleans where he played for the Pelicans for parts of four seasons (1887, 1892–1894) and adopted the city as his home. Despite Powers' entreaties, Campau never managed the New Orleans Pelicans for him. He played and managed until 1905 when he became an umpire. After two years, however, he turned to thoroughbred racing as a handicapper and placing judge at several racetracks in the United States, Canada, and Cuba before returning to the Fair Grounds in New Orleans. Campau passed away in New Orleans on April 3, 1938.

Charles "Count" Campau strikes a gloveless fielder's pose on this 1887 Old Judge N172 tobacco card. He was a prolific hitter and base stealer for the New Orleans Pelicans (Library of Congress).

While Campau was Powers' first choice to manage the Pelicans, when the 1894 season began it was Powers himself who had to step in as manager. For his part, Powell spent 1890 with the Spokane Bunchgrassers in Washington and also with the Hamilton Hams/Montreal aggregation in Canada, returning to Seattle in the Pacific Northwest League for the 1891 season. Yet he was agreeable when asked to return to New Orleans for the 1892 season.

When Powers took control as manager in 1894, Powell elected to play for league rival, the Nashville Tigers.

Managers across the Southern League once again engaged in their annual mad scramble to sign players within the league's $1,000 monthly salary limit in time to bring them to their city for spring training in early March. Former New Orleans players unwilling to sign under the league's salary limit were easily replaced by other players quickly. Irrespective of skill level, baseball players tended to rise up like mushrooms in spring. Returning players could either sign or test the market elsewhere. The sooner managers could cement their rosters, the better their chances of pulling together a strong contender. New Orleans usually had something of a competitive advantage by booking professional teams to train at Sportsman's Park in New Orleans. During the 1894 spring training season, the Pelicans were willing opponents for the Baltimore Orioles, the Boston Beaneaters, and the Detroit Wolverines.

The Southern League returned to the optimal eight-team format and once again found itself entangled in the middle of a contentious struggle to keep their owners and managers from selling off their best players to major league teams in order to keep their franchises afloat. This practice not only dampened the quality of play but alienated the legions of local fans who each had their favorite players who were now playing elsewhere. Nonetheless, there was an inexplicable yet undeniable tone of optimism as the beginning of the first half of the 1894 season approached. Scheduled to run from early April through the end of June, the first half was captured by Memphis with Mobile and Charleston right on their heels. With the first half under their belts owners felt like they could finally exhale. But it was not going to be so easy.

On June 20 Macon surrendered its franchise after fifty-five games with a disappointing record of 14 wins and 41 losses (.254). It was thought that the franchise would move to Montgomery, but Chattanooga and Little Rock were also possible alternatives. At the end of the first half of the season a week later on June 27, Charleston and Savannah dropped out of the league and the first-place Mobile franchise was transferred to Atlanta. This once again left four teams to soldier on—Atlanta, New Orleans, Memphis, and Nashville. League president J.B. Nicklin believed the remainder of the season could not only be salvaged but could be profitable as well. The league stipulated that stronger teams, meaning those still able to travel and compete, could elect to play the second half if they chose. However, not far into the second half of the split season, it was discovered on June 8 that the second-place Memphis Giants reneged on their commitment to the league not to sell off players by sending William Wadsworth, their best pitcher (16 wins—7 losses and a .696 winning percentage), and Charles Lutenberg, their best hitter (.319 batting average), to Louisville. In all, Memphis manager Frank Graves sold five players and received between $1,500 and $1,800 at the end of the season. The proceeds of the sale may or may not have covered Memphis' accumulated losses for 1894. He may well have sold or optioned other players prior to June. While this restored some much-needed liquidity to the failing Memphis franchise, the move incurred the ire of many of the other three teams who honored their agreement not to sell off players during the season and, who now refused to play Memphis, bringing the whole league down like a house of cards, effectively ending the 1894 season on July 10th after only eight games into the second half of the season.

The New Orleans Pelicans finished in fifth place for the first half of the season with a record of 30–30 (.500) but was only 4–5 (.444) in the second half when the league once again collapsed. Owner/manager Henry Powers informed his team captain and field manager Count Campau to tell his players that they would be paid in full if the team disbanded. Powers kept his word to his players at great personal expense. In a move reminiscent of Toby Hart, Powers also announced that he intended to explore moving to the Texas League for the 1895 season.

After much debate, the 1894 pennant was awarded to Memphis. The initial optimism that ushered in the 1894 season had withered when teams pressured to maintain their financial integrity began selling off their best players in order to survive, a strategy that backfired badly. Although Memphis won the pennant, they could not last past the first half of the season. New Orleans compiled a record of 34 wins and 35 losses (.493), which was only good enough for fifth place, well off the pace.

Year after year, backers of baseball did all they could to give their cities a winning team. They brought some of the best minor league players through the Southern League, but at great expense. Every ballpark had an available flagpole to hoist the pennant, but thus far many of them remained vacant. Between 1885 and 1894 there were six cities were played in the Southern League—Chattanooga, Little Rock, Macon, Mobile, Montgomery, and Nashville—that had yet to raise the league flag.

Final Results of the 1894 Southern League Season

Team	Won	Lost	Pct	GB
Memphis Giants	42	23	.754	
Mobile/Atlanta	43	25	.632	-4.5
Charleston Seagulls	33	23	.600	-6
Savannah Modocs	30	27	.526	-10
New Orleans Pelicans	*34*	*35*	*.493*	*-13.5*
Nashville Tigers	30	38	.441	-17
Atlanta Atlantas	21	37	.362	-19.5
Macon Hornets	15	41	.268	-24.5

During the January 1895 meeting in Chattanooga the main concern on the minds of the owners was for all of the teams in the group to live through the season and complete their schedule. The $1,000 guarantee was repeated for 1895 and was to be deposited by the first of February. The $1,000 monthly salary limit and $100 per month league dues were renewed, and the revenue sharing arrangement saw visiting teams being given 50 percent of the gate receipts with a minimum of $60 per game being established. The formula for the league's sinking fund was revised: given that the average daily attendance was worth approximately $200 per day, this was multiplied by the number of teams remaining in the league, with the result being assessed the league's 3 percent fee for the sinking fund. For example, if there were eight teams currently in league play, the $200 per game times eight teams totaled $1,600 which would be multiplied by 3 percent or $48, making each team's share approximately $6 for every game played.

The Great Depression that had started in 1873 was still lingering seventeen years later, yet there was a slight hint of confidence for improvement in the 1895 campaign. Only time would tell how long this optimism would last. The now customary annual argument of the Southern League versus the Texas League dominated the new year. In a reversal of prior opinion, Galveston now actually favored bringing New Orleans and Shreveport into the league, walking back their prior stance that the Texas League should be limited to Texas teams. At the same time, Southern League officials were meeting at the Reed House in Chattanooga and the lingering animosities of the past against New Orleans were dredged up and revisited. It was not strictly their displeasure with the past leadership of Toby Hart, but also with the outsized and disproportionate influence of New Orleans as the largest city in the league. No longer enjoying the influence he once had, Hart withdrew his bid to join the Texas League. Powers, on the other hand, was more acceptable to the other Southern League owners, probably because Powers was a willing and silent investor in other Southern League teams, among them Chattanooga and Birmingham.

Although Powers could not convince Count Campau to accept the manager's slot at New Orleans, because he also owned the Chattanooga franchise he was successful in convincing him to take the helm there in 1895. Campau expressed his strong opinion that the league's past failures were due to "excessive salaries," long jumps between cities driving up travel costs, and poor decisions from the pool of umpires.

No winter meeting would be complete without the possibility of the Southern League merging with another league to help stabilize operations. The Texas League was the first alternative considered during January, but there was so much dissent among Texas League owners that they actually put together a small committee made up of George Dermody, Alex Easton, and E.R. Cheesborough to express their opposition to the other Texas League owners during their meeting in Dallas. The Southern League talks then centered around the Central League who had given a home to Southern League teams in the past. In the end, the proposal was discussed and tabled, but in mid–January the Southern League was reorganized and Nashville, Memphis, Little Rock, and Evansville were admitted to the Southern League. Thus the 1895 league meetings ended with the announcement that the franchises that defaulted during 1894—being Mobile, Charleston, Macon, and Savannah— would be awarded to Little Rock, Evansville, and Memphis, resulting in a full slate of eight teams set to start the season. Those teams were New Orleans, Atlanta, Montgomery, Chattanooga, Memphis, Little Rock, Nashville, and Evansville. The inclusion of a team from Indiana in the Evansville Blackbirds marked the first and only time the Southern League would have a member north of the Mason-Dixon line in the league. The entire circuit was approximately 5,000 miles so travel was going to be a significant concern. A unanimously backed proposal called for renewed negotiations with the railroad companies to provide volume ticket discounts.

A bright sign for New Orleans was the return of Abner Powell as manager and it was generally anticipated that the 1895 Southern League season would came off with only a few minor setbacks, but no major problems. With a salary limit of $1,000 per month being maintained for another season, Powell and other Southern League managers now accustomed to the hurdle and were actively signing players to fill out their rosters. Their teams were completed a little later in the season than expected. The Pelicans could look forward to a challenging spring training season with the St. Louis Browns, the Louisville Colonels, the Baltimore Orioles, and the New York Giants all settling in for the spring in New Orleans. The New York Giants remarked that "the trip [to New Orleans] will undoubtedly be of great benefit to the team and the boys should return to begin the fight for the pennant in the very pink of condition."[44]

The good news was that spring training in New Orleans had grown into a profitable side business for the owners and management of the New Orleans Pelicans. With four major league teams in town, practice sessions at the ball park had to be carefully scheduled and other facilities pressed into service for practice when Sportsman's Park hosted an exhibition game. The bad news was that with four major league teams in town the New Orleans Pelicans were rarely needed as a sparring partner for an exhibition game.

In an unusual change to the schedule, the Pelicans faced off against the Montgomery Colts on April 25, and were administered with a full coat of kalsomine, falling 9 to 0 in a rare Opening Day shutout.[45] By mid–May the Pelicans were lodged in sixth place out of eight teams. The league limped along until July 18 and was somehow able to complete the first half of the 1895 season, but both Little Rock and Memphis dropped out shortly thereafter, having played sixty-nine and seventy-two games, respectively. The remaining six teams struggled through the next thirty days, with teams playing between twenty-three to twenty-eight games in the second half before calling it quits for the season. The New Orleans squad continued their slow crawl out of the cellar, posting 46 wins and 55 losses (.455), putting them in fourth place. Their performance was even more disappointing in that there were six of their starting nine players who batted over .300 for the season. At .384 Robert Stafford led the team in hitting and was second in the league only to the .404 batting average achieved by Chattanooga's Lew Whistler. The Atlanta Crackers captured their third Southern League pennant. Despite their occasional hiccups, New Orleans and Atlanta proved to be two of the few bright spots in the league during its first ten years in operation. In fact, 1895 was the first time in the last three seasons that the Southern League finished with more than four teams.

Most Southern League teams wrestled with low attendance and it was well-known that smaller teams relied on larger teams like New Orleans to provide an above average attendance. In fact, their 50 percent of the gate receipts often made the difference in covering the travel expenses for getting their team to the next city. But attendance was not a sure bet and certainly the Pelicans fought an uphill battle for much of the 1895 season. For instance, a charity game between two social clubs, the Boston Club and the Pickwick Club, was played on May 10, 1895, at Sportsman's Park to benefit the Home for the Incurables. The gentlemen of the Boston Club convincingly defeated the gentlemen of the Pickwick Club by the score of 32 to 3 before a respectable crowd of 1,200 spectators.[46] Taking into account that this was a charity game, the event still easily out-drew the Pelicans who were sadly only averaging between 500 and 800 per game.

Final Results of the 1895 Southern League Season

Team	Won	Lost	Pct	GB
Atlanta Crackers	70	37	.654	
Nashville Seraphs	69	38	.645	-1
Evansville Blackbirds	66	38	.635	-2.5
New Orleans Pelicans	**46**	**55**	**.455**	**-21**
Chattanooga/Mobile	37	63	.370	-29.5
Montgomery Grays	40	70	.364	-31.5
Memphis Giants	32	37	.464	NA
Little Rock Travelers	25	47	.347	NA

Shortly after the end of the 1895 season, a whole new set of league officers were elected. President J.B. Nicklin was retiring, and Henry Powers became the new league president and J.L. Mueller of Mobile was named vice-president. The board included Monroe L. Bickert of Atlanta, Solon Jacobs of Birmingham, R.L. White of Nashville, and Robert Armour of Memphis. Their plate was full dealing with the concerns of owners whose investors and shareholders had withstood the barrage of bills to continue to bring baseball to their cities with no tangible return on their investment. There was constant competition to secure the best players and teams from rival leagues such as the Texas League, the Southeastern League, and the Central League.

Powers gave a newspaper interview during which he expressed his confidence in the overall financial strength of the Southern League and his disappointment that the New Orleans franchise would once again lose money.[47] Powers was spot on in his assessment of the financial capacity of the Southern League. Memphis had $2,000 and the promise of a new ballpark courtesy of the local street railway company, and Little Rock had $5,000 in reserves. During the January meeting in Memphis, discussions centered around a proposed move up from Class B to Class A and the attempts from rival leagues to poach rival cities. And once again there were a number of complaints against Henry Powers and New Orleans lodged by other owners. What used to be a couple of rival teams who harbored their individual grudges against New Orleans had deteriorated into a gaggle of petty squabbles from other teams for a variety of inconsequential reasons. Grievances no longer originated from the competitive fire of something that may have occurred on the field during a game but sunk to the level of bickering over the color of their uniforms and the timing of a trade for a player. In the end, all of the parties left the meeting agreeing to complete the league with six teams—New Orleans, Montgomery, Columbus, Atlanta, Birmingham, and Mobile.

New Orleans had assembled its strongest team since 1887, and a return to their traditional Opening Day opponent on April 16, 1896, saw the Pelicans outlast Mobile 9 to 8 in a slugfest during which both clubs had on their hitting shoes, with New Orleans smacking fourteen hits and Mobile pounding out fifteen hits. By the start of May New Orleans was in second-place, right on the heels of Montgomery. The Pelicans dismantled the rest of the field in both halves of the season behind the hitting of John Huston, whose twenty-seven doubles led the league, and skipper Abner Powell, whose ninety-seven runs also led the league. The pitching corps was led by twenty-two game winner Lucien Smith, whose total wins and thirty-four complete games also topped all Southern League hurlers. The league ended the season with six teams, having lost Atlanta on July 4 and Birmingham on July 12.

The New Orleans populace had apparently grown bored with waiting for electrifying baseball with the Pelicans playing winning baseball in front of large stretches of unoccupied seats, many games drawing fewer than 100 fans whose meager cheers could barely be heard over the drone of crickets chirping. Nonetheless, the Pelicans captured their third Southern League pennant, their first since 1889, finishing seven games ahead of the Montgomery Colts. After the fact, those few New Orleanians who actually attended the games had earned the right to howl, but it did not stop even the infrequent rooters from rooting and the fickle cranks from shrieking in delight. With the rest of the league in almost constant disarray, the decision was made during the winter meetings in Montgomery not to operate during 1897.

Final Results of the 1896 Southern League Season

Team	Won	Lost	Pct	GB
New Orleans Pelicans	67	30	.744	
Montgomery Colts	60	37	.667	-7
Mobile Blackbirds	39	59	.398	-28
Columbus Babies	35	60	.368	-32
Atlanta Crackers	36	36	.500	NA
Birmingham Barons	26	41	.388	NA

There was no baseball in any of the Southern League cities in 1897, and their players were scattered around the country. With the closure of the Southern League during 1897, a number of the Pelican players caught on with other teams. Abner Powell returned to his home state of Pennsylvania to play for the New Castle Quakers of the Interstate League and the Wilkes-Barre Coal Barons in the Eastern League. The Pelicans' leading hitter, shortstop John Huston, signed with the Galveston Sandcrabs in the Texas League along with outfielder William York and catcher John Gondling. Native New Orleanian and fan favorite, third baseman Joe Dowie, went to the Texas League with the Dennison-Sherman Twins and the Waco Tigers. This scenario was repeated in cities across the south.

The Southern League's best hitter, Montgomery's Ed Deady, played with Detroit, Indianapolis, and Minneapolis in the Western League. The best pitcher, Montgomery's Win Kellum also played with Indianapolis while Mobile pitcher Rudolph "Skel" Roach played with Wilkes-Barre in the Eastern League and Kentucky in the Western League.

With an entire year to reflect on the problems of the 1896 season, owners felt uncharacteristically confident that they would reverse course in 1898. The league got off to a strong start to the 1898 season on April 10 with eight teams, but ongoing lack of fan interest early in the season should have been a reminder of years past and a harbinger of the year ahead. But the fans' lack of support for their team was not as a result of ongoing bad play or from disaffected fans abandoning baseball altogether. Rather, it was a combination of continued economic hardship and their concerns over the looming tensions between Spain and America. The fiery "yellow journalism" rhetoric of newspapermen Joseph Pulitzer and William Randolph Hearst fueled the fires of war, and businessmen nationwide feared that war would only deepen the recession in an already fragile and uncertain economy.

In the past, New Orleanians would turn to diversions like baseball to escape the pressing concerns of economic uncertainty and recession. Now they would add the fear of war with Spain to the mix. But the baseball public was so starved for the return of professional baseball that their pent-up demand was satisfied in the short-term. With all of the accumulated uncertainty it took an inordinate amount of time for the league to finalize the participants for the 1898 season. On January 1 the league already had agreements in place with the usual six teams and were still confident of adding Montgomery and Augusta within the next two weeks. However, the final team wasn't signed until February 5, and then it took another month for the season schedule to be confirmed at the March 6 meeting in Birmingham. The season was set to run for four months from April 15 until August 15. In an attempt to shore up the finances of the league and the current teams, owners agreed to set aside 5 percent of gross receipts to the league's sinking fund, an increase from 3 percent, and to send 50 percent of the gross receipts to visiting teams on holidays.[48] Despite these fiscally responsible moves on the part of the league, there were some owners who were still hesitant to commit to the Southern League. Their pre-season confidence was beginning to erode.

Ignoring all of the commotion whirling around him and confident that his team would be playing somewhere in 1898, Abner Powell had begun signing players for New Orleans in early January. Between January 20 and February 18, he signed infielder Frank Graney, pitcher Ed Sheehan, pitcher W.W. Setley, pitcher F.T. Wayne, second baseman J. Goldie, L. Bennett, two pitchers named Burris and Haeger, catcher Fred Abbott, P.W. Mahan, catcher/outfielder Jack Hess, and Danny Boland. Of these players only six made the Opening Day roster. Bennett, Burris, Mahan, Hess, and Boland played elsewhere in 1898.

To celebrate the return of professional baseball to the city, New Orleans Mayor Walter Flower led an Opening Day trolley parade on Friday, April 15, to escort both teams from the St. Charles Hotel to the ballpark for the first game to be played at the city's new ballpark, Athletic Park. The new facility was accessible via the Canal and Claiborne Railroad line or through some of the city's newly asphalt paved roads. Athletic Park featured better grandstand views which were closer to the action on the diamond. On Saturdays and Sundays there would be a brass band to entertain fans beginning thirty minutes before the game.[49]

There were more than 1,000 fans in the stands at Athletic Park to celebrate Opening Day, but who were forced to watch the Mobile Blackbirds down the Pelicans in ten innings 5 to 4.[50] The game was tied at two runs apiece after five innings and the deadlock held fast until the tenth inning. Mobile then jumped on Pelicans pitcher F.T. Wayne for three runs in the top of the frame and the New Orleans rally fell a run short and they dropped their first game of the new season.

Mobile versus New Orleans
April 14, 1898[51]

Innings	1	2	3	4	5	6	7	8	9	10	Total
Mobile	0	0	1	0	1	0	0	0	0	3	5
New Orleans	0	0	0	0	2	0	0	0	0	2	4

The first half of the 1898 season ended in mid–May and some teams were beginning to falter. Last place Montgomery with only 9 wins against 19 losses (.379) folded after twenty-four games and there were rumors that in spite of their position in second-place Augusta at 14 wins and 9 losses (.605), was likely to follow within days. As it turned out, Augusta, managed to stay the course, but as an added distraction Atlanta leveled allegations that both New Orleans and Mobile were shirking their payments to the league's sinking fund and that Birmingham had paid less than $10 thus far. None of Atlanta's complaints were of much interest to the majority of Southern League fans whose attention was drawn and riveted to the details of the Spanish-American War that had broken out on April 21 just a week after Opening Day. Their ongoing concerns about the war and its potential impact on an already fragile economy were top of mind, overshadowing everything, including and especially baseball. Although Atlanta's allegations against New Orleans were soon proved to be unfounded, many saw this as another excuse to shutter the league to keep from hemorrhaging even more money.[52] Throughout the season New Orleans seemed to have a firm grip on sixth place, ending with a record of only 10 wins against 15 losses (.400) and finishing 8½ games behind Augusta. After a scant thirty games, the 1898 season was the shortest season in Southern League history. From April 10 until May 19, the collapse only took a mere thirty-nine days.

Final Results of the 1898 Southern League Season

Team	Won	Lost	Pct	GB
Augusta	20	8	.714	
Charleston	20	10	.667	-1
Savannah	15	11	.577	-3
Atlanta	14	15	.483	-6.5
Birmingham	13	16	.488	-7.5
New Orleans Pelicans	*10*	*15*	*.400*	*-8.5*
Mobile	11	18	.379	-9.5
Montgomery	9	19	.321	-11

The final indignity came in the 1899 season. The winter meetings in mid–December of 1898 began with a reasonable plan to field eight teams. However, at the mid–January league meeting in New Orleans, and over the objections of several owners, Abner Powell put forward a proposal to move forward with only four teams.[53] While there was no clear consensus in favor of Powell's proposal, no one had a better solution and the league was declared complete with only four viable teams—the New Orleans Pelicans, the Mobile Blackbirds, the Shreveport Tigers, and the Montgomery Steers. As expected, it was Atlanta, Charleston, and Birmingham who objected to the change that left them out of the Southern League and searching for a new league to call home. To no one's surprise, Powell's four-team proposal was adopted, as much out of frustration and exhaustion from the ongoing bickering as anything else. Their frustration was understandable and unfortunate. No one was making any money and no one was entirely confident that the new four-team scheme would be successful. There was still the hope that between Memphis, Little Rock, and Birmingham at least two of the three would join the league in enough time to revise the league schedule and have at least six teams. That hope dissolved under the ongoing disagreements regarding financial requirements, mainly the minimum mandatory forfeit deposit and reserve fund. Even though these payments to the league were pro-rated on a monthly basis, the razor-thin margins, or lack thereof, only added to the monthly deficits that could easily and frequently weigh on the weaker teams.

With the inclusion of Shreveport for 1899 came the inevitable inquiries regarding New Orleans joining the Texas League, this time coming from representatives from Houston and Dallas. There were tedious and often contentious discussions about merging the two leagues into two four-team circuits to be called the Southeastern League. The Pelican's Henry Powers was trying to develop a workable plan, but the entire situation was still unsettled by mid–March, making it increasingly more difficult for managers to sign players with any degree of certainty of where they might be playing. But ever the optimist, Abner Powell was an experienced baseball hand who again knew that his New Orleans Pelicans team was certain to be playing somewhere in the next thirty days and, with practiced stealth, quietly assembled a team of seasoned players. As time wore on, Powell's four-team format was ratified without any hope of adding new teams, and the smaller Southern League headed almost reluctantly toward Opening Day.

The Pelicans went on the road to face Mobile on April 13, 1899, before a scant 600 fans. Mobile scored two runs in the second-inning which was all they needed to whitewash the Pelicans by the score of 2 to 0. Mobile's pitcher Chamberlain held New Orleans to six hits, none bunched, and only two Pelicans made it as far as third base during the game. New Orleans' pitcher Jim Delaney only gave up seven hits, but they did all of their damage in the second-inning.[54]

By May 7 New Orleans was firmly in second place with a record of 10 and 8 (.555) behind Mobile, who seemed to be destined to win the pennant. Yet on May 25 the first-place Mobile disbanded "for want of patronage." When the Montgomery group threw in the towel it was Dallas Hams, formerly of the Texas League, who picked up the franchise.

On Wednesday, May 31, 1899, New Orleans' fans peered across the diamond at the unfamiliar faces of the Dallas players. There was no way of knowing at the time but this would be the final game New Orleans played in the Southern League.

Dallas versus New Orleans
May 31, 1899[55]

Innings	1	2	3	4	5	6	7	8	9	Total
Dallas	5	0	0	0	0	6	2	1	1	9
New Orleans	0	0	2	0	1	0	0	0	0	3

The visitors scored five runs in the first inning which as it turned out would have been enough to win the game, but then tallied another four runs in the last three innings. Both teams tallied nine hits during the game and the Pelicans were guilty of four errors in the first inning that cost them the game. It was a disappointing end to a disappointing season, ending with a

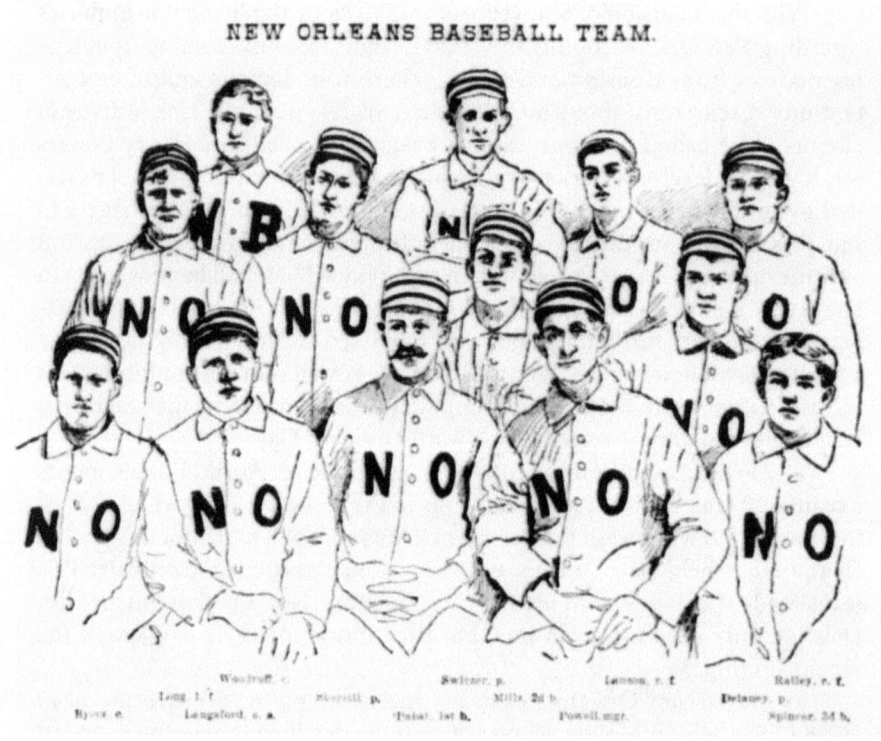

An engraving of the 1899 New Orleans Pelicans. The team posted a dismal 19–21 (.475) record in 1899 before the Southern League collapsed after only fifty-two days (*Semi-Weekly Times-Democrat*, April 21, 1899).

whimper on June 3 after only fifty-two days. The four-team format proved to be competitive even though Mobile led the pack from wire to wire. Once again, the most popular sport in Louisiana was crippled "for want of patronage."

New Orleans finished in third-place behind the pitching of Art Switzer, who at 6'10" was the tallest player in baseball, but who was so thin he could have been an advertisement for malnutrition. His 49 strikeouts helped him put up a 10–5 (.667) record. The Pelicans ending 1899 season with 19 wins and 21 losses (.475), in third place just four and one-half games behind the Mobile Blackbirds. Pelican second baseman Sam Mills captured the Southern League batting title (.393) and also led the league with sixty-four hits in forty games.

Final Results of the 1899 Southern League Season

Team	Won	Lost	Pct	GB
Mobile Blackbirds	23	16	.590	
Shreveport Tigers	21	23	.490	-4
New Orleans Pelicans	**19**	**21**	**.475**	**-4.5**
Montgomery/Dallas	19	23	.452	-5.5

Powell and several members of the Pelicans team, including pitcher Art Switzer, first baseman Ed Pabst, catcher Bill Byers, and second baseman Sam Mills, headed north to Paterson, New Jersey, to play in the Atlantic League for the remainder of the season.[56]

In a reversal of roles, when Montgomery folded on May 2 threatening to halt play in the Southern League, it was the Dallas Hams, shut out of the Texas League, that came to the rescue. They assumed Mobile's schedule starting on May 5. When the Southern League threw in the towel on June 3, Mobile moved to the Texas League to replace the Houston Buffalos, buying another thirty days for yet another dying circuit.

No one was really focused on the death of the Southern League which had been a long time in coming and was expected by almost everyone. Instead, all eyes along the Gulf Coast, indeed nationwide, were riveted on news reports of a new outbreak of yellow fever in New Orleans. The city's Board of Health of the City of New Orleans was quick to downplay any rumor of an epidemic or of a possible quarantine, describing instead the single fatality in late May as that of a seventeen-year-old Italian girl being an isolated incident. In an abundance of caution, and not wishing to repeat the death toll of fifty-seven people in 1898, the New Orleans Board of Health cautioned all transportation lines, hotels, restaurants, and other public businesses to take the usual precautions against spreading the disease. In the end there were twenty-three deaths in New Orleans from yellow fever during 1899. Life in the city returned to normal, but professional baseball was gone with no hope of returning. The Southern League had started in 1885 with such promise and it was thought that professional baseball had finally gained a secure foothold in the South, particularly with the success of the New Orleans and Atlanta franchises, but it never gained the stability needed to ensure its success.

Number of Games Played on the League Schedule
By Year—Fewest and Most Games Played

Year	Fewest Games	Team	Most Games	Team
1885	92	Memphis	104	Augusta
1886	52	Augusta	97	Charleston
1887	22	Mobile	114	New Orleans
1888	50	(Three Teams)	56	New Orleans
1889	36	(Two Teams)	55	New Orleans
1892	120	(Two Teams)	124	Montgomery
1893	90	Augusta	95	Montgomery
1894	55	Charleston	69	New Orleans
1895	69	Memphis	110	Montgomery
1896	72	Atlanta	98	Mobile
1898	25	New Orleans	30	Charleston
1899	39	Mobile	43	Shreveport

There were opportunities to make money in baseball, although infrequent. Unlike the amateur team tours by New Orleans teams beginning in 1869, barnstorming exhibition tours of American professional baseball players to Cuba were almost always profitable and continued until well into the 20th century. Abner Powell led one such tours in late December of 1899 and early January of 1900. His aggregation left New Orleans on the Southern Pacific steamer *Aransas* on Thursday, December 28, 1899. Powell was joined in the venture by his old friend Toby Hart. The team included players from the National, Western, and Southern leagues and was thought to be abroad for about thirty days. They planned to play two games per week on Thursdays and Sundays with one of the four teams in Havana as their opponent.

Powell wrote to Hart following their first game on January 4, 1900, telling him that his squad had defeated the Cubans by the score of 29 to 10 and that the team cleared $249 from the gate receipts. They played again on Sunday, January 7, winning 9 to 6 in front of a crowd estimated to be between 4,000 and 5,000 people for which his share of the gate was $666. They returned to New Orleans on Thursday, January 25, following a dispute with the Cuban ballpark owner who Powell claimed reneged on their contract.

However, the United States was in almost continual recession from 1890 through 1896. And though the recession of 1890–1891 was shorter than the recession of 1887–1888, it was far more pronounced in its impact. Still struggling to recover from back-to-back recessions, the country went into a panic in 1893 with the failure of the Reading Railroad and the subsequent collapse of the country's financial markets. This was followed by the panic of 1896, seen as the peak of a recessionary cycle that lasted from 1893 through 1896. With non-stop deflationary pressure, the national economy tottered along as best it could, but the most fragile economies in the South came quite close to hitting rock bottom. With little or no discretionary income available for professional baseball, and an ample supply of high caliber amateur baseball games available at more affordable prices, the business of professional baseball was nowhere close to being a sure thing.

But it was not only the Southern League and the New Orleans Pelicans that were impacted by economic events. Other leagues found themselves taking on water and discontinuing operations mid-season, closing for an entire season, or folding altogether. Among them were the Texas League, the American Association, the Players League, the Northwestern League, the Union Association, and the Eastern League. Some lasted a single season, some found themselves merging with other leagues. Given the miserable success rate for professional baseball leagues in the last quarter century of the 19th century, the relative success of the Southern League, particularly in its early years, is remarkable. Teams enjoyed strong fan following, even if there were not always able to back their teams at the ticket window. Players developed intense rivalries and these rivalries were not lost on the business and political leaders in their respective communities. A winning baseball team was just another metaphor for a successful city.

New Orleans was successful from the outset, as much for their baseball talent as for their frugality. Long known for having the lowest payroll in the league, it was their low overhead and their fan support, albeit sporadic, that allowed their franchise to persevere, despite consistently losing money from operations. Even during their worst seasons, the Pelicans never found the basement. They endured cold bats when the baseball looked like an aspirin coming out of the pitcher's hand; periods when even an experienced fielder had trouble with a can of corn; and when every ball hit their way was cold coffee. But every ball club goes through such periods. Fortunately for the Pelicans they had fewer of these slumps than their competition.

It took a cooperative effort to build a successful baseball alliance between the city and the franchise. New Orleans was fortunate to have the leadership of men such as Toby Hart, Thomas Brennan, Charles Genslinger, Abner Powell, and Henry Powers in the professional arena, and William F. Tracey, Conrad Leithman and a host of others in the amateur arena. In establishing the Southern League, the first professional league below the Mason-Dixon Line, the owners and investors in their respective franchises sought to capitalize on the growing national popularity of baseball. And more often than not the New Orleans franchise owners had to dig into their own pockets every season to keep the team afloat, not to mention the supplemental financial assistance they regularly provided other teams that would never be repaid.

The turn of the century found Abner Powell, Charles Frank from Memphis, and Newt Fisher from Nashville—all veterans of the now defunct Southern League—drumming up renewed interest in Southern baseball. They formed the Southern Association from the ashes of the failed Southern League. Both major league and minor league baseball would survive as a business concern. Like its predecessor, the new Southern Association began life on shaky legs, endured their early growing pains, and managed to persist for sixty years through good economic times and both recessions and depressions, through two world wars, through record-breaking fan attendance and stadiums that looked nearly empty. In the end it would be considered a success as the league achieved Class AA status and produced a steady stream of major leaguers, All-Stars, and future Hall of Famers, of which New Orleans could claim their share.

Between 1887 and 1959, New Orleans never missed an Opening Day, never folded mid-season unless forced to by the league's total collapse, and only begrudgingly sold their franchise to Little Rock at the conclusion of the 1959 season. With New Orleans gone, the Southern Association could not survive and closed down after the 1960 season.

Standing on the shoulders of all of those intrepid, adventurous young men who elevated a child's game into an exciting, addictive, and competitive sport during the 19th century, baseball would not only become the country's National Pastime, but by World War II was considered to be so vital to the very fabric of American life that on January 15, 1942, President Franklin D. Roosevelt issued what has become known as the Green Light Letter to the Baseball Commissioner to recommend that baseball continue to operate for the good of the country during the Second World War.

Appendix
What's in a Name?

Ballparks

The following list was compiled from published articles and game reports from various city newspapers. In the early days of baseball in New Orleans, newspaper reporters relied on the club secretary or scorer to provide the team roster and score. Eventually, as the game grew in popularity, the newspaper assigned reporters to cover games, but there were far more games being played on any single day than the paper could reasonably afford to send. So the news desk would frequently receive envelopes full of game results and news of the formation or reorganization of clubs.

Ballparks that appear on this list may have been referred to under an alternative name. The date shown is the first mention in print that I have found to date. It is highly likely that a ballpark existed prior to the date shown. If the reader notices any errors or omissions, please send me the appropriate documentation.

Algiers Green (1877)
Annunciation Square (1874)
Art Street (at the foot of) (1874)
Bannon's Park (1884)
Base Ball Green (1881)—*corner of Louisiana Avenue and Dryades Street*
Bee Green (1877)—*on Washington Avenue*
The Beef Lot (1886)—*perhaps located in the city of Carrollton*
Bellecastle and Magazine Street (1884)
Bienville Street (1866)—*Lone Star's grounds* (near the Fair Grounds)
Bingaman/Bingamon Race Course (1860)—*Algiers*
Blaffer's Park (Blatter's) (1884)
Branch Green (1893)
Broad Street Green (1879)
Campbell Green (1881)
Canal Street (at the head of)

Canal Street (1870) (at the Fourth Canal)—*also identified with Stonewall's Green*
Carney's Park (1882)
Carrollton Park (1893)—*this may be an alternative name for Ferran's Park*
Carver's Park (1884)—*junior teams called the New Orleans Base Ball Park (on Canal Street)*
Chandler's Park (1870) (proposed)
City Park (1884)
Claiborne Green (1875)
Claiborne Street (1859)—*between Union Street and Bagatelle Street*
Clara Street Green (1881)
Clouet Street (1870) (at the foot of)
Coliseum Square (1877)
Common and Rocheblave Street (1881)
Congo Square
The Crescent City Base Ball Park (02-08-1880)—*later Sportsman's Park, "back half of the Half-Way House"*
Customhouse Street (at the foot of) (1866)
Delachaise Grounds (1859)
Dufossat Street and Chestnut Street (1881)
Eighth Street Green (1882)
Erato Street Green (1879)
Esplanade & Broad Street (at the foot of) (1870)
Esplanade & White Street (at the corner of) (1869)
Exposition Park (1884)—*on the infield of the Audubon Driving Course*
Fair Grounds (1869)
Ferran's Park (1893)
First Field (1881)
Fourth & Franklin Street (at the corner of)
Freetown (1881)—*on Westbank of New Orleans*
Gaiennie Street Green (1882)
Galvez Green (1880)
Girod Street (at the foot of) (1877)
Gretna Green (1874)
Hancock Green (1874)—*corner of Dryades Street and Louisiana Avenue*
Henry Clay Avenue (1884)
Jackson Green (1876)
Jefferson Green (1882)
Keller's Green (1884)
Kettle Park (1879)—*corner of Poeyfarre and Foucher Streets*
Lafayette Square (1874, 1877, 1879)
Lapeyrouse and Galvez Streets (1873)
Locust Park (1879)
Loeper's Park (1879)—*4300 Bienville—Conti—Napoleon (Hennessey)—Alexander*

Logan's Green (1877)
Logan Street Green (1886)—*Carrollton*
London Green (1881)
Louisa Street (at the foot of)
Louisiana Avenue & Bacchus Street (Baronne Street) (at the corner of) (1867)
Louisiana Avenue & Dryades Street (at the corner of) (1872)
Louisiana Base Ball Park (Association)—*Henry Clay (Palmer Ave)—Long Street (Freret Street)—and Victor Street (Magnolia Street) (1870) (Sixth District)*
Mack's Green (1881)—*corner of Conti and Rocheblave Streets*
Magazine Street & St. Joseph Street (corner of) (1870)
Magnolia Garden (1883)—*at West End*
Masonic Lot (1881)—*opposite Tivoli Circle on St. Charles and Calliope Streets*
Maylie's Green (1882)
McCarthy Square (1875)
McCarty Square (1876)—*between Burgundy, North Rampart, Pauline and Jeanna (Alvar) Streets in the Third District*
McDonoghville (1877)—*on the Westbank in present day Gretna*
Metairie Course (1868)—*Lone Star's grounds*
Milan Green (1884)
Monck/Mouck's Park (1884)
Montegut Street (at the foot of) (1877)—*the Montegut Green (1881)*
Morgan's Green/Morgan's Depot (1877)—*Algiers*
Napoleon Avenue (1870)
Nashville Station of Carrollton Railroad (1866)
Natchez Green (1881)
The New Orleans Base Ball Park (1884)—*the NO Baseball Park Association—4500 block of Canal Street bounded by Olympia/Murat/ Customhouse (Iberville) streets*
Oak Grove Park (1879)—*"below the slaughterhouse" (St. Bernard?)*
Oakland Park (1872)
Ogden Park (two squares above Louisiana Avenue on Prytania Street) (1877)
Oil Factory Green (1882)
The Old Paper Mill (1860)—*in the Third District*
Orange Green (1879)
Orleans Park (1877)
Piety Street (at the foot of)
Pioneer Green (1872)—(in the rear of the Second District)—*on Esplanade, at the foot of Ursuline Street*
Piper's Green (1882)
Poland Street Green (1874)
Poydras Green (1882)

Prytania Street Car Station Green (1886)
Rackett Grounds/Old Racket/Roquette Green—*Annette Street* (at the foot of—Third District)
Robin Street (at the foot of) (1873)
St. Charles and Milan (1885)
Sister's School Green (1885)
Soniat Station of Carrollton Railroad (1867)
Southern Green (1870)—*corner of Magnolia and Poydras*
Sportsman's Park (1886)—*formerly Crescent City Base Ball Park*
Stickerbush Green/Stickney Bush Green (1882)—*corner of Camp and Amelia Streets*
Stone Lot Green (1879)
Stonewall's Green—*Fourth Canal (Canal Street) (1870) at Loeper's Park*
Thalia Street Lot (1879)
Thalia Street Green (1881)
Three Oak Green (1881)
Tivoli Circle
U.S. Barracks (1879)
Valence Green (1890)
White & Ursuline Streets (at the corner of) (1874)

Teams

The following list was compiled from published articles and game reports from various city newspapers. In the early days of baseball in New Orleans, newspaper reporters relied on the club secretary or scorer to provide the team roster and score. Eventually, as the game grew in popularity, the newspaper assigned reporters to cover games, but there were far more games being played on any single day than the paper could reasonably afford to send. So the news desk would frequently receive envelopes full of game results and news of the formation or reorganization of clubs.

Teams that appear on this list may have played a single game, a single season, or for many years. The date shown is the first mention in print that I have found to date. It is highly likely that teams existed prior to the date shown. If the reader notices any errors or omissions, please send me the appropriate documentation.

340's (1877)
A&R's (1884)
Acme Base Ball Club (1886)
Active Base Ball Club (1870)
Actives (1882)—*Poydras Street produce clerks*
C. Adams/Adams Base Ball Club (1881)
Tommy Adler Base Ball Club (1882)

Adrien/Adrien Brothers (1884)
Aetna Base Ball Club (1872)—*black team—(1877) former Franklin players*
Algiers Joy Base Ball Club (1881)
Alleghenies (1883)
Allens Base Ball Club (1882)
Allright Base Ball Club (1874)
Aloe Base Ball Club (1871)—*Algiers (?)*
Altogether Base Ball Club (1879)—*formerly Our Boys Base Ball Club*
Always Sure Base Ball Club (1879)—*Third District*
Amaranth Social Club (1879)
Amateur Base Ball Club (1874)—*(formerly The Richmonds?)*
American District Telegraph Nine (1884)
American Rice Mill Base Ball Club (1884)
T. Anderson Base Ball Club (1877)—*named for the "Mayor of Storyville," Thomas C. Anderson*
Arctic Base Ball Club (1875)
Arlington Base Ball Club (1872)—*junior team—Central High School Club (1881)—J.D. Houston Base Ball Club (1881)*
Armchair Base Ball Club (1882)
William Armshaw Base Ball Club (1882)
Atlantic Base Ball Club (1860)
Athletes Base Ball Club (1896)
Athletics Base Ball Club (1869) *(reorganized 1873)*
Athletic Base Ball Club (1885)—*black team*
Atlantic Base Ball Club (1867)—*Algiers*
Aunt Richard's Base Ball Club (1882)
Avenue Base Ball Club (1886)—*junior team*
Dr. L. Azabary Base Ball Club (1879)
B'Hoys Base Ball Club (1873)
Eugene Babad (1884)
J.C. Bach Base Ball Club (1884) *(reorganized 1886)*
Gabe Bachemine Base Ball Club (1886)
A.S. Badger Base Ball Club (1879)
I.N. Bakers Base Ball Club (1884)
William Baker Base Ball Club (1877)
Baltic Base Ball Club (1871)
Baltimore Base Ball Club (1879)—*female baseball club*
Banditti Club (1874)
Banquois (1884)
Barber Base Ball Club (1884)
Alf. Barnes Base Ball Club (1884)
T. Barret Base Ball Club (1882)
Barry Base Ball Club (1879)
T.J. Bath Base Ball Club (1884)

V.E. Baumgarien/Baumgarden Base Ball Club (1882)
Bayou St. John Base Ball Club (1884)
Beauregard Base Ball Club (1870)
O. Becker Base Ball Club (1882)
P. Becker Base Ball Club (1884)
J. Beecher Base Ball Club (1884)
W. J. Behan Base Ball Club (1879)
J. Behrman Base Ball Club (1882)
Beiden Base Ball Club (1879)
Belle Castle Base Ball Club (1884)
Belle Lee Base Ball Club (1869)
H.A. Bellman/Belmont Base Ball Club (1881)
A.A. Belmont Base Ball Club (1882)—*(possibly named for August Belmont who wife's uncle was John Slidell)*
John A. Benedict Base Ball Club (1881)—*former Washington Base Ball Club players*
John E. Bensel Base Ball Club (1881)
R.S. Benton Base Ball Club (1882)
(Dr.) Otto Berger Base Ball Club (1881)
Bernard Base Ball Club (1884)
Mike Berry Base Ball Club (1879)—The Berry Nine (1881)
Patrick Berry Base Ball Club (1882)
The Best Olive Base Ball Club (1890)
J. Bertucci Base Ball Club (1882)
Philip Best Brewing Company Base Ball Club (1886)
Bittle Base Ball Club (1879)—*Ninth Ward*
B. Bitters Base Ball Club (1881)
Black Elephant Base Ball Club (1875)
Peter Blaise Base Ball Club (1881)
The Blakes (1880)
Blanco Base Ball Club (1884)
Fred A. Blanks Base Ball Club (1880)
Leon Blessings Base Ball Club (1881)
Blinkey Base Ball Club (1875)
Blockhead Base Ball Club (1882)
Bloom's Nine (1879)
Blue Caps Base Ball Club (1884)
Blue Cloud Base Ball Club (1877)
Blue Stocking Base Ball Club (1869)
The Blue Stocking Mutuals (1872)
A. Blume Base Ball Club (1882)
A.A. Bohne Base Ball Club (1881)
Bon Ton Base Ball Club (1881)
Bordel Base Ball Club (1886)—*black team*

Borges Base Ball Club (1886)—*Later P.J. Caldwell Base Ball Club (1886)*
Boss Nine (1879)
Boston Base Ball Club (1881)—*black team*
Boston Base Ball Club (1874)
Boston Nine (1876)—*female baseball club*
Boulevard Base Ball Club (1886)
Boyle Base Ball Club (1884)
Boys Base Ball Club (1876)
L.W. Bradley Base Ball Club (1882)
E.A. Brandsos Base Ball Club (1884)
Braselman Combination (1884)
Harry Breen Base Ball Club (1886)
Brenard/A. Brenard Base Ball Club (1884)
H.F. Brennan Base Ball Club (1881)
Nick Brennan Base Ball Club (1882)
Thomas Brennan Base Ball Club (1879)
Brewster Base Ball Club (1881)
C.A. Brisset Base Ball Club (1884)
D. Broderick/Brodick Base Ball Club (1879)
W. Brophy Base Ball Club (1884)
Tom Brothers Base Ball Club (1885)—*junior team*
D. Brown Base Ball Club (1883)
Ed. Brown Base Ball Club (1884)
H. Brown Base Ball Club (1886)—*black team*
M. Brown Base Ball Club (1884)
Robert L. Brown Base Ball Club (1886)
John H. Brownlee Base Ball Club (1886)
The Bruisers (1877)
Geo. Bruno/Bruneau Base Ball Club (1881)
Buckeye Base Ball Club (1872)
J.W. Buckhart Base Ball Club (1882)
Buffalo Bills Base Ball Club (1881)
The Buffers (1877)
Eugene F. Buhler Base Ball Club (1882)
L. Buhler Base Ball Club (1882)—*junior team*
Bulldozer Base Ball Club (1877)—*Second District*
Buncy Bells (1881)—*changed to A.G. Maylies (Sept. 1881)*
William Burges Base Ball Club (1886)
T. Burke Base Ball Club (1883)
E.A. Burke Base Ball Club (1879)
Buster Custers Base Ball Club (1881)
William Butler Base Ball Club (1881)
Butts Base Ball Club (1886)
S. Caleca Base Ball Club (1886)

P./P.J. Caldwell Base Ball Club (1886)—*formerly the Borges Base Ball Club (1886) and Bob Lamson players*
Calhoun Base Ball Club (1882)
J.C. Callahan Base Ball Club (reorganized 1883)
F.P. Callejas Base Ball Club (1884)
P. Caminita/P. Cominita Base Ball Club (1884)
The Canal Ducks (1872)—*junior team*
Canal Street Pleasure Club (1886)
The Canary Club (1881)
Capitol Base Ball Club (1870)—*junior team*
W. Carroll/Carroll Base Ball Club (1884)
Carwashers Base Ball Club (1883)
Bert Casey Base Ball Club (1884)
Pat Casey Base Ball Club (1884)
D. Cavanaes/Cavanacs Base Ball Club (1882)
Dan Cavanaugh Base Ball Club (1883)
A.F. Caymo Base Ball Club (1881)
F.P. Cellogas Base Ball Club (1884)
Centennial Base Ball Club (1875)
Champion Base Ball Club (1869)—*Seventh District*
The Charmers (1872)
The Cheap John Base Ball Club (1879)
Cherokee Base Ball Club (1882)
E.R. Chevally Base Ball Club (1879)
Chicago Base Ball Club (1882)—*junior team*
Chinward Base Ball Club (1884)
City Items Base Ball Club (1882)
Claiborne Base Ball Club (1875)
J. Paris Childress Base Ball Club (1879)
The Clara Guards (1877)
William Clements Base Ball Club (1881)
Clerks Base Ball Club (1886)
Grover Cleveland Base Ball Club (1886)
Cleveland Avenue Base Ball Club (1886)
Cleveland Avenue Boys (1886)—*formerly the Galvez Boys*
Clippers (New Orleans) (1872)—*junior team*
Clippers (Mandeville) (1872)
Coakley Base Ball Club (1882)
Charles Cochrane Base Ball Club (1884)
Walter/W.L. Cohen Base Ball Club (1885)—*formerly The Pickwicks (black team)*
Coleman Mill Factory Base Ball Club (1880)
Coliseum Nine Base Ball Club (1886)
Coltecnne Base Ball Club (1884)—*junior team* (spelling questionable)
Compress Men (1894)

Coughlin Base Ball Club (1882)
Columbia Base Ball Club (1877)
Columbus Base Ball Club (1877)
Comet Base Ball Club (Sept 1860) *(reorganized 1868)*
Comet Base Ball Club (1884)—*junior team*
Comic Base Ball Club (1875)
P.J. Commer Base Ball Club (1881)—*junior team—former Louisiana Base Ball Club players*
Commercial Base Ball Club (1879)
J.P. Conners Base Ball Club (1881)
Continental Base Ball Club (1870)
Larry Conroy Base Ball Club (1881)
William Cooper Base Ball Club (1881)
Copor (1881)
A.J. Cosgrove Base Ball Club (1880)
Cotton Plant Base Ball Club (1881)
Cotton Yard Men (1894)
The Crabs (1879)
J. Cravens Base Ball Club (1886)
The Crawmeats Base Ball Club *(reorganized 1879)*
Creole Base Ball Club (1866)
Crescent Base Ball Club (1870)—*reorganized 1879*
Crescent Browns Base Ball Club (1886)
Crescent City Base Ball Club (1869)
Crescent City Combination (1883)
Crescent Insurance Company Base Ball Club (1884)
Crescent Light Guards Base Ball Club (1886)
The Crescent Rifles (1882)
Cricket Base Ball Club (1874)—*The Crickets (1881)*
Crusader Base Ball Club (1867)
John Cruso Base Ball Club (1886)
D. Cullan Base Ball Club (1882)
E.H. Curry Base Ball Club (1882)
J. Curry Base Ball Club (1884)
F. Custer Base Ball Club (1881)
Custer Buster Base Ball Club (1881)
Daddies Base Ball Club (1886)
The Daisy Club (1877)
E.R. Dalton Base Ball Club (1884)
George N. Daner Base Ball Club (1885)
Senator Daniels Base Ball Club (1883)
Danite Base Ball Club (1879)
James Darrow Base Ball Club (1884)
A.C. Daunoy Base Ball Club (1884)

J. Danynois Base Ball Club (1882)
Dauntless Base Ball Club (1882)—*former Arlington (junior) and Lotta players—changed to Arlington Base Ball Club (1882)*
R.C. Davey Base Ball Club (1881)
John Davis Base Ball Club (1886)
Geo. Degby/Digby Base Ball Club (1881)—*former Mike Rickerts players—changed to Owen Woods Base Ball Club (1881)*
A.W. Delavallades Base Ball Club (1882)
Delmonte Base Ball Club (1886)
P. Demots Base Ball Club (1883)—*formerly the D. McCarthy Base Ball Club*
J. Delords Base Ball Club (1881)
Delta Base Ball Club (1875)
Democratic Base Ball Club (1879)
The Democrats (1872)—*black team (1886)*
Tony Demote Base Ball Club (1886)
Joe Desposito Base Ball Club (1879)—*formerly the M.J. Harts (1881)*
Detroit Base Ball Club (1881)
Deuce of Hearts Base Ball Club (1884)
L. Dever Base Ball Club (1886)
Dexter Base Ball Club (1870)
Diamond Base Ball Club (1877)
Dicks Base Ball Club (1881)
Thomas Dillon Base Ball Club (1882)
John A. Dix Club (1874)
Charley Dodge Base Ball Club (1881)—*workers in Pullman car shop of Jackson Railroad Depot*
Donahoe Base Ball Club (1881)
Bridgit Donahue Base Ball Club (1883)
Ed Donnelly Base Ball Club (1879)
P.A. Donnelly Base Ball Club (1885)—*junior team*
John Dooley Base Ball Club (1884)
The Dots (1872)
The Doughnuts (1880)
John Dowie Base Ball Club (1885)
John Doyle Base Ball Club (1879)
P.H. Doyle Base Ball Club (1884)
The Dread Not Base Ball Club (1869)
Dr. E. Dreifus/Dreyfus Base Ball Club (1879)—*changed to Charles Schreiber Base Ball Club (August 1879)*
Dew Drops Base Ball Club (1886)
Dryades Market Base Ball Club (1881)
Ferdinand Dudenheffer Nine (1879)
The Dudes (1884) and The Dudines (1886)—*benefit teams*
Duffys Base Ball Club (1886)—*formerly The Schencks*

Luke Duffy Base Ball Club (1881)
Thomas Duffy Base Ball Club (1879)
Duffy Malt Whiskey Base Ball Club (1886)
James J. Dugan Base Ball Club (1881)
J.H. Duggan Base Ball Club (1882)
C. Dumeyer Base Ball Club (1886)
O. Dumstre Base Ball Club (1886)
A.J. Dumont Base Ball Club (1881)—*black team*
Dunn Base Ball Club (1882)
Alf. Dupre Base Ball Club
Eugene Dupre Base Ball Club (1882)
The Dussees (1884)
Durning E Base Ball Club (1884)
J.B. Durnin Base Ball Club (1881)
J. Dutrey Base Ball Club (1884)
H. Duvalle Base Ball Club (1881)
Pat Eagan/P. Egan/Eagan Base Ball Club (1882)
Eagle Bakery Nine (1884)
Eagle Base Ball Club (1870)
Echo Base Ball Club (1874)
Eckford (Ecford) Base Ball Club (1874)
Eclipse Base Ball Club (1881)
Egg Dealers (1871)
T.H. Ehlers Base Ball Club (1884)
El Dorado Base Ball Club (1877)—*Garden District*
Elite Base Ball Club (1882)
E. John Ellis Base Ball Club (1882)
Elks & Reindeers Base Ball Club (1894)
Elmo Base Ball Club (1882)
Empire Base Ball Club (1859)
Esculent Base Ball Club (1872)
B. Estalope Base Ball Club (1882)—*former La De Dah Base Ball Club players*
The Eurekas (1885)—*former Ponsettis*
Evening Star Base Ball Club (1874)
Excelsior Base Ball Club (1868)—*(1874—"several Excelsior clubs")*
Exposition Nine/The Expositions (1884)
V. Fabian Base Ball Club (1884)
William Fagan Base Ball Club (1879)
J.B. Faget Base Ball Club (1879)
Fairfax Base Ball Club (1874)
L. Falk Base Ball Club (1887)
The Fanks (1881)
The Fannius (1884)
The Farantas (1884)

The Farraks (1881)
Jas. Farrell Base Ball Club (1881)
The Fashions (1869)
D. Feany Base Ball Club (1882)—*junior team*
Fearless Base Ball Club (1869)
Feldmyer Base Ball Club (1882)
A.M. Felts Base Ball Club (1884)
Female Base Ball Club (1886)
Fenian Base Ball Club (1875)—*Irish*
Chas. H. Fenner Base Ball Club (1881)
Frank Fenner Base Ball Club (1879)
R. Fernandez Base Ball Club (1882)
Filmore Base Ball Club (1882)—*junior club*
P.J. Finney Base Ball Club (1882)
Fire Fly Base Ball Club (1869)
Fireman's Insurance Company Base Ball Club (1884)
The Fischers/A. Fischer Base Ball Club (1885)—*black champions of Carrollton*
C. B. Fischer Base Ball Club (1886)
William E. Fitzgerald Base Ball Club (1879)
The Fitzpatricks (1879)—*deputy criminal sheriffs*
Flaherty Base Ball Club (1877)—*junior team*
The Flanders (1885)—*junior team*
Fletcher Base Ball Club (1893)
L. Fleming Base Ball Club (1879)
The Flints (1883)
The Flip Flaps (1886)—*Young Men's Gymnastics Club team*
The Flirts/The Lazy Flirts (1874)—*renamed The Reverigerre Base Ball Club (1874)*
J.B./E.B. Flores Base Ball Club (1882)
Florida Base Ball Club (1870)—*junior team*
George W. Flynn/Flynn Base Ball Club (1884)
G.T. Ford Base Ball Club (1881)
P.H. Ford Base Ball Club (1881)
P.T. Ford Base Ball Club (1881)—*formerly John Hoffman Base Ball Club*
T.J. Ford Base Ball Club (1883)—*junior team*
Foresters Base Ball Club (1881)
George W. Foster Base Ball Club (1898)
Franklin Base Ball Club (1877)—*formerly the Aetnas*
J.J. Frawley Base Ball Club (1882)
J. Frederick Base Ball Club (1886)
Freedom Base Ball Club (1872)—*junior team*
C. Freese/Freece Base Ball Club (1885)—*Sixth District—junior team*
J.H. Frerichs/Ferriches Base Ball Club (1881)
Fruit of the Loom Base Ball Club (1882)

Fulton Base Ball Club (1879)
Chas. Funk Base Ball Club (1881)
The Futures (1882)
The G&P's (1884)
Gable Base Ball Club (1884)
Gallagher Base Ball Club (1881)
Galvez Boys Base Ball Club (1886)
Capt. Galvin Base Ball Club (1882)
Gangers Base Ball Club (1879)—*female baseball club (?)*
Garden City Base Ball Club (1871)
Garden Gates Base Ball Club (1874)
M.D. Gardner Base Ball Club (1879)
John Garic Base Ball Club (1879)
E. Garnier Base Ball Club (1881)
The Garrigans *(see McGarrigan Base Ball Club)*
Gascard Base Ball Club (1884)
Gaspard Base Ball Club (1880)
The Gatti Base Ball Club (1899)
John Gauche & Sons Nine (1884)
General Longstreet Base Ball Club (1874)
H. Gessner Base Ball Club (1884)
Gilliam Base Ball Club (1886)
P. Gillon Base Ball Club (1881)
Pat Glennon Base Ball Club (1879)—*became the Remy Clarke Base Ball Club (November 1879)*
James Glynn Base Ball Club (1882)
Leon Godchaux Base Ball Club (1890)
Go Easy Base Ball Club (1877)
Golden Crown Nine (1883)—*crew of the steamboat Golden Crown*
Golden Rule Base Ball Club (1883)—*crew of the steamboat Golden Rule*
Golden Thread Base Ball Club (1875)
Good For Nothing Base Ball Club (1879)
P. Graham Base Ball Club (1881)
Grand Dukes Base Ball Club (1881)
J.L. Grasshoff Base Ball Club (1886)
Grasshopper Baseball Club (1871)
Greeley Base Ball Club (1872)—*employees of the Republican "office" of NO*
Green Stocking Base Ball Club (1870)—*junior team*
Emile Grillot Nine (1881)
S.T. Gately Base Ball Club (1882)
Gus. Gast Base Ball Club (1880)
W.F. Goldthwaite Base Ball Club (1882)—*junior team*
Fred Good Base Ball Club (1882)
G.W. Green Base Ball Club (1882)

J.V. Guillotte Base Ball Club (1881)—*former Washington Base Ball Club players; named for ex-Mayor of N.O.*
M. Hackett Base Ball Club (1881)
L.P. Hackmeyer Base Ball Club (1884)
D. Haggerty Base Ball Club (1880)
R.M. Hahn Base Ball Club (1881)
Charles A. Haifleigh Base Ball Club (1879)
C.H. Haights Base Ball Club (1882)
Hakenjos Base Ball Club (1886)
J.A. Haley/J. Healy Base Ball Club (1881)
Hall Mutual Base Ball Club (1877)
Hamilton Base Ball Club (1882)
Hard Hitters Base Ball Club (1882)—*junior team*
Hardin Base Ball Club (1884)—*black team (?)*
Headers & Anti-Headers (1884)—*cyclists*
Hancock Base Ball Club (1871)—*later the National Base Ball Club (May 1871)*
Handstands Base Ball Club (1886)
H. Hankin Base Ball Club (1884)
Jack Harkaway Base Ball Club (1874)
P.M. Harnan Base Ball Club (1879)
T.M. Harlee Base Ball Club (1883)
E.J. Hart Base Ball Club (1886)
The Harts (1881)
The Hasty Tappers (1884)
Hon. John Hayes Base Ball Club (1884)
J.J. Hayes Base Ball Club (1884)
Haymaker Base Ball Club (1870)
Healy Base Ball Club (1884)
D.C. Hennessey Base Ball Club (1879)
Jim Hennessey Base Ball Club (1882)
P. Hess Base Ball Club (1882)
Jack/Jacob Hettinger Base Ball Club (1882)
Hickey Base Ball Club (1881)
T.J. Higgins Base Ball Club (1881)
J.S. Hodgins Base Ball Club (1886)
John Hoffman Base Ball Club (1879)—*changed to P.T. Ford Base Ball Club (1881)*
The Hole in the Wall Base Ball Club (1879)
L. Hollman Base Ball Club (1881)
T.J./Thomas J. Holmes Base Ball Club (1882)
Home Base Ball Club (1860)—*volunteer firemen*
The Hop Bitters Base Ball Club (1879)—*became the C.T. Howard Base Ball Club (1880)*
Hop Bitters Base Ball Club (1886)

Hope Base Ball Club (1868)—*(reformed by 1874 merger of Mississippi and Washington clubs)*
Alex. Horn Base Ball Club (1881)
Hourbright Base Ball Club (1879)
J.D. Houston Base Ball Club (1881)—*junior team—formerly the Arlington Base Ball Club*
William T. Houston Base Ball Club (1880)
C.T. Howard Base Ball Club (1880)
Howard Base Ball Club (1874)
R.S. Howard Base Ball Club (1880)
A. Huber Base Ball Club (1882)
Louis J. Huber Base Ball Club (1884)
E.R. Hunt Base Ball Club (1886)
The Hunters & Genslingers/The H&G's (1884)
Eli D. Hunter Base Ball Club (1883)
William E. Hunter Base Ball Club (1884)
Ida Base Ball Club (1872)
Idlewild Dramatic Club (baseball team) (1873)
Illgs Base Ball Club (1882)
Imperial Base Ball Club (1877)
Independent Base Ball Club (1882)
Innocent Base Ball Club (1874)
Iolanthe Base Ball Club (1883)
Irad Base Ball Club (1877)
Irish Wonders (1896)
Isaacson Base Ball Club (1879)
W. Israel Base Ball Club (1886)—*junior team*
"The Items" Base Ball Club (1886)—*newspaper team*
Jackson Base Ball Club (1874)—*junior team*
Jacksons (1870)—*of Carrollton*
Jackson Base Ball Club (1886)—*black*
Jackson Barracks Nine (1874)—*soldiers*
Jackson Press Base Ball Club (1879)
Jesuit Base Ball Club (1879)
Joseph Janfroids Base Ball Club (1881)
Jefferson Base Ball Club (1879)
E.J. Johnson Base Ball Club (1879)
F.R. Johnson Base Ball Club (1881)
Joseph Johnson Base Ball Club (1881)
W. F. Johnson Base Ball Club (1884)
Jonas Base Ball Club (1872)
Junior Base Ball Club (1866)
P.J. Kammer Base Ball Club (1881)—*former Louisianas*
P. Kane Base Ball Club (1882)

Katies (1881)—*Gretna*
Keating Base Ball Club (1882)
Keena/William Keenan Base Ball Club (1884)
Corporal Keenan Base Ball Club (1884)
Burt Kelly Nine (1884)—*clerks of civil district court*
Geo. Kelly Base Ball Club (1881)
P. Kelly Base Ball Club (1882)
Tom Kelly Base Ball Club (1882)
John C. Kendry Base Ball Club (1884)
P. Kenny Base Ball Club (1881)
Keno Base Ball Club (1873)
Kenton Base Ball Club (1883)
Kernon Base Ball Club (1882)
Kenair Base Ball Club (1880)
Frank Kennedy Base Ball Club (1884)
Kennedy Base Ball Club (1879)
John E. Kennedy Base Ball Club (1881)
C. Kents Base Ball Club (1883)
James J. Kent Base Ball Club (1886)
Theodore H. Kerr Base Ball Club (1884)
Ketchum Base Ball Club (1883)
Kiks Base Ball Club (1886)
J.M. Kimberger/Kinberger Base Ball Club (1884)
Ferdinand Kirsch Base Ball Club (1882)
Jake Kirsch Base Ball Club (1884)
Ed. Klotz Base Ball Club (1882)
J. Klotz/Klutz Base Ball Club (1884)
The Knickerbockers (1874)
Geo. Koeffer Base Ball Club (1881)—*junior team*
Koenig Base Ball Club (1882)
T.J. Kohl Base Ball Club (1886)
Tom Koop Nine (1884)—*clerks of civil district court*
J. Kray Base Ball Club (1884)
The Kraus Nine (1879)
Ku-Klux Base Ball Club (1879)—*Fourth District*
Kuhn Base Ball Club (1879)
La De Dah Base Ball Club (1882)—*changed to the Estalope Base Ball Club (1882)*
Lhote & Co. Base Ball Club (1883)
C.V. Lacoste Base Ball Club (1879)
J.V. Lacoste Base Ball Club (1879)—*formerly The J.F. Markey Base Ball Club*
"Ladies Pets" (1881)
Lafayette Base Ball Club (1881)
Lafayette Hook and Ladder Fire Company (1883)
O. Lagman Base Ball Club (1887)

F. Lamandres Base Ball Club (1881)
V.J. Lambert Base Ball Club (1882)
Lambour Base Ball Club (1898)
Leon Lamothe Base Ball Club (1879)
Bob/Robt. Lamson Base Ball Club (1881) *former Little Rocks Base Ball players*
Emile Lananze Base Ball Club (1882)
Landwehr/Landwer Base Ball Club (1881)—*Germans*
Laners Base Ball Club (1881)
The Lanters (1881)—*Germans*
The Lasses (1890)—*female team*
The Last Ditchers (1872)
Laurel Base Ball Club (1881)
H.T. Lawler Base Ball Club (1875)
W.J. Lawler Base Ball Club (1881)—*formerly the Wild Indians*
Samuel Laycock Base Ball Club (1882)
C. Lazard Base Ball Club (1894)
Lazy/Old Lazy Base Ball Club (1871)—*later the Boston Base Ball Club (1874)—(1875) former Rose Buds*
Leber Base Ball Club (1884)
G. LeBreton Base Ball Club (1881)
Leche Base Ball Club (1879)—*Jackson School*
R.E. Lee Base Ball Club (1864)
C.J. Leeds Base Ball Club (1874)
M. Lehman Base Ball Club (1886)—*junior team*
Gus Lehmann Base Ball Club (1886)
L. Lehmann Base Ball Club (1881)
P. LeLoup Base Ball Club (1887)
Kyley William J. Lemps Base Ball Club (1886)
The Leos (1898)
The Leppets (1882)—*formerly the Ropers*
Levee Cotton Clerks Base Ball Club (1879)
E.S. Levy Base Ball Club (1879)
Levy & Meyer Base Ball Club (1879)—*employees of the Natchez Cotton Press*
D. Lewis Base Ball Club (1882)
J.R. Lewis Base Ball Club (1882)
Liberty Base Ball Club (1860)-*volunteer firemen (reorganized 1874)*
"Liberty & Erato Street Nine" (1881)
The Lightweight Base Ball Club (1869)
The Lightning Bugs (1872)—*Daily Picayune operators*
Lightwing Base Ball Club (1871)
A.C. Lindauer Base Ball Club (1882)
Little Brown Jugs Base Ball Club (1882)
D. Littlefield Base Ball Club (1881)
Little Giant Base Ball Club (1874)

Little Rocks (1881)—*changed to Robt. Lamson Base Ball Club (1881)*
Live Oak Base Ball Club (1886)
Moses Loeb/M. Lobe & Company Base Ball Club (1879)
Lone Star Base Ball Club (1859)—*founded by mechanics at Leed's Foundry, club room at 93 St. Charles Avenue (1870)*
William D. Long Base Ball Club (1882)
L.F. Longmore Base Ball Club (1882)
Lonsdal Base Ball Club (1886)
Lotta Base Ball Club (1871)—*junior team*
Louisiana Base Ball Club (1859)
Louisiana Brewing Company Base Ball Club (1886)
Louisiana Electric Base Ball Club (1886)
The Louisianas (1872)—*junior team—changed to P.J. Commers Base Ball Club (1881)*
Louisiana Base Ball Club (1886)—*black*
Louisiana Browns (1877)
Louisiana Field Artillery Base Ball Club (1882)
The Louisiana Reds (1884)—*junior team*
The Louisiana Rifles (1886)
P. Lubie Base Ball Club (1877)
Chas. T. Lucke Base Ball Club (1882)
C. Ludock Base Ball Club (1881)
L. Luzenberg Base Ball Club (1886)
A. Lynch Base Ball Club (1886)
The I.L. Lyons Base Ball Club (1884)
J.P. Lytle Base Ball Club (1884)
Joe Mack Base Ball Club (1886)—*junior team*
P. Mack Base Ball Club (1886)
Wm. Mack Base Ball Club (1882)
Minnie Maddern Base Ball Club (1883)
Magenta Base Ball Club (1881)
E.F. Maginnis Base Ball Club (1884)
Magnolia Base Ball Club (1859) (1886)
Ed Maber Base Ball Club (1879)
William Mahoney Base Ball Club (1886)
Malley & Sons (1884)
(Dr.) J.M. Malter Base Ball Club (1882)
Mamie Base Ball Club (1877)
Jules Manaud/Manand Base Ball Club (1881)
Mandeville Clippers Base Ball Club (1872)
Marengo Base Ball Club (1886)—*Jefferson City*
Marigny Base Ball Club (1882)
H. Markel Base Ball Club (1882)
John F. Markey Base Ball Club (1879)

What's in a Name? 225

The Marks (1879)
Marks Isaacs Base Ball Club (1881)
Gus Marks Base Ball Club (1881)
Marsden's Peetoral Balm Nine (1884)—*former employees of G. R. Finlay & Co.*
R. Martine and Brookers Base Ball Club (1882)
F.P. Martinez Base Ball Club (1884)
August Marx Base Ball Club (1882)—*junior team*
Mascot/Mascottes Base Ball Club (1882) *(reorganized 1886)*
Masdexexarts Base Ball Club (1879) *(also Massadexis/Masdesexart)*
Maseppas Base Ball Club (1877)—*Gretna*
Mason Base Ball Club (1896)
Victor Mauberet Base Ball Club (1881)
The Mauberret Base Ball Club (1894)
May 2nd and Kane Base Ball Club (1879)
Mayflower Base Ball Club (1882)
A.G. Maylie Base Ball Club (1881)—*formerly Buncy Bells*
McCall Base Ball Club (1879)
James/Jas. McCann Base Ball Club (1881)
D. McCarthy Base Ball Club (1882)
McCarthy & Raymond Base Ball Club (1884)
John J. McFarlane Base Ball Club (1886)
McFallen Base Ball Club (1886)
McLean Base Ball Club (1881)
John J. McCloskey Base Ball Club (1885)
McCluskey Base Ball Club (1884)
J. McCord Base Ball Club (1881)—*changed to Geo. Daily Base Ball Club (1881)*
James McCormack/McCormick Base Ball Club (1881)
George McEvoy Base Ball Club (1881)
T.S. McEvoy Base Ball Club (1882)
M.J. McFarland Base Ball Club (1882)
James/Jas. McGarrigan Base Ball Club (1881)—*changed to Phil Reillys (Third Ward)*
W.J. McGeehan Base Ball Club (1883)—*junior team*
McGelon Base Ball Club (1884)
McHale Base Ball Club (1879)
J.B. McKernan Base Ball Club (1882)
McMillan Base Ball Club (1879)
McNeil Base Ball Club (1881)
Nelson McStea Base Ball Club (1884)
Mechanics Base Ball Club (1881)
P. Mealies Base Ball Club (1879)
H. Meister Base Ball Club (1881)
Melpomenia Base Ball Club (1859)
The Memory Base Ball Club (1893)

H. Mentrop Base Ball Club (1884)
D. Mercier's Sons Employees (1884) *men's clothing store*
W.H. Merkel Base Ball Club (1879)
Merry Nine Base Ball Club (1886)
J. Mesritz Base Ball Club (1879)
Mexican Gulf Base Ball Club (1882)
Wm. Mieding Base Ball Club (1882)
Mikado Base Ball Club (1886)—*named for the Gilbert & Sullivan comic opera*
Miller & Diechmann Base Ball Club (1884)—*mercantile employees*
Billy Miller's Hard Wood Nine (1882)—*former old-time R.E. Lee Base Ball Club players*
A. Misses Base Ball Club (1882)
Mississippi Base Ball Club (1870)—*junior team—(merged with Washington in 1874 as Hope Base Ball Club)*
Tom Mitchel Base Ball Club (1881)—*junior team*
John Mitchell Base Ball Club (1881)
Mixologists Base Ball Club (1879)
Modoc Base Ball Club (1875)
M. Moelker Base Ball Club (1884)—*otherwise known as the Scheib junior team*
Moerlein Base Ball Club (1886)
Norman/N. Mohr Base Ball Club (1884)
D.C. Moise Base Ball Club (1882)
Montgomery Base Ball Club (1882)
W.H. Moon Base Ball Club (1886)
T.J. Mooney Base Ball Club (1884)
T.F. Moore Base Ball Club (1879)
P.S. Moran Base Ball Club (1882)
R.C./Ralph Morgan Base Ball Club (1881)
Morgan Base Ball Club (1866) (1872)—*junior team*
Morgan Railroad Base Ball Club (1884)
Dan Moriarty Base Ball Club (1879)
Morning Star Base Ball Club (1870)
Jimmy Morrisey Base Ball Club (1882)
Morse Base Ball Club/Morse Nine (1870)—*employees of the Western Union Telegraph Co.*
Mortar & Pestle Club (1884)
Move On Base Ball Club (1879)
Mueller Base Ball Club (1882)
Muffer Base Ball Club (1877)
Muldoon Base Ball Club (1881)
P. Mulholland Men (1884)
Dennis Mullen Base Ball Club (1884)
Capt. Murphy Base Ball Club (1881)

J.C. Murphy Base Ball Club (1884)
D. Murray Base Ball Club (1885)—*former J. Sherman Base Ball Club*
Mike Murray Base Ball Club (1881)—*junior team*
Musgrove Base Ball Club (1882)
Mutual Base Ball Club (1870)
Munna/John Munna Base Ball Club (1871)
The Nameless Nine (1874)—*changed to Chas. H. Fenner Base Ball Club (1881)*
The National Base Ball Club (1860)
M.L. Navara/Navara's Chinese Palace Base Ball Club (1882)
NEOLA Base Ball Club (1896)
Ne Plus Ultra Base Ball Club (1859)
M.E. Nester/Nestor Base Ball Club (1879)—*reorganized in 1883 with former Buncy Bell players*
New Bedford Base Ball Club (1880)—*formed by Frank Bancroft of Hop Bitters (NY) to play in NO*
New Orleans Boy's Base Ball Club (1879)
New Orleans Base Ball Club (1886)—*Gulf League team*
News Dealers Base Ball Club (1882)
New Orleans Chess, Checkers & Whist Base Ball Club (1884)
New Orleans News Company Nine (1882)
New Orleans Pelicans (1859)
Next Timers (1879)
F.T. Nicholls Base Ball Club (1877)—*reorganized in 1879*
Night Hawk Base Ball Club (1884)
Nine Brothers Base Ball Club (1886)
Nine Little Dutchmen (1882)—*junior team*
Nine Orphans Base Ball Club (1879)
Nine Star Base Ball Club (1875)
Nolan Base Ball Club (1874)
J.H. Nolting Base Ball Club (1881)
Nonpareil Paso Base Ball Club (1872)—*junior team*
J. Noreric Base Ball Club (1887)
Norman Base Ball Club (1875)
Northeastrn Railroad Employees (1885)—*freight office versus baggage room*
North Star Base Ball Club (1881)
J. Noveh Base Ball Club (1886)
Nugent & Johnson Base Ball Club (1884)
F.J. Nusloch Base Ball Club (1882)
James O'Donnell Base Ball Club (1881)
J.J./Joe O'Hara Base Ball Club (1884)
T./O'Leary Base Ball Club (1884)
Hy. Ollie Base Ball Club (1882)
O'Neal Base Ball Club (1882)
W.T. O'Reilly Base Ball Club (1882)

O'Shaugnessy Base Ball Club (1879)
Offner Base Ball Club (1882)—*employees of Offner's*
Ogden Base Ball Club (1879)
"Old Timers" and "Old Wrecks" (1882)—*military organizations*
Old Hickory Club (1879)
Old Tops Base Ball Club (1879)
J.J. Oliver Base Ball Club (1881)
Joe Oliver Base Ball Club (1884)
The Olivias (1877)
Olympic Base Ball Club (1882)
Onward Base Ball Club (1867)—*junior team*
Oriental Base Ball Club (1871)
The Originals (1877)
The Original OBBC Base Ball Club (1879)—*Third District*
Original Echo Base Ball Club (1874)
Oriole Base Ball Club (1886)
"Orleans" and "Factors" (1883)—*press teams*
Orleans Base Ball Club (1860) (reorganized 1871)
Orleans Social and Base Ball Club (1877)
The Orleans Base Ball Club (1884)—*black team*
R. Otero Base Ball Club (1882)
Oser Base Ball Club (1881)
The Our Boys Base Ball Club (1876)—*became the Altogether Base Ball Club (1877)*
Gary Owens Bitters Club (1879)
Oxidental Base Ball Club (1870)—*junior team*
P.B.S. Pinchbacks (1888)—*black team*
Pacific Base Ball Club (1877)—*junior team—black*
Palmetto Base Ball Club (1866) (1874)—*junior team*
Paragon Base Ball Club (1882)
The Pastimes (1874)
Pearline Base Ball Club (1882)
Peek-a-Boo Base Ball Club (1884)
Pelican Base Ball Club (1859) *(reorganized 1865)*
Pender Base Ball Club (1881)
R.C. Pendergrast Base Ball Club (1882)
J.C. Pepper Base Ball Club (1884)
W.S. Perry Base Ball Club (1881)
The Petries (1884)
Pfeiffer Base Ball Club (1887)
Philadelphia Base Ball Club (1874)
Philadelphia Fire Company No. 14 Base Ball Club (1883)
P. Philbin Base Ball Club (1879)
R. Phillip Base Ball Club (1881)—*changed to P. Kane Base Ball Club (1883)*
Phoenix Club (1881)

Pluck & Luck Base Ball Club (1881)—*Algiers*
The "Picayunes" & The "Times" (1871)—*Daily Picayune and Times-Democrat newspaper teams*
T. Piglord Base Ball Club (1882)
Pickwick Base Ball Club (1869)
Pickwicks (1882)—*black team*
Pie Base Ball Club (1875)
G. Pietri Base Ball Club (1884)
W.S. Pike Base Ball Club (1874)
L. Pimken Base Ball Club (1883)
Pinafore Base Ball Club (1881)
Pine Knot Base Ball Club (1880)
Pioneer Base Ball Club (1877)
Piper Base Ball Club (1875)
G. Pitard Base Ball Club (1879)
Pocahontas Base Ball Club (1881)—*junior team*
Poets Base Ball Club (1881)—*black (?)*
Poinsettia Base Ball Club (1884)
W. Polchow Base Ball Club (1884)
R.G. Ponsetti Base Ball Club (1884)—*name changed to C.A. Brissets (1884)*
The Poor Scrub Nine (1884)
W.M. Porter Base Ball Club (1882)
Porter & Childs Base Ball Club (1884)
Powell Base Ball Club (1875)
Presas Base Ball Club (1881)
Price Current Base Ball Club (1874)
Pride of New Orleans Base Ball Club (1882)
A.C. Pritchet Base Ball Club (1882)
Providence Base Ball Club (1880)
Alex. Pujols Base Ball Club (1881)
Thomas Pye/Pyes Base Ball Club (1886)
Quickstep Base Ball Club (1870)
Quinette Base Ball Club (1874)
J.P. Quinn Base Ball Club (1884)
H. Rain Base Ball Club (1886)
Rankel Base Ball Club (1882)
James Rankin/J.D. Rankin Base Ball Club (1877)
Red Cloud Base Ball Club (1877)
Red Head Base Ball Club (1881)
Red Hots (1868)—*firemen*
Red Jackets (1866)
Red Star Shoe Company Base Ball Club (1884)
Red Stockings (1870)
The Reds & Blues (1894)

The Red Warriors (1882)
The Redon Base Ball Club (1882)
E. Regan Base Ball Club (1882)
The Regulators (1881)
J.A. Reinecke Club (1881)
Remy Clarkes Base Ball Club (1879)—*formerly the Pat Glennon Base Ball Club (1879)*
Bud Reno Base Ball Club (1886)—*possibly named for sports promoter Bud Renaud*
Reverigerre Base Ball Club (1874)
P.J. Reynolds Base Ball Club (1886)
The Rhamers (1884)
J. Rheinhard Base Ball Club (1879)
Rice & Hayes Base Ball Club (1885)—*female team*
H./Hunt Richards Base Ball Club (1882)
Louis A. Richards Base Ball Club (1879)
Jno. P. Richardson Base Ball Club (1884)
Richmond Base Ball Club (1866)
Mike Rickers/Rickard/Rickerts Base Ball Club (1881)
L.J. Ricks Base Ball Club (1886)
Phil Rielly/Reilly/Riley Base Ball Club (1879)
The Right Ways (1872)
The River Nine (1881)
Riverside Base Ball Club (1873)—*(1875)—former Jackson team*
H.J. Rivet Base Ball Club (1879)
J.G. Roche Base Ball Club (1879)
Rockford Base Ball Club (1875)
Robert H. Rodetzkie Base Ball Club (1884)
John Rogers Base Ball Club (1882)—*junior club*
W.A. Rogers Base Ball Club (1879)
E. Rolland Base Ball Club (1884)
Rollaway Base Ball Club (1882)
G. Roman Base Ball Club (1884)
W.H. Rooney Base Ball Club (1881)
A.J. Rose Base Ball Club (1879)
Rose Base Ball Club (1875)—*later the Lazy Base Ball Club*
Dan A. Rose Base Ball Club (1884)
Rosebud Base Ball Club (1881)
Owen Roper Base Ball Club (1881) *(junior club)—The Leppets (1882)*
Rough on Rats Base Ball Club (1881)—*junior team*
Rousseau Base Ball Club (1869)
Manuel C. Royes Base Ball Club (1879)
Ruby Base Ball Club (1877)
E.V. Ruel Base Ball Club (1884)

Manuel Ruler Base Ball Club (1882)
Amos Runkel/Ruckel Base Ball Club (1882)
H.P. Ryan Base Ball Club (1886)
St. Mary Base Ball Club (1879)—*junior team*
Samuels Base Ball Club (1883)
Saraboneyard/Sarah Boneyard Base Ball Club (1881)
The Scale Hands (1894)
The Scalpers (1881)
Schaffer Base Ball Club (1885)—*junior team*
P. Scheib Base Ball Club (1884)
Schellang Base Ball Club (1881)
Schencks Base Ball Club (1886)—*later became the Duffys*
J. Scherman/Shirman/Sherman Base Ball Club (1885)—*later became the D. Murray Base Ball Club*
Jos. Schlitz Base Ball Club (1886) *brewery team*
Schilling Base Ball Club (1894)
Schneider Base Ball Club (1884)—*Germans*
Charles Schreiber Base Ball Club (1879)—*formerly Dr. Dreyfus*
T. Schreiber Base Ball Club (1886)
Wm. Schreiber Base Ball Club (1881)
A. Schwartz & Sons Base Ball Club (1882)
T. Scoggin Base Ball Club (1886)
The Screw Guzzles (1868)—*firemen*
P. Seighers Base Ball Club (1881)
Septoline Oil Nine (1882)
Seymour Base Ball Club (1886)
The Shamrocks (1884)
Shannon Base Ball Club (1886)—*black*
J.T. Shaw Base Ball Club (1884)
M.J. Sheehan Club (1879)
F. Sheridan Base Ball Club (1882)
J. Sheridan Base Ball Club (1884)
Shoo-Fly Base Ball Club (1870)
Jack Short Base Ball Club (1886)
James Siepkins Base Ball Club (1881)
P. Shilling Base Ball Club (1884)
The Silk Stockings (1881)
Silver Crescent Base Ball Club (1884)
H.B. Simms Base Ball Club (1881)
R.E. Simon Base Ball Club (1881)
P.H./Primrose H. Simpson Base Ball Club (1883)
H. Singer Base Ball Club (1884)
The Single Stars (1871)
Sitting Bull Base Ball Club (1881)

The Slow Boys Base Ball Club (1874)
Slow Steps Base Ball Club (1874)
Smeadley Base Ball Club (1886)
J. Smeary Base Ball Club (1884)
L.W. Smith Base Ball Club (1883)
C. Smyth Base Ball Club (1884)
Soapina Base Ball Club (1890)
Sol Lions Base Ball Club (1879)
The Somersaults (1886)—*Young Men's Gymnastics Club team*
The Somerset Nine (1879)
Sonie Base Ball Club (1882)—*junior team*
Southern Base Ball Club (1866)—*clubroom at the corner of Gravier and St. Charles*
Southern Brewery Base Ball Club (1886)
Southern Express Base Ball Club (1872)
Southern Pacific Base Ball Club (1887)
Southern Policy Club (1877)
Southern Star Base Ball Club (1871)
Southwestern Base Ball Club (1877)
The Spade Base Ball Club (1875)
The Sparks (1872)—*Daily Picayune clerks* (Daily Picayune clerks) (1880)
Spoopendyke Base Ball Club (1881)
M. Sporls Base Ball Club (1881)
M. Sport Base Ball Club (1883)
Squirrel Tails (1868)—*firemen (?)*
Standard Base Ball Club (1883)
Starck Base Ball Club (1882)
Henry W. Staub Base Ball Club (1881)—*junior team*
Stauffer, Macready & Co. Nine (1884)
The "Steamship" & "Railroad" teams (1874)
Stenck Base Ball Club (1882)—*junior team*
J. Steppe Base Ball Club (1884)
Jake Stevens Club (1881)
A. Steward Base Ball Club (1882)
John Stewart Club (1881)
Stickers (1882)
Still Waters Base Ball Club (1877)
Stonewall Club (1866)—*Algiers*
Stonewall-Lee Base Ball Club (1882)
Henry Stouder Base Ball Club (1881)
The Strikers Base Ball Club (1877)
Dan Sullivan Base Ball Club (1880)
John L. Sullivan Base Ball Club (1882)—*named for the celebrated heavyweight boxing champion*

M. Sullivan Base Ball Club (1886)—*black*
The Summer Gang (1870)—*junior team*
The Sunflowers (1882)
Surprise Base Ball Club (1870)
P. Swago Base Ball Club (1880)
J. Swain Base Ball Club (1886)
The Swamp Angels (1881)
Sweet By-and-By Club (1881)
Switzer Base Ball Club (1881)
J.M. Swoop Club (1881)—*junior team*
J. Syme & Co. Base Ball Club (1884)
Charles Tackleberry Base Ball Club (1884)
Taylor Brothers Base Ball Club
John Teen Base Ball Club (1881)
J. Tennyson Base Ball Club (1882)
W.S. Terry Base Ball Club (1881)
Ben Theard Base Ball Club/The Theards (1888)
J.B. Thierry Club (1881)—*Algiers*
The Thomies (1882)
S. Thompson Base Ball Club (1886)
Larry Thorn Base Ball Club (1885)
The Tiger Club (1870)
Prof. L. Timken Base Ball Club (1883)
Tiro al Bersaglio Society
Toney Base Ball Club (1882)
F. Tournes Base Ball Club (1884)
Jas. Tracey Base Ball Club (1881)
Trahant Base Ball Club (1871)
The Treme Market Butchers (1890)
The Turflights (1872)
The "Tugboat" and "Railroad Mother Hubbards" (1884)
I.L. Twitchel Base Ball Club (1884)
J.W. Twomey Base Ball Club (1882)
"U.B.S" and "I.B.S" Base Ball Club (1886)—*New Basin Canal longshoremen*
The Ubiquitous Base Ball Team (1870)—*postal workers*
Union Base Ball Club (1886)
Union Moustache Base Ball Club (1884)
United Nine (1881)
University of Louisiana Base Ball Club (1881)
Unknown Base Ball Club (1881)—*changed to Joseph Janfroids Base Ball Club (1881)*
The New Orleans Unions (1884)—*black team*
The Universities (1877)
Variety Base Ball Club (1872)
Jules Victor Base Ball Club (1882)

A./Vidous Base Ball Club (1886)—*Carrollton*
Violet Base Ball Club (1872)—*(1875) former XYZ's*
Thomas Vizard Base Ball Club (1879)
John Voelker Base Ball Club (1882)
F.W. Volchmann Base Ball Club (1884)
Volunteer No. 1 Base Ball Club (1884)—*firemen*
F. Voss Base Ball Club (1879)
G.W. Vredenberg (Vandenberg?) Base Ball Club (1881)
Happy Wagner Base Ball Club (1881)
P. Waldemann Base Ball Club (1881)
Walk Away Base Ball Club (1872)
Walk-A-Bouts (1877)
Thos. F. Wall Base Ball Club (1882)
F.P. Walle Base Ball Club (1881)
Walsh & Creevy Base Ball Club (1886)
J.M. Walters Base Ball Club (1882)
W.H. Warners Base Ball Club (1884)
H.C. Warren Base Ball Club (1882)
Washington Artillery Base Ball Club (1882)
Washington Avenue Base Ball Club (1882)
Washington Base Ball Club (1860)—*merged with Mississippi Base Ball Club in 1874 as Hope Base Ball Club*
Washington Marks Base Ball Club (1879)—*Washington Market—Wash Marks (1881)*
Washington No. 20 Base Ball Club (1884)—*firemen*
Paul Waterman Base Ball Club (1879)
The Waters (1885)
Webb Base Ball Club (1874)
The Webers/Websters (1885)
George Weber Brewing Company Base Ball Club (1886)
J.C. Weber Base Ball Club (1879)
T.S. Weber Base Ball Club (1885)—*female team*
Weisler Base Ball Club (1884)
Welcome Base Ball Club (1877)—*Carrollton*
C. Welker Base Ball Club (1882)
D.E. Wells Base Ball Club (1879)
Western Union Base Ball Club (1884)
J. Wharton Base Ball Club (1881)
Whitney Base Ball Club (1875)
C.B. White Base Ball Club (1879)
White League Base Ball Club (1874)
White Star Base Ball Club (1882)
White Stockings Base Ball Club (1871)—*Algiers*
"White & Thalia Street Nine" (1881)

Whitmore Base Ball Club (1881)
Wide Awake Base Ball Club (1868)
Wild Girod Base Ball Club (1881)
Wild Indians (1877)
Oscar Wilde Base Ball Club (1882)—*named for the noted British writer and wit*
F. Wilford Base Ball Club (1884)
T.S. Wilkinson Base Ball Club (1886)
Charles Will Base Ball Club (1881)
Willings Base Ball Club (1886)
The Will Nots (1884)—*junior team*
Dan Wilson Base Ball Club (1881)
W.S. Wilson Base Ball Club (1881)
Wilson Base Ball Club (1886)—*black*
Nick Wiltze (sp?) Base Ball Club (1884)
The Winships (1880)
The Wintersaults (1886)—*YMGC (gymnasts) team*
The Wintersmiths (1886)—*YMGC (gymnasts) team*
T. Wolf Base Ball Club (1884)
D. Woods Base Ball Club (1881)
M. Woods Base Ball Club (1883)
Worcester Base Ball Club (1881)
John Wragg Base Ball Club (1884)—*junior team*
J.S. Wright Base Ball Club (1877)
XYZ Base Ball Club (1875)—*former members of the Jackson and Pike clubs*
Young Adams Base Ball Club (1871)
Young Americans Base Ball Club (1881)
Young Sara Base Ball Club (1884)
Zabrey Base Ball Club (1879)
Richard Zank Base Ball Club (1882)
E.C. Ziegler Nine (1881)
E.E. Ziegler Base Ball Club (1880)
Zimmerman Base Ball Club (1882)

Chapter Notes

Preface

1. *New York Daily Herald*, October 7, 1845.

Introduction

1. Henderson, Robert W. *Ball, Bat and Bishop: The Origin of Ball Games.* New York: Rockport Press, 1947.
2. *The Daily Delta*, May 22, 1860.
3. *Ibid.*, May 22, 1860.
4. *The Daily Picayune*, November 11, 1891, and November 23, 1891.
5. Wright, Marshall D. *The Southern Association, 1885–1962.* Jefferson, NC: McFarland, 2002.
6. *The Daily Picayune*, August 20, 1859.
7. *Ibid.*, May 28, 1882.

Chapter One

1. Alvarez, Mark. *The Old Ball Game.* Alexandria, VA: Redefinition, 1990.
2. Newberry, John. *A Little Pretty Pocket-Book,* 1767, page 43 .
3. *The Daily Picayune*, August 14, 1859.
4. *The New Orleans Crescent*, April 30, 1860.
5. *The Evansville Daily Journal* (Evansville, LA), July 23, 1858; *The Independent American* (Troy, AL), April 21, 1858; *The Daily Journal* (Wilmington, NC), July 10, 1858; *The Semi-Weekly Standard* (Raleigh, NC), July 30, 1859; *The Greensboro Times* (Greensboro, NC), May 26, 1860; *The Abbeville Press and Banner* (Abbeville, SC), August 13, 1858; *The Alexandria Gazette* (Alexandria, VA), June 8, 1858; *The Louisville Daily Courier* (Louisville, KY), June 30, 1858; *The Nashville Union and American* (Nashville, TN), July 24, 1858.
6. Kirsch, George B. *Baseball in Blue & Gray: The National Pastime During the Civil War.* Princeton: Princeton University Press, 2003.
7. *The Daily Picayune*, November 25, 1863.
8. *The Daily Delta*, August 30, 1859.
9. Husman, John Richmond. "Ohio's First Baseball Game." *Baseball: A Journal of the Early Game* (Spring 2008). Jefferson, NC: McFarland.
10. *The Daily Picayune*, November 26, 1866.
11. *Ibid.*, August 1, 1869.
12. *The True Delta*, January 25, 1857.
13. *New Orleans Republican*, May 19, 1870.
14. *The Daily Picayune*, July 8, 1872.
15. *Ibid.*, May 24, 1874, and July 7, 1874.

Chapter Two

1. Goldstein, Warren. *Playing for Keeps.* New York: Barnes & Noble, 2000.
2. *The Daily Picayune*, May 7, 1893.
3. *Ibid.*, April 23, 1872.

Chapter Three

1. *The Daily Delta*, October 4, 1859.
2. *The Daily Picayune*, October 16, 1866.
3. *Ibid.*, March 28, 1875.
4. *Ibid.*, May 6, 1875.
5. *Ibid.*, May 13, 1888.

6. *Ibid.*, July 12, 1858.
7. *The Daily Delta*, June 7, 1859.
8. *Ibid.*, May 18, 1859.
9. *The Daily Picayune*, June 24, 1859.
10. *Ibid.*, July 30, 1859.
11. *Ibid.*, August 3, 1859.
12. *Ibid.*, August 13, 1859.
13. *Ibid.*, August 20, 1859.
14. Thorn, John. *Baseball: A Journal of the Early Game* 6, no. 32 (Fall 2012).
15. *New Orleans Crescent*, April 13, 1860.
16. *The Daily Picayune*, June 20, 1861.
17. *New Orleans Republican*, April 26, 1870.
18. *The Daily Picayune*, September 6, 1859.
19. *The New Orleans Crescent*, August 29, 1859.
20. *The Daily Picayune*, September 23, 1859.
21. *Ibid.*, October 7, 1859.
22. *The New Orleans Republican*, June 7, 1870.
23. *The New Orleans Times*, December 1, 1869.
24. Rader, Benjamin. *Baseball: A History of America's Game.* Urbana: University of Illinois Press, 2002.
25. *The Daily Picayune*, December 22, 1859.
26. *The Times-Democrat*, December 29, 1869; *The Times Picayune*, December 30, 1869.
27. *The Times Picayune*, May 14, 1870.
28. *Ibid.*, February 4, 1887.
29. *Ibid.*, April 26, 1870.
30. *Ibid.*, April 27, 1870.
31. *Ibid.*, April 29, 1870.
32. *The New Orleans Republican*, April 30, 1870.
33. *The Daily Picayune*, May 1, 1870.
34. *Chicago Tribune*, May 7, 1870.
35. *The Daily Picayune*, March 13, 1886.
36. *The New York Times*, March 13, 1886; *The Daily Picayune*, March 13, 1886.
37. *The Daily Picayune*, January 12, 1873.
38. *The Times-Democrat*, December 9, 1875.
39. *The Daily Picayune*, October 27, 1875.
40. *Ibid.*, June 16, 1883.
41. *Ibid.*, March 5, 1869.
42. *The New Orleans Delta*, August 4, 1858; *The New York Times*, August 11, 1858.
43. *The Daily Picayune*, February 13, 1880.
44. *Ibid.*, March 18, 1880.
45. *Ibid.*, February 28, 1884.
46. *The Philadelphia Inquirer*, December 7, 1860; *The Chicago Tribune*, December 10, 1860.
47. *New Orleans Crescent*, September 6, 1860; *The Daily Delta*, March 16, 1861.
48. *The Daily Picayune*, February 14, 1885.
49. *Ibid.*, July 22 and August 9, 1884.
50. *Ibid.*, November 13, 1886.
51. *Ibid.*, March 28, 1898.
52. *Ibid.*, April 14, 1898; *The Times-Democrat*, April 15, 1898.
53. *The Daily Picayune*, April 14, 1898.
54. *The New Orleans Crescent*, June 18, 1860.
55. *Ibid.*, July 2, 1860.
56. *The Daily Picayune*, April 26, 1868.
57. *Ibid.*, June 16, 1872.
58. *Ibid.*, September 18, 1882.
59. *Ibid.*, November 25, 1877.
60. *The Daily Democrat*, May 12, 1879.
61. *The Daily Picayune*, June 26, 1879.
62. *Ibid.*, March 24, 1882; *The Times-Democrat*, March 28, 1882; *The Daily Picayune*, May 5, 1882.
63. Fairall, Herbert S. *The World Industrial and Cotton Centennial Exposition.* Iowa City: Republican Publishing Company, 1885.
64. *The Times-Democrat*, November 17, 1885.
65. *Ibid.*, November 17, 1885.
66. *The Daily Picayune*, December 6, 1885.
67. *Ibid.*, February 17, 1893.

Chapter Four

1. *The Daily Picayune*, December 16, 1859.
2. These figures are derived from the list of teams found in the Apendix. It is a work in progress as new periodicals become available for review from time to time. Baseball researchers are invited to send any additions, revisions, corrections, or errors to me, along with the appropriate documentation.
3. *The Daily Picayune*, May 19, 1878.
4. *Ibid.*, March 27, 1877.
5. *Ibid.*, June 12, 1872.
6. *New Orleans Crescent*, February 7, 1860, and February 16, 1860.
7. *Ibid.*, October 21, 1859.
8. *The Daily Picayune*, January 10, 1866.
9. *Ibid.*, January 10, 1866.

10. *Ibid.*, August 6, 1879.
11. *The New Orleans Daily Democrat*, August 22, 1879.
12. *The Daily Picayune*, September 7, 1879.
13. *Ibid.*, September 14, 1879.
14. *Ibid.*, May 13, 1886.
15. *Ibid.*, May 20, 1886.
16. *Ibid.*, September 23, 1884.
17. *Ibid.*, May 15, 1886.
18. *Ibid.*, May 24, 1886.
19. *Ibid.*, May 24, 1886.
20. *Ibid.*, June 19, 1886.
21. *The Times-Democrat*, September 11, 1888.
22. *Ibid.*, October 12, 1888.
23. *The Daily Picayune*, February 8, 1884.
24. *The Times-Democrat*, April 28, 1884.
25. *The Daily Picayune*, May 12, 1884.
26. *Ibid.*, May 26, 1884.
27. *Ibid.*, June 26, 1884.
28. *Ibid.*, June 8, 1884.
29. *Ibid.*, June 15, 1884.
30. *Ibid.*, July 12, 1884.
31. *Ibid.*, July 17, 1884.
32. *Ibid.*, September 6, 1884.
33. *Ibid.*, May 19,1888.
34. *Ibid.*, May 13, 1888.
35. *Ibid.*, May 15, 1888.
36. *Ibid.*, September 23, 1889.
37. *Ibid.*, May 29, 1879.
38. *Ibid.*, May 30, 1879.
39. *The New Orleans Daily Democrat*, June 4, 1879.
40. *The Daily Picayune*, December 25, 1884.
41. *Evening Telegraph* (Philadelphia), March 30, 1867.
42. *New Orleans Republican*, April 16, 1875.
43. *The Times-Democrat*, August 23, 1875.
44. *The Daily Picayune*, April 4, 1880; *The New Orleans Daily Democrat*, April 4, 1880.
45. *The Daily Picayune*, June 17, 1886.
46. *Ibid.*, June 18, 1886.
47. *Ibid.*, June 22, 1886.
48. *Ibid.*, June 23, 1886.
49. *Ibid.*, December 21, 1869.
50. *Ibid.*, August 29, 1881.
51. *Ibid.*, September 12, 1881.
52. *The Times-Democrat*, May 9, 1886.
53. *Ibid.*, October 18, 1886.
54. *The Daily Picayune*, October 25, 1886.
55. *The Daily Picayune*, October 25, 1886.
56. *Ibid.*, November 15, 1886.
57. *Ibid.*, November 5, 1888, July 8, 1889.
58. *Ibid.*, March 20, 1886.
59. *Ibid.*, May 31, 1887.
60. *Ibid.*, January 8,1888.
61. *The Daily Picayune*, January 9, 1893; *The Louisiana Review*, April 26, 1893; *The Times-Democrat*, May 7, 1893; *The Daily Picayune*, May 14,1893.
62. *The Times-Democrat*, January 31, 1886.
63. *The Daily Picayune*, February 17, 1886.
64. *Ibid.*, March 11, 1886.
65. *The Mobile Register*, June 16, 1886.
66. *The Daily Picayune*, March 28, 1886.
67. *Ibid.*, April 26, 1886.
68. *Ibid.*, June 17, 1886.
69. *Ibid.*, June 21, 1886.
70. *Ibid.*, August 25, 1886.
71. *Ibid.*, August 16, 1881.
72. *Ibid.*, September 19, 1883.
73. *The Montgomery Advertiser*, November 26, 1884.
74. Wright, Marshall D. *The Southern Association, 1885–1962.* Jefferson, NC: McFarland, 2002.
75. *The Daily Picayune*, December 7, 1886.
76. *Ibid.*, December 17, 1886.
77. *Ibid.*, December 15, 1885.
78. *Ibid.*, April 18, 1887.
79. *The New York Times*, August 23, 1886; *The Louisville Courier-Journal*, August 23, 1886.
80. *The Times-Picayune*, August 8, 1953.
81. *The Times-Democrat*, June 10, 1898.

Chapter Five

1. *The Daily Picayune*, September 17, 1883.
2. *The Times-Democrat*, June 8, 1869.
3. *The Daily Picayune*, August 17, 1869.
4. *Ibid.*, August 17, 1869.
5. *The Times-Democrat*, August 26, 1869.
6. *The Daily Picayune*, August 26, 1869.
7. *The Times-Democrat*, August 27, 1869.
8. *The Daily Picayune*, July 17, 1870.
9. *Ibid.*, July 21–August 15, 1870; *The Chicago Tribune*, July 21–August 15, 1870.
10. *The Daily Picayune*, August 16, 1870.
11. O'Neal, Bill. *The Texas League, 1888–1987.* Austin: Eakin Press, 1987.
12. *The Daily Picayune*, July 25, 1872.

13. *Ibid.*, August 25, 1872.
14. *Ibid.*, July 19, 1872.
15. *Ibid.*, July 21, 1872.
16. *Ibid.*, July 22, 1872.
17. *Ibid.*, July 22–August 3, 1872.
18. *Ibid.*, October 6, 1908.
19. *Ibid.*, August 1–21, 1883.
20. United States Department of Commerce, Bureau of the Census, *Historical Statistics of the of the 1840, 1860, and 1870 Census.*
21. *The Daily Picayune*, November 4, 1886.
22. *The Times-Democrat*, December 12, 1886.
23. *The Daily Picayune*, January 1, 1887; January 8, 1887.
24. *The Times-Democrat*, January 11, 1887.
25. *The Daily Picayune*, April 28, 1887.
26. *Ibid.*, October 5, 1887; October 29, 1887; November 1, 1887; *The Tines-Democrat*, October 1, 1887; October 4, 1887.
27. United States Department of Commerce, Bureau of the Census, *Historical Statistics of the of the 1880 and 1890 Census.*
28. *The New York Times*, October 31, 1887 and November 5, 1887; *The Daily Picayune*, November 7, 1887.
29. *The Daily Picayune*, December 19, 1886; April 17, 1887; May 9, 1887.
30. *The Times-Democrat*, July 22, 1888; September 8, 1888.
31. *Ibid.*, October 2, 1888.
32. *The Daily Picayune*, October 20, 1888.
33. *Birmingham Evening News*, May 15, 1889.
34. *The Times-Democrat*, October 2, 1888.
35. *The Daily Picayune*, January 19, 1890.
36. *Ibid.*, February 2, 1890.
37. *Ibid.*, April 11, 1892.
38. *Ibid.*, October 2, 1892.
39. *Ibid.*, November 1, 1892.
40. *Ibid.*, April 30, 1893.
41. *Ibid.*, February 17, 1893.
42. *Ibid.*, October 5, 1893.
43. *Ibid.*, February 25, 1894.
44. *The New York Sun*, December 13, 1894.
45. *The Daily Picayune*, April 26, 1895.
46. *The Times-Democrat*, May 11, 1895.
47. *Ibid.*, August 16, 1895.
48. *Ibid.*, January 17, 1899.
49. *Ibid.*, April 14, 1898; *The Times-Democrat*, April 15, 1898.
50. *The Daily Picayune*, April 15, 1898.
51. *Ibid.*, April 15, 1898.
52. *Ibid.*, May 21–24, 1898.
53. *Ibid.*, January 17, 1899.
54. *The Times-Democrat*, April 15, 1899.
55. *The Atlanta Constitution*, June 1, 1899.
56. *The Daily Picayune*, June 4, 1899; *The Times-Democrat*, June 5, 1899.

Bibliography

Books

Alvarez, Mark. *The Old Ball Game.* Alexandria, VA: Redefinition, 1990.
Augustin, George. *History of Yellow Fever.* New Orleans: Searcy & Plaff, 1909.
Block, David. *Baseball Before We Know It: A Search for the Roots of the Game.* Lincoln: University of Nebraska Press, 2005.
Chetwynd, Josh. *Baseball in Europe: A Country by Country History.* Jefferson, NC: McFarland, 2008.
Fairall, Herbert S. *The World Industrial and Cotton Centennial Exposition.* Iowa City: Republican Publishing Company, 1885.
The Friends of the Cabildo. *New Orleans Architecture—Volume VII: Jefferson City.* Gretna, LA: Pelican Publishing Company, 1989.
The Friends of the Cabildo. *New Orleans Architecture—Volume VIII: The University Section.* Gretna, LA: Pelican Publishing Company, 1997.
Frommer, Harvey. *Old-Time Baseball: America's Pastime in the Gilded Age.* New York: Taylor Trade, 2006.
Goldstein, Warren. *A History of Early Baseball.* New York: Barnes & Noble, 2000.
Henderson, Robert W. *Ball, Bat and Bishop: The Origin of Ball Games.* New York: Rockport Press, 1947.
Kirsch, George B. *Baseball in Blue & Gray: The National Pastime During the Civil War.* Princeton: Princeton University Press, 2003.
Melville, Tom. *Early Baseball and the Rise of the National League.* Jefferson, NC: McFarland, 2001.
Morris, Peter. *But Didn't We Have Fun? An Informal History of Baseball, 1825–1908.* Lincoln: University of Nebraska Press, 1995.
Nemec, David. *The Beer and Whiskey League.* New York: Lyons & Burford, 1994.
Nystrom, Justin A. *New Orleans After the Civil War: Race, Politics and a Birth of Freedom.* Baltimore: Johns Hopkins University Press, 2010.
O'Neal, Bill. *The Texas League: A Century of Baseball.* Austin: Eakin Press, 1987.
Rader, Benjamin. *Baseball: A History of America's Game.* Urbana: University of Illinois Press, 2002.
Ritter, Lawrence S. *The Story of Baseball.* New York: William Morrow, 1990.
Ryczek, William J. *When Johnny Came Sliding Home: The Post-Civil War Baseball Boom, 1865–1870.* Jefferson, NC: McFarland, 1998.
Somers, Dale A. *The Rise of Sport in New Orleans, 1850–1900.* Baton Rouge: Louisiana State University Press, 1972.
Sullivan, Dean A., ed. *Early Innings—A Documentary History of Baseball, 1825–1908.* Lincoln: University of Nebraska Press, 1995.
Tygiel, Jules. *Past Time: Baseball as History.* New York: Oxford University Press, 2000.

Ward, Geoffrey C., and Ken Burns. *Baseball: An Illustrated History.* New York: Alfred A. Knopf, 2000.
Wright, Marshall D. *The Southern Association in Baseball, 1885–1961.* Jefferson, NC: McFarland, 2002.

Government Publications

U.S. Department of Commerce, Bureau of the Census
Historical Statistics of the 1840 U.S. Census
Historical Statistics of the 1860 U.S. Census
Historical Statistics of the 1870 U.S. Census
Historical Statistics of the 1880 U.S. Census
Historical Statistics of the 1890 U.S. Census

Newspapers

The Abbeville Press and Banner (Abbeville, SC) 1858
The Atlanta Constitution (Atlanta, GA) 1899
The Birmingham Evening News (Birmingham, AL) 1889
The Chicago Tribune (Chicago, IL) 1860–1870
The Daily Delta (New Orleans, LA) 1859–1863
The Daily Journal (Wilmington, NC) 1858
The Daily Picayune (New Orleans, LA) 1859–1900
The Evansville Daily Journal (Evansville, LA) 1858–1859
The Evening Telegraph (Philadelphia, PA) 1867
The Greensboro Times (Greensboro, NC) 1860
The Independent American (Troy, AL) 1858
The Independent Monitor (Tuscaloosa, AL) 1860
The Louisiana Review (New Orleans, LA) 1893
The Louisville Courier-Journal (Louisville, KY) 1886
The Louisville Daily Courier (Louisville, KY) 1858
The Mobile Register (Mobile, AL) 1886
The Montgomery Advertiser (Montgomery, AL) 1884
The Nashville Union and American (Nashville, TN) 1858
The New Orleans Crescent (New Orleans, LA) 1859–1860
The New Orleans Daily Democrat (New Orleans, LA) 1879–1880
The New Orleans Delta (New Orleans, LA) 1858
The New Orleans Republican (New Orleans, LA) 1870
The New Orleans Times (New Orleans, LA) 1869
The New York Daily Herald (New York, NY) 1845
The New York Sun (New York, NY) 1894
The New York Times (New York, NY) 1858–1886
The Philadelphia Inquirer (Philadelphia, PA) 1860
The Semi-Weekly Standard (Raleigh, NC) 1859
The Tennessean (Nashville, TN) 1860–1861
The Times-Democrat (New Orleans, LA) 1863–1900
The True Delta (New Orleans, LA) 1857

Articles

Husman, John Richmond. "Ohio's First Baseball Game." *Baseball: A Journal of the Early Game* (Spring 2008).

Lalire, Gregory. "Baseball in the West." *Wild West Magazine*, March 31, 2011.
Soniat, Meloncy C. *The Faubourgs Forming the Upper Section of the City of New Orleans.* New Orleans: The Louisiana Historical Society, 1937.
Thorn, John. From *Baseball: A Journal of the Early Game* (Fall 2012).

Exhibitions

Waco at Bat: The History of Baseball in Waco, Historical Waco Foundation

Index

For team names keyword, see the Appendix.

A. Blume Base Ball Club 212
A. Brenard Base Ball Club 213
A. Fischer Base Ball Club 21, 125, 218
A. Huber Base Ball Club 221
A. Lynch Base Ball Club 224
A. Misses Base Ball Club 226
A. Schwartz & Sons Base Ball Club 231
A. Steward Base Ball Club 232
A./Vidous Base Ball Club 234
A.A. Belmont Base Ball Club ("Belmonts") 212
A.A. Bohne Base Ball Club 128, 212
A&Rs 210
Abbott, Fred 95, 199
A.C. Daunoy Base Ball Club 215
A.C. Lindauer Base Ball Club 223
A.C. Pritchet Base Ball Club 229
Acid Iron Earth Base Ball Club (AL) 116, 135–137, 147
Acme Base Ball Club 210
Active Base Ball Club (IL) 159
Actives 210
Adair, Robert 179
Adams, Lionel 126
Adams Base Ball Club 210
Adrien/Adrien Brothers 211
Aetna Base Ball Club 21, 125–126, 211
A.F. Caymo Base Ball Club 214
A.G. Maylie Base Ball Club 225
Airey, T.L. 103
Aixler, A. 112
A.J. Cosgrove Base Ball Club 215Coughlin 109
A.J. Dumont Base Ball Club ("Dumonts") 21, 125, 127, 217
A.J. Rose Base Ball Club 230
Alex. Horn Base Ball Club 221
Alex. Pujols Base Ball Club 229

Alexander, Gus 112
Alf. Barnes Base Ball Club 211
Alf. Dupre Base Ball Club ("Dupres") 118, 217
Algiers Green 60, 207
Algiers Joy Base Ball Club 211
Alleghenies 211
Allen 65–67
Allen, R. 96
Allens Base Ball Club 211
Allison, Doug 51
Allright Base Ball Club 211
Aloe Base Ball Club 211
Alston, J.J. 73
Altogether Base Ball Club 211
Always Sure Base Ball Club 211
Amar 124
Amaranth Social Club 211
Amateur Base Ball Club 211
American Association 100, 117, 144, 183, 205
American District Telegraph Nine 211
American Exposition 100–102, 138, 177
American Rice Mill Base Ball Club 211
Amos Runkel/Runkel Base Ball Club 231
Annunciation Square 15, 61, 207
Anthracite League 145
Archinard Base Ball Club ("Archinards") 147–148
Arctic Base Ball Club 211
Arlington Base Ball Club 211
Armchair Base Ball Club 211
Armour, Robert 196
Arnold 123
Art Street 207
A.S. Badger Base Ball Club ("Badgers") 127, 211
Association of Gymnastic Clubs 108

244　Index

Athletes Base Ball Club 211
Athletic Base Ball Club 125, 147, 211
Athletic Base Ball Club (IL) 156
Athletic Club League 108
Athletic Park 87, 91, 93–95, 104, 199
Athletics 119
Atkinson 142
Atlanta (GA) 138, 163, 168, 175, 178, 181–182, 185–186, 197
Atlanta Atlantas Base Ball Club (GA) 138–139, 168–170, 192–193
Atlanta Crackers (GA) 146–147, 195–198, 200–201, 204
Atlanta Firecrackers (GA) 185–187
Atlanta Windjammers (GA) 187–188
Atlantic Base Ball Club 211
Atlantic Base Ball Club ("Atlantics") 18, 77–78, 80, 119–120, 211
Atlantic Base Ball Club (MO) 152–153
Atlantic League 145–146, 203
Audubon Park 60, 72, 99, 103, 132
August Marx Base Ball Club 225
Augusta (GA) 138, 163, 199–200, 204
Augusta Browns Base Ball Club (GA) 138–139, 162, 168–170
Augusta Electricians 187–188
Aunt Richard's Base Ball Club 211
Austin (TX) 158–159, 179
Austin Senators (TX) 184
Auxiliary Sanitation Association 121
Avenue Base Ball Club 211
A.W. Delavallades Base Ball Club 216
Aydelotte, Jacob 140–142

B. Bitters Base Ball Club 212
B. Estalope Base Ball Club 217
Bach, J.C. 138
Baker 160
Baker, F.W. 102
Baker, Judge 81
Bal Nuptiale 23
La Balle au Bâton 23
La Balle Empoisonée 10, 23
Baltic Base Ball Club 211
Baltimore (MD) 43, 165, 172
Baltimore Base Ball Club (LA) 120–121, 211
Baltimore Orioles (MD) 19, 142, 145, 192, 195
Banditti Club 211
Banker's League 108
Bannon's Park 207
Banquois 211
Barber Base Ball Club 211
Barleycorn, John 80
Barnes, Ross 2

Barrett 109
Barry Base Ball Club 211
Barstow 65–67
Barthe, Joseph 112
Base Ball Green 207
Baumgarden Base Ball Club 212
Bayou St. John Base Ball Club 212
Beanham, W.H. 72
Beauregard, Pierre Gustave Toutant (P.G.T.) 88, 92
Beauregard Base Ball Club 212
Beauvais 65–67
Bee Green 60, 207
Beef Lot 207
Behan 135, 140–141
Behan, William J. 99
Beiden Base Ball Club 212
Bell 65–67, 76
Belle Castle Base Ball Club 212
Belle Lee Base Ball Club 212
Bellecastle and Magazine Street 207
Belmont Base Ball Club 212
Ben Theard Base Ball Club ("Theards") 93, 233
Bennett, L. 199
Benton, Frank 111
Berkery 116
Bernard Base Ball Club ("Bernards") 113–114, 118, 212
Bert Casey Base Ball Club 214
Bertel (Bertell) 74, 110
Best Olive Base Ball Club 212
B'Hoys Base Ball Club 211
Bickert, Monroe L. 196
Bidwell 65–67
Bienville, Jean-Baptiste Le Moyne de 10, 38, 62
Bienville Street 98, 207
Billy Miller's Hard Wood Nine 226
Bingaman Course 96, 207
Birmingham (AL) 134, 137–138, 168–170, 175, 194, 196, 199
Birmingham Barons (AL) 197–198, 200–201
Birmingham Grays (AL) 186–188
Birmingham Ironmakers (AL) 176
Birmingham Maroons (AL) 178–182
Bishop's Hotel 85
Bittle Base Ball Club 212
Bittle Battle 25
Bixamos, Charles 91
Black Elephant Base Ball Club 212
Blaffer's Park 207
Blakes 212
Blanco Base Ball Club 212
Bloomington Base Ball Club (IL) 156

Bloom's Nine 212
Blue Caps Base Ball Club 212
Blue Cloud Base Ball Club 212
Blue Stocking Base Ball Club 125, 127, 212
Blue Stocking Mutuals 212
Bluff City Base Ball Club (TN) 152–153, 156
Bob/Robt. Lamson Base Ball Club ("Lamsons") 114, 213, 223
Boetticher, Major Otto 35
Boisseau 126
Bokenfohr, William 136
Boland, Danny 199
Bomberry 116
Bon Ton Base Ball Club 212
Bond 74
Bond, George 71
Bordel Base Ball Club 125, 212
Borges Base Ball Club ("Borges") 114, 214
Born 65, 67
Boss Nine 213
Boston (MA) 27, 165
Boston Base Ball Club (LA) 125, 213, 223
Boston Beaneaters (MA) 80, 137, 176, 192
Boston Club 125, 196
Boston Commons 12
Boston Nine (LA) 121, 213
Bothner 116
Boudousquiè, Charles 69
Boulevard Base Ball Club 213
Boullemet, J.S. 103
Boyle Base Ball Club 213
Boys Base Ball Club 213
Brainard, Asa 2, 76, 79–80, 152
Branch Green 207
Brandenburg, C.D. 151
Brännboll 28
Braselman Combination 213
Brautball 23
Brebéuf, Jean de 9
Brenard/A. Brenard Base Ball Club 213
Brennan, Jack 140–142, 147
Brennan, Nick 163
Brennan, Thomas C. 87, 116, 137–138, 147, 162–163, 170, 173–174, 205
Brewster Base Ball Club 213
Bridgit Donahue Base Ball Club 216
Brien, Honorable J.G. 135
Bright 140–141
Britton, J.D. 133
Broad Street Green 207
Brodick Base Ball Club 213
Brooklyn (NY) 1, 74, 165, 184
Brooklyn Atlantics (NY) 79
Brooklyn Bridegrooms (NY) 137
Brooklyn Grays (NY) 19

The Brotherhood 182
Brown 96
Brown, Bob 116
Browning, Pete 50
The Bruisers 213
Bruneau Base Ball Club 213
Bruning's Restaurant 85
Buckeye Base Ball Club 213
Bud Reno Base Ball Club 230
Buddendorf, Joseph C. 151
Buffalo Bills Base Ball Club 213
The Buffers 213
Bulldozer Base Ball Club 213
Bumetz 109
The Buncy Bells 213
Burdett, Oliver 65–67
Burke, Edward 99
Burke, Ella 121–122
Burris 199
Burt 74
Burt Kelly Nine 222
Burthe, Dominique Francois 72
Buster Custers 106, 213
Butler, C.W. 133
Butler, William J. "Bill" 19, 126, 136, 142, 163
Butts Base Ball Club 213
Byers, Bill 203
Byrne, T.L. 134

C. Adams/Adams Base Ball Club 210
C. Dumeyer Base Ball Club 217
C. Freese/Freece Base Ball Club 218
C. Kents Base Ball Club 222
C. Lazard Base Ball Club 223
C. Ludock Base Ball Club 224
C. Smyth Base Ball Club 232
C. Welker Base Ball Club 234
C.A. Brisset Base Ball Club 213
Cain 110
Calhoun Base Ball Club 214
Campau, Charles ("Count") 2, 147, 190–191, 193–194
Campbell Green 207
The Canal Ducks 214
Canal Street 20, 33, 40, 65, 84–86, 88–89, 93, 104, 113, 117, 146, 153, 207–214
Canal Street Pleasure Club 214
The Canary Club 214
Canfield 126
Capitol Base Ball Club 214
Capprice 96
Capt. Galvin Base Ball Club 219
Capt. Murphy Base Ball Club 226
Carney's Park 208
Carroll Base Ball Club 214

Carrollton (City) 14–15, 58, 60, 73, 99, 104, 207, 209, 218, 221, 233–234
Carrollton Avenue 93, 95, 104
Carrollton Gardens Resort 104
Carrollton Park 103, 208
Carrollton Railroad 60, 62, 76, 209–210
Carson 124
Carter, H. 103
Cartwright, Alexander 2, 9, 31–32
Cartwright, Ed 139–142, 147, 171
Carver's Park 208
Carwashers Base Ball Club 214
Catholic League 108
Cavanacs Base Ball Club 214
C.B. Fischer Base Ball Club 218
C.B. White Base Ball Club 234
Centennial Base Ball Club 214
C.H. Haights Base Ball Club 220
Chadwick, Henry 8, 31, 68, 116
Champion Base Ball Club 18, 214
Chandler 96
Chandler, M.K. 151–152
Chandler's Park 208
Charles A. Haifleigh Base Ball Club 220
Charles Cochrane Base Ball Club 214
Charles Schreiber Base Ball Club 231
Charles Tackleberry Base Ball Club 233
Charles Will Base Ball Club 235
Charleston (SC) 169
Charleston Seagulls (SC) 147, 169–176, 178–182, 187–188, 192–193, 195, 200–201, 204
Charley Dodge Base Ball Club 216
The Charmers 214
Chas. Funk Base Ball Club 219
Chas. H. Fenner Base Ball Club 218
Chas. T. Lucke Base Ball Club 224
Chattanooga (TN) 138–139, 192–194
Chattanooga Chatts 186–187
Chattanooga Lookouts (TN) 168–170, 175, 178, 182, 195–196
Chattanooga Warriors (TN) 187–188
Cheap John Base Ball Club 214
Cheesborough, E.R. 194
Cherokee Base Ball Club 214
Chess, Checkers and Whist Club 117
Chicago (IL) 19, 75, 108, 156–157, 159–160, 184
Chicago Base Ball Club (LA) 214
Chicago Unions 145
Chicago White Stockings ("White Stockings") 19, 80, 93, 95, 100, 156
Childs 115
Chilton, J.P. 133
Chinward Base Ball Club 214
Cincinnati (OH) 75, 77, 121, 151–152, 154–157, 172

Cincinnati Red Stockings ("Red Stockings") 19, 51, 76–80, 100, 142, 144–145, 152–153, 156, 163–164, 166
City Items Base Ball Club 214
City League 104, 147–148
City Park 60, 85, 99, 146, 208
Civil War 2–4, 8, 11, 16, 18, 20, 33–36, 39–40, 42, 48, 56, 88, 97, 105, 107–108, 110, 112, 122, 155, 165; Confederates 34–36, 68, 88, 92; Union 4, 34–36, 39, 61, 88–89, 151–152, 165
C.J. Leeds Base Ball Club 223
Claiborne Base Ball Club 214
Claiborne Green 208
Claiborne Street 208
The Clara Guards 214
Clara Street Green 208
Clerks Base Ball Club 214
Cleveland (OH) 19, 43, 139, 184
Cleveland Avenue Base Ball Club 214
Cleveland Avenue Boys 214
Cleveland Indians (OH) 93
Cleveland Spiders (OH) 137
Clinton, J.P. 133–134
Clippers 214
Clouet Gardens 60
Clouet Street 208
Club de Béisbol de Almendares (Almendares Base Ball Club) 19
Club de Béisbol de la Habana (Havana Base Ball Club) 19–20
Club de Béisbol de Matanzas (Matanzas Base Ball Club) 19
Coakley Base Ball Club 214
Coburn 109
Cohen, E. 126
Cohen, Walter L. 126, 128
Coleman Mill Factory Base Ball Club 214
Coliseum Nine Base Ball Club 214
Coliseum Square 61, 208
College baseball 130–134
Collie, J.B. 65–67
Colored Amateur League 108, 127, 130
Coltecnne Base Ball Club 214
Columbia Base Ball Club 215
Columbus (GA) 128, 135, 138, 163
Columbus Babies (GA) 197–198
Columbus Base Ball Club (LA) 215
Columbus Stars Base Ball Club (GA) 168–169
Comet Base Ball Club 18, 153, 215
Comic Base Ball Club 215
Commercial Base Ball Club 215
Commercial League 106, 108, 119
Common and Rocheblave Street 208
Compress Men 214

Congo Square 15, 208
Conlon 110
Conners 110
Conniff, J.R. 133
Continental Base Ball Club 215
Copor 215
Corbett, James J. 161, 189
Corporal Keenan Base Ball Club 222
Cotton Plant Base Ball Club 215
Cotton Yard Men 215
Coughlin Base Ball Club 215
The Crabs 215
Cram 109
Crambert, Fannie 121–122
Crawford, G.T. 151
Crawmeats Base Ball Club 215
Creole 11–14, 69, 99
Creole Base Ball Club 215
Creole Course 96–97
Crescent Base Ball Club 110, 112–113, 159, 215
Crescent Browns Base Ball Club 215
Crescent City Base Ball Club 93, 159, 215
Crescent City Base Ball League 18, 87, 108, 113–114, 130, 168
Crescent City Base Ball Park 84, 87, 89, 91, 208, 210
Crescent City Combination 215
Crescent City Cricket Club 64
Crescent Insurance Company Base Ball Club 215
Crescent Light Guards Base Ball Club 131, 215
The Crescent Rifles 215
Cricket 2–3, 10, 18, 22, 26, 28–29, 31, 33, 42, 53, 56, 62, 64, 68–70
Cricket Base Ball Club ("Crickets") 215
Crooks 152
Crusader Base Ball Club ("Crusaders") 97, 215
Cruso, John 116, 136
C.T. Howard Base Ball Club 87, 220–221
Cuban League 20
Curry Base Ball Club ("Currys") 118
Curtis, W.P. 102
Curtis & Walmsley 93
Custer Busters Base Ball Club 106, 215
Customhouse Street 208
Cutler, Colonel William A. 45, 48
C.V. Lacoste Base Ball Club 222

D. Broderick/Brodick Base Ball Club 213
D. Brown Base Ball Club 213
D. Cavanaes/Cavanacs Base Ball Club 214
D. Cullan Base Ball Club 215
D. Feany Base Ball Club 218

D. Haggerty Base4 Ball Club 220
D. Lewis Base Ball Club 223
D. Littlefield Base Ball Club 223
D. McCarthy Base Ball Club 216, 225
D. Mercier's Sons Employees 226
D. Murray Base Ball Club 227, 231
D. Woods Base Ball Club 235
Daddies Base Ball Club 215
The Daisy Club 215
Dallas (TX) 158–159, 179, 183, 194, 201
Dallas Hams (TX) 180, 201–203
Dallas Tigers (TX) 183
Dan A. Rose Base Ball Club 230
Dan Cavanaugh Base Ball Club 214
Dan Moriarity Base Ball Club 226
Dan Sullivan Base Ball Club 232
Dan Wilson Base Ball Club 235
Danite Base Ball Club 215
Dauntless Base Ball Club 216
Dauvray, Helen 176
Davis, Jefferson 182
Dayton (OH) 138
D.C. Hennessey Base Ball Club 220
D.C. Moise Base Ball Club 226
D.E. Wells Base Ball Club 234
D.E. Wells Base Ball Club 234
Deady, Ed 198
Delachaise, Philippe August 62–63
Delachaise Estate 18, 31, 41, 64
Delachaise Grounds 41, 60–64, 70–71, 88, 109–110, 124, 208
Delachaise Street 62–63
Delamore, A. 96
Delamore, G. 96
Delaney, Jim 104, 201
Delgado Community College 134
Delmonte Base Ball Club 216
Delta Base Ball Club 216
Democratic Base Ball Club 125, 216
Democrats/Democratic Base Ball Club 125, 216
Dempsey, Jack ("Nonpareil") 91, 185
Denegre, Walter 102–103
Dennis Mullen Base Ball Club 226
Dennison-Sherman Twins (TX) 198
Denny, Jerry 177
Depassan 110
Dermody, George 194
Detroit (MI) 19, 190
Detroit Base Ball Club (LA) 216
Detroit Wolverines (MI) 163, 192, 198
Deuce of Hearts Base Ball Club 216
Dew Drops Base Ball Club 216
Dexter Base Ball Club 216
Diamond Base Ball Club 216
Dickerson, Lewis P. "Buttercup" 137

Dicks Base Ball Club 216
Didilake, George 151
Digby Base Ball Club 216
Dillard University 134
Dr. E. Dreifus/Dreyfus Base Ball Club 216
Dr. J.M. Malter Base Ball Club 224
Dr. L. Azabary Base Ball Club 211
Dr. Otto Berger Base Ball Club 212
Doll, G.W. 72
Donahoe Base Ball Club 216
Donnelly, P.A. 113
Donnelly Base Ball Club 130
Donovan, Phil 151
Dooley, John 36
Dorsey, C.H. 179
The Dots 216
Doubleday, Abner 2, 8–9, 31
The Doughnuts 216
Dowd 126
Dowie, Joe 19, 115, 139, 183, 198
Dowling, Jack 134
Doyle 110
Drake, Ellis 45, 48
Dread Not Base Ball Club 216
Dreyfus Base Ball Club 216
Drohler, C.P. 163
Druby (Drouby) 172
Dryades Market Base Ball Club 216
The Dudes 216
Dudley, W.S. 102
Dueling 5, 85–86
Duffee 140–141
Duffy Malt Whiskey Base Ball Club 217
Duffys Base Ball Club 216
Dufossat and Chestnut Street 208
Dunn, James 110, 116
Dunn Base Ball Club 217
Durning E Base Ball Club 217
The Dussees 217

E. Garnier Base Ball Club 219
E. John Ellis Base Ball Club 217
E. Regan Base Ball Club 230
E. Rolland Base Ball Club 230
E. Tournes Base Ball Club 233
E. Voss Base Ball Club 234
E.A. Brandsos Base Ball Club 213
E.A. Burke Base Ball Club 213
Eagan Base Ball Club 217
Eagle Bakery Nine 217
Eagle Base Ball Club 217
Eagle Base Ball Club (KY) 156
Eagle Base Ball Club (MO) 152–153
Early, Jubal 92
Eastern League 145–146, 198, 205
Eastin 74

Easton, Alexander 179, 194
E.B. Flores Base Ball Club 218
E.C. Ziegler Nine 235
Echo Base Ball Club 217
Eckford (Ecford) Base Ball Club 87, 217
Eclipse Base Ball Club 217
Eclipse Base Ball Club (TN) 123–124
Eclipse Course 96
Eclipse Park (KY) 144
Ed Donnelly Base Ball Club 216
Ed. Brown Base Ball Club 213
Ed. Klotz Base Ball Club 222
Edward Maber Base Ball Club ("Mabers") 112, 224
E.E. Maginnis Base Ball Club 224
E.E. Ziegler Base Ball Club 235
Egg Dealers 217
Eggler 74
Egypt 7
E.H. Curry Base Ball Club 215
Eight Street Green 208
E.J. Hart Base Ball Club 220
E.J. Johnson Base Ball Club 221
El Dorado Base Ball Club 217
Eldred, Harry 139
Eli D. Hunter Base Ball Club 221
Elite Base Ball Club 217
Elkin's Hotel 85
Elks & Reindeers Base Ball Club 217
Elmira/Oswego Pioneers (NY) 146
Elmo Base Ball Club 217
Elysian Fields (NJ) 1
Emerson, Walter 113
Emile Grillot Nine 219
Emile Lananze Base Ball Club 223
Empire Base Ball Club ("Empires") 18, 70–71, 88, 106, 108, 110, 217
Empire Base Ball Club (MO) 152–153, 156, 159–160
E.P. Callejas Base Ball Club 214
E.R. Chevally Base Ball Club 214
E.R. Dalton Base Ball Club 215
E.R. Hunt Base Ball Club 221
Erato Street Green 208
Ernest 109
E.S. Levy Base Ball Club 223
Esculent Base Ball Club 217
Esplanade & Broad Street 208
Esplanade & White Street 208
Eugene Babad Base Ball Club 211
Eugene Dupre Base Ball Club 217
Eugene F. Buhler Base Ball Club 213
The Eurekas 217
E.V. Ruel Base Ball Club 230
Evansville (IN) 159–160, 195
Evansville Blackbirds (IN) 195–196

Evening Star Base Ball Club 217
Ewing, Buck 101, 177
Excelsior Base Ball Club 217
Excelsior Base Ball Club (PA) 122
Exposition Nine 138, 217
Exposition Park 99–102, 208
The Expositions/Exposition Nine 138, 217

F. Custer Base Ball Club 215
F. Good Base Ball Club 219
F. Lamandres Base Ball Club 223
F. Sheridan Base Ball Club 231
F. Wilford Base Ball Club 235
Fabian, Henry 183
Faget Base Ball Club ("Fagets") 113, 217
Fair Grounds 42, 75, 96–97, 100, 120, 132, 191, 207–208
Fairchild, L.W. 102
Fairfax Base Ball Club 217
The Fanks 217
The Fannius 217
Faranta Base Ball Club ("Farantas") 88, 113
The Farraks 218
Farrar, E.H. 102
Farrell, Jonathan T. 163
Farrell (Farrel) 116, 126
The Fashions 218
Faubourg Delachaise 62–63
Faubourg Marigny 13–15
Faubourg Plaisance 62
Fay, Fred 151
Fearless Base Ball Club 18, 218
Feldmyer Base Ball Club 218
Female Base Ball Club 218
Female Baseball 93, 120–122, 132, 211, 213, 218–219, 223, 230, 234
Fenian Base Ball Club 20, 218
Fenner, Erasmus Darwin 131
Ferdinand Dudenheffer Nine 216
Ferdinand Kirsch Base Ball Club 222
Ferran's Park 103–104, 208
Ferren 129
Ferriches Base Ball Club 218
Ferris 65–67
Ferry 124
Feytel 124
Filmore Base Ball Club 218
Fire Fly Base Ball Club 218
Fireman's Insurance Company Base Ball Club 218
First Field 208
The Fischers/A. Fischer Base Ball Club 21, 125, 218
Fisher 96
Fisher, Newt 146, 206
Fitzgerald, Jonathan T. 87, 179

The Fitzpatricks 218
Fitzsimmons, Bob 185
F.J. Nusloch Base Ball Club 227
Flaherty Base Ball Club 218
Flanders, Clem 113
Flanders Base Ball Club ("Flanders") 114, 218
Fletcher Base Ball Club 218
The Flints 218
The Flip Flaps 218
The Flirts/The Lazy Flirts 218
Florida Base Ball Club 218
Florida Mallorys 162
Flower, James 103
Flower, Mayor Walter 199
Flynn 140–141
Flynn Base Ball Club 218
Foley, Thomas "Tom" 80
Folger 65–67
Ford, Patrick 80–82
Ford, Thomas J. 81–82
Forest City Base Ball Club (IL) 156
Foresters Base Ball Club 218
Forshee 65–67
Foster, Governor Murphy J. 133
Foucher, L.F. 72
Foucher, Marie Antonine 62
Foucher Street 63, 208
Fourth & Franklin Street 208
Foutz, Dave 101
Fowler 129
Fox 110
F.P. Cellogas Base Ball Club 214
F.P. Martinez Base Ball Club 225
F.P. Walle Base Ball Club 234
F.R. Johnson Base Ball Club 221
Frank 132
Frank, Charles 146, 206
Frank Fenner Base Ball Club 218
Frank Kennedy Base Ball Club 222
Franklin, Benjamin 62, 69
Franklin Base Ball Club 125–126, 218
Frascati Park 135–136
Fred A. Blanks Base Ball Club 212
Freece Base Ball Club 218
Freedom Base Ball Club 218
Freeman, Harry H. 121
Freetown 60, 208
French Quarter 12, 15, 39–40, 69, 153
Fruit of the Loom Base Ball Club 218
F.T. Nicholls Base Ball Club 227
Fuller, Harry 140–141, 171
Fuller, W. "Shorty" 141, 170–171
Fulton Base Ball Club 219
The Futures 219
F.W. Volchmann Base Ball Club 234

G. LeBreton Base Ball Club 223
G. Pietri Base Ball Club 229
G. Pitard Base Ball Club 229
G. Roman Base Ball Club 230
Gabe Bachemine Base Ball Club 211
Gable Base Ball Club 219
Gaiennie Street Green 208
Gainesville (FL) 163
Gallagher 151–152
Gallagher Base Ball Club 219
Gallier, James 69
Galpin's Chop House 107
Galveston (TX) 179
Galveston Giants (TX) 179–180, 183
Galveston Sand Crabs 94–95, 194, 198
Galvez Boys Base Ball Club 219
Galvez Green 208
Galvez Street 208
Gambling 4, 14, 37, 85, 92, 166–167, 173
G&P Base Ball Club ("The G&P's") 118, 219
Gangers Base Ball Club 121, 219
Garden City Base Ball Club 219
Garden Gates Base Ball Club 219
Garig, William 133
The Garrigans 219
Gary Owens Base Ball Club 228
Gascard Base Ball Club 219
Gaspard Base Ball Club 219
Gates, A. 133
Gatti Base Ball Club 104, 219
Geiss 141, 171
Geitzen, Charles H. "Pretzels" 137
General Longstreet Base Ball Club 219
Genslinger, Charles H. 87, 91, 118–119, 138, 168, 170, 184–185, 187–190, 205
Geo. Bruno/Bruneau Base Ball Club 213
Geo. Degby/Digby Base Ball Club 216
Geo. Kelly Base Ball Club 222
Geo. Koeffer Base Ball Club 222
George McEvoy Base Ball Club 225
George N. Dauer (Daner) Base Ball Club ("Daners") 128, 215
George W. Flynn Base Ball Club 218
George W. Flynn/Flynn Base Ball Club 218
George W. Foster Base Ball Club 147, 218
George Weber Brewing Company Base Ball Club 234
George Weber Brewing Company Base Ball Club 234
Gilliam Base Ball Club 219
Girod Street 20, 61, 153, 208
Go Easy Base Ball Club 219
Golden Crown Base Ball Club 219
Golden Rule Base Ball Club 219

Golden Thread Base Ball Club 219
Goldie, J. 199
Gondling, John 198
Good for Nothing Base Ball Club 219
Gordon, Frank 103
Gounoud, Charles 70
Gouville 109
Grace 110
Grahm 110
Grand Dukes Base Ball Club 219
Graney, Frank 199
Grasshopper Base Ball Club 219
Graves, Abner 8
Gray 110
Greeley Base Ball Club 219
Green Stocking Base Ball Club 219
Gretna Green 208
Grinnell 65–67
Grove City Base Ball Club (IL) 156
Grover Cleveland Base Ball Club 214
Grunwald Hall 117
G.T. Ford Base Ball Club 218
Guillett, Stanislaus 65–67
Guillot, Ernesto 19
Guillot, Nemesio 19
Guillotte, Mayor Joseph Valsin (J.V.) 139, 161
Gulf League 18–19, 75, 90, 108, 114, 116, 118, 130, 134–139, 147, 168–169, 183–184, 227
Gus Lehmann Base Ball Club 223
Gus Marks Base Ball Club 225
Gus. Gast Base Ball Club 219
G.W. Green Base Ball Club 219
G.W. Vredenberg/Vandenberg Base Ball Club 234
Gymnasiums 16–17, 119

H. Brown Base Ball Club 125, 213
H. Gessner Base Ball Club 219
H. Hankin Base Ball Club 220
H./Hunt Richards Base Ball Club 230
H. Markel Base Ball Club 224
H. Meister Base Ball Club 225
H. Mentrop Base Ball Club 226
H. Rain Base Ball Club 229
H. Singer Base Ball Club 231
H.A. Bellman/Belmont Base Ball Club 212
Haegar 199
Hahn, Frank George "Noodles" 137
Hakenjos Base Ball Club 220
Half-Way House 84–87, 97
Hall Mutual Base Ball Club 220
Hamilton Base Ball Club 220
Hamilton Hams 145–146, 183, 191
Hancock Base Ball Club 18, 153, 220
Hancock Green 208

Handstands Base Ball Club 220
Hanefy, John 110, 151
Hanley 126
Hanlon 136
Hannon, H. 126
Hannon, J. 126
Happy Wagner Base Ball Club 234
Hard Hitters Base Ball Club 220
Hardin Base Ball Club 220
Harry Breen Base Ball Club 213
Harry H. Freeman's Female Base Ball Club 121
Hart, Joel T. 69
Hart, Toby 18–19, 71–72, 76, 84, 87–91, 100, 113–114, 116, 118, 121, 134–135, 137–139, 143, 147, 155–157, 162, 168–170, 173–175, 178–179, 181–185, 193–194, 204–205
Hart, W.O. 89
The Harts 220
Harwood, William 45, 48
The Hasty Tappers 220
Hatfield 74
Haymaker Base Ball Club 220
Hays 141
H.B. Simms Base Ball Club 231
H.C. Warren Base Ball Club 234
Headers & Anti-Headers 220
Healy, John J. "Egyptian" 137
Healy Base Ball Club 220
Hearst, William Randolph 198
Hennessy 74, 126
Hennessy, James 151
Henry, Colonel 86
Henry Clay Avenue 208
Henry Stouder Base Ball Club 232
Henry W. Staub Base Ball Club 232
Hess, Jack 199
Hess, Louis 117
Hezekiah & Company 120
H.F. Brennan Base Ball Club 213
Hickey Base Ball Club 220
Higginbotham, T.R. 65–67
Higgins 109
Higham 74
Hillerich, John 50
H.J. Rivet Base Ball Club 230
Hoboken (NJ) 1
Hogan, J. 113
The Hole in the Wall Base Ball Club 220
Holiday 65–67
Holland, Willard 184
Holtzman, John T. 107, 151
Home Base Ball Club 18, 108, 220
Hon. John Hayes Base Ball Club 220
Hop Bitters Base Ball Club 220
Hop Bitters of New York 87, 227

Hope Base Ball Club 153, 221, 226, 234
Hourbright Base Ball Club 221
Houston, J.D. 133
Houston (TX) 69, 183, 201
Houston Buffaloes (TX) 94–95, 203
Houston Red Stockings (TX) 179–180
Howard, Charles T. 92
Howard, J.N. 72, 77
Howard Base Ball Club ("Howards") 98, 123, 221
Howell, Joseph T. 86
H.P. Ryan Base Ball Club 231
H.T. Lawler Base Ball Club 223
Hunt, Charles M. 102
Hunt Richards Base Ball Club 230
Hunter & Genslinger 87, 91, 118, 184
Hunter & Genslinger Base Ball Club ("H&G") 113–114, 118, 221
Hunters Base Ball Club 113, 118
Hurling 23
Huston, Jack 182–183, 197–198
Hy. Ollie Base Ball Club 227

Iberville, Pierre Le Moyne 10
Iberville Street 88, 122, 209
Ida Base Ball Club 221
Idlewild Dramatic Club 221
I.L. Lyons Base Ball Club 224
I.L. Twitchel Base Ball Club 233
Illgs Base Ball Club 221
Imperial Base Ball Club 221
I.N. Bakers Base Ball Club 211
Independent Base Ball Club 221
Indianapolis (IN) 80, 152, 156–157, 198
Indianapolis Hoosiers 19, 117, 142, 163, 176
Innocent Base Ball Club 221
Integrated baseball 89, 97, 122–130
Intercollegiate Athletic Association 133
International Association 183
International League 145
Interstate League 145, 198
Iolanthe Base Ball Club 221
Irad Base Ball Club 221
Irish Wonders 221
Iron Horse 105
Irvin, Jonathan J. 163
Isaacson Base Ball Club 221
The Items Base Ball Club 221

J. Beecher Base Ball Club 212
J. Behrman Base Ball Club 212
J. Bertucci Base Ball Club 212
J. Cravens Base Ball Club 215
J. Curry Base Ball Club 215
J. Danynois Base Ball Club 216
J. Delords Base Ball Club 216

Index

J. Dutrey Base Ball Club 217
J. Frederick Base Ball Club 218
J. Healey Base Ball Club 220
J. Klotz/Klutz Base Ball Club 222
J. Kray Base Ball Club 222
J. McCord Base Ball Club 225
J. Mesritz Base Ball Club 226
J. Noreic Base Ball Club 227
J. Noveh Base Ball Club 227
J. Paris Childress Base Ball Club 214
J. Rheinhard Base Ball Club 230
J. Scherman/Shirman/Sherman Base Ball Club 231
J. Sheridan Base Ball Club 231
J. Smeary Base Ball Club 232
J. Steppe Base Ball Club 232
J. Swain Base Ball Club 233
J. Syme & Co. Base Ball Club 233
J. Tennyson Base Ball Club 233
J. Wharton Base Ball Club 234
J.A. Haley/J. Healey Base Ball Club 220
J.A. Reinecke Base Ball Club 230
Jack Harkaway Base Ball Club 220
Jack/Jacob Hettinger Base Ball Club 220
Jack Short Base Ball Club 231
Jackson Barracks Base Ball Club 221
Jackson Base Ball Club 125, 221
Jackson Green 208
Jackson Press Base Ball Club 221
Jackson Square 15, 60, 62
Jacksons 221
Jacob Hettinger Base Ball Club 220
Jacobs, Solon 196
Jaeger's Silver Coronet Band 97
Jake Kirsch Base Ball Club 222
Jake Stevens Base Ball Club 232
James Darrow Base Ball Club 215
James Glynn Base Ball Club 219
James J. Dugan Base Ball Club 217
James J. Kent Base Ball Club 222
James/Jas. McCann Base Ball Club 225
James/Jas. McGarrigan Base Ball Club 225
James McCormick Base Ball Club 225
James O'Donnell Base Ball Club 227
James Rankin/J.D. Rankin Base Ball Club 229
James Siepkins Base Ball Club 231
Jamison 124
Jas. Farrell Base Ball Club 218
Jas. McCann Base Ball Club 225
Jas. McGarrigan Base Ball Club 225
Jas. Tracey Base Ball Club 233
J.B. Durnin Base Ball Club 217
J.B./E.B. Flores Base Ball Club 218
J.B./Faget Base Ball Club ("Fagets") 113, 217
J.B. McKernan Base Ball Club 225

J.B. Thierry Club 233
J.C. Bach Base Ball Club ("Bachs") 93, 113, 121, 138, 147, 162, 211
J.C. Callahan Base Ball Club 214
J.C. Murphy Base Ball Club 227
J.C. Pepper Base Ball Club 228
J.C. Weber Base Ball Company 234
J.D. Houston Base Ball Club 211, 221
J.D. Rankin Base Ball Club 229
Jefferson Base Ball Club 221
Jefferson City 14, 41, 58, 62, 64, 71, 88, 224
Jefferson Green 208
Jefferson Parish 84, 86, 126
Jesuit Base Ball Club 221
J.G. Roche Base Ball Club 230
J.H. Duggan Base Ball Club 217
J.H. Frerichs/Ferriches Base Ball Club 218
J.H. Nolting Base Ball Club 227
Jim Hennessey Base Ball Club 220
Jimmy Morrisey Base Ball Club 226
J.J. Frawley Base Ball Club 218
J.J. Hayes Base Ball Club 220
J.J./Joe O'Hara Base Ball Club 227
J.J. Oliver Base Ball Club 228
J.L. Grasshoff Base Ball Club 219
Joe Desposito Base Ball Club 216
Joe Mack Base Ball Club 224
Joe O'Hara Base Ball Club 227
Joe Oliver Base Ball Club 228
John A. Benedict Base Ball Club 212
John A. Dix Club 216
John C. Kendry Base Ball Club 222
John Cruso Base Ball Club 215
John Davis Base Ball Club 216
John Dooley Base Ball Club 216
John Dowie Base Ball Club 216
John Doyle Base Ball Club 216
John E. Bensel Base Ball Club 212
John E. Kennedy Base Ball Club 222
John E. Markey Base Ball Club 224
John Garic Base Ball Club 219
John Gauche & Sons Nine 219
John H. Brownlee Base Ball Club 213
John Hoffman Base Ball Club 220
John J. McCloskey Base Ball Club 225
John J. McFarlane Base Ball Club 225
John L. Sullivan Base Ball Club 232
John Mitchell Base Ball Club 226
John Munna Base Ball Club 227
John Rogers Base Ball Club 230
John Stewart Club 232
John Teen Base Ball Club 233
John Voelker Base Ball Club 234
John Wragg Base Ball Club 235
Johnson 124
Johnson, A.B. 75

Index

Johnson, W. 133
Johnson, William Preston 131
Johnson's Island (OH) 35–36, 151
Johnstown (PA) 147
Jonas Base Ball Club 221
Jones, H.B. 65–67
Jones, J.H. 41, 64–67, 70
Jos. Schlitz Base Ball Club 231
Joseph Janfroids Base Ball Club 221
Joseph Johnson Base Ball Club 221
J.P. Conners Base Ball Club 215
J.P. Lytle Base Ball Club 224
J.P. Quinn Base Ball Club 229
J.P. Walters Base Ball Club 234
J.R. Lewis Base Ball Club 223
J.S. Hodgins Base Ball Club 220
J.S. Wright Base Ball Club ("Wrights") 87, 113, 235
J.T. Shaw Base Ball Club 231
Jules Manaud/Manand Base Ball Club 224
Jules Victor Base Ball Club 233
Julier, Conrad C. 112
Junior Base Ball Club 221
J.V. Guillotte Base Ball Club 220
J.V. Lacoste Base Ball Club 222
J.W. Buckhardt Base Ball Club 213
J.W. Swoop Base Ball Club 233
J.W. Twomey Base Ball Club 233

Kaiser, John 75
Kansas City (MO) 159
Kansas City Blues (MO) 184
Katies 222
Kauffman, Maurice J. 87, 113, 170, 177
Keating Base Ball Club 222
Keefe, Tim 101, 177
Keller's Green 208
Kellum, Win 198
Kelly 96, 140–141
Kelly, D.M. 72
Kelly, John F. 134–135, 186
Kelly, King 177
Kelly, M.J. 103
Kenair Base Ball Club 222
Kenna/William Kenna Base Ball Club 222
Kennedy 109, 126
Kennedy Base Ball Club 222
Kennedy Base Ball Club 222
Keno Base Ball Club 222
Kenton Base Ball Club 222
Kentucky Base Ball Club (KY) 152–153
Kernon Base Ball Club 222
Kethum Base Ball Club 222
Kettle Park 208
Kiks Base Ball Club 222
Kinberger Base Ball Club 222

Kingman 96
Klein 124
Klusman 140–142
Klutz Base Ball Club 222
K.M. Kimberger/Kinberger Base Ball Club 222
Knappan 23
Knickerbocker Base Ball Club ("Knickerbockers") 31–32, 34, 105
Knickerbocker Rules 32, 66, 105
Knockball 29
Knucke 23
Koenig Base Ball Club 222
The Kraus Nine 222
Ku-Klux Base Ball Club 222
Kuhn Base Ball Club 222

L. Buhler Base Ball Club 213
L. Dever Base Ball Club 216
L. Falk Base Ball Club 217
L. Fleming Base Ball Club 218
L. Hollman Base Ball Club 220
L. Lehmann Base Ball Club 223
L. Luzenberg Base Ball Club 224
L. Pimken Base Ball Club 229
La De Dah Base Ball Club 222
Labouisse, Peter 102–103
Lacrosse 7–10, 23
Ladies' Athletic Association 120
Ladies' Day 4, 143, 170, 172–173
Ladies Pets 222
Lady Nine of Baltimore 120
Lady Nine of Boston 120
Lafayette, Marquis de 15, 69
Lafayette Base Ball Club 222
Lafayette Cemetery Number One 69
Lafayette City 14, 58, 62
Lafayette Hook & Ladder Fire Company 222
Lafayette Square 15, 61–62, 69, 208
Lafitte, J.A. 103
Lambour (Lambeau), Mike 116, 163
Lambour Base Ball Club 223
Lamothe's Turf Exchange 142
Landon 74
Landry, William A. 116, 163
Landwehr/Landwer Base Ball Club ("Landwehrs") 20, 113, 118, 223
Landwer Base Ball Club ("Landwehrs") 20, 113, 118, 223
Laner 74
Laners Base Ball Club ("Laners") 20, 223
The Lanters 223
Lapeyrouse and Galvez Street 208
Lapta 28
Larkin, Nick 151

Index

Larry Conroy Base Ball Club 215
Larry Thorn Base Ball Club 233
The Lasses 121, 223
The Last Ditchers 223
Lauer, Gus 76
Laurel Base Ball Club 223
Lawrence, T.H. 112
The Lazy Flirts 218
Lazy/Old Lazy Base Ball Club 223
Leber Base Ball Club 223
Leche Base Ball Club 223
Legendre, James 102
Lehman, Augustus 181
Leithman, "Governor" Conrad 76, 116, 118, 134, 170, 205
Leo Base Ball Club ("Leos") 104, 223
Leon Blessings Base Ball Club 212
Leon Godchaux Base Ball Club 219
Leon Lamothe Base Ball Club 223
Leonard 160
The Leppets 223
Levee Cotton Clerks Base Ball Club 223
Levi 74
Levis, S.H. 179
Levy 124
Levy & Meyer Base Ball Club 223
Levy Base Ball Club 147
Lewis, Mayor John L. 85
L.F. Longmore Base Ball Club 224
Lhote & Co. Base Ball Club 222
Liberty & Erato Street Nine 223
Liberty Base Ball Club 18, 108, 223
Liberty Base Ball Club (IL) 156
Liberty Base Ball Club (MO) 156
Light House Hotel 85
The Lightning Bugs 223
Lightweight Base Ball Club 223
Lightwing Base Ball Club 223
Little Brown Jugs Base Ball Club 223
Little Giant Base Ball Club 223
Little Rock (AR) 192–193, 195, 201, 206
Little Rock Travelers 196–197
Little Rocks 224
Livaudais, Francoise Dugas 62
Live Oak Base Ball Club 224
L.J. Ricks Base Ball Club 230
Locust Park 208
Loeper's Park 93, 98–99, 127, 208–210
Logan Street Green 209
Logan's Green 209
Lombard, J.E. 133
London Green 209
Lone Star Base Ball Club ("Lone Stars") 18, 20, 73, 75–80, 87, 89, 91, 106–108, 111, 115–116, 124–125, 151, 153, 155–163, 184, 224

Lonsdal Base Ball Club 224
Lorch, Adam 76, 116, 163
Lotta Base Ball Club 224
Louis A. Richards Base Ball Club 230
Louis J. Huber Base Ball Club 221
Louisa Street 209
Louisiana Amateur Base Ball Association 115, 118–119, 163
Louisiana Avenue & Bacchus Street 209
Louisiana Avenue & Dryades Street 209
Louisiana Base Ball Association 18, 84, 88, 105, 108–112, 153
Louisiana Base Ball Club 18, 41, 64–66, 68, 70, 88, 105, 108, 119, 125, 215, 224
Louisiana Base Ball League 108, 112, 130, 137
Louisiana Base Ball Park 71–72, 76, 80, 82–84, 89, 98, 209
Louisiana Base Ball Park Association 72, 76, 87–88
Louisiana Brewing Company Base Ball Club 224
Louisiana Browns 224
Louisiana Club 102
Louisiana Electric Base Ball Club 224
Louisiana Field Artillery Base Ball Club 224
The Louisiana Reds 224
The Louisiana Rifles 224
Louisiana State Lottery Company 92
Louisiana State University (LSU) 132–134
Louisiana Tigers Brigade 36
The Louisianas 224
Louisville (KY) 50, 75, 80, 108, 144, 151–156, 162
Louisville Colonels (KY) 144, 187, 192, 195
Louisville Eclipse (KY) 50
Louisville Slugger 50
Loyola University of New Orleans 134
L.P. Hackmeyer Base Ball Club 220
Lucie 96
Luke Duffy Base Ball Club 217
L.W. Bradley Base Ball Club 213
L.W. Smith Base Ball Club 232
Lyons, L. 103

M. Brown Base Ball Club 213
M. Hackett Base Ball Club 220
M. Lehman Base Ball Club 223
M. Lobe Base Ball Club 224
M. Moelker Base Ball Club 226
M. Sporls Base Ball Club 232
M. Sport Base Ball Club 232
M. Sullivan Base Ball Club 125, 233
M. Woods Base Ball Club 235
Mack, Connie 146
Mack's Green 209

Macon (GA) 138, 168–170
Macon Central City (GA) 117, 187–188
Macon Hornets (GA) 192–193, 195
Magazine Street & St. Jospeh Street 209
Magenta Base Ball Club 224
Maginnis 115
Magnolia Base Ball Club ("Magnolias") 18, 61, 70, 96, 108, 224
Magnolia Garden 209
Magnolia Street 72, 209–210
Magnon 96
Mahan, P.W. 199
Maley 110
Malley & Sons 224
Mamie Base Ball Club 224
Manand Base Ball Club 224
Mandeville, Bernard Xavier Phillippe de Marigny 13–15, 72
Mandeville Clippers Base Ball Club 224
Manhattan Athletic Club 190
Manuel C. Royes Base Ball Club 230
Manuel Ruler Base Ball Club 231
Marengo Base Ball Club 224
Marigny Base Ball Club 224
Marion (N) 142
Marion Base Ball Club (IN) 152
The Marks 225
Marks Isaacs Base Ball Club 225
Marsden's Peetoral Balm Nine 225
Martin 74
Martin, Francoise Xavier 62
Martinez 110
Mascot/Mascottes Base Ball Club 225
Mascottes Base Ball Club 225
Masdexexarts Base Ball Club 225
Maseppas Base Ball Club 225
Mason, Charles 19
Mason Base Ball Club 225
Mason-Dixon Line 5, 20, 195, 205
Masonic Lot 60, 209
Massachusetts Association of Base Ball Players 31
Massachusetts Game 29, 31, 66
Mauberet Base Ball Club 225
Maubret, L.E. 133
May 2nd and Cane Base Ball Club 225
Mayer, D.A. 87, 170
Mayflower Base Ball Club 225
Maylie's Green 209
McCall Base Ball Club 225
McCardy 109
McCarthy & Raymond Base Ball Club 225
McCarthy Base Ball Club ("McCarthys") 114
McCarthy Square 209
McCarty Square 209

McCloskey, John J. 179
McCluskey Base Ball Club 225
McClusky 110
McCormick 116
McCormick, William 163
McCoy, A. 109
McCoy C. 109
McDonnell's Restaurant 107
McDonoghville 60, 209
McDonough, John 69
McDonough Park 60
McEnery, Governor Samuel D. 82
McFallen Base Ball Club 225
McGelon Base Ball Club 225
McGuirk, Tom 182–183
McHale Base Ball Club 225
McKeough, E. 135
McKeough, F.M. 76, 112
McKinley, Governor William 139
McLean Base Ball Club 225
McManus, H.M. 71, 88
McMillan Base Ball Club 225
McNamara, Michael (Lt.) 36, 151
McNeil Base Ball Club 225
McVey 140–142
McVey, Cal 2
M.D. Gardner Base Ball Club ("Gardners") 118, 219
M.E. Nester/Nestor Base Ball Club 227
Mechanics Base Ball Club 225
Meister, C. 96
Meister, G. 96
Melpomenia Base Ball Club ("Melpomenias") 18, 108–109, 225
The Memory Base Ball Club 225
Memphis (TN) 79–80, 99, 108, 111, 128, 138, 146, 151–157, 160, 175, 185, 197, 204, 206
Memphis Browns Base Ball Club (GA) 168–169, 176
Memphis Giants (TN) 187–188, 192–193, 195–197, 201
Memphis Grays (TN) 169, 173, 178–182
Meridian (MS) 89, 162
Meridian Base Ball Club (MS) 162
Merry Nine Base Ball Club 226
Metairie Cemetery 87, 182
Metairie Course 86, 96–97, 100, 126, 209
Metairie Road 84, 86
Metropolitan Club 91, 184, 190
Mexican Gulf Base Ball Club 226
Mikado Base Ball Club 226
Mike Berry Base Ball Club 212
Mike Murray Base Ball Club 227
Mike Rickers/Rickard/Ricketts Base Ball Club 230

Milan Green 209
Miller 160
Miller, Billy 134
Miller, Joseph H. "Cyclone" 117, 137
Miller & Diechmann Base Ball Club 226
Mills, Abraham G. 8
Mills, C. 74
Mills, E 74
Mills, Sam 203
Mills Commission 8
Milneburg 59, 98
Minch 109
Minneapolis Millers 117, 198
Minnie Maddern Base Ball Club 224
Mississippi Base Ball Club 221, 226
Mixologists Base Ball Club 226
M.J. McFarland Base Ball Club 225
M.J. Sheehan Base Ball Club 231
M.L. Navra/Navra's Chinese Palace Base Ball Club 227
Mobile (AL) 19, 23, 90, 122, 127–128, 134, 136, 139–140, 168, 170, 175, 178–179
Mobile Base Ball Club (AL) 116, 136–137, 139–140
Mobile Blackbirds (AL) 95, 181–188, 192–193, 195–198, 199–201, 203–204
Mobile Swamp Angels (AL) 137, 140–142, 173–174–176, 181
Modoc Base Ball Club 226
Moerlein Base Ball Club 226
Monck/Mouck's Park 209
Moneal, William 115
Monrovia Base Ball Club (PA) 122
Montegut Street 209
Montgomery (AL) 134–135, 138, 162, 198
Montgomery Base Ball Club (LA) 226
Montgomery Colts (AL) 187–188, 192–193, 195–200
Montgomery Gladiators (AL) 147
Montgomery Grays (AL) 196
Montgomery Lambs (AL) 187
Montgomery Steers (AL) 201–204
Mooney, R.H. 115
Morgan 124
Morgan Base Ball Club 226
Morgan Railroad Base Ball Club 226
Morgan's Depot 60, 209
Morgan's Green/Morgan's Depot 60, 209
Morning Star Base Ball Club 226
Morris, F.B. 134
Morris, John 92
Morse Base Ball Club 20, 226
Morse Nine 106, 226
Mortar & Pestle Club 226
Moses Loeb/M. Lobe Base Ball Club 224
Mouck's Park 209

Move On Base Ball Club 226
Mueller, J.L. 196
Mueller Base Ball Club 226
Mueller Base Ball Club 226
Muffer Base Ball Club 226
Muldoon Base Ball Club 226
Mundinger, George 19, 116–118, 126, 142, 163
Munna/John Munna Base Ball Club 227
Murphy, Andrew H. "Cap" 81
Murphy, Henry 141, 171
Murphy, John 81–82
Murray, A.J. 103
Musgrove Base Ball Club 227
Mutual Base Ball Club 42, 227
Mutual Base Ball Club (MO) 159
Mutual Base Ball Club of New York *see* New York Mutuals
Mutz, Joseph 117

N. Mohr Base Ball Club 226
The Nameless Nine 227
Napoleon Avenue 209
Nashville (TN) 128, 138, 146, 156–157, 173–175, 195, 206
Nashville Americans Base Ball Club (TN) 168–169
Nashville Blues (TN) 176–177
Nashville Seraphs (TN) 195
Nashville Station 60, 209
Nashville Tigers (TN) 145, 187–188, 192–193
Nashville Volunteers ("Vols") (TN) 146
Natchez Green 209
National Association of Base Ball Players (NABBP) 20, 31, 48, 50, 74–75, 122
The National Base Ball Club 227
Navra's Chinese Palace 20, 227
Navra's Chinese Palace Base Ball Club 227
Ne Plus Base Ball Club 227
Neihoff, Bert 141
Nelson 74
Nelson McStea Base Ball Club 225
NEOLA Base Ball Club 227
Nestor Base Ball Club 227
New Basin Canal 13, 84–86, 89, 93, 97, 233
New Bedford Base Ball Club 227
New Castle Quakers (PA) 145, 198
New England Game 29
New Orleans Amateur League 108, 115, 118–120, 168
New Orleans Base Ball Association 90, 112
New Orleans Base Ball Club 136, 227
New Orleans Base Ball Company 170, 187
New Orleans Base Ball Park 87, 89–91,

Index

104, 114–115, 121, 123, 127–128, 158, 162, 184, 208–209
New Orleans Base Ball Park Association 87–88
New Orleans Bicycle Club 91, 184
New Orleans Boy's Base Ball Club 227
New Orleans Chess, Checkers & Whist Base Ball Club 227
New Orleans Fire Department 81, 117
New Orleans News Company Nine 227
New Orleans Opera House 59, 69–70
New Orleans Pelicans ("Pelicans") 1, 4, 19, 56, 76, 87, 89–91, 94–95, 104, 106, 116–117, 139, 141–147, 170, 172–203, 205, 227
New Orleans Unions 233
New York Base Ball Club 1
New York Game 32, 66
New York Giants 80, 100–102, 176–178, 195
New York Knickerbockers 53, 79, 172
New York Mutuals ("Mutuals") 19, 73–74, 80, 100, 164, 166
New York State League 146
Newark Colts (NJ) 145–146
Newcomb College 130–131
Newman 124
Newsboys' Band 142
Next Timers 227
Nicholls, Governor Frances T. 92
Nick Brennan Base Ball Club 213
Nick Niltze Base Ball Club 235
Nicklin, J.B. 192, 196
Night Hawk Base Ball Club 227
Nine Brothers Base Ball Club 227
Nine Little Dutchmen 227
Nine Orphans Base Ball Club 227
Nine Star Base Ball Club 227
Nolan Base Ball Club 227
Nonpareil Paso Base Ball Club 227
Norman Base Ball Club 227
Norman/N. Mohr Base Ball Club 226
North Star Base Ball Club 227
Northeastern Railroad Employees 227
Northwestern League 117, 145, 205
Norton 109
Nugent & Johnson Base Ball Club 227

O. Becker Base Ball Club 212
O. Dumestre Base Ball Club 217
O. Lagman Base Ball Club 222
Oak Grove Park 209
Oakland Park 86, 97, 100, 123, 126–127, 209
Offner Base Ball Club 228
Ogden Base Ball Club 228
Ogden Park 98, 125, 209
Oil Factory Green 60, 209

Oina 28
O'Keefe, C.A. 77, 151–152
Old Cat 8, 26–27
Old Hickory Club 228
Old Lazy Base Ball Club 223
Old Paper Mill 209
Old Racket Green 210
Old Timers 228
Old Tops Base Ball Club 228
Old Wrecks 228
O'Leary Base Ball Club ("O'Learys") 118, 227
Olympic Base Ball Club 228
Olympic Base Ball Club (PA) 29
Olympic Club 91, 139, 161, 184–185, 189–190
Olympic Theatre 161
O'Neal Base Ball Club 227
Onward Base Ball Club 228
Orange Green 60, 209
Oriental Base Ball Club 228
Original Echo Base Ball Club 228
The Originals 228
Oriole Base Ball Club 228
Orleans & Factors 228
Orleans Base Ball Club 21, 125, 228
Orleans Park 209
Orleans Social and Base Ball Club 228
Orleans Theatre 69
Oscar Wilde Base Ball Club 235
Oser Base Ball Club 228
O'Shaughnessy Base Ball Club 228
Oswego Pioneers (NY) 146
Oteri, Joseph 181
Our Boys Base Ball Club 210, 228
Our Boys Base Ball Club (FL) 162
Owen Roper Base Ball Club 230
Owens, Dan 115
Oxidental Base Ball Club 228

P. Becker Base Ball Club 212
P. Caminita/P. Cominita Base Ball Club 214
P. Cominita Base Ball Club 214
P. Demots Base Ball Club 216
P. Eagan Base Ball Club 217
P. Gillon Base Ball Club 219
P. Graham Base Ball Club 219
P. Hess Base Ball Club 220
P. Kane Base Ball Club 221
P. Kelly Base Ball Club 222
P. Kenny Base Ball Club 222
P. LeLoup Base Ball Club 223
P. Lubie Base Ball Club 224
P. Mack Base Ball Club 224
P. Mulholland Men 226

P. Philbin Base Ball Club 112, 228
P./P.J. Caldwell Base Ball Club 213, 214
P. Scheib Base Ball Club 231
P. Seighers Base Ball Club 231
P. Shilling Base Ball Club 231
P. Swago Base Ball Club 233
P. Waldemann Base Ball Club 234
P.A. Donnelly Base Ball Club 216
Pabst, Ed 203
Pacific Base Ball Club 228
Pacific Northwest League 145–146, 183–184, 191
Palant 28
Palm Grove Base Ball Club (MO) 75
Palmer Park 60
Palmetto Base Ball Club 228
Paragon Base Ball Club 228
Parker 109
Parker, E.T. (Sherriff) 39
The Pastimes 228
Pat Casey Base Ball Club 214
Pat Eagan/P. Eagan/Eagan Base Ball Club 217
Pat Glennon Base Ball Club 112–113, 219, 230
Pat Glennon Base Ball Club ("Glennons") 219
Paterson Giants (NJ) 145–146, 203
Patrick Berry Base Ball Club 212
Patterson 74
Paul Waterman Base Ball Club 112, 234
P.B.S. Pinchback Base Ball Club 21, 125, 228
Pearline Base Ball Club 228
Peek-a-Boo Base Ball Club 228
Pelican Base Ball Club ("Pelicans") 18, 75–77, 105, 108, 153, 228
Pelican Cricket Club 64
Pelican Hook & Ladder No. 4 117
Pelican Park 95
Pelican Regiment 36
Pelota 10
Peltz, John 19, 142, 163
Pender Base Ball Club 228
Pensacola (FL) 122, 134–135, 137, 162–163, 188
Pensacola Mallorys Base Ball Club (FL) 162
Peoria Reds 145
Pesäpallo 28
Pescay (Pascay), Charles 41, 64–70
Peter Blaise Base Ball Club 212
Peters, Henry 134, 187
Petrie Base Ball Club ("Petries") 127–128, 162, 228
Pfeiffer Base Ball Club 228

P.H. Doyle Base Ball Club 216
P.H. Ford Base Ball Club 218
P.H./Primrose H. Simpson Base Ball Club 231
Phelan, Dick 183
Phil Rielly/Reilly/Riley Base Ball Club 230
Philadelphia (PA) 121–122, 142, 165, 172
Philadelphia Athletics (PA) 142
Philadelphia Base Ball Club 228
Philadelphia Centennials (PA) 19
Philadelphia Fire Company No. 14 Base Ball Club 228
Philadelphia Pythians Base Ball Club (PA) 122
Philbin, S. 112
Philip Best Base Ball Club 212
Phillips 109
Phoenix Base Ball Club 228
Picayune Base Ball Club ("Picayunes") 106, 229
Pickwick Base Ball Club ("Pickwicks") 18, 21, 97, 124–126, 128, 214, 229
Pickwick Club 102–103, 125
Pie Base Ball Club 229
Pierce, Charles Hatch (Lt.) 36
Piety Street 209
Pinafore Base Ball Club 229
Pine Knot Base Ball Club 229
Pioneer Base Ball Club 229
Pioneer Green 60, 209
Piper Base Ball Club 229
Piper's Green 209
Pitkin, R.K. 107
Pittsburg Pirates (PA) 187
Pittsburgh (PA) 19
Pittsburgh Alleghenys (PA) 163
P.J. Caldwell Base Ball Club 213
P.J. Commer Base Ball Club 215
P.J. Finney Base Ball Club 218
P.J. Kammer Base Ball Club 221
P.J. Reynolds Base Ball Club 230
Plattsmier, A.L. 109
Plattsmier A.A. 109
Player's League 183
Pluck & Luck Base Ball Club 229
P.M. Harnan Base Ball Club 220
Pocahontas Base Ball Club 229
Poets Base Ball Club 125, 229
Poinsettia Base Ball Club ("Poinsettias") 118, 229
Poland Street Green 209
Polhemus, Mark 2, 181, 183, 187
Pommeroux 115
The Poor Scrub Nine 229
Pope 109

Porter 115
Porter & Childs Base Ball Club 229
Portland (OR) 184
Potts, J.J. 133
Pottsville Maroons (PA) 145
Powell, Abner 2, 4, 87, 89, 95, 115, 139, 140–147, 170–173, 176–179, 183, 185, 187–188, 190–192, 195, 197–201, 203–206
Powell, James 173
Powell Base Ball Club 229
Powell's Garage 146
Powers, Henry 76, 93, 181, 184, 189–194, 196–197, 201, 205
Poydras Green 209
Presas Base Ball Club 229
Price 124, 129
Price Current Base Ball Club 229
Pride of New Orleans Base Ball Club 229
Primrose H. Simpson Base Ball Club 231
Prof. L. Timken Base Ball Club 233
Providence Base Ball Club 229
Prytania Street Car Station Green 210
P.S. Moran Base Ball Club 226
P.T. Ford Base Ball Club 218
Pujol, Jules 115–118, 141, 171
Pulitzer, Joseph 198
Pyes Base Ball Club ("Pyes") 114, 229

Quickstep Base Ball Club 229
Quinette Base Ball Club 229

R. Fernandez Base Ball Club 218
R. Martine and Brookers Base Ball Club 225
R. Otero Base Ball Club 228
R. Phillip Base Ball Club 228
Racetracks 96, 191
Rackett Grounds/Old Racket/Rouquette Green 210
Radbourn, Charles Gardner "Old Hoss" 137
Railroad Mother Hubbard 233
Rain check 20, 143–144
Rainey 124–125
Ralph Morgan Base Ball Club 226
Rankel Base Ball Club 229
Rareshide, J.B. 88
R.C. Davey Base Ball Club 216
R.C. Pendergrast Base Ball Club 228
R.C./Ralph Morgan Base Ball Club 226
R.E. Lee Base Ball Club ("Lees") 18, 73–80, 88, 93, 98, 106, 111, 113, 115–118, 134–136, 151, 153, 158–162, 223, 226
R.E. Simon Base Ball Club 231
Recasner 123
Reconstruction 2, 4, 85, 95

Red Cloud Base Ball Club 229
Red Head Base Ball Club 229
Red Hots 20, 229
Red Jackets 229
Red Star Shoe Company Base Ball Club 229
Red Stockings 229
The Red Warriors 230
Redon, Marsh 128, 142, 160–162
Redon Base Ball Club 230
The Reds & Blues 229
The Regulars 119, 230
Reilly, Phillip 181, 184
Reilly Base Ball Club 230
Reilly Base Ball Club 230
Reinecke, J.A. 113
Remy Clarke Base Ball Club ("Clarkes") 93, 113, 115, 119, 160, 163, 219, 230
Renfroe 123
Reverigerre Base Ball Club 230
Reynolds 124
R.G. Ponsetti Base Ball Club ("Ponsettis") 113, 229
The Rhamers 230
Rice, Grantland 146
Rice & Hayes Base Ball Club 121, 230
Richard Zank Base Ball Club 235
Richmond Base Ball Club 230
Richmond Virginians (VA) 145
Richtor 109
Rickard Base Ball Club 230
Rickerts Base Ball Club 230
The Right Ways 230
Riley Base Ball Club 230
The River Nine 230
Riverside Base Ball Club 230
Riverside Base Ball Club (IN) 159–160
Riverside Boxing Club 85
R.M. Hahn Base Ball Club 220
Roach, Rudolph "Skel" 198
Robert H. Rodetzkie Base Ball Club 230
Robert L. Brown Base Ball Club 213
Robin Street 210
Robinson 126
Robt. Lamson Base Ball Club ("Lamsons") 114, 213, 224
Rochester Bronchos (NY) 191
Rockford Base Ball Club 230
Rollaway Base Ball Club 230
Roosevelt, Franklin Delano 206
Roosevelt, Theodore 8
Rose Base Ball Club 230
Rosebud Base Ball Club 230
Rough on Rats Base Ball Club 230
Rounders 10, 12, 25, 27–29, 30–31–32, 37, 50, 56

Rouquette Green 210
Rousseau Base Ball Club 230
Rowing Club League 108
R.S. Benton Base Ball Club 212
R.S. Howard Base Ball Club 221
Ruby Base Ball Club 230
Runkel Base Ball Club 231
Ryan, Edward (Lt.) 36

S. Caleca Base Ball Club 213
S. Thompson Base Ball Club 233
St. Charles and Milan Street 210
St. Charles Hotel 161, 176–177, 199
St. John Boat House 85
St. Louis (MO) 19, 43, 75, 80, 108, 129, 138, 143, 151–157, 159–160, 172
St. Louis Browns 100–102, 147, 195
St. Louis Cardinals 163
St. Louis Cathedral 5, 15, 85
St. Mary's Base Ball Club 231
St. Mary's Market 105
St. Petersburg (FL) 147
Saint-Saëns, Camille 70
Samuel Laycock Base Ball Club 223
Samuels Base Ball Club 231
San Antonio (TX) 179
San Antonio Cowboys (TX) 180
San Francisco (CA) 165
Saraboneyard/Sarah Boneyard Base Ball Club 231
Sarah Boneyard Base Ball Club 231
Savannah (GA) 162–163, 169, 173, 175–176, 178, 191, 195, 200
Savannah Dixies (GA) 162
Savannah Electrics (GA) 187–188
Savannah Forest City Base Ball Club (GA) 163
Savannah Modocs 192–193
Savannah Oglethorpes (GA) 163
Saxon, W.L. 76, 134
The Scale Hands 231
The Scalpers 231
Schachern, Joseph 184
Schaffer Base Ball Club 231
Schellang Base Ball Club 231
Schencks Base Ball Club 231
Schilling Base Ball Club 231
Schneider Base Ball Club 20, 231
Schwartz, David 72, 76
Scott 65–67, 124, 160
The Screw Guzzles 20, 231
Scully, Ed 112
Seattle Hustlers (WA) 145–146, 191
Selleck 65, 67
Selma (AL) 135, 162
Selma Christians (AL) 146

Senator Daniels Base Ball Club 215
Septoline Oil Nine 231
Setley, W.W. 199
Seymour Base Ball Club ("Seymours") 114, 231
Shaffer, Charles 135
Shakspeare, Mayor Joseph A. 62, 92, 119
The Shamrocks 231
Shannon Base Ball Club 125, 231
Shea, Mike 19, 115
Sheehan, Ed 199
Shenandoah (PA) 142
Sheridan, Richard 135
Sherman Base Ball Club 231
Sherry 109
Shinty 23
Shirman Base Ball Club 231
Shoo-Fly Base Ball Club 231
Shreveport (LA) 119, 137, 204
Shreveport Tigers (LA) 201, 203
The Silk Stockings 231
Silver Crescent Base Ball Club 231
Simmes, L.L. 107
Simms, William (Capt.) 36
Simonin 173–174
The Single Stars 231
Sister's School Green 210
Sitting Bull Base Ball Club 231
Skinner, E.K. 76
Slaball 28
The Slow Boys Base Ball Club 232
Slow Steps Base Ball Club 232
Smeadley Base Ball Club 232
Smith 96
Smith, A.S. 103
Smith, Benjamin Franklin 63
Smith, Lucien 2, 197
Smith, William "Bill" 163
Smith, W.T. 96
Soapina Base Ball Club 232
Society for the Prevention of Cruelty to Children 120
Sol Lions Base Ball Club 232
Solomon 124
The Somersaults 120, 232
The Somerset Nine 232
Soniat Station 210
Sonie Base Ball Club 232
La Soule 10, 23
Southern Amusement Company 187, 190
Southern Association 146, 206
Southern Athletic Club 133
Southern Athletic Park 93
Southern Base Ball Club ("Southerns") 18, 36, 61, 70, 75–78, 80, 97, 105–107, 111, 151–158, 232

Southern Brewery Base Ball Club 232
Southern Express Base Ball Club 232
Southern Green 210
Southern Intercollegiate Athletic Association 134
Southern League Base Ball Club 170
Southern League of Colored Baseballists 108, 122, 126–127
Southern League of Professional Base Ball Clubs ("Southern League") 5, 18–19, 56, 75, 89–91, 104, 108, 116–117, 128, 130, 134, 137–148, 151–158, 168–170, 173, 175–176, 178–186, 188–190, 192–206
Southern Pacific Base Ball Club 232
Southern Policy Club 232
Southern Star Base Ball Club 232
Southern University 134
Southwestern Base Ball Club 232
Southyard, Charles 65–67
The Spade Base Ball Club 232
Spalding, Albert (Al) 8, 11, 47, 51–52
Spanish Fort 59–60, 85, 98, 122
The Sparks 232
Spies, Harry 19
Spokane Bunchgrassers (WA) 145, 183, 191
Spoopendyke Base Ball Club 232
Sportsman's Park 4, 19, 87, 89–91, 93, 103–104, 114, 121, 128, 136, 139, 162, 170, 177, 184, 188, 192, 195–196, 208, 210
Squirrel Tails 232
S.T. Gately Base Ball Club 219
Stafford, Robert 196
Stagg, J.P. 65–67
Standard Base Ball Club 232
Stanley Steamer 146
Starck Base Ball Club 232
Stauffer, Macready & Co. Nine 232
Steel 109
Stenck Base Ball Club 232
Stevenson 115
Stickerbush Green/Stickney Bush Green 210
Stickers 232
Stickney Bush Green 210
Still Waters Base Ball Club 232
Stinson 96
Stith, Gerald 63
Stoball 26
Stockton, G.K. 76
Stone Lot Green 210
Stonewall Club 232
Stonewall Green 98, 210
Stonewall-Lee Base Ball Club 232
Stoolball 7, 23, 25–26, 28, 56
The Strikers 232
Strondbach 109

Strong 96
Sullivan 127
Sullivan, John L. 161, 182
Sullivan, Ted 186
Sully, Thomas 103
The Summer Gang 233
Summersgill, H.T. 134
Sunday Blue Laws 38
The Sunflowers 233
Surprise Base Ball Club 233
Swamp Angels 137, 139, 142; *see also* Mobile Base Ball Club
The Swamp Angels 233
Swanson 96
Sweet By-and-By Club 233
Switzer, Art 203
Switzer Base Ball Club 233

T. Anderson Base Ball Club 211
T. Barrett Base Ball Club 211
T. Burke Base Ball Club 213
T. Piglord Base Ball Club 229
T. Schreiber Base Ball Club 231
T. Scoggin Base Ball Club 231
T. Wolf Base Ball Club 235
Taylor Bros. Base Ball Club 120, 233
Tebeau (Thibau), Al 170
Tennison (Tennyson) 160
Texas League 94, 179–180, 182–185, 193–195, 197–198, 201, 203, 205
Texas-Southern League 145, 179
T.F. Moore Base Ball Club 226
T.H. Ehlers Base Ball Club 217
Thalia Street Green 210
Thalia Street Lot 210
Théatre de l'Opéra 69
Thebault, E.I. 124, 151
Theodore H. Kerr Base Ball Club 222
Thèque 23
Thibault (Thebault), Richard M. 160
Thomas Brennan Base Ball Club ("Brennans") 87, 113, 115, 117–118, 126, 137, 162, 213
Thomas Dillon Base Ball Club 216
Thomas Duffy Base Ball Club 217
Thomas J. Holmes Base Ball Club 220
Thomas Pye/Pyes Base Ball Club ("Pyes") 114, 229
Thomas Vizard Base Ball Club 234
The Thomies 233
Thomm Brothers 130
Thorp, Thomas 187
Thos. F. Wall Base Ball Club 234
340s 210
Three Oak Green 210
The Tiger Club 233

Tilton 74
Tiro al Bersaglio Society 20, 233
Tivoli Circle 60–61, 209–210
T.J. Bath Base Ball Club 211
T.J. Ford Base Ball Club 218
T.J. Higgins Base Ball Club 220
T.J. Kohl Base Ball Club 222
T.J. Mooney Base Ball Club 226
T.J./Thomas J. Holmes Base Ball Club 220
T.M. Harlee Base Ball Club 220
Tom Brothers Base Ball Club 213
Tom Kelly Base Ball Club 222
Tom Koop Nine 222
Tom Mitchel Base Ball Club 226
Tommy Adler Base Ball Club 210
Toney Base Ball Club 233
Tony Demote Base Ball Club 216
Toole, Steve 19
Townball 1, 7–8, 10, 29–32, 37, 50, 56
Tracey, William F. 72, 77, 107, 111, 115, 124–125, 151, 155
Tracy 96
Trahant Base Ball Club 233
The Treme Market Butchers 233
Tremont Hotel 179
T.S. McEvoy Base Ball Club 225
T.S. Weber Base Ball Club 121, 234
T.S. Wilkinson Base Ball Club 235
The Tugboats 233
Tulane Athletic Association 131–132
Tulane University 130–133
The Turflights 233
Turner 126
Twain, Mark 8, 16, 23
Tweed, William Marcy "Boss" 75
Twomey, J.S. 151
Tyler, E.A. 69

The Ubiquitous Base Ball Club 20, 233
Union Association 145, 205
Union Base Ball Club (MO) 152–153, 156
Union Base Ball Club of New Orleans 21, 123, 125, 127–130, 233
Union Course 96
Union League 145
Union Moustache Base Ball Club 233
United Nine 233
U.S. Barracks 210
The Universities 233
University of Alabama 134
University of Louisiana Base Ball Club 233
University of Mississippi 134
University of New Orleans 134
University of Texas 134
Unknown Base Ball Club 233

V. Fabian Base Ball Club 217
Valence Green 93, 210
Van Benthuysen, E. 102
Vandenberg Base Ball Club 234
Varden, Dolly 97
Varieties Base Ball Club (MO) 159–160
Variety Base Ball Club 233
V.E. Baumgarien/Baumgarden Base Ball Club 212
Veach, William Walter "Peek-a-Boo" 117, 137
Verlander 65–67
Victor Mauberet Base Ball Club 225
Vidous Base Ball Club 234
Violet Base Ball Club 234
Violett, E.R. 103
V.J. Lambert Base Ball Club 223
Volunteer No. 1 Base Ball Club 234
Voyard 110

W. Brophy Base Ball Club 213
W. Carroll/Carroll Base Ball Club 214
W. Israel Base Ball Club 221
W. Polchow Base Ball Club 229
W.A. Rogers Base Ball Club 230
Waco (TX) 158–159
Waco Tigers (TX) 198
Waite, Charles C. 51–52
Walk-a-Bouts 234
Walk Away Base Ball Club 234
Walker, W.W. 85
Wall, J.J. 107, 151
Wall, S.F. (Capt.) 36
Wallace, A. 96
Walsh & Creevy Base Ball Club 234
Walter L. (W.L.) Cohen Base Ball Club ("Cohens") 124–130, 214
Ward 110
Ward, Frank "Piggy" 183
Ward, John Montgomery 176–177
Warren, R.E. 151
Wash Marks Base Ball Club 112, 234
Washington Artillery Base Ball Club 234
Washington Avenue Base Ball Club 234
Washington Base Ball Club ("Washingtons") 18, 42, 87, 108, 112, 212, 220, 221, 226, 234
Washington Fire Company No. 20 112, 234
Washington Marks Base Ball Club ("Wash Marks") 234
Washington Nationals 74, 142, 145
Washington No. 20 Base Ball Club 234
Washington Senators 147, 163
Washington Square 15, 60
Waterman 124

Waterman, C.C. 133
Waters Base Ball Club ("Waters") 135, 162, 234
Waud, Albert R. 86
Waverly House Hotel 173
Wayne, F.T. 199
Webb Base Ball Club 234
The Webers/Websters 234
Websters 234
Wedig (Weydig), J. 113
Weisler Base Ball Club 234
Welcome Base Ball Club 234
Wells, Jacob 170–172
Werden, Perry 2
West End 59–60, 64, 85, 98, 209
West End Boat Club 119
West End Hotel 59
West End Rowing Club 85
West End Theatre 161
Western Association 184
Western Interstate League 147
Western Union Telegraph Company 93, 106, 226, 234
W.F. Goldthwaite Base Ball Club 219
W.F. Johnson Base Ball Club 221
W.H. Merkel Base Ball Club 226
W.H. Moon Base Ball Club 226
W.H. Rooney Base Ball Club 230
W.H. Warners Base Ball Club 234
White, James "Deacon" 53
White, R.L. 196
White & Thalia Street Nine 234
White & Ursuline Streets 210
White League Base Ball Club 234
White Motor Company 146
White Star Base Ball Club 234
White Stockings Base Ball Club 234
Whitmore Base Ball Club 235
Whitney Base Ball Club 234
Wide Awake Base Ball Club 235
Wild Girod Base Ball Club 235
Wild Indians 235
Wilkes-Barre Coal Barons (PA) 145–146
The Will Nots 235
William Armshaw Base Ball Club 211
William Baker Base Ball Club 211
William Burges Base Ball Club 213
William Butler Base Ball Club 213
William Clements Base Ball Club 214
William Cooper Base Ball Club 215
William D. Long Base Ball Club 224
William E. Fitzgerald Base Ball Club 218
William E. Hunter Base Ball Club 221
William Fagan Base Ball Club 112, 217
William J. Lemps Base Ball Club 223

William Kenna Base Ball Club 222
William Mahoney Base Ball Club 224
William T. Houston Base Ball Club 221
Williams 110, 126
Willings Base Ball Club 235
Wilson, Sylvester Franklin 122
Wilson Base Ball Club 125, 235
Windsor Hotel 138
Winkle, William Van 144; *see also* Wolf, Jimmy "Chicken"
The Winships 235
The Wintersaults 235
The Wintersmiths 235
W.J. Behan Base Ball Club 212
W.J. Lawler Base Ball Club 223
W.J. McGeehan Base Ball Club ("McGeehans") 118, 225
W.M. Porter Base Ball Club 229
Wm. Mack Base Ball Club 224
Wm. Mieding Base Ball Club 226
Wm. Schreiber Base Ball Club 231
Wolf, Jimmy "Chicken" 144
Wolters 74
Wooden 109
Worcester Base Ball Club 235
Worchester Ruby Lugs (MA) 137
World Industrial and Cotton Centennial Exposition 89, 99–100, 138
Woulfe, Jas. J. "Jimmy" 19, 76, 163
Wright, George 76, 79
Wright, Harry 79
W.S. Perry Base Ball Club 228
W.S. Pike Base Ball Club 229
W.S. Terry Base Ball Clun 233
W.S. Wilson Base Ball Club 235
W.T. O'Reilly Base Ball Club 227

Xavier University 134
XYZ Base Ball Club 235

York, William 198
Young 65–67, 124
Young, G.W. 75
Young, Thomas 174
Young Adams Base Ball Club 235
Young Americans Base Ball Club 235
Young Men's Democratic Association (Y.M.D.A.) 119
Young Men's Hebrew Association 106
Young Sara Base Ball Club 235
Youngstown (PA) 147

Zabrey Base Ball Club 235
Zimmerman Base Ball Club 235

www.ingramcontent.com/pod-product-compliance
Lightning Source LLC
Chambersburg PA
CBHW051214300426
44116CB00006B/570